"He'll Work It Out"

By

Taryn C. Atkins

Copyright © 2017, 2018 by Taryn C. Atkins
He'll Work It Out
TCA Productions Inc
ISBN: 978-0615914718

All Rights Reserved. No part of this book may be reproduced or transmitted in any form or by any means, electronic or mechanical, including photocopying, recording, or by any information storage and retrieval system without the written permission of the author, except where permitted by law.

Printed in the United States of America

2

This book is a work of fiction. Names, characters, places, and incidents either are products of the author's imagination or are used fictitiously. Any resemblance to actual persons, living or dead, events, or locales is entirely coincidental.

~Table Of Contents~

THE MUST HAVE ITEMS
ii - vii

CHAPTER 1 - Pg. 1.
~Family, Friends, Acquaintances & Their Issues~

CHAPTER 2 - Pg. 73.
~Free Will + Choices + Options = The Path~

CHAPTER 3 - Pg. 153.
~Victimized in Spirit, in Soul & in Body~

CHAPTER 4 - Pg. 193.
~Our Actions Have Consequences~

CHAPTER 5 - Pg. 251.
~One's Remorse, One's Loathing & One's Compliance~

CHAPTER 6 - Pg. 276.
~Uncovered Lies, Relinquished Desires & Revealed Truths~

CHAPTER 7 - Pg. 312.
~Unconditional Love Can Recover & Make Whole~

CHAPTER 8 - Pg. 391.
~His Ways Are Not Our Ways~

**SHARE YOUR THOUGHTS
OR WRITE A REVIEW
Pg. 479.**

~Simply said To 5~

~And in the order the Lord Blessed Me with Them~

To My Lord & Savior Jesus Christ, The Alpha & Omega, The True Living God. Who I give All Praise to for entrusting me with "He'll Work It Out. I'm simply the vessel He used to bring it forth, He is truly the Author & Finisher and it's all for His Glory & Honor.

To My Parents, the late James & Marilyn Atkins, for always being there, believing in me, investing in me and encouraging me every step of the way. When others thought I wouldn't, couldn't, shouldn't or can't, you told me I could, and to keep on keeping on. You already had three boys & a girl, and then after two miscarriages most people would've stopped. You brought forth naturally five but in total 7. I'm blessed to be the 7th child of a 7th child. So, I know I'm meant to be here! Thank the Lord it was in His plan for you to keep going and bring me on thru, without the two of you none of this would be possible. Mommy & Daddy, I did it and this is the first of many to come. So, until we see each other again, for you will always be remembered, truly missed & forever loved.

To AVC, the late Evangelist Elaine Hicks-Crawford & Dr. Robert Thomas My Brother & Friend; I thank the Lord for using you as the vehicle to introduce me to the Great I Am that I Am. Robert it was your alter call, at that AVC Picnic where the Lord first tugged at my heart and where I surrendered my life to the Lord Jesus Christ. I love you very much, and you will always be a part of my family.

To the late Apostle John H. Boyd Sr., of the New Greater Bethel Ministries. I'm blessed to be able to say you were my first Pastor and Bethel my Boot Camp. It was his teaching and guidance that helped lay the foundation for my relationship with the Lord. Your words of wisdom relayed to us in your many sayings are forever in my heart. You, Mother Margie Boyd, Pastor John Boyd II, Lady Valerie Boyd, Dr. Gail Johnson & the entire Boyd family will always be deeply loved by me.

To Bishop Aretha Wilson, the Pastor & Overseer of Kingdom Ambassadors Global Ministries in Lynbrook, NY; I'm Blessed, Favored & Extremely Honored to call you <u>My Pastor</u>, <u>My Mentor</u> & <u>My Spiritual Mother</u>. Pastor, it was you who instilled in us to be progressive without compromise. You placed in us the will & strength to endure the process of being formed, fashioned & fortified by God. I Praise & Thank God for your guidance & eagle eyes to see that which I can't, had I gone on in my flesh & power HWIO would never have become the weighty, driving & powerful piece of dramatic writing it is today. Nor would I be the person I am. I love you pastor with all my heart, and this daughter is happy to present to you the first of my fruit.

~*Preface*~

"He'll Work It Out" is guaranteed to capture your attention and keep you intrigued page after page. The Lord inspired me to write this story because of my past struggles and experiences. I've noticed that humanity has come to think that they in their limited power can fix everything. The late Bishop John H. Boyd said, "God can do more for you in 5 minutes, then you can do for yourself in a lifetime." That being said. When we, in our own power stop trying to fix ourselves, someone or some situation. When we take our hands off allowing God to have His way and allow God's will to be done. I've found that God has a way of working it all out.

"He'll Work It Out" is sure to entertain because everyone can find themselves or someone they know within its pages, it will enrich and cultivate lives because somewhere on your journey you too will have to let go of something, someone or some situation and let God have His way. This story is for families and individuals from all races and walks of life because we all can identify. We all have disagreements within our families; we all struggle with something, and we all have at one time or another been affected be it good or bad by someone's beliefs, feelings, and actions. I want to let people know when you've come to the end of your rope, done all you can, and nothing seems to work. Let go and let God.

I've been that person who looked for love in other places right, wrong & in between because of issues and situations I went through. I've been that person who did things outside the norm to escape from hurts & disappointments. I've been that person who allowed themselves to be mistreated by others because I didn't yet see my value. I've been that person who was victimized by others that couldn't see beyond their fears & idiosyncrasies and unable to show compassion or empathy for my struggles and shunned rather than showed unconditional love. But, when they let go, and I let go, and allowed God to come in He worked it out.

It's taken ten years to compose and after several proof readings, rewrites & revisions, late nights, frustrations, tears & prayers; I've learned that to produce something of substance, significance and true quality takes prayer, commitment & time. Real diamonds don't get created in microwaves. Now with it all said and done; I give all Glory & Honor to God and count myself blessed for the Lord inspiring me to write this story. I wrote this, so it may help others, it's written from a place of truth & honesty, being transparent & real about my feelings when I went through my struggles.

Reader approach this book with an open mind, spirit and soul, you won't be disappointed. HWIO is the first of more to come.

~And to Those a "Thank You" Goes~

While on this journey creating "He'll Work It Out" aka HWIO through its various stages and finally becoming an entertaining & intriguing piece of work. God blessed me to have remarkable people by my side be it for a moment or years.

To my Siblings: & Family: James Jr., Marilyn, Frank, Kenny & my entire family both far and near. I love and appreciate each of you. I know you all love me, believe in me and support me. Most of all you're excited & blessed to see my dreams coming true.

To my KAGM Family: Thanks for your words of encouragement & all your prayers. Like all families, we have our times, but we love each other deeply and have each other's back always. I love you all from the depths of my heart.

My Covenant Relationships: Carla Cantres love ya, the dreams created at 8-10 are coming forth; Thanks for always believing in me. Barbara Lewis, I love & miss you but glad you're able to look down and see I'm finally doing it. Letonya Mays, Karyn Rayner, Florence Pauls, Edress Jenkins, Mother Brenda Hill, Sis. Ada Blakely, Min. Aurelia Workmen & Tanisha Thompson "Thanks for great wedding vows." My love & thanks to each of you for all the ways you've been there for me. Those times when I needed harsh criticism or words of encouragement, you were there praying for & with me, you were there for me to vent to, cry to, and share times of laughter together too. When I wasn't where I needed to be, you yet believed in & respected me because you saw the call of God on my life and where He was taking me.

Much Appreciation, Gratitude & Love To: Sean Mackey, a dear friend who assisted me with the very early stages of this baby in its play form and the first two chapters of the second edition. Joy Pittman a truly brilliant lady who edited the first manuscript. Andrew Faison a long time close friend & creative comrade, for the countless hours you've taken with me in editing this second edition, and much love to your wife Michelle Cruz, for her patience during the process. As well as others such as: Pastor Viniell Jones, Elder Leon Smith, Pastor Walter Sargeant, Mother Megan Sargeant, Mother Thelma Taylor, Dr. Carlett Jones, Evangelist D. Taylor, Elder May Glover, Colette Livingston, Desiree Perrin, James & Rachel Blackwell, Katrina Faulkner, Gail Kirkland, Natasha Kirkland, Donna Anderson, Lori Wright, Ronnie Summerset & the late Tandra Summerset, Aisha Williams, Joy Pittman, Takiah McClean, Evelyn McArthur, Veltria Roman, Alexandra Pena, Jason Keith & Raeanne Davis and Omar Benjamin. Be it the Play, 1st or 2nd Editions some have read, reread & even proofed, and some have even invested. Lakeya Johnson love my logo & Brian Wallace love your excellent graphics for the new book cover & trailer. All here have believed in & encouraged me to press forward, they never saw HWIO as a minor thing and are equally excited about it finally coming forth.

To All Those Talented Actors & Actresses: Who gave their time, commitment & dedication to rehearsals for HWIO Workshops. It's because of you that, not only the story but your talent assisted me in making each character more in depth, well rounded & most of all real. Extra special thanks, much love & appreciation to those who are still yet with us on this journey. Words cannot express the special place each of you have in my heart. Plus, I look forward to all the new talent destined to be a part of the HWIO family.

~Blessing, Peace & Favor To You All + Much Love Always, Taryn C. Atkins~

~Introduction~

"He'll Work It Out" is not your typical inspirational piece, but a pioneering work of dramatic fiction, with real life issues brought forth with a raw intensity and a fresh courageousness. This narrative is sure to capture your attention and engage your entire being. HWIO will surely entertain, intrigue, enrich and cultivate lives while it keeps you immersed in every page, as it reminds one there is no distance or depth that God can't reach. All families have issues and this one isn't exempt. The story centers on an African American suburban family who experiences trials and tribulations down through the years, and in the face of their fighting and dysfunctions. It's through the faith and nurturing of the family matriarch that teaches them to trust in God. They come to learn that no matter what life throws at you, somewhere on your journey, you will have to let go and let God work it out.

~CHAPTER 1~

~Family, Friends, Acquaintances & Their Issues~

~THE BIRTHDAY PARTY~

It's the Spring of 2003, Maven Babcock's home is always full of life and on this late Saturday afternoon it bubbles over. The house keeps the scent of Mop & Glo and Murphy's Oil Soap, they're embedded in the floors and trim. Throughout the years, as the sunset approaches and the dimming sunlight passes over the walls; It seems to never take any of the spirit or liveliness out of the peach color they're painted. Maven loves peach and brown; She says they show the color of life. Peach revealing those vibrant and joyous times, as seen in her memories of giving birth to her daughters. While brown displays a time of modification and transformation, exhibited in the Fall of 2002 when she laid to rest her brother Jimmy, making her the last of eleven siblings.

Maven's brothers and sisters simply called her Mae, but over her years she's received a few monikers. She's the adored and highly esteemed Mother Babcock at her long-time church home, and lovingly called Mama Mae by her neighbors. This handle even caught on with some of her family. She's lived in this New York suburban area for close to forty years. Her home still has a refreshingly new take on traditional style, reminiscent of classic row houses in places like Savannah, Charleston, and her own Georgia. When Mae's husband Luke passed in 1996, her family took over the responsibility of keeping their home in pristine condition.

It's fascinating how she keeps each of her families' photos encased in a uniquely designed mahogany picture frame. They're displayed on the walls and mantles around the house. It's when you enter the living room one can see this is where they're showcased. An antique grandfather clock stands against the wall behind the dining room table; It chimes out five times communicating the hour.

"He'll Work It Out" Chapter 1. Taryn C. Atkins

The dining room table is equipped for this day of celebration with a stack of royal blue plastic Solo cups, clear Chinet dinner and dessert plates with matching cutlery. There are trays of appetizers, among them homemade recipes that no Babcock family gathering can do without. A large bowl of ginger ale punch with fruit floating on top sits by the centerpiece of bright colored balloons; Each inscribed in a calligraphy style with dazzling metallic silver ink, and the words upon them read "Happy Birthday Mama Mae".

The festivities began at noon, with it now being a little after 5 p.m.; There are a few cups and dinner plates scattered about the room. One could see by reviewing them, that the appetizers and the main meal is pleasing to all. The common factor the tableware shares is each held a drop of punch, a naked bone and a meager remnant of food with a used napkin and eating utensil.

Mae endeavors to keep an atmosphere of peace, love and joy in her home. She cultivates it with music stemming from her old cassette player. It's stationed front and center on the fireplace mantel. When looking at it you can't believe it's still able to bring forth any sound at all, but amazingly it plays her favorite gospel music and preaching cassettes without a hitch.

Mae's of average height and build with a little cushion added. She loves cooking and appreciates a well-prepared meal. Nevertheless, she does her best with the help of the Lord to stay in good health; Only wearing glasses because of astigmatism. Her milk chocolate hue is rich and smooth as silk. Today her gorgeous silver-gray hair is up in a bun with bangs. She always reflects elegance whether she's relaxing in her favorite pajamas, dressed in her Sunday best or like on this late afternoon she sports a casual top, denim skirt, and sandals.

Mama Mae sits in the center of her sofa with a heartwarming smile on her lips, delighted to be surrounded by her family. She reaches out in front of her, picks up her Solo cup from a coaster on top of a brown leather antique trunk that's used as a coffee table. She takes the fork out the cup, drinks the remaining punch and then uses the fork to eat the leftover chunks of pineapple. She licks her lips and wiggles, doing a little dance showing her enjoyment of the fruit as she places the cup back on the coaster.

As Mama Mae watches all those in attendance, she leans to the side and tucks under her arm one of the paisley print sofa pillows. Each pillow matches the earthy color arrangement of her home. She surveys her spacious living room from right to left, taking in and admiring each family member.

Her eyes go to her teenage grandson Reginald Wesley Jacobs aka Reggie. Mama Mae smiles with a deep affection in her eyes. She remembers sitting in pediatrics with Leah, hearing the doctor say Reggie has a growth disorder, and for a time it appears he would never grow. When Reggie hit his teens, all doubt is gone. Although his father Wes isn't around much, his mother knows they share many traits. Reggie has his tall well-conditioned physique, charm and temper. Along with his mom's almond tint, taste, talent and easygoing personality. He's clad in a t-shirt, Levi khaki cargo shorts and a pair of Converse. Reggie's framework is sprawled across the loveseat as he checks out the baseball game on the TV in spurts, being more involved with playing Tekken Advanced on his Gameboy.

Her eyes move to the formal dining room, where her nephew James Speaks is seated a few feet behind Reggie at one end of the table. James is in his mid-twenties. Mama Mae's siblings ran the gamut regarding skin, hair and eye color. The range spans from ebony with blue eyes to golden honey with gray eyes. James falls smack in the middle of that ratio. He sits finishing off his third plate of food. Although James isn't a rather stocky guy; His appetite always left people in awe. James wears his usual gear: overalls, a t-shirt and work boots. And like a cherished pet, his tool belt rests on top of his metal toolbox beside his chair. James returns from repairing some appliances and cars around the neighborhood. He's a handy asset around her home and is always available to his aunt. James puts down his napkin and stretches letting out a manful moan, showing he's satisfied by the meal.

"Ah-choo!"

"He'll Work It Out" Chapter 1. Taryn C. Atkins

Around the room the heads of various ones pop up and turn replying 'God bless you' to the woman bending slightly over in the corner.

"Oh, my goodness," she said. "Thanks everybody."

Mama Mae's eyes go to the other end of the dining room table. Where by the china hutch against the wall Nola Harris, a friend of the family straightens up wiping her nose with a tissue. Nola balls up the used tissue stepping over to Mama Mae's daughter Shayna Babcock-Greye.

"I'll be back," Nola said. "Allergies, I gotta wash my hands."

"There's a small bathroom," Shayna said. "Out the living room door, and to your right."

"Ya can't miss it." James said.

"I've been here before," Nola said, she walks away making a face at James. As she passes the sofa she glances at Mama Mae. "Right Mama?"

"You sure have," Mama Mae said with a nod. She smiles at Nola. "And sometimes without Shayna."

"Hello!" Nola said, snapping her fingers.

Nola throws the tissues in a small garbage pail by the living room door as she pushes it open and walks through. She's Shayna's best friend, they were dorm buddies in college, but after graduation they lost touch. They've been joined at the hip ever since reconnecting in 1998; After bumping into each other at an art gallery that Shayna was auditing for her job. Nola was there just taking in the creative expressions. Shayna was headed to the receptionist up front when she heard Nola's voice. She knew it could be nobody else but her.

Nola's voice took people off guard because it didn't match her ginger hair and ivory complexion. In college, their friends always said they needed to exchange voices. Nola returns to the living room and reconvenes with Shayna. She appears to tower over Shayna as they talk but it's the black fedora Nola wears that lengthens her frame. It accents her off the shoulder white peasant blouse, black cropped pants and sling-back heels.

A smile comes across Mama Mae's face as she observes her daughter Shayna. Even though she's in her late thirties, Mama Mae

"He'll Work It Out" Chapter 1. Taryn C. Atkins

recalls that little girl clinging to her side while taking her first steps. Shayna's an alluring and independent woman. She's fetching as usual, years of modern and jazz dance preserves her exquisite frame. Her silky mocha texture is adorned in a beautiful flowing gold spring sundress with matching heels.

It's amazing how nothing gets by Mama Mae. She watches as Shayna scrutinizes the appetizers on the dining room table. While covertly, keeping tabs across the room on her teenage daughter Gisele Greye aka Gigi. She chats on her cell phone sitting comfortably on the living rooms grand bay window. Gigi's attire for the day is a velour Juicy Couture tracksuit with Nike Air Max's. Her outfit stands out and blends well with the color scheme of her grandmother's home. Gigi's clothes accent her delicious coffee with cream tint, a beautiful blend she receives from her parents. A smile appears on Mama Mae's face again as she reflects watching her granddaughter Gigi. You see anytime Gigi visits; Mama Mae can find her tucked in the corner of that bay window. It's Gigi's favorite spot in the house.

"Yes!"

The resounding jubilation comes from the opposite side of her, it takes her eyes to her son-in-law Clifford Greye aka Cliff.

"Get it going." Cliff said, gesturing toward the television a few feet in front of him. "Come on guys!"

He relaxes in the recliner watching the game. Cliff and Shayna got married after their college graduation, even though her parents wanted them to wait. Luke and Mae eventually grew to like Cliff, taking comfort in knowing he's a good man and the right one for their daughter.

Cliff's the hazelnut cream in Gigi's tone, their youngest Regina resembles Shayna and Mama Mae. His daughters regard him as their personal Superman with no glasses included. The one whose view of him has changed is his personal Lois Lane, Shayna. Cliff throws his hand behind his head as he lays back in the recliner. He dons a Nautica crew t-shirt, Lee carpenter jean shorts, and suede loafers. The size of the recliner always amazes Mama Mae because somehow it takes tall, stocky, muscular men like her Luke and Cliff, and appears to swallow them up.

"Alright, it's looking good!"

Mama Mae hears the voice of her daughter Leah Babcock aka Lee, roar out from inside the kitchen. Mama Mae peers over her left shoulder at the kitchen door off to the side. Leah makes her entrance into the living room. She keeps the kitchen door open for a moment with one hand, while holding a wine glass in the other and looks back inside.

"Now, just keep an eye on it." Leah said.

Leah's a splendid fusion of her parents' genes and is eye-catching in her chic denim skirt outfit. It compliments her semi voluptuous and curvy frame. The high heels she effortlessly sports, draws attention to her calves. Mama Mae's eagle eyes lock on Leah sipping from the wine glass as she makes her way to the sofa.

That better not be wine. Mama Mae thought.

As Leah crosses in front of the TV, Cliff screws up his face annoyed at her for disrupting his view. Mama Mae ponders on the fluid in Leah's glass and before Leah can take a seat.

"What's that?" Mama Mae said.

"Soda Mama." Leah said, resting a hand on her hip. "Just black cherry soda."

Leah exhales taking a seat by Mama Mae. She goes to put her glass down on the coffee table but Mama Mae stops her. Mama Mae reaches over to the nearest end table, takes a coaster from it and gives it to her.

"I know," Leah said, taking the coaster. "How could I forget Mama, it's one of the family heirlooms."

"Yes, that's right," Mama Mae pats the trunk like it's an old friend. "This belonged to my father and that silverware in the kitchen belonged to my mother."

Shayna becomes attentive to their conversation and turns toward them.

"They were given to me and your dad when we got married. They don't make'em like that anymore and I don't want'em messed up."

"Okay Mama," Leah glances up, huffs and looks at her mother. "I'm back, please go on with your story."

Before Mama Mae could get a word out.

"Mama, I am the oldest," Shayna points toward the kitchen. "That silverware in there should be mine."

Leah slowly shakes her head as she studies Shayna.

"Unbelievable," Leah said. "You know what, you can have that silverware, cause that grandfather clock," She points in its direction. "Is mine. So, whatever." Leah rolls her eyes at Shayna and turns to Mama Mae. "Go on."

"So..." Mama Mae glances at Shayna for a second, then returns to Leah. "Like I was saying."

The family members continue what they're doing but stay attentive to Mama Mae as she entertains them with her story.

"We're on the porch at my brother Jimmy's house. James was 'bout thirteen and hanging out front with his friends. My brother Jimmy yells, "James! Come here boy!" James has the nerve to yell back. "Wait! I'm doing somethin!" Well, before I could bat an eye, my brother was on him with the belt."

Those around snicker and giggle. James watches Mama Mae as he gets up from his seat.

"Aunt Mae," James said. "You telling that story again?"

"I sure am." Mama Mae said with a chuckle.

"Well, let me pick it up from there,"

"Go on boy." Mama Mae said laughing.

James stands by the loveseat. He's been up here a year, but his southern drawl has blended well with the New York accent.

"So, I'm standing there right, all of a sudden I feel..." He moves his hand like he's snapping a whip and makes a whip sound. "I took off running! Digging in too, or so I thought. I felt the belt again!" He snaps the invisible whip and makes the whip sound once more. "Man, I didn't know my Dad could move like that! I was going up hills, down hills, and Dad was still on me! Man, I learned my lesson that day. When I got back home, all I could do was that stuttering, barely breathing-cry kids do. Y'all know it! Kids do it after getting that beating that wears their as-" He glances at Mama Mae. "That wears

"He'll Work It Out" Chapter 1. Taryn C. Atkins

their behind out! I'm twenty-five, and still flinch! Just thinking about that beating."

As everyone laughs, each of their faces contort as they flash back to their own memorable behind beating. Leah stares at James.

"Baby, I know the one," Leah said. "When it's over, your parents have the nerve to tell you..." She skims their faces. "Come on. Y'all know the line, say it with me."

Mama Mae looks around at everyone as they join Leah and say in unity.

"You know that hurt me, more than it hurt you." Leah sucks her teeth. "I'm sorry but I don't think so."

"Amen to that." James said.

"Ya got that right!" Reggie said.

Leah eyes Reggie, "Oh, really."

"I'm just saying." Reggie said.

James goes toward the loveseat but checks out Reggie spread out on it. He shakes his head and gestures to Reggie, then goes to the dining room table, grabs a chair, puts it next to Cliff and sits.

"That's Yankees verses Oakland?" James said.

"Yep." Cliff said, keeping his eyes on the game.

While they focus on the game, Mama Mae takes Leah's hands in hers and admires the design on her nails. As they talk and laugh. Nola observes them, a smile forms on her face seeing Mama Mae have a good time with her family. Nola leans over and gently bumps her shoulder against Shayna's.

"Mama Mae's enjoying herself," Nola said. "It's great everyone made it but, what happened to the folks from the neighborhood? You did invite them?"

"Well," Shayna said, with a dismissive wave of her hand. "I wanted just the family. So, I didn't bother mentioning it."

"Shayna, it's Mama Mae's party."

"Please, Nola those folks hear free food and come running with all their Bebe's kids."

Nola shakes her head. "You still should've invited them."

Shayna shrugs her shoulders while nibbling on one of the

appetizers. She shakes her head as she spies on Gigi.

Bet she's talking to that child again. Shayna thought.

Shayna sucks her teeth and huffs as she continues eyeballing Gigi. She glances at Nola and points to Gigi.

"Look at that."

Nola turns around and scouts Gigi.

"You believe she's still on that phone."

Nola tilts her head slanting her eyes at Shayna.

"Shayna, it's a shiny new toy. Let the girl enjoy it."

Nola turns back toward the dining room table and drinks her punch. Shayna's attention stays on Gigi.

Under her breath, Shayna said. "She's been on that phone since we got here."

Gigi checks the time on the grandfather clock and notices her mother watching her; She huffs, shaking her head and curtly turns her back to her mother. Gigi gazes out the window continuing with her call.

"Goodness... My mom's watching my every move... What? Please, I wish I could break out... Lexi, it's not happening... She's already laid down the law and my dad is not gonna come up against it." She chuckles. "Yeah I know... Like she really cares that I'm here, but hey, she gotta keep up appearances."

The doorbell rings, in one swift motion Reggie jumps to his feet and puts down his video game on the coffee table.

"Nobody move! I got it!" Reggie said.

Reggie brushes off his clothes and checks his breath. The doorbell rings again and James moves to get up.

"I'll go get it." James said.

"I told you, I got it!" Reggie said. He calms himself.

"Relax, like I said. I got this."

On hearing the doorbell ring once more, Reggie gets ready to rush out the living room but stops. James grins observing Reggie, as he composes himself and struts through the living room door with a swagger. James looks at Leah.

"What is up with him?"

"Oh, you'll see."

"He'll Work It Out" Chapter 1. Taryn C. Atkins

Gigi peeks over her shoulder and sees her mother's eyes still fixed on her.

What's her issue? Gigi thought.

Gigi lets out a harsh breath as she returns her focus to the phone conversation

"Hmph... I wish... You're lucky you're done... I've got one more final exam... No actually, two more and that's it... Oh, did you see them on campus today? Well, remember to tell them what I said... Yes... I'm sure... Lexi, please... Just tell her okay... I said I'm sure... Thank you... Look, I gotta go..." Gigi's mouth curves into a smile. "I hear em back there..." Her eyes twinkled as she blushed a bit. "Tell Bobbie I said hello too... Alright... I'll call you later... Bye."

Gigi places her cell in her tracksuit pocket. When Shayna notices, she abruptly puts down her plate and eyes Nola as she brushes off her hands. Gigi stands and stretches.

"I'm taking care of this right now." Shayna rushes off toward Gigi.

"Shayna don't," Nola said.

Nola reaches out to grab Shayna's arm but misses. Cliff clocks Shayna heading toward Gigi with anger in her eyes.

Here we go. Cliff thought, sitting up concerned about the interaction to take place.

Shayna's brash movement makes the rest of the family attentive to the situation at hand.

"Oh my Lord," Mama Mae said.

Gigi's back is to Shayna as she approaches. She comes up behind Gigi, grabs her upper arm and snatches Gigi around to face her.

"Hey!" Gigi said.

"What the!" James said.

"Jesus!" Leah said.

"Ow!" Gigi said.

"Shayna!" Cliff said.

"Come on now!" Mama Mae said.

"Take it easy!" Cliff said.

"He'll Work It Out" Chapter 1. Taryn C. Atkins

"Ma," Gigi said. "What's wrong?"

"Well, it's about time!" Shayna said, releasing Gigi's arm. "It's ridiculous how long you've been on that cell phone!"

"Ma please." Gigi said, rubbing her arm.

"Shayna what's going on?!" Cliff said.

"Cliff!" Shayna turns to him taking a brash tone. "I'll handle this!" She shifts back to Gigi. "Gisele, it's just disrespectful! We're here spending time with your grandmother on her birthday, and all you've done is talk on that cell phone! How many people have that number anyway!?"

Under her breath, Gigi said, looking away crossing her arms. "Why do you even care?"

"Excuse me!?" Shayna said, putting her hands on her hips. "Listen," She points at Gigi. "I'll ask whatever I want about that phone!"

"Take it easy Shayna." Nola said, advancing toward them.

Shayna gives no reply, just cuts her eyes at Nola as she comes over.

"Grandma," Gigi casts her eyes on Mama Mae, moving toward her, she extends her hand out. "Do you feel I was disrespecting you?"

"Of course not baby." Mama Mae said.

Gigi stops a foot or two from the coffee table.

"See," Gigi turns to her mother. "Grandma's not upset."

"That's not the point!" Shayna steps to Gigi. "I'm your mother and we spoke about that phone before we left."

"Come on now," Leah said. "Let the girl be!"

"Y'all need to take it down some," James said, gesturing for them to lower their voices. "We don't know who came in."

Shayna's eyes dart to James.

"Well, I'm speaking to my daughter."

"And I'm just saying, everybody don't need to know."

"He'll Work It Out" Chapter 1. Taryn C. Atkins

After answering the front door, Reggie and his friend are in the foyer approaching the living room. Reggie overhears a portion of the bickering going on behind it. He fakes a cough to drown out the sound of the altercation. Reggie places his hands on his friend's shoulders and moves them to the side of the living room door. He steps back, glances at his friend, showing his pearly whites and winks.

"Wait here."

His friend stares at him with a lopsided grin, Reggie bust through the living room door. As he charges into the living room, all eyes go to him.

"Lord Jesus!" Mama Mae said.

"Boy are you crazy?!" Leah said.

They watch as Reggie motions with his head to the living room door. He speedily does his best to sound like Jim Carrey from "The Mask."

"Look who's here!" Reggie said. "The one and only Ms. Kisha Carrington!"

Reggie holds the living room door open, through it steps a pretty refine and studious young lady; Whose a mix of Ethiopian and Colombian. Kisha wore a lovely GAP top, jeans, and flat sandals. Reggie pretends to be a news reporter on assignment, holding an invisible microphone to his mouth. He looks into the unseen video camera in front of him.

"Ms. Carrington's the one accepted to and soon to leave for... Well, audience she has yet to choose. Will she possibly give us an answer today? Let's ask shall we. So Kisha, where will you attend college? Will it be Yale, Howard or Brown? What can you tell us?

Reggie extends his hand, putting the intangible mic close to Kisha's mouth waiting for her to speak. Reggie stares into Kisha's eyes, as she gazes into his, she leans into the unseen mic, cracks her mouth and slaps Reggie's hand out her way.

"Stop it," Kisha said.

Kisha nudges Reggie to the side. She glances at him smiling and shaking her head as she strolls by him.

"Silly."

"He'll Work It Out" Chapter 1. Taryn C. Atkins

Kisha walks to the sofa giving a wave to all.

"Hi everybody."

All but Shayna and Gigi greet Kisha. Nola waves hello but quickly moves in front of Shayna and Gigi.

Nola whispers to Shayna, "Please keep it down."

Nola tries her best to block Kisha's view of what's going on between Shayna and Gigi. Cliff keeps his eyes on them. Nola looks at them and motions toward the grand bay window.

"Let's move over there."

Shayna, Gigi and Nola proceed to the grand bay window. Gigi rushes to it and plops down with arms crossed. Nola eyeballs Cliff and they slightly nod to each other, silently agreeing it's best to put space between the situation at hand and visitors. Shayna stands on one side of Gigi and Nola's on the other. Shayna calms her tone and actions but continues to fuss at Gigi. Cliff reclines in his chair and returns to watching his sports. Reggie follows Kisha to his family and he notices what's going on between Gigi and her mom. He realizes it's the source of the commotion he heard outside in the hall. Kisha rubbernecks a bit, trying to check out what's happening between Gigi and her mother, but Leah draws her attention.

"So, Kisha!" Leah said. "All those universities want you! I'm sure your parents are so proud of you."

"Thank you," Kisha said. "Yeah, they're happy, and annoyed too. Since I haven't decided on one yet. Well, no matter where I attend-I knew I couldn't leave without seeing Mama Mae." She sits next to Mama Mae and gives her a big hug. "Happy Birthday!"

"Thank you baby, and congratulations." Mama Mae said, reciprocating the hug. "It's always great to see ya and you're looking beautiful as always."

They release each other. Reggie takes a seat on the arm of the sofa next to Kisha. He taps her on the shoulder and she glances up at him.

"You missed Mario," Reggie said. "He stopped by before heading to that interview at Princeton."

"He's worked hard for this," Kisha said. "I'm happy for

him."

"He's nervous," Reggie said. "He convinced his mom, dad, and his little brother to drive there with him."

"Yeah, Kisha, you should've seen him," James said with a chuckle. "He's dressed in his preppy best, face all clean shaven, hair neat, slicked and hair sprayed stiff. He'll blend right in."

"Come on now, leave our friend alone," Kisha said.

"James," Reggie said laughing a bit. "I've got two Ivy League best friends, and both fit right in with Chad, Becky, and Boomer."

"Biff and Buffy too," James said.

James and Reggie laugh while slapping each other high five.

"Whatever you two," Kisha said. She nudges Reggie. "So, still no college for you?"

"Yes Kisha," Leah said sucking her teeth. "Even after seeing what's happening with you and Mario. He still doesn't want to go to college. You believe that."

"Really now?" Mama Mae said. She looks over her glasses at Reggie. "I didn't know that."

"Oh, you didn't tell your grandmother that," Leah said.

"Grandma, no worries." Reggie said. "Things are gonna be great! I'm going on the road with my Dad. He'll be managing me too. Y'all just watch, I'll have a record deal in no time."

"You can still go to college." Kisha said. "Some of the best artists earned their degrees while pursuing their career."

"Mm-hmm," Leah said, she looks at Reggie and motions to herself. "That's exactly what I said." She gestures to Kisha. "Please talk some sense into him."

"Mom, I haven't crossed off college," Reggie said. "I'm just seventeen; I've got time for college. Right now, I really want to go on the road with dad." He bends down and ties his sneakers. *You said you were okay with that.* He thought. Reggie straightens up, "Kisha you hungry?

I'm hungry. I'll meet you in the kitchen."

"I'll be right there," Kisha said.

Reggie heads to the kitchen door, he stops and peeks back at Kisha as he points to the door.

"Kisha," Reggie said. "We can have a private conversation in there." He focuses on his mom. "With no interruptions."

Leah glimpses over her shoulder at him, "Yeah, whatever."

Mama Mae studies Reggie standing at the kitchen door.

"Boy you betta stop," Mama Mae said. "You ain't too grown for my belt."

"That's right," James said. "And I know you still got that belt Aunt Mae, don't ya?"

"Sure do," Mama Mae nods, peering over her glasses at Reggie. "Reggie remembers, it's right in this here trunk."

When Reggie sees Mama Mae about to open the trunk, he does a double take and rushes into the kitchen. They all have a good laugh watching him flee for safety. Leah glances back at the kitchen door for a second and then focuses on Kisha.

"Kisha he's playing it cool right now." Leah said. "When you leave though," She points toward the kitchen. "That boy's gonna miss you."

"There's something there." Mama Mae said with a smile.

"I see it when you look at each other."

Kisha smiles as she observes Mama Mae and Leah.

"We're friends, that's all." Kisha said. "All three of us have been best friends since fifth grade. Besides, he's gonna love being on the road with his dad. Hopefully, we'll all keep in touch. I mean it would be great if we stay friends but life has a way of changing things. Right Mama Mae?"

Kisha expects a response full of wisdom but instead she hears snoring. When Kisha and Leah look at Mama Mae, they see she is dozing and they both laugh. They lower their volume so they won't wake her. James notices his aunt is asleep.

"I knew that would happen," James said. "Yesterday

Pastor called the intercessors to the church for 7 p.m., to have all night prayer. Aunt Mae didn't get back till early this morning."

Cliff glances at Mama Mae, sees she's asleep and returns his focus to the game.

"She's alright though?" Leah said.

"She's okay, just tired." Cliff said. "Probably thought she could sleep late today."

"Yeah," James said. "She didn't expect this get-together."

Kisha stands preparing to depart into the kitchen.

She softly rubs Mama Mae's shoulder. "We'll let her sleep."

"Yeah let her rest." Leah looks at Kisha. "Anyway, I'm telling you Kisha. My son cares for you."

"And on that note," Kisha points to the kitchen door as she heads for it. "I'm going in the kitchen."

Kisha retreats into the kitchen. While Mama Mae naps, James and Cliff focus on the game. Leah tries to watch the sporting event too but after a few moments, she sighs from disinterest.

"Oh My God! This is boring!" Leah said. "How can you watch this!? I'm sure a live game is better."

James and Cliff look at each other.

"I know she didn't just say that." Cliff said.

A smirk is on James' face as he stares at Cliff; He sticks his thumb out and gestures toward Leah. Cliff shakes his head and puts his attention back on the game. James leans slightly forward and eyes Leah.

"A live game is much better." James said. "We even had airline tickets to go see it. You wanted us to be here today though, ain't that right Cliff."

Cliff pulls two tickets for today's game out of his shirt pocket; He holds them in the air and takes a gander at Leah.

"Yes, and so we're here," Cliff said.

Cliff puts the tickets away and returns to watching the game.

"And I appreciate your sacrifice," Leah said. She leans back on the sofa. "So I'll let you two watch the game."

"We'd appreciate that," James said.

"He'll Work It Out" Chapter 1. Taryn C. Atkins

James and Cliff go back to watching the game. While Mama Mae naps, she repositions herself and for a quick second lets out a roaring snore. Leah watches Mama Mae laughing a little as she picks up Reggie's Gameboy off the coffee table and tries to play it.

Shayna restrains her voice with Kisha in the living room. When Shayna glances over her shoulder and sees Kisha exit, her volume rises. Cliff, James and Leah nonchalantly keep their eyes on what's happening by the bay window. Cliff sees Shayna hasn't let up on Gigi, and notices his daughters face shows signs of being overwhelmed.

"Ma, I got three or four calls at the most." Gigi said.
"And you've been on it from the moment we got here!" Shayna said. "Did you even say Happy Birthday to your grandmother?"
"Of course I did."
"Still, the amount of time you've been on that phone is rude."
"Ma come on! Will you please stop it?"
"I told you about that phone before we got here."

Cliff, bothered by what's happening between them, gets up from the recliner. He grabs his plate and glass off the end table.

Under his breath, Cliff said, "Give the girl a break."

Leah hears his statement as she plays with the Gameboy. Cliff heads to the dining room table. Leah looks up and shakes her head watching Shayna go off on Gigi. Leah goes to say something to Mama Mae but she's still asleep. She pats her mother's leg trying to wake her. Mama Mae's eyes slowly open.

"Mama look." Leah points to Shayna and Gigi. "It's a shame what she puts that child through."

Mama Mae adjusts her position as she views Shayna and Gigi. Cliff stands at the dining room table snacking on appetizers and drinking punch. James also shakes his head witnessing Shayna tear into Gigi.

"All she's doing is pushing her away." James said.
"Doing a good job too." Leah said.

Mama Mae shakes her head watching Shayna get on Gigi.

"He'll Work It Out" Chapter 1. Taryn C. Atkins

"I've told Shayna to lighten up on her." Mama Mae said.

"Yeah well, Shayna only listens to Shayna," Leah said.

Mama Mae drifts back to sleep. Leah keeps an eye on the situation across the room while playing with the Gameboy. James watches the Yankees play as Cliff snacks at the dining room table. Nola tries to calm the tension.

"Shayna! Stop fussing with her."

Shayna gives Nola the evil eye taken aback by her statement.

"This is between me and my daughter."

"And you're blowing this out of proportion."

Shayna ignores Nola and returns to dealing with Gigi.

"Listen, that phone rang so much; It makes you look fast."

Nola steps back, throwing up her hands and shaking her head. Gigi abruptly stands.

"So... so now I'm fast?!"

Cliff hearing Gigi's voice, puts down his plate and turns to them.

"Ma, you have no idea but... Whatever."

Gigi storms off. All those in the room see Gigi rush away from her mother except Mama Mae who's still knocked out. Gigi heads for the living room door.

"Gigi wait a second," Cliff said.

Gigi doesn't stop, she gets to the living room door and as she's about to push her way through.

"Gigi stop!" Cliff said.

The movement and banter in the room makes Mama Mae stir in her sleep. Gigi doesn't move or turn around. She folds her arms as Cliff approaches her. Tears well up in her eyes but she fights to hold them back. Cliff stops a few feet behind her.

"Where you going?"

Gigi drops her arms turning to him. "I want to leave!"

"We're celebrating with Mama Mae. Look, I know your mom is getting on you about your new cell, but it's--"

"It's just another thing wrong with me. Apparently I'm fast now!" Gigi steps away from Cliff folding her arms as she glances at the ceiling. "Fast..." She softly said to herself. "Please, that's the least of my worries."

"What? I... I didn't hear you."

Some tears escape as Gigi turns to her father. She looks at him wiping them from her cheek.

"Dad what did I do? Cause, I don't get it. Mom has an issue with everything I do. It's like... She can't stand me."

Gigi gazes off to the side while Cliff speaks to her.

"Come on now." Cliff saddened by her comment. "Your mom and I love you."

Across the room, Nola tries to talk to Shayna but she's focused on Cliff and Gigi. Cliff tries to soothe the hostility that's boiling between his wife and daughter.

"Listen, I promise. We'll all talk once we're back home. Let's try to enjoy ourselves, it is grandma's birthday."

Gigi wipes her face again as she looks to her father.

"Fine..."

"That's my girl. Come here."

Cliff opens his arms and Gigi steps right into them. She buries her head in his chest. Cliff tilts his head to the side, he lays it gently on top of hers and they hug.

"I love you, my gummy bear," Cliff softly said.

"I love you too, my Papa bear," Gigi said cracking a smile.

"You know I'm here for you, no matter what."

"I know, thanks dad."

They release each other. Gigi steps back wearing a small smile on her face, she points to the kitchen door.

"I'm gonna go help Gina."

Cliff nods his head and seeing Gigi smile provokes a toothy grin from him. Gigi turns to go to the kitchen and her eyes meet her mother's. Shayna glares at her, Gigi peers back shaking her head as she walks through the kitchen door.

Shayna's eyes quickly go to Cliff. He turns around and they lock on to each other staring intensely. Shayna's brows drew together as Cliff's forehead creased. Shayna huffs, rolling her eyes at him. She folds her arms as she turns her back to him and faces Nola. Cliff went back to the dining room table. He huffs under his breath as he glances at Shayna shaking his head.

All this makes no type of sense. Cliff thought.

Cliff picks up his empty cup and standing there with his back to everyone stares at the bottom of it, losing himself for a moment. Cliff swiftly shakes his head bringing himself out of it. He rubs his hand over his face and scouts the punch bowl with the long silver ladle leaning against it. He grabs the spoon, scoops up some punch and pours it into his glass. Cliff stares at the glass of punch, takes a breath, exhales and drinks it down.

Gigi steps into her grandmother's traditional wood kitchen with its harvest gold range oven, dishwasher, classic white refrigerator and matching appliances. She takes in the sight of the brown, tan and gold paisley tiled floor for a moment. Gigi slowly lifts her head up, places her hand on the edge of the kitchen counter and leans against it. As Gigi takes in her surroundings, she sees pans of food on the stove and kitchen counters. They contain the main menu of the day and are filled with good down-home eats, such as: fried chicken, barbecue ribs, grilled salmon, macaroni and cheese, candied yams with marshmallows, lasagna, potato salad, peach and apple cobbler, plus a sweet potato pie. There are also three pots sitting on top of the stove which contain collard greens, corn, and fried okra.

Reggie and Kisha sit at the kitchen table. They glance at Gigi for a quick second and then continue their conversation while eating their stacked plates of food. Regina Greye aka Gina is bent over, checking out the contents of the oven. On hearing, someone walk into the kitchen, Regina closes the oven, she picks up the spoon and mixing bowl sitting on the kitchen counter. She turns around, sees her sister standing there and advances to her.

Gigi closes her eyes and stands there trying to recover from the argument with her mother. The voices in the kitchen muffle as she takes in a deep breath. The air is filled with the delicious aroma of all the foods around her and the sweet circular loaf baking in the oven. She holds the air in for a few seconds, then slowly exhales. She feels herself calm down. Gigi hears the faint sound of Regina's childlike voice increasing in volume as it calls to her.

"Gigi... Hey, Gigi... Hello."

Gigi opens her eyes, they focus on Regina who's standing a few feet from her. It's clear to see even at Regina's young age, she's a natural beauty and will grow to be a lovely lady. Regina pushes her silver rim glasses back up on her nose. They couldn't hide her almond shape eyes, high cheek bones nor the concern on her face.

"Gigi, you okay?" Regina said. "Reggie told me mom was getting on you."

"I'm all right," Gigi said. "Same stuff just a different day."

Regina admires her big sister, she especially loves her fashion sense. Regina wore one of Mama Mae's aprons which her petite frame swims in. Under it, she has on an almost identical track suit. Except Regina's is fuchsia and with it, she wore a white top and white Keds. As Regina stands there using a long wooden spoon in a plastic mixing bowl. She holds the bowl somewhat tilted in the crook of her left arm. Regina sighs as she keeps whipping the spoon around in the bowl.

"Feels like I've been stirring this forever."

Gigi glances down into it and sees that Regina is stirring a light beige creamy substance. As she observes Regina, she smiles seeing that Regina is unaware that a dollop of the substance is on her cheek.

"Cream cheese frosting?" Gigi said.

"Yeah, hope the cake turns out right," Regina said.

Gigi reaches out to Regina's face, extending her finger she scoops the frosting off her sister's cheek and samples it.

"Mmmph, tastes good."

Reggie, seeing what Gigi did gets a disgusted look on his face.

"Oh that's nasty!" He said. "You don't know how long that's been hanging there."

"Oh please, she just made it."

"Still, eating it off her face Gigi. That's gross."

"She's my sister," Regina said.

"I don't care, still nasty."

Gigi waves off Reggie not bothered by his opinion.

"He'll Work It Out" Chapter 1. Taryn C. Atkins

"Forget him, come on Gina. Let's see if the cake is ready."

They both walk to the oven, in the living room Shayna points at Nola.

"See, you should've listened to me." Shayna said.

"Hold on." Nola said. "Get your hand out my face."

Shayna puts her hand down and folds her arms.

"I told you not to buy her that cell phone."

"Please. Gigi just celebrated her eighteenth birthday, plus she made the Dean's List. She deserved that gift. Why are you on her back so much? Tell me that! What's with you?"

"It's like... she tries to get on my nerves."

"Shayna it's not her, it's you and you need to ease up."

"Please don't tell me how to talk to my daughter."

"That's what you call what you just did?"

Cliff takes a deep breath, turns around and heads toward Shayna. As he approaches, Shayna's back is to him, he touches her on the shoulder and she swiftly turns to him.

"What's going on now?" Cliff said.

Cliff slides his hand down her arm, Shayna moves away.

"Didn't you get the story from her?!" Shayna said.

Shayna's voice draws Leah and James attention again.

"Please lower your voice, everyone already heard you fussing with Gigi about her cell. What's the big deal?"

"Nothing, like you would even understand."

Cliff reaches out to put his hand on Shayna's shoulder, but she huffs and pushes pass him.

"Shayna." Cliff said.

You'll take her side anyway. Shayna thought marching off toward the sofa.

Cliff and Nola watch Shayna, astonished by her actions. Shayna plops down by Mama Mae and wakes her up.

"My Lord! What's going on?!" Mama Mae said.

"It's Alright Mama," Leah said patting her mother's leg.

"It's Shayna being Shayna."

Shayna turns to Leah, "What's that suppose to mean!?"

"Oh please," Leah said turning to Shayna. "You know

exactly what I mean!"

Shayna moves to the edge of the sofa. "Listen here Leah!"

"What!?" Leah moves to the edge of the sofa too.

"Listen you two stop it!" Mama Mae said. "I'm not gonna have all that in this house. Not today! You hear me?"

Shayna slides back on the sofa and crosses her legs; She rolls her eyes at Leah and turns her head. Leah sucks her teeth as she moves back on the sofa as well; She picks up her wine glass and takes a few sips. The room falls a bit silent, but you hear the baseball game. Under it music softly comes from mama's cassette player it's the chorus from Vanessa Bell Armstrong's "Peace Be Still."

Cliff and Nola look at each other for a second. Cliff shakes his head, as he turns around and throws his hands up in the air. Nola pats him on the back sharing his frustration with her best friend. He goes back to the dining room table. Nola walks to the loveseat and sits down. Cliff pours himself another glass of punch and returns to the recliner to watch the game. They all sit saying nothing. Nola quietly takes a few deep breaths to relax herself. She notices something smells a little funny and sniffs the air twice.

"Is... is there something burning?" Nola said.

James scoots his chair up and points at Leah. "See, I knew it!"

"Don't start James." Leah said.

Nola sniffs the air again; A concerned expression appears on her face. She eyes Leah and moves to get up.

"Maybe... maybe I should go check."

"No sit-down." Leah gestures to Nola. "Everything's alright."

Nola sits, she crosses her legs and brushes some lint off her pants. Mama Mae sniffs the air too and inspects the room.

"So umm... where's Regina?" Mama Mae said.

James stands with his finger pointed in the air, "Aunt Mae, that's a good question."

James walks to the sofa studying Shayna and Mama Mae for a moment or two. He motions to Shayna to scoot down. She gawks at him with an attitude and only moves a little. James moves his hand vigorously at Shayna, gesturing for her to move further. She glares at him, sucking her teeth and loudly huffs as she goes to the end of the sofa. James sits in between her and Mama Mae. He leans over to his aunt.

"Aunt Mae, frankly I'm a bit nervous." James scopes Leah and Shayna, then leans in a little closer to his aunt. "See they ain't gonna tell ya, but I will." He peeks around at them again and back at his aunt. "Regina's in the kitchen, making your birthday cake."
"Really." Mama Mae said with a concerned look on her face. Catching herself, she smiles. "Really, that's nice."
"Mm-hmm," James shakes his head. "I wouldn't smile yet."

Shayna still having an attitude sits there with her arms and legs cross, as she bounces her top leg. She hears James' comment and turns to Mama Mae, looking around James.

"Pay him no mind Mama. My baby's been practicing and her baking has..." Shayna checks James. "Improved."

James leans over to his aunt while looking at Shayna.

"Mm-hmm see that Aunt Mae, it's that long pause between has, and improved that scares me."
"James, stop it," Leah said. She pats Mama Mae's leg once again. "Mama watch, you'll love it."
James pretends to sneeze. "Don't think so."
"Stop that," Leah hits James' leg.

Nola admires her newly manicured nails.

"Leah," Nola said. "Your girl Meeko, did a lovely job on my hands and feet; I'm going to her from now on."
"She's wonderful." Leah said. "My question is, why are you so quiet about that engagement ring sitting on your finger?"
"Child you're late," Mama Mae said as she glances at Leah. "I spotted that while y'all were yelling surprise." She darts to Nola. "I didn't want to spoil your good news. Dray's a good man and funny too, it's wonderful when a man knows how to make ya laugh. Yeah, I sure did love that about my Luke. I'm happy for you two. Finally

making it right before God. You'll see, being husband and wife is a blessed and beautiful relationship. Congratulations darling."

"Thanks," Nola said. "For me it's about time. I'm about to be forty and we've been together for five years."

Shayna looks at her, "You still have a few years before forty Nola. I'm thirty-eight, you're a year younger."

"Yeah, but you and Cliff got married at twenty."

"Well, how old is Dray?" Leah said.

Shayna watches Nola with a little smirk on her face.

"Go ahead Nola, tell them his age."

Everybody turns their head in Nola's direction. Nola glances at Shayna and fidgets in her seat seeing all eyes on her.

"It's not like I'm robbing the cradle." Nola said.

"Okay, so how old?" Mama Mae said.

"Or how young?" Leah said.

"Dray's... thirty," Nola said.

"A younger man huh," Leah said. "Well my oh my."

"Now wait a minute." Mama Mae said with a smile. "That means... you were thirty-two and Dray was twenty-five when you two met."

They all look at Nola again waiting for a reply. Nola blushes as she eyes Mama Mae and nods.

"Yes ma'am, that's correct."

James swiftly stands, throwing his hands in the air like a touchdown happened.

"It's Official Ladies and Gentlemen." James said. "We've got ourselves..." He points to Nola. "A cougar in the room."

Everybody in the room cracks up with laughter. James even jokingly growls a little as he looks at Nola.

James raises his hand approaching Cliff, "Can I get some."

Cliff and James high five each other. Shayna loses the attitude as she laughs with everyone. While James is standing though, Shayna repositions herself on the sofa.

"Oh, stop it." Nola said. "Come on it's just seven years."

"He'll Work It Out" Chapter 1. Taryn C. Atkins

Seven years. She thought. Nola laughs a bit and raises her hand. "Okay, I'm guilty; I'm a cougar."

Nola laughs along with everyone else. The laughter dies down but it help lighten the atmosphere in the room. James goes to sit back down but his spot is gone; He reviews Mama Mae and Leah, and squeezes into the space between them. It forces Leah to move down to her end of the sofa. Mama Mae and Leah look at him like "Really." James ignores their stares and directs his attention to Cliff laying back in the recliner watching the television.

"So," James accentuates a southern twang, "How old are you?"

"Me?" Cliff glances at James. "I'm thirty-eight, like Shayna."

"My Lord, and you been married to *her*," James gestures with his head toward Shayna. "Since you were twenty?"

"Yeah.?"

Cliff returns to watching baseball. James scrutinizes Shayna with confusion scratching his head. He flashes to Cliff and being in awe of him lays his hand on Cliff's shoulder.

"Brother, I'm sending up a special prayer for you. Cause that's amazing."

I know that's right. Leah thought as she fixes her earring.

Nola and Mama Mae laugh at James statement as does Cliff. Shayna beams at James with attitude.

"Oh, you think you're funny huh?" Shayna said.

"Funny?" James looks at Shayna. "I'm serious, note my serious face." He points at his face.

Mama Mae chuckles and nudges him. "Be nice boy."

"She's already upset." Nola said slightly laughing. "Don't make it worse."

"Whatever." James said.

"Anyway, Nola congratulations," Leah said. "I'm thirty three and I'll be glad when it's me. Y'all set a date? What's the plan? What's the colors?. Big wedding, small wedding, casual, formal? Gurl spill all the details."

"We're having the wedding next year." Nola said.

"He'll Work It Out" Chapter 1. Taryn C. Atkins

"Nothing large, just family and friends. Big plans for the honeymoon, we'll be gone three weeks. We're still making arrangements but we're going on a European cruise. We'll be visiting a few places, so far it's England, France, Greece and Italy. We're trying to squeeze in Spain too."

"Honey," Shayna enthusiastically motions to Nola, "Check out St. Martin in the Caribbean. Get yourselves one of those private island villas. Oh, it's beautiful and so romantic. You'll love it."

"Okay but umm..." Nola smiles but gazes at Shayna a little confused. "I thought you and Cliff went to Hawaii."

"Me too." Mama Mae said looking at Shayna.

As everybody stares at Shayna, in her peripheral vision she sees Cliff sit up in the recliner. He stares at her with a puzzled expression. After a moment or two Cliff shakes his head as he rolls his eyes turning away. Cliff puts his attention back on the game. Shayna glances at their faces as she leans back on the sofa.

"Why are y'all staring?!" Shayna said. "A co-worker showed me pictures of her honeymoon. That's all! My goodness!"

"Well Nola," Mama Mae said. "I'm sure that trip is gonna cost y'all a pretty penny for sure."

"Oh it is," Nola said. "Which is why we haven't taken any vacation for two years. That honeymoon is gonna be worth it."

"I know that's right," Leah said. "Well congratulations again, I am thrilled for you two."

"Yeah congratulations Nola," James said. "Where is Dray? Us guys were supposed to play basketball at the park."

"He sends his apologies. Dray and his friend Paris, are at the airport seeing a Marine buddy of theirs off. He's headed for the Persian Gulf."

"Man," Cliff said, shaking his head looking at Nola. "A lot of our troops have been sent there."

"I know," Nola said. "A few women I know got sent too."

"Our troops are getting it done though," James said. "I heard last month they captured Baghdad and finally ended Saddam Hussein's regime."

"After twenty-four years of havoc, it's about time," Cliff said. "I mean, don't get me wrong; I appreciate our troops. It's not easy doing what they do."

"You know what though, after Pearl Harbor," Leah said. "Roosevelt handled his business. When 9/11 happened, I feel if JFK or Clinton had been in office, instead of George Jr. I believe they would've handled their business too."

"I think it's about time the USA had a change of color in the white house anyway," James said.

"Our time is coming." Mama Mae said. "I heard about this black politician down in Illinois, by the name of Barack Obama, he's running for the US Senate. He may be our first black president."

"You prophesying Aunt Mae?" James said.

"No, but Psalms 75:6 and 7 says, "For promotion cometh neither from the east, nor from the west, nor from the south. But God is judge: he putteth down one, and setteth up another." All I'm saying, is God has the last word."

Nola sniffs the air again, she glances at Leah and gets up.

"I'm gonna go check on Regina."

"Yes please do," James said.

Before Nola gets to the kitchen door, Kisha and Reggie come out. Both moaning and showing signs that they've fully enjoyed an excellent meal. Nola smiles at them as she proceeds into the kitchen. Kisha and Reggie plop themselves down on the loveseat and lean on each other for support. James and Cliff get back into watching the game. While Leah enjoys playing with Reggie's Gameboy. Mama Mae turns to Shayna.

"Hey," Mama Mae said. "I know Regina just turned fifteen but next year will be here before you know it. Have you started planning her Sweet Sixteen party?"

"He'll Work It Out" Chapter 1. Taryn C. Atkins

Shayna loses the attitude and allows excitement to fill her. Leah puts the video game on the coffee table and pays closer attention to their conversation.

"Well, I've got a few ideas," Shayna said. "I thought a party cruise on a little yacht would be great. After all, Gina's been doing so good in school. I haven't settled on it, but either way. It'll be a day she'll never forget."

Kisha and Reggie continue to lean on each other as the "itis" weighs heavily on them. Reggie has given in to it and is knocked out. Kisha yawns and smiles as she looks at Shayna.

"A party cruise? That sounds perfect." Kisha said.

Kisha drifts off to sleep. Leah gets up, takes her glass off the coffee table and strolls to the dining room table.

"Well, I'm sure Regina's day will be perfect," Leah said. "I know Gigi won't ever forget hers."

"Leah," Mama Mae said shaking her head. "Don't start."

"It's true though Mama," Leah said taking a small plate from the stack on the table. She glances at Cliff. "Am I right Cliff?"

"Yeah," Cliff nods. "You're right."

Leah scrutinizes the appetizers, she places some on her plate and nibbles on a few. Leah pours herself some punch.

"Oh! I see," Shayna leers at Cliff. "I'm the bad guy; I recall us making the decision together that day, remember."

"I do remember," Cliff stares at her. "I can admit it was the wrong decision too."

Shayna huffs and looks away folding her arms. Leah puts her plate down on the table, picks up her glass and turns toward Shayna.

"Shayna, I get it. Gigi came home drunk. I understand being upset with her, but grounding her, the same week as her sixteenth birthday. You could've gone a little easy on her. You only turn sixteen once, that's all I'm saying."

Leah drinks some of the punch in her glass.

Shayna shakes her finger at Leah, "Well I had my reasons." She turns to Cliff. "Apparently you feel different. Maybe, you'd have rather she go with you to AA, then you would have company!"

"My God Shayna!" Mama Mae said staring at her.

"Did... did she actually say that?" James said.

"Yes she did," Leah shakes her head looking hard at Shayna. "You are something else."

They all stare at Shayna floored by her statement.

"How dare you," Mama Mae said. "Yes, Cliff's made mistakes. We all have at some point and time. The only perfect person I know of is Jesus. Cliff's been working hard to get himself together and God is bringing him through. Then you go say something like that. You should be ashamed of yourself."

"Calm down Aunt Mae," James said.

"Yeah don't get all upset Mama," Leah said.

"It's okay Mama Mae," Cliff watches Shayna, as he leans forward, pulling the lever on the side of the recliner he sits up. "See that day." He shakes his head and laughs a bit. "Shayna just didn't want Gigi celebrating with Lexi. I've tried to tell her, whether we like it or not Lexi's her best friend."

"And she's a bad influence," Shayna said.

"Because you say so."

"Yes!"

Cliff shakes his head and returns his attention back to the game. Leah takes one of the dining room chairs and turns it around so she can face everybody. She takes a drink from her glass of punch.

"Bad influence?" Leah nibbles on the appetizers on her plate. "I don't see it. Lexi's not a hood rat or anything. She's smart, got to Columbia on a scholarship, and okay, her parents aren't like us. Lexi is always kind and respectful to all of us. Unlike you Shayna, who gives her attitude every time you see her."

For several minutes the kitchen door has been wedged open, while Nola assists Regina in preparing the cake. Gigi stands looking through the cracked door, listening attentively to all that's being said.

"Look I'm sorry okay," Shayna said. "Why are we even talking about this, what's done is done. It was two years ago. Let it go."

"Wow, do you ever take responsibility?" Leah said.

Shayna murmurs to herself, "Oh please."

Shayna looks away, folding her arms and crossing her legs disregarding Leah. Cliff keeps his eyes on her.

"Shayna," Cliff said. "You knew Gigi didn't want any extravagant Sweet Sixteen party anyway. You did. All she wanted was to go with her friends to some house party, and we should of let her go. That's why she snuck out in the first place."

Mama Mae turns to Shayna taking her hand.

"Sweetheart," Mama Mae said. "You're so hard on Gigi, and these teenage years are important. You don't want to be pushing her away, that's all we're saying. Lord knows, I know it's not easy being a parent, it takes time, effort, a lot of love and patience. God will grace you to do it. Just ask him. I did..." She laughs a little.

"And still do sometimes."

Mama Mae puts her arms around Shayna, hugs her, leans her head against Shayna's and loves on her. As Shayna takes in Mama Mae's love, her attitude melts away. Leah returns to the sofa retaking seat. Mama Mae releases Shayna from her embrace and Shayna kisses Mama Mae on her cheek. The room is silent for a few moments and the seriousness in the atmosphere is thick. Reggie wakes up, stretches and lets out a long, boisterous yawn. He can't close his mouth to stop it; Everyone watches Reggie and his yawn even wakes up Kisha. Once the yawn is finish Reggie looks at his mother rubbing his stomach.

"Oh man! Ma, that food was slamming! You out did yourself!"

"Yes Ms. Leah," Kisha said. "Everything tasted so good!" She pats her stomach. "I went up about two sizes, but it was so worth it."

"I'm glad you enjoyed it," Leah said.

"I'll jump in on that," James said. "Cause you did put ya

"He'll Work It Out" Chapter 1. Taryn C. Atkins

foot in it cousin,"

Mama Mae takes Leah's hand in hers, "Yes, everything was delicious." She takes note of everyone. "This was a beautiful surprise. You've made my heart glad. I love y'all, thank you so much."

"We love you too Mama," Leah said.

Leah moves to the edge of the sofa, she turns to Mama Mae and reaches out putting her arms around her mother. Leah hugs her tight and kisses her mom several times on the cheek. James leans back trying to move out the way from all the affection. When Leah releases Mama Mae there is lipstick prints all on her cheek.

"We got ya too," Leah rubs her lipstick off. "You were totally caught off guard."

"Yeah y'all got me good." Mama Mae said.

"Well, I'm glad Mama," Shayna still in a mood. "I thank God for Nola; I practically did everything myself." She glances at Leah. "Some folks didn't do much."

"Didn't do much?" Leah said. "I was cooking all day."

"Well, decorating isn't easy either."

"You know what--"

"Come on now you two, please." Mama Mae said. "Can we just enjoy each other?"

"Sorry Mama." Shayna said. "I should've ignored lurking demons."

"Lurking demons!" Leah said. "Listen Shayna--"

"Now y'all stop it!!" Mama Mae said. "Sweet Jesus walk through here!"

The living room goes silent again. Under the sound of the baseball game the soft melody plays of the Take 6 song "If We Ever Needed The Lord Before". Reggie and Kisha have drifted off to sleep once again. After a few moments.

"I'm sorry Mama," Shayna said. "So, tell me, did you finally get the tape you wanted from that Friday night revival service? You said Pastor's son Elder Gorham preached a good word."

"Yes, yes I did." Mama Mae said. "God is indeed using him too. Elder Gorham said Every believer is a Son of

God. He preached from... Romans 8:19. He talked about how creation waits with expectation for the manifestation of the sons of God. Said how we're not on this earth just to make a living, but to make a difference. He said, "The world needs us more than ever, no more church just behind four walls."

"Would've loved to hear that one," Cliff said.

Mama Mae glances at Cliff, "Buy the tape son, five dollars." She looks around at her family. "Folks need to hear sermons like that. Good solid preaching and teaching of the word of God. Straight out the bible and not watered down. So many preachers caught up in the glitz and glamor nowadays, not concerned about souls like they used to be."

James sits up nodding his head, "Yeah it's all about how many people are in the pews, and the amount of bucks going in the basket. Some pastors let folks get away with anything."

"Well, I thank God my Pastor is truly living for the Lord." Mama Mae said. "Pastor Gorham even prophesied to Reggie." She points at him. "Said God called him to be a preacher, don't you forget that either Reggie."

Reggie still half asleep nods his head, "I know grandma."

"Well, I don't know about prophecy," Leah said. "I've seen too many so called..." She does quotation signs in the air. "Prophets" on that put in for prophecy kick."

Leah surveys her family, they glance at each other and then focus on her with puzzled expressions.

"Meaning," Leah said. "The more you put in the offering, the better your prophecy."

Leah laughs, as do James and Cliff. Almost in unison Mama Mae and Shayna's faces tighten and become stern as they both fold their arms. James and Cliff laugh until they notice the seriousness beaming off of Shayna and Mama Mae's face.

Both play off their laughter by pretending to cough and put their attention back on the baseball game. Leah notices James and

Cliff's sudden change. She takes in the sight of her mother and Shayna's stern countenance.

"Oh come on, that's funny. A bit true too, even in your church mama."

"What did you say?" Mama Mae said focusing on Leah.

James quickly stands doing the time out sign, "Hold it! Time Out!" *Let me get out the way.* He thought.

James turns to those sitting on the sofa.

"Aunt Mae, Leah, can y'all please move down towards Shayna?"

Mama Mae and Leah appease James and shift their positions.

"Thank you so much," James sits on the opposite side of Leah, and leans over to her. "You asked for it." He peeks at his aunt giving the time in sign. "Time In!" He leans over to Leah again. "This is gonna be good."

Leah nudges James. Mama Mae's eyes are locked on Leah.

"Are you talking about my Pastor?"

"Mama, you know there are pastors hooking and crooking out there."

"Whatever those pastors do is between them and God. My pastor's no crook. So don't put him in that equation."

"Mama, all I'm saying is that--"

"Leah Rowena Babcock! I don't want to hear it!"

Mama Mae's voice wakes up Reggie and Kisha, they sit up wondering what's going on rubbing the sleep from their faces.

Leah looks away murmuring, "Not the whole name."

"See I recall, God using Pastor Richard Gorham when you first got saved. Lest we forget the crying and giving up all at the altar last year."

"Which went out the window once Wes got to town," Shayna said adding her two cents.

"Oh and wasn't it Lady Alma Gorham who tarried with you. Prayed you through."

Shayna's two cents doubles to four, "Also gone once Wes was back in town."

"Why don't you shut up Shayna!" Leah said.

Reggie and Kisha say nothing; They look at each other from time to time and listen.

"As a matter of fact," Mama Mae said. "Lady Gorham made sure you left the church that day Holy Ghost filled."

Leah drops her head, "Oh here we go."

"Oh yeah, here we go!" Mama Mae said nodding her head. "I remember you eee tah tahing from the church, to the car, in the car and all the way home."

Leah returns her attention to her mother.

"Alright Ma, All I'm saying--"

"No, I'm saying! There is no time to be playing games with God! The last thing you need to be doing is talking about Pastor. He's the one praying for your soul Leah."

"I wasn't specifically talking about him."

"Still! God has been merciful because of his prayers and mine. I've said it before and I'll say it again. The only thing that comes out of shacking up is a place in hell."

"You keep waiting for that ring though." Shayna said doubling her four cents to eight.

James sees Leah inching up in her seat on the sofa.

"Calm down Lee," James nonchalantly whispers to Leah. "Don't get up, please don't get up."

James shakes his head, as he leans back on the sofa turning his attention back to the television.

James thought. *It's about to go down in five, four, three, two–*

James swiftly sits up, looks at Shayna, gestures to her while right in sync with Mama Mae mouthing her exact words.

"Shayna Rochell Babcock-Greye!" Mama Mae said.

James quickly leans back, his actions never noticed by Mama Mae. Shayna stares at her mother stunned.

"Ma really... You gonna use the whole name."

"She sure did." James snickers.

"Cause you need to mind your business!" Mama Mae said.

"Yes! And stay out of mine!!" Leah said.

"Whatever," Shayna shows Leah her wedding ring. "At least I'm legal."

"He'll Work It Out" Chapter 1. Taryn C. Atkins

"Alright." James said under his breath. He taps Cliff. "Here we go."

"You're also a PUNK!" Leah gets up, pointing at Shayna. "When your so call perfect world got a little rocky a year ago, you jump ship and disappear for almost two weeks, to God knows where!"

"It's none of your business where I went!" Shayna gets up. "But for your information. Cliff knew I went on a business trip for my job. Happy now, big mystery solved."

"All I know, a week had already went by; When I'm told you hadn't come home and nobody heard from you either."

Reggie and Kisha sit there keeping quiet and listening. James listens also but pretends to watch the game.

James mumbles to himself, "Ahhh, family get togethers. Good times, good times."

Shayna locks her eyes on Cliff. "So you're telling my family our business now."

Cliff peers at Shayna, shakes his head but gives her no answer. He turns the TV off and leans back in the recliner. As Cliff goes to sit the remote on the end table, James takes it from him.

"Hey man," James said. "I'm still watching that."

James takes the remote and turns the TV back on. Cliff leans back in the recliner trying to stay calm, regardless of the current commotion.

"It wasn't him," Leah said. "The girls came to me, worried sick about you. Wondering what happen to you, why did you leave, you had them thinking they were the reason you left."

"Well they weren't." Shayna said. "I needed that trip okay; I had to get away. So, that business trip was right on time. It helped take my mind off of situations here. At least for a little while."

"Well Shayna, what I have with Wes isn't perfect, but I never ran from them either. I never ran leaving my son or his father to just figure it out."

"Wait, what you have with Wes-isn't it what you and

several other women have with Wes. Because he spends more time gone than here."

Reggie stands up with a quickness. "Don't talk about my father!"

"Reggie sit down," Kisha grabs his hand and tries to pull him back down in the seat.

"No Kisha," Reggie glances at Kisha pulls his hand from her. "She has no right."

Cliff watches and listens as he lays back in the recliner.

"Reggie, I'll handle this." Leah said. "Now sit down."

Kisha moves to the edge of the loveseat, staying between Reggie and Shayna.

"Ma," Reggie motions toward Shayna, "Who does she think she is, saying that about dad."

"I'm your aunt." Shayna said. "And I'm talking to my sister. So you need to watch your mouth."

"You need to watch yours." Reggie said.

Mama Mae quickly gets up, motioning to Reggie saying, "Quiet Reggie!"

As Mama Mae makes her way to him, Shayna moves to the side allowing her to pass.

"Go on outside with Kisha." Mama Mae said. Reggie doesn't move. "I said go on Reggie." Mama Mae motions to Kisha. "Kisha, please take that boy outside. He doesn't need to get involved in this."

"Yes ma'am," Kisha said. "Come on Reggie."

Kisha gets up, she darts pass Reggie grabbing his hand. When she pulls him Reggie doesn't budge, she pulls him harder causing him to move. He pulls his hand away, but follows Kisha out the living room door. Shayna eyeballs Leah.

"Guess he's not ready for the truth."

Leah moves toward Shayna.

"You know Shayna," Leah said, "I've been wondering, did you only rush back from your "business trip", after learning it was Gina hit by a car."

"Let me tell you--" Shayna said moving toward Leah.

"What! Tell me!" Leah said heading toward Shayna.

"He'll Work It Out" Chapter 1. Taryn C. Atkins

Before either can do anything, Mama Mae rushes between them.

"Back Up! Mama Mae pushes Shayna, she eyes Leah and shoves her too. "I said Back Up!!"

Leah and Shayna back away from each other.

"Mama," Leah motions to Shayna. "She has no right--"

"Well you shouldn't--" Shayna points at Leah.

"Jesus!!" Mama Mae said. "Both of Y'all Shut Up and Sit Down!!! I'm tired of all the fussing now! You're sisters! My God!! You should get along!!"

The kitchen door quietly closes. Gigi turns around to see Regina is standing a few feet behind her, looking extremely excited holding a slanted birthday cake in her hands.

"Okay, it's ready!" Regina said. "Let's go!"

"No... not yet." Gigi said. She looks at the slanted cake.

"I... I think it needs more frosting."

"Really?" Regina said.

"Yeah, plus look, you forgot the candles. Can't have a birthday cake with no candles."

Regina gives the cake the once-over, "Oh yeah, can't forget those. Okay, we'll be ready to go out in a little while."

Regina takes the cake back to the counter and adds frosting. Nola watches Gigi, seeing the concerned look on her face, she knows something is wrong and goes to her.

"I know Gigi." Nola whispers. "I heard them arguing."

"Yeah." Gigi said keeping a soft tone. "Mom and Aunt Leah are going at it."

"I know," Nola said. "It was hard keeping Regina distracted, so she wouldn't notice."

"Well, let's keep her in here a little bit longer," Gigi said. "It's best she not know what's going on out there."

"Yeah we'll wait a moment before we go out."

"I'll listen out and tell you when."

"Okay, leave Regina to me."

"Thanks Aunt Nola."

Nola takes the candles off the table and goes to Regina.

"Okay, found the candles, lets put them on the cake."

"He'll Work It Out" Chapter 1. Taryn C. Atkins

Back in the living room, Cliff tries to relax while James stays focused on the television. Leah and Shayna slowly sit down on the sofa. Mama Mae shakes her head as she watches them. Leah makes eye contact with her mother and quickly looks away. Mama Mae glances at Shayna, who also turns away. As Mama Mae retakes her seat she taps James on his knee.

"James," Mama Mae said.

"Yes Aunt Mae." James said.

"Go get Reggie and Kisha please." Mama Mae said. "And let Reggie know it's over! Tell him, I said he betta not walk up in here with any attitude toward anybody either."

"I'll tell him." James said as he gets up. He picks up the remote and turns off the TV. "You relax Aunt Mae." He points at Leah and Shayna. "Don't let these two run your pressure up."

"You right about that baby."

Shayna and Leah both eyeball James with serious faces. He returns the look as he heads toward the living room door.

"That's my Aunt Mae, so y'all can evil eye me all y'all want. Ain't nobody scared."

James steps out of the living room. He walks to the front door, opens it and steps outside. He enjoys the Spring breeze for a moment and then checks Reggie and Kisha sitting on the porch bench.

Everyone in the living room sits in silence. The kitchen door slowly opens and Gigi peeks through the cracked door. After a few moments, James, Reggie and Kisha walk back into the living room. Reggie and Kisha sit on the loveseat, and James sits at the end of the sofa by Leah. Gigi slowly closes the kitchen door.

The living room is quiet but this time, the silence is deafening; Not even Mama Mae's gospel music is heard. Everyone sits mute until Gigi's voice bellows from the kitchen.

"Okay everybody! Get ready!!"

Everyone stands and moves into position around the birthday girl waiting for the birthday cake. Cliff moves the recliner out the way as Leah turns off the living room lights.

"I know the lights are out grandma," Reggie said. "You still have to close your eyes."

"Oh, okay." Mama Mae said.

Mama Mae closes her eyes. Reggie stands behind Mama Mae covering her eyes with his hands.

"Reggie, my eyes are closed." Mama Mae said.

"Yeah I know," Reggie said. "You peek sometimes though."

Mama Mae laughs tickled by Reggie's statement, "Lord knows you got me. Tell the truth and shame the devil."

Everybody laughs.

"Alright y'all, we're ready out here." James said.

Those in the kitchen make their entrance, but with the lights off; All that can be seen are two floating golden flames, which appear to be leaning to the side. The floating flames make their way to the middle of the room and touchdown on the coffee table.

"Here we go." James said. He stomps on the floor as he counts out loud. "One, two, one two three!"

Leah flicks on the lights and Reggie uncovers Mama Mae's eyes. Everyone starts to sing happy birthday, each one cracking their voices on purpose as they sing. Mama Mae scrunches up her face as she listens to the unified screeching voices. It's at this moment when everyone forgets about all the fussing and confusion that went on. They joyfully sing horribly as they dance around the room together, celebrating the life of the family matriarch. Watching their ecstatic faces makes Mama Mae's heart glad.

They sing and dance around, doing the chorus three times. They all stop where they are on the last one and hold the note. Instead, of the sound of sweet harmony they all once again crack and shriek their voices. When all the birthday celebratory dancing and singing is finished, they all find a place to be seated around Mama Mae.

James grabs a dining room chair and takes a seat by the loveseat. Seated in the loveseat is Reggie, Kisha, and Nola. By them sitting on the sofa is Leah, Gigi, Mama Mae and next to her Regina. Cliff and Shayna sit together in the recliner.

"He'll Work It Out" Chapter 1. Taryn C. Atkins

Now the room is quiet again but no loud outburst caused it. This time, it's because all eyes were focused on the two layered, slanted, cream cheese frosted birthday cake with the two burning number candles sitting on top. Regina scooted off the sofa to kneel down by the coffee table. Regina smiled as she delighted in breaking the silence.

"Ta-Dah!!" Regina said. "Happy Sixty-Seventh Birthday Grandma!! I made it from scratch, it's your favorite too! Red Velvet!"

"Thank you baby," Mama Mae said with a big smile.

"Sixty-seven grandma! You better go head!!" Reggie said.

"I pray I look like you when I get there." Kisha said.

"Gurl I do too!" Leah said. She raises her hand in the air, "Praise the Lord thank ya for good genes."

"Amen to that!" Shayna said.

"Well, hope I can get in on that good gene action by association." Nola said.

"Me too for that matter." Kisha said.

"I ain't mad at ya." Nola said. "Get in on it gurl."

Nola extends her hand to Kisha, and they high five each other. Everyone laughs, the atmosphere is back to being as it should be, full of peace, joy and love.

"So Aunt Mae," James laughs. "How do you like your mini me's first baking masterpiece?"

Mama Mae looks at James for a quick second as she takes in the slanted cake.

"Its..." Mama Mae focuses on Regina, takes her hand and rubs it. "It's a beautiful cake baby! I bet it taste good too."

James pretends to sneeze saying, "I don't think so."

Regina considers James, then observes everyone around her. She gets up off the floor and sits next to Mama Mae again.

"Well," Regina said. "Okay, it didn't come out, exactly like I wanted it. I'm sure it taste good grandma."

Reggie slowly raises his hand saying, "Excuse me, but umm... I call for a second opinion."

Kisha shoves Reggie. "Don't do that."

Reggie glances at Kisha. "I'm just saying."

"Grandma," Regina pouts a bit. "I'm sorry but it's from my heart."
Reggie raises his hand again, "I think I speak for everyone when I say, it's our stomachs we're worried about."
"Stop it." Kisha shoves Reggie again.
"Ignore him." Mama Mae puts her arm around Regina.
"Baby I love it, thanks for making it for me."

Mama Mae gives Regina a big hug and as they release each other Regina has a big smile on her face. She glances at Reggie and sticks her tongue out at him. As they all laugh, Reggie points at Regina.

"Yeah alright mini mama," Reggie said. He playfully punches into his hand. "I'll get you later."
Mama Mae smiles looking at everyone.
"Thank you, everybody." Mama Mae said. "Thank you so much for throwing me this birthday party. My heart is so full." She glances at Shayna and Leah as she looks around at everyone else. "I apologize for all the confusion that took place. Y'all should know by now, I'm gonna speak the truth. I love y'all, but I'm gonna always tell the truth."
"Aunt Mae we know you love us." James said. "And we love you right back. Now make a wish, the candles are melting."
"I'll say a little prayer." Mama Mae closes her eyes, smiles, then opens them. "Alright, It's my birthday; I want to sing the song I taught my girls."
"Well, alright!" Cliff said. "Get to singing ladies."

Shayna, Leah, Gigi and Regina move into their places. Leah and Shayna move behind the sofa and stand behind Mama Mae. Gigi and Gina are already in place, one sitting on each side of Mama Mae. Everyone sits in the living room waiting to enjoy, the sweet sounds to come. Reggie eyes his mother.

"Ma, you never told me you could sing," Reggie said.
"I've never heard you and you be joking around in the shower."

"Leah's been singing since high school." Mama Mae said.
"Does dad know?"
"How do you think I met your father?" Leah said.

Instead of music coming from the cassette player, the atmosphere is filled with the melodious voices of Mama Mae, Shayna, Leah, Gigi, and Regina. They join together singing in five part harmony the acapella version of one of Mama Mae's favorite songs "God Will Take Care Of You."

~THE MASQUERADE~

Ten Years Have Passed. It's a late Sunday afternoon, during the month of May in the Spring of 2013, and the Full Gospel Temple service ended about thirty minutes ago. The corridor where the church offices are is so luminous from the natural light coming through the row of picture windows. The lighting accentuates the rice bowl colored walls, as well as the custom hand-scraped walnut floors, which matches the beams in the hall ceiling. What truly set off this section of the church when entering it, you walk through a beautiful pair of arched, hand carved, solid wood double doors which have a French country architectural style to them.

One of the office doors opens and through it steps Minister Pauls. She is a honey caramel tint, although fashionable she's modest in attire and lovely. Her Donna Karan glasses look studious on her. Minister Pauls has her dark hair up in a French twist, she wears a dark blue, Jones New York fishtail skirt suit, an ivory silk shell with matching pearl earrings and necklace, and dark blue Nine West patent leather pumps.

She holds her cell phone to her ear as she places her black Coach briefcase on the floor, she closes her office door and wiggles the doorknob to make sure it's locked. As Minister Pauls gets ready to walk away from her office, she fixes her Michael Kors tote bag strap on her shoulder, picks up her briefcase and starts down the hall. She takes a few steps, but stops to focus on the conversation she's engaged in on her cell.

"Dylan, like I've said to you before, for every temptation God provides a way of escape... Yes, but you have to pray too, ask Jesus to keep you. God will keep you Dylan if you want to be kept... When you're disappointed, you call Sean and end up falling again... Sean will never take your salvation seriously if you keep sleeping with him... Dylan, bottom line, if you want to keep your deliverance, you'll do whatever it takes." She takes a few steps down the corridor. "2 Corinthians 6:17, in the amplified version states. "So, come out from among [unbelievers], and separate (sever) yourselves from them, said the Lord, and touch not [any] unclean thing; then I will receive you kindly and treat you with favor." She stops walking. "That means, if you must change your circle of friends then that's what you need to do... You have to get serious and stop playing." She checks her watch. "Dylan I've gotta go; I have a meeting to get to. We're scheduled for a session this Tuesday coming."

The sound of footsteps are heard on the corridor floor. Regina strolls through the open double doors, dressed in a pretty peach spring pants suit and heels. Minister Pauls back is turned. Regina approaches her, but slows her pace once she hears Minister Pauls talking on her cell.

"Dylan, have faith, Jesus can get you through this. All you have to do is call on Him."

Minister Pauls turns around and notices Regina coming down the hall. She smiles and waves hello to her as she listens to the party on her cell phone. Regina slowly advances toward her.

"You're busy." Regina softly said. "We'll talk later."

Minister Pauls looks at Regina covering her cell, "I'm almost done." She uncovers her phone. "Alright Dylan, I've got to go; Like I said, I've got a meeting to get to... I'll see you Tuesday God willing. Okay... Talk to you then. Take care." She taps her phone ending her call, slips it into her handbag and smiles at Regina. "Well it's great to see you, come give me a hug."

Minister Pauls spreads her arms wide and they embrace.

"It's great to see you too." Regina said. They release each other. "Sorry to disturb you."

"Please, I was just finishing up." Minister Pauls said. "Look at you, no glasses, all grown up and you're so beautiful. I am loving that twist out on you."

"Thank you," Regina said. "It took a moment to work with it, but I'm glad I went natural. You look fantastic."

"Oh stop, I'm speechless." Minister Pauls said. "You're a grown woman now. Has it been that long."

"Yes it has. I still remember being at the airport that day when you left for California."

"Wow... You... you remember that? You were like nine."

"I've always had a good memory. Which is why, even though you look a little different. I knew who you were when you started coming here. I saw you a few times too, we even said hello in passing. You didn't realize who I was though, not until you saw me with my parents."

"I was stunned too." Minister Pauls said. She glances at the corridor wall and gestures to them. "Let's go over here."

Minister Pauls heads toward the corridor wall and Regina follows. Lined up against them, which emphasized the area, are three long restored, vintage wooden church pews. Minister Pauls walks to the middle pew and places her bags on it. Regina reviews them.

"Ahh yes," Regina said. "The signs of a woman in ministry, the oversize handbag, briefcase and tote."

Regina snickers as she sits down next to the bags.

"I know it's terrible." Minister Pauls said.

"Oh I do know, mines are in my car." Regina said.

They both laugh for a moment.

"You know Gina, I've been a member here for about two years now. I'm still surprised; I didn't see you guys when I first started attending services. I mean, this congregation is pretty large, but I was here about six months before we even bumped into each other. I didn't even know Mother Babcock was your grandmother until last year."

"Well, that's not surprising to me." Regina sits back and

crosses her legs. "We all have such different schedules. It's hard sometimes for us to even catch up with each other at home. Besides, we don't always come to service together either. As you can see though, its a small world."

Minister Pauls nods her head, "So true." She reaches into her tote bag, as she looks through it, in a soft tone she utters to herself. "Apparently smaller than I thought." She takes a soft peppermint out her bag, as she unravels it. "So you're twenty-five now?" She places the peppermint in her mouth and smiles. "Are the brothers chasing you down?"

"They try, but Thank God for Jesus."

"I know that's right."

Minister Pauls smooths down the back of her skirt as she sits down and leans back on the bench crossing her legs.

"You look great!" Regina said. "Okay you tell, I don't want to say the wrong age and get in trouble.

"You're sweet," Minister Pauls said. "I'm forty-five now."

"Like I said, you look fantastic. And I'm sure the brothers are chasing you down."

"Like you said, they do try." Minister Pauls looks in her tote bag again. "I've been so busy, getting settled in here and at my new place." She takes out a few soft peppermints. "I'm sorry; I love these things."

She hands Regina some of the peppermints.

"Thanks, me too. They're addicting."

They both open a mint up and pop it in their mouth.

"You know I have to ask." Regina said. "Where and when did you get saved... Minister Pauls?"

"I got saved while out in California." Minister Pauls said. "It's been about thirteen years now. I was invited to church by one of my patients and well, the rest is history."

"Well Praise God."

"Yes, Praise God. Okay so, what are you doing now? I'm sure you went to college."

"Of course, mom wouldn't let me get away with that."
"Of course not. So where did you go?"
"I went to City College up in Harlem."
"Harlem? Your mom didn't fight you on that."
"You know she did. She wanted me to go to a private university, but I held my ground."
"Good for you. Go on."
"So I got my BA in Performing Arts; I've been acting, singing and doing a little dancing here and there. Right now I'm attending K.L.B.I. I mean Kingdom Life Bible Institute; I'm going for my Bachelors in Theology and maybe later my Masters."
"A triple threat, plus a preacher, that's alright. Please let me know the next time you're performing, and when you have your first preaching engagement."
"I'll do that, but now wait, I know by now you're a threat too. When I was a kid, you already had two Bachelors, one in Accounting and the other in... Psychology."
"That's amazing, and you're correct."
"Now I know you did some of your residency here, but isn't that why you went to California?"
"One of the reasons." Minister Pauls said.
"So come on," Regina said. "Tell me all the credentials."
Minister Pauls shakes her head. "No."
"You've got to do this for me..."
"Stop it, I don't usually talk about it that's all."
"Oh come on, please... it's me."

Minister Pauls looks away shaking her head and fiddles with her earring. She glances at Regina shaking her head again. They sit in silence for a few seconds as Minister Pauls contemplates Regina's toothy grin filled with anticipation. It causes her to crack a smile too.

"Fine..." Minister Pauls said. "I've got my Masters in Accounting and my Ph.D., in Psychology. I'm licensed and certified. Okay."

Regina uncrosses her legs as she sits up.

"Then it's Dr. Pauls," Regina said with a big smile. She

claps her hands a few times. "Impressive."

"Anyway, I didn't see Mother Babcock in service and she's always here. Is she alright?"

"Grandma's fine, today's her birthday so she's in her pj's relaxing at home. That's why I won't be at the meeting, I'm headed there."

"Well, she deserves to relax."

"You just changed the whole conversation, Dr. Pauls."

Regina repositions herself slightly on the pew as she leans back, extends her arm resting it on the back of the pew.

"Yes I did." Minister Pauls folds her hands in her lap. "So now, is everything good with you?"

"Well," Regina's mood dampens. "It... it could be better."

"Uh-oh, I remember that tone. What's going on?"

Regina sighs, "This... friend of mine is in a real stressful situation, and since you counsel people. I thought I could talk to you about them."

"Alright, I'm here. What's the situation?"

"Well, my friend came out to their parents, it went terrible and they had to move out."

"Okay, but be honest with me. If this is you, you can tell me. Or do I need to get the milk and Oreo's like old times."

Regina smiles, "I'll still have milk and cookies when I'm working something out. It's not me though, truthfully."

"Alright, so how can I help?" Minister Pauls said as she glances at her watch. "Oh my goodness." She rushes to her feet. "I totally forgot about the leadership meeting." She swiftly opens her briefcase. "I am so sorry Gina." She takes a business card out. "Listen, here's my card. My numbers on it of course." She gives Regina the card and a quick hug. "Please call me, let's finish talking about this okay. I'm sorry I have to rush off like this. "

"No problem."

"He'll Work It Out" Chapter 1. Taryn C. Atkins

Minister Pauls grabs her bags and quickly walks away, heading for the corridor doors. Before walking through them, she stops and turns back to Regina.

"I'm always here for you Gina regardless." Minister Pauls starts to move away. "Let me go, give your friend my card in case they want to talk." Minister Pauls turns to leave. As she walks away, she raises her hand and waves. "And don't be a stranger, call me!"

"I will!" Regina said. "And thanks again!"

"Glad to help."

Minister Pauls rushes off.

Regina focuses on the card as she crosses her legs. "Well Lord, this couldn't hurt."

~LEADERSHIP MEETING~

Moments later, in the Full Gospel Temple Ministries elegant and massive dining hall. Which besides ministry events it's used for wedding receptions, banquets and other gatherings. The radiance around the room comes from several glistening gold trim chandeliers; Each of their creatively carved crystal pieces illuminates every section. The glossy shine of the oak mocha stained floors was brilliant under their lights.

While waiting for the meeting to start, the sound of various conversations flow throughout the room from leaders and lay members present. The attendees sit in beige vinyl padded stacking chairs. They have been set up around six long cream folding tables. The tables are positioned in the center of the room in the shape of a rectangle. This way, everyone in attendance could easily see each other. A round table is also setup off to the side, Sister Carlton the late fifties, church cougar and gossip, is sitting there with Sister Richardson the early thirties, second generation busy body. They sit slowly finishing their lunch. Well, that was their story anyway.

Elder Mays, a full-figured, refine and stylishly dressed lady in her early fifties, is one of the leaders in the church. As she sits there, she flips the top page of the writing tablet she has in her hand. Elder Mays places it on the table in front of her and puts her uniquely designed pen on top of it. She picks up the paper with the meetings agenda and carefully scans it.

Lady Gorham stands next to her at the head of this rectangle. She's a statuesque, pleasant and classy lady; who's also in her early fifties. Lady Gorham always looks so chic, today the First Lady is wearing a gorgeous custom made NoelLe Martin silky twill pink suit. She is studying the meetings agenda on the table and takes note of the topics that will be discussed. Her head is down, and you can't see her charming face because she's wearing an exquisite silky pink hat with a white bow trimmed in silver, which matches her suit perfectly.

Lady Gorham takes her seat next to her husband, Pastor Gorham. He's in his late fifties, a stately, tall and stocky man. The Pastor does his best to stay somewhat fit. He dresses snazzy and quite dapper. This Sunday, he sports an Armani, light gray, pin-striped three-piece suit, a light gray shirt with a pair of light gray, patent leather Ferragamo shoes. His tie, handkerchief and socks match his wife's attire. They're a regal couple with such presence, approachable and down to earth too. Pastor Gorham leans in and whispers a few words to Lady Gorham. She shakes her head in agreement picking up a small bottle of water in front of her and takes a few sips.

Lady Gorham checks the seats a few feet behind her for one of her armor bearers or nurses. Marsha a graceful and trendy young lady in her late twenties is seated there. Lady Gorham beckons for Marsha to come. She quickly comes over and after Lady Gorham says a few words to her. Marsha goes to a little suitcase she has by her seat, reaches into the side pocket and pulls out a baggie filled with cough drops and soft peppermints. Marsha takes out a few, then comes back and hands some to Lady Gorham and Pastor Gorham. Elder Mays leans in and says a few words to Marsha. She then places a few of the cough drops and mints in Elder Mays hand too.

Before Marsha sits down, she gives some to Elder Rayner too. He's an older man in his early sixties, who dresses rather sporty for his age, and his handlebar mustache always makes him look so distinguished. Elder Rayner sits on the other side of Pastor Gorham.

Marsha takes her seat next to Gilbert, a preppy and educated man of thirty-four, he's one of Pastor Gorham's armor bearers. He taps Marsha on her arm and before he could even say anything, Marsha hands him a few mints too. Pastor Gorham rises to his feet. When all in attendance notice the sound of all conversation ceases.

> "Good Afternoon Saints." Pastor Gorham said "I see a few of the leadership are on vacation. Nevertheless, we're still going to have this brief meeting. After having preached, I'm drained so..." He motions to his wife. "When I finish my beautiful wife, Lady Delinda, will continue with the meeting." He looks at her. "Is that alright?"

Lady Gorham gazes at her husband with a beaming smile.
"That's fine Pastor Robert."
"Excellent." Pastor Gorham said, He turns his attention back to those at the meeting. "I won't be long saints. There's no evening service, so come and go with me tonight. I'm preaching at Kingdom Ambassadors Global Ministries, in Lynbrook, NY. Where the lovely and highly anointed woman of God, Bishop, Dr. Aretha Wilson is Overseer and Pastor.

I'm excited to have been asked to bring forth the word there. Y'all know Dr. Wilson doesn't play with the word of God or her members. She said she's a little shy, but my God, you would never know it by the way she preaches and teaches, and don't get me started on her praying. See, besides being anointed, Dr. Wilson's well studied and proficient in the holy scriptures. That little lady is powerful, she operates in all five ministry gifts and she's a seer too.

Dr. Wilson doesn't play, she doesn't let just anybody walk up into her pulpit and feed her flock either. They eat well there saints. God's presence resides there too, it's truly a place where you can encounter God and experience change.

Before I even got this invitation; I've seen her preach, heard a lot about her and her RAW Gatherings too. So, I went to visit her. We're sitting in her office, sharing our experiences with God and both of us being a pastor and all. Well, she had to step out for a moment. I'm sitting there and in the corner of her desk, was a few bibles stacked up. There was a Thompson Chain, a Scofield, Dakes and even a Complete Jewish Bible. She had good ones there.

As I sat there; I inspected her library. A pastor's personal library says a lot about them. Saints, y'all know, I've been studying the word a while, been involved in ministry since I was about fifteen, served while my father was pastor, right here. Well, I scanned the titles and subjects in her library. The authors I saw were, Wigglesworth, Tetsola, Horton, Ray, Bynum, Nee, Munroe, Boyd, McCullough, Bloomer, Shaw and Lahaye. I... I got a bit nervous, even started sweating. I rushed, got my pen and pad out, and started jotting down names and titles.

Well, she came back in her office, saw me sitting there, leaning on her desk and writing away. She put her hand on my shoulder, asked me if I was alright and what I was doing. I told her the truth. Yes I did. I looked up at that little lady and said after viewing your library. I see, I gotta step up my game a little more. Listen, I got a few degrees under my belt but Dr. Wilson's library, made me feel like a second-year college student.

So I count it an honor to know Dr. Aretha Wilson and be in fellowship with another worker in the vineyard, who makes you want to expand your capacity, study harder and learn more about the God we serve. Iron sharpens iron saints.

I'm excited to go tonight, service starts at 7:30 sharp, so join me. I'm turning this meeting over to the First Lady now. Pray for me saints, and I'll see y'all in Lynbrook. Lady Gorham."

Gilbert stands up. Pastor Gorham takes his wife's hand, assisting her as she stands. Pastor Gorham leans in and kisses her softly on the cheek before leaving. Gilbert picks up Pastor Gorham's briefcase sitting by his chair. Pastor Gorham then follows Gilbert as he walks toward the main doors of the dining hall. Gilbert opens one of the main doors and hold it. Pastor Gorham gives a wave and walks through. Gilbert leaves out right behind him. After Lady Gorham watches her husband go, she peruses the room.

"Okay let's begin." Lady Gorham said. "This year--"

Music blares out, everyone in attendance looks to see where it's coming from. Cliff glances down on the table in front of him and realizes it's his cell. Shayna, who's sitting next to Cliff, looks at him a bit miffed. Cliff looks at the display and quickly answers. He holds the phone to his ear and covers his mouth.

"Hello?" Cliff whispers. "Hey... Hold on a moment." He stands. "I apologize Lady Gorham; I have to take this call."

"No problem Deacon Greye." Lady Gorham said.

Cliff steps away from the meeting, leaving through the side doors of the dining hall. Shayna folds her arms watching him leave, annoyed by Cliff's urgency toward the call. Lady Gorham notices Minister Pauls rush in through the main doors.

"Excellent timing Minister Pauls." Lady Gorham said. "I was just about to say how this year, you, Minister McDaniels and Mother Livingston are organizing our Women's Fellowship Luncheon. How is it going ladies?"

Lady Gorham sits down as Minister Pauls walks to the empty seat between Minister McDaniels and Mother Livingston.

"It's going well Lady Gorham." Minister Pauls said. She

takes her seat and gestures to Minister McDaniels. "I'm going to let Minister McDaniels fill you in further."

While Minister Pauls gets herself together. Minister McDaniels stands, she's in her mid thirties, a relatively pretty woman but not into all the designer clothing labels. As Minister McDaniels holds her iPad in her hands, the sizeable Star Trek emblem on the cover is seen by all. She taps the front of the iPad a few times.

Minister McDaniels said, "Well Lady Gorham, we've decided the theme will be Women of Virtue and Substance. The menu will consist of various types of Caribbean food." She looks around at others present in the meeting. "One more thing; I wanted to remind those who signed up this month. Saturday coming we'll be going out to witness. If anybody else would like to join us, please meet us in the sanctuary at 9 a.m. We're praying for thirty minutes and then going out. Thank you."

Minister McDaniels puts her iPad down and takes her seat. Minister Pauls moves her chair back a little then stands.

"Well, Lady Gorham." Minister Pauls said. "Things are moving along, we're finalizing arrangements but there are a few other items that we need to get done. We could use some extra help." She sits back down. "It would be greatly appreciated."

"Alright, who can assist these ladies?" Lady Gorham said.

Lady Gorham puts a cough drop in her mouth, looks around at the leaders and lay members at the meeting. All but especially the women in the room do their best to avoid eye contact with her. As Lady Gorham scans the area, Minister Pauls goes in her briefcase, takes out an elegant, black lace hand fan and places it on the table.

"Okay," Lady Gorham said. "I'll choose."

Lady Gorham once again surveys those to her left and right. She looks across the room and her eyes go to Shayna. Who is sitting there with her head down, focused on writing a few notes in her notepad.

"Deaconess Greye can you please assist Minister Pauls and the other ladies?" Lady Gorham said.

"Oh…" Shayna said. She looks up a bit surprised. "Lady Gorham, I'm no good at organizing things."

"It will be fine." Minister Pauls said. She gestures to the ladies sitting by her. "We'll all help out with showing you what needs to get done, won't we ladies." Minister McDaniels and Mother Livingston nod agreeing with her. "So see, no worries."

Shayna smiles, putting her pen down as she looks across the room at the three women.

"Ladies, I do appreciate your help. I do." Shayna said. She looks at Lady Gorham. "Lady Gorham, I'll mess up everything. It's better to get somebody else."

"It won't be a lot of work Deaconess Greye." Minister McDaniels said. "There's just a few area's left where we'll be needing assistance."

"You being a CPA is great." Minister Pauls said. "Your work as an Auditor, you could keep us on track with our budget." She looks at Lady Gorham. "I could do that too Lady Gorham, but since I'm running around handling specific arrangements. Plus doing counseling sessions. It would be terrific if we had someone who could just focus on the budget." She looks at Shayna. "Deaconess Greye, your help would definitely be appreciated."

"Well Deaconess Greye," Lady Gorham said. "Looks to me like your assistance is needed. So, would you be able to lend them a hand?"

Shayna smirks as her eyes go to Minister Pauls. Shayna slowly shakes her head looking down at the table for a second taking in a deep breath. She exhales raising her head, glancing at Minister McDaniels and Mother Livingston and puts on a smile as she looks at Lady Gorham.

"Lady Gorham honestly," Shayna said. "Besides my job having me on three large company audits this month. My mother hasn't been feeling well and--"

"What?!" Mother Livingston said.

"He'll Work It Out" Chapter 1. Taryn C. Atkins

Shayna stunned by being interrupted stares at Mother Livingston, who in her seventies, dressed in a classic and stunning white suit with a fabulous matching hat. She is at times considered the cordial yet mean and blunt church mother. Her eyes are fixed on Shayna somewhat confused by her statement.

"I saw Mother Babcock a few days ago." Mother Livingston said. "She looked fine. Deaconess Greye, please, I'm sure you're capable of giving some of your time to assist us."

The two ladies off to the side in the peanut gallery are finishing their lunch and keep their eyes and ears open to the meeting taking place. They pay close attention what's being said and to the different emotions coming from the faces in attendance. Shayna smiles, looks nonchalantly at the various faces around the table. While under the table Shayna uses her hand to rub and squeeze her thigh, heated by Mother Livingston statement. Shayna fights to hold back her annoyance while focusing Mother Livingston.

"No disrespect Mother Livingston," Shayna said. "I'm sure my mother may not tell you everything. I am her daughter after all." She looks around at those in the meeting. "That being said, I'm sure you all noticed my mother wasn't in attendance today. Well, that's because she's feeling a bit under the weather and she didn't want anyone to worry." She looks at Lady Gorham. "I simply want to keep myself available for my mother."

Minister Pauls remembers what Regina said about her grandmother. Minister Pauls stares at Shayna for a moment, under her breath, she huffs picks up her fan, opens it and fans herself. Minister Pauls glances at Shayna again and shakes her head.

"I'm not trying to be difficult Lady Gorham," Shayna said. Minister Pauls murmurs to herself, "Sure you're not."
Shayna said with a stern expression, "Mother Livingston, Minister McDaniels, and of course, you Minister Pauls. I hope each of you can understand my situation here."
"Well, after all. I'm just your mother's closest friend." Mother Livingston said. "My apologies Deaconess Greye, and of course we understand."

"Yes, we do." Minister McDaniels said.

"Of course." Minister Pauls said with a smirk."

Lady Gorham said, as she cleared her throat. "Yes Deaconess Greye, no problem. We'll keep Mother Babcock in our prayers. So, is there anyone else who can possibly assist these ladies?"

A few seats to the right of Lady Gorham, a hand raises and energetically waves in the air. It's Sister Cantres, she's in her late twenties, a fetching Dominican young woman, newly saved and full of zeal.

"Hello Lady Gorham, I'm Juanita Cantres. I don't mind helping, I've done event planning before." She looks at Shayna. "I'm no CPA though," Her eyes dart back to Lady Gorham. "I've got a little accounting experience. So, I'd be glad to lend a hand."

Lady Gorham's eyes go to Elder Mays as she leans in toward her. Under her breath she said, "Marcella, what's her name again?"

Elder Mays looks at Lady Gorham, reaches out and taps her hand.

"You remember Sister Cantres." Elder Mays said. "She's a new member of the ministry, a lovely young lady too, and so personable."

"Juanita right?" Lady Gorham studies Sister Cantres. "Yes, I do remember us speaking at the new members class. Thank you for jumping in to help out."

Minister Pauls eyes Sister Cantres, gives her a smile and waves, "We appreciate it too Sister Cantres."

Lady Gorham smiles looking at the young lady, "It's outstanding to see you're anxious to get to work in the ministry." She points to Minister Pauls and Minister McDaniels. "These ladies will be sure to see you after the meeting." She claps her hands together again. "Now, any other announcements? It's been a long day, I'm sure everyone wants to get home."

Shayna looks down at Cliff's empty seat, she softly huffs and shakes her head a bit.

Where in the world is he? Shayna thought.

Shayna looks up, as the man seated next to Cliff's empty chair raises his hand and stands. It's Minister Thomas, he's in his early forties, and a impressive melting pot. His warm beige hue is deeper from the tan it holds. He is roughly five-ten and keeps himself in decent shape. A real gentlemen, who loves the Lord. As he threads his hand through his thick and wavy, medium length highlighted dirty blond hair. Minister McDaniels and the ladies in the peanut gallery sigh to themselves. Before he speaks he mildly tugs on the edge of his Hugo Boss pinstriped suit jacket.

"Good afternoon saints." Minister Thomas said. "I wanted to remind the brothers about the men's all night prayer this coming Wednesday. Something special happens when real men of God pray. Our own Elder Bernard Rayner will lead off the prayer, ain't that right." He points across the room at Elder Rayner. "He's gonna call down the Lord's fire and glory for us?"

Elder Rayner stands to his feet, raising one hand as he looks on Minister Thomas.

Elder Rayner said, "Well, to God be the glory son. I'm gonna let the Lord use me however He sees fit, but all we do is for God's glory. That is the one thing we must never forget." He looks around at the men in the room. "The late Bishop John H. Boyd Sr., a great man of God, a true Father and General in ministry once said. "God can do more for you in five minutes, then you can do for yourself in a lifetime." He glances at Minister Thomas again. "So son, when we all hit the altar Wednesday night and pray, we're gonna let God be God. Is that alright. God bless."

As Elder Rayner sits. The men about the room respond to him and Minister Thomas nods his head in agreement.

"Amen, amen." Minister Thomas said. He looks around at the men in the meeting. "So brothers be sure to come on out for the prayer Wednesday night, we'll be starting at 10 p.m. We know the women are always before God praying. Well, it's time for the men to step up and travail before God in prayer too. I'm looking forward to it. So I hope to see each and every brother here Wednesday night."

As Minister Thomas sits, Cliff walks through the side doors returning to his seat. Cliff sits down, looks at his wife and sees the indignation on her face. Cliff turns his attention toward Minister Randall, who's raising his hand. He's in his late twenties, a sharp, espresso toned brother of average height, with a sleek athletic build. He sports a buzz cut and a short tapered beard. As Minister Randall stands, he adjusts his Ray-Ban eyeglasses. He's an old soul, although he's the church youth minister.

"God Is Good!" Minister Randall said.

All those in the room reply, "All The Time!"

"And All The Time!" Minister Randall said.

All those in the room respond, "God Is Good!"

"Alright, y'all sound real good." Minister Randall said. "I'm here to tell everyone to please remember the youth service this Friday Night. It'll start at seven sharp. The Youth Department has put together a wonderful program. The Gospelfest winning and world traveling choir, The Angelic Voices for Christ, with director Evangelist Elaine Hicks-Crawford will be giving us a few selections.

Our guest speaker will be Dr. Aretha Wilson of Kingdom Ambassadors Global Ministries, many of us have heard Dr. Wilson before, and as pastor said she's an anointed and powerful woman of God. Who truly has a heart for God's people.

I know I'll be going out there tonight to fellowship with our pastor. All are invited to come to the youth service. Also please remember, next year in February the whole church is going to Dr. Wilson's annual RAW Gathering. She already knows we're coming and is excited to have us. So, don't forget to come out to the youth service and register for RAW now. Thank you."

"He'll Work It Out" Chapter 1. Taryn C. Atkins

Minister Randall takes his seat and Lady Gorham stands as she looks around the room into the various faces at the meeting.

"I've heard Dr. Wilson preach," Lady Gorham said. "And she's no joke. Plus that choir AVC is awesome and anointed too. So please everyone come on out to the youth service, invite others you know and also register for RAW. Pastor and I are registered already and we want the whole church there. Remember last year, for Thanksgiving. Our covering asked for our entire church to be at their big family and friends day. Well, we all went and had a great time too. Pastor and I want that same turn out for RAW. So register now. Okay, any more announcements, questions or comments?"

Elder Mays glances at Lady Gorham as she stands up.

"Oh, Lady Gorham." Elder Mays said. "We forgot to give that praise report to the saints."

"Right, go ahead." Lady Gorham said sitting back down.

Elder Mays looks around the room, "Well saints we've got good news to share! The ministry got blessed y'all, and currently Brother James is driving back from Washington D.C., with a beautiful, fully loaded, twenty-four passenger tour bus."

All those in attendance get happy, they express their excitement and clap their hands about the blessing.

"Yes, it's wonderful saints." Elder Mays said. "They're on vacation now but the van was jointly purchased and given to the ministry by the Harley and Hicks families. Look at God, now the church can pick up and take home those who are elderly or disable. We can go to shelters now and bring folks to service, as well as to the food pantry. Praise the Lord Saints. God is supplying all our needs."

As Elder Mays retakes her seat, Lady Gorham stands proclaiming.

"Well Praise The Lord Everybody!! That's sure nuff a Praise Report! God is good y'all! I told ya, "He'll Work It Out." Let's give God some praise."

"He'll Work It Out" Chapter 1. Taryn C. Atkins

Everyone there, and even the ladies off to the side take a moment and give the Lord praise. Some clap, others lift their hands, but all raise their voice and give God praise for what He's done. Lady Gorham slowly stops clapping.

"It's been a high time in the Lord all day." Lady Gorham said. "So, if there's nothing more to be said."

All are quiet as Lady Gorham looks around the room.

"Remember we're a family." Lady Gorham said. "So please support one another. Alright, let us dismiss. Mother Livingston, can you please do the honors."

"Please bow your heads," Mother Livingston said. "Lord, as we leave this place but never your presence, take us over the highways and byways safely. We bind up all dangers and accidents, seen and unseen, and ask you oh Lord that you watch over us until we meet again. In the mighty and matchless name of Jesus! Amen."

Everybody repeats together, "Amen."

They all start to gather their things and move about the room preparing to leave. Minister McDaniels heads over to Sister Cantres. Marsha gathers up Lady Gorham's things. Elder Mays, Lady Gorham and Elder Rayner speak among themselves for a few moments. As the three of them talk. Marsha stands a few feet back and off to the side, waiting for Lady Gorham. Minister Randall marches over to help Mother Livingston get ready to go home. Minister Thomas and Cliff look at each other as they stand up.

"Deacon Greye." Minister Thomas said.

"Minister Thomas," Cliff said.

They shake hands, embrace and release each other.

"It's always good to see you Cliff."

"Same here."

Minister Thomas looks around Cliff and waves at Shayna.

"Greeting's Deaconess Greye, all is well?" Minister Thomas said.

Cliff moves to the side as Shayna looks up at Minister Thomas and smiles.

"Yes, all is well." Shayna said. "And you? Is everything alright? Cliff and I was just saying, its been a moment since you've been by the house."

"Yeah, I've been busy at work and getting this trip in order." Minister Thomas said. "I've booked my flight; So I'll be gone for the month of June as usual."

"Well, have a safe trip. Come by for dinner when you get back."

"I will, please say hello to Mother Babcock and give her a kiss for me too."

"I'll be sure to do that."

Shayna continues getting her things together as Minister Thomas returns his attention to Cliff.

"Right, your annual trip to Mississippi." Cliff said. "Casey I've known you for 7 years now, when will the brothers get to go with you? I'd love a chance to do some fishing."

"Maybe one day, but I don't go to do stuff like that." Minister Thomas said.

"Really," Cliff said. "I always thought it was some big vacation so you and your family could get together."

"It's more of an anniversary thing." Minister Thomas said. "Every June the founder of The Wilkins Foundation comes to the cabin and we show our respect by spending time with him."

"Right, the guy who looked out for you and your sister after your parents died."

"Yeah, when the rest of my so called "siblings" left home; They forgot all about Mississippi and everyone with it. When our parents died, the foundation looked out. Everything happened so fast. It was a rough time, especially for me. The founder came in, handled everything and even took care of us for a while. So we show our respect once a year. We squeeze in family time too though."

"Well that's good, I believe in spending time with family. I've always meant to ask, who watches the cabin during the rest of the year?"

"This guy Paton takes care of it for us." Minister Thomas said. "His family owns the electronics and hardware

"He'll Work It Out" Chapter 1. Taryn C. Atkins

store in town. They've had it since I was little. Paton and I went to school together. He was two years behind me, had to take those special classes." He chuckles. "My friends and I gave him a hard time about it too, but after my parents died we became friends. Paton knows we come up every June. So he gets the place ready for us, does an excellent job too."
"I'm a country boy at heart." Cliff said. "I'd love to see it one day."
"My parents loved that place; They put their heart and soul into it too. It's a sweet two story, ranch style cabin with: four bedrooms, three full baths, living room, dining room, kitchen, a huge finished basement, two car garage and a decent amount of land too. Neighbors are a few miles away."
"That sounds alright."
"Man, we almost lost it when they died. It's all we have left of them."
"I'm know it holds a lot of memories."
"It sure does, and we make new ones every year," Minister Thomas said. "Paton was doing some remodeling in the bedrooms and basement when we left last year. He finished up last month, he usually sends pictures but I haven't gotten any yet. Guess we'll see things when we get there."
"Now although it's business," Cliff said. "You're there for a month. So take time to enjoy yourself."
"Oh I make sure I do. After all, it's only once a year. That's the way I look at it. I reserve two nights for the old gang to come visit; I emailed their invites in April. They're mostly my sister's friends though. They always look forward to seeing her."
"I'm sure she feels the same."
"Well, with her living all high class now." Minister Thomas slightly laughs. "They give her a hard way to go." Cliff snickers. "Her friends want to make sure she remembers where she comes from, we all go through

that."

"Yeah, we don't want her to forget her place."

"If you want, I can watch Rudi for ya." Cliff said.

"I don't leave Rudi." Minister Thomas said. "He goes every year too, wouldn't be a family trip without him."

"Oh okay, what breed is he anyway? You've had two just like him."

"Rudi's an English Foxhound. My sister was ten when our parents died. I got one for her; I figured besides me, she'd love another companion. So we've always had one. Let me go, I'm on duty for James and Lady Gorham's leaving out soon. I'll see you at the men's prayer."

"Alright Casey, remind me again a week before you go. So I can make sure your duties here are covered."

"Will do."

Minister Thomas walks away, he heads toward Lady Gorham and waits off to the side with Marsha. As Shayna slowly prepared her things to leave, Brother Hamlin who is seated on Shayna's left, reaches his hand out and places it on Shayna's shoulder catching her attention.

"You have a good night Deaconess Greye." Brother Hamlin said.

"You too Marcus," Shayna said. "Say hi to Patricia for me."

"I'll be sure too."

Brother Hamlin gets up out his seat, he's in his late 30's, a chestnut complexion, husky build and he's just a tad shorter than Cliff. He's always so polished, like he put on a brand new outfit straight off the rack. Brother Hamlin approaches Cliff, extending his hand to him and they shake.

"Alright, Deacon Greye." Brother Hamlin said. "I'll see you at the Men's Prayer."

"Marcus, call me Cliff man," Cliff said. "And yes you will see me there."

Brother Hamlin goes to walk away, but Cliff stops him.

"Hold up," Cliff said. "You okay, cause you're not usually all scraggly and disheveled like this. Everything alright?"

"Just keep me and mine in your prayers." Brother Hamlin said. "My wife's sister Kia, has done this complete turn around, has the whole family on edge. Tricia's all upset. So as you see, I haven't been getting much rest."

"Well talk to me, what's going on with Kia?"

"Brother, I'll have to tell you that story another time. I've got to get home and get some type of sleep; I'm working a double tonight but I'll see you at the Men's Prayer."

"Okay, I'll be praying."

"Thanks Cliff."

"Take it easy."

They shake hands again and Brother Hamlin leaves. Cliff stretches a bit, then takes his suit jacket off the back of his chair, as he puts it on he turns to Shayna.

"I'm gonna get the car," Cliff said. "I'll meet you out front."

"So..." Shayna said, looking up at Cliff, folding her arms.

"Important call?"

Cliff sees she's upset, he glances at the ceiling and returns his eyes to Shayna. She sits in silence for a few seconds with her eyes fixed on him.

"It was her right?" Shayna stands to get her things together. "She called you again, didn't she?"

"Let's not talk here."

Sister Carlton and Sister Richardson sit back in the cut, slyly encroaching their presence, watching and listening intently to everything that's going on, and with the leadership meeting finished, their eyes fix on Deacon and Deaconess Greye across the room.

The tension rises between Cliff and Shayna as they get their things together preparing to leave. Shayna tries to keep her tone down and her expressions in check, to keep up appearances to the church members still around them.

"So you're still letting her call you?" Shayna said shoving her bible and notepad into her tote. "Cliff, I'm getting sick and tired of you doing this."

"Who else is she going to call?" Cliff said.

Shayna abruptly turns to Cliff, pointing at him replying,

"Did we or did we not have an agreement?"

"Yes, but..."

Various church members have already left and Lady Gorham is now ready to leave out too. Minister Thomas walks a few feet in front of Lady Gorham, Elder Mays and Elder Rayner trail behind her followed by Marsha. As they all head towards the main doors of the dining hall, Lady Gorham looks back into the room.

"Good evening everyone." Lady Gorham said. "Hope to

see you all in Lynbrook."

Right behind Lady Gorham all those with her also say their good nights, sounding in somewhat unison. Shayna cuts her disagreement with Cliff, puts a smile on and with the rest of those in the room, she waves and says good night to Lady Gorham. Once Lady Gorham's gone Shayna returns to her emotionally heightened discussion with Cliff. Minister Randall and Mother Livingston accompanied by Minister Pauls move toward the main doors of the dining hall.

"Mother Livingston you take it easy." Minister Pauls said. "Minister McDaniels will be meeting with the caterer tomorrow morning. If it's okay with you Mother, we can meet at your home tomorrow afternoon, and discuss the details regarding the fellowship, alright?"

"That's fine." Mother Livingston said.

"Excellent, good night Mother, and I'll see you tomorrow."

"Okay, good evening Minister Pauls."

"Alright," Minister Randall said looking at Minister Pauls. "I got Mother, thanks. Have a good one."

"You too Minister Randall. You're looking handsome in that suit brother."

He smiles, "Thank you, you always look lovely Minister Pauls."

"Thank you, have a good evening now."

"You too."

Mother Livingston waves her hand as she and Minister Randall head out the door. Minister Pauls walks back to her seat and starts putting her belongings into her briefcase. Shayna and Cliff talk, but tension continues to rise between them.

"We had an agreement but come on." Cliff said.

"Come on nothing!" Shayna quickly snaps back. "You know what? You could understand how I feel. Could you at least do that."

While Minister McDaniels talks to Sister Cantres, she signals to Minister Pauls to come over. Minister Pauls looks at her and motions to Minister McDaniels.

"I'll be right there." Minister Pauls said.

Minister Pauls takes her tote bag puts it on her shoulder and picks up her briefcase. Shayna snatches her tote off the table, puts it on her shoulder as she walks away from Cliff.

"Shayna wait." Cliff said.

Watching Shayna rush off, Cliff shakes his head as he turns away. Minister Pauls proceeds to Minister McDaniels and Sister Cantres. Shayna glances back at Cliff for a moment, Minister Pauls happens to notice a small dust bunny on the shoulder of her suit jacket and wipes it off. The flies on the wall are the only ones that see the imminent collision. As Minister Pauls happens to look up, Shayna looks in front of her. Both come to an immediate halt, stopping inches from the other and scarcely avoiding bumping into one another. Shayna nonchalantly looks around and notices that only a few members still linger. Minister Pauls laughs amused by what almost took place.

"My goodness," Minister Pauls said, laughing a bit amused by what almost took place. "That was close, I didn't even see you. Please, excuse me Deaconess Greye."

Shayna huffs, and motions in the direction she's going, "No excuse me."

Across the room, Minister McDaniels once again gestures to Minister Pauls to come over. When Minister Pauls sees her, she raises her hand telling her to wait a moment. Shayna already agitated tries to walk away, but unknowingly Minister Pauls gets in her way. While Minister Pauls is focused on Minister McDaniels, Shayna's jaw clenches and her head slightly shakes as she looks Minister Pauls up and down. Minister Pauls returns her attention to Shayna and tries to be amicable to her.

Minister Pauls said, "Well, I just wanted to say--"

"I've got to go." Shayna said.

Shayna goes to walk around her, but Minister Pauls deliberately steps in front of her.

"Now see," Minister Pauls smiles while saying under her breath. "You're not being civil about this."

Shayna in like manner said, "No I'm not, and I don't have to be either. You could've joined another church. You're here now, fine. Just stay out of my face. I wouldn't want to have to--"

"Have to what?" Minister Pauls said.

Shayna casually looks around seeing if any church members are watching. The flies on the wall look away for a moment but bring their eyes back to the situation at hand. Shayna returns her attention to Minister Pauls.

"Listen here--" Shayna said.

"No, let me explain something." Minister Pauls said, pointing at Shayna as she steps in a tad closer. "This, is a two-way street. You tell my secret; I'll be sure everyone knows yours." She slides her glasses down, peers over the rim and nods. "Understand? Deaconess Greye." She fixes her glasses, and smirks. "You have a good evening."

As Minister Pauls goes about her business, Cliff turns around and sees her walking away from Shayna. He moves toward Shayna looking concerned. Minister Pauls sees Cliff coming in her direction. Shayna stands there numb. Minister Pauls and Cliff head toward each other. He glances at Shayna again, seeing her back is to them. Cliff approaches Minister Pauls quickly casing the room to see who's still there. She smiles as they meet each other.

"Good evening Deacon Greye." Minister Pauls said.

"Good evening." Cliff said. He casually uses his head to motion toward Shayna. "So what was that about?"

"What that?" Minister Pauls said, looking at Cliff as she

points over her shoulder toward Shayna. "That was nothing." She smiles and laughs a bit. "We almost bumped into each other, that's all."

Cliff nods his head, "Oh, okay."

"There's lint on your suit."

Minister Pauls reaches out to brush off the shoulder of Cliff's jacket but he grabs her wrist.

"Don't."

They hold their gaze for a second, Cliff quickly releases her hand and walks away.

"Have a good evening."

Minister Pauls stands there, she peeks over her shoulder in his direction and grins.

"You too."

Cliff goes to Shayna. Minister Pauls approaches Minister McDaniels and Sister Cantres.

"So ladies, ready to go?" Minister Pauls said.

"Yes we are." Minister McDaniels said.

They all proceed to the side doors of the dining hall. As they talk with Sister Cantres, her eyes sparkle with enthusiasm.

"I'm looking forward to working together." Sister Cantres said. "Like I said in the meeting; I've done event planning before. So I've got great ideas."

"That's wonderful." Minister McDaniels said. "We look forward to hearing them. Right Minister Pauls."

A subtle smile forms on Minister Pauls lips.

"Yes." Minister Pauls said. "I have a few ideas too."

Sister Cantres and Minister McDaniels walk through the side door. Before Minister Pauls steps out, she looks back in the room and waves to Sister Carlton and Sister Richardson.

"Have a blessed night ladies."

Sister Carlton and Sister Richardson glance at each other, then back at Minister Pauls and casually wave. Minister Pauls smiles and leaves out the side door. Besides the flies on the wall, Cliff and Shayna are the only ones left in the dining hall. Cliff steps in front of Shayna, softly slides his hands over her shoulders and down her arms. His touch snaps her back.

"Sweetheart," Cliff said. "Can we please talk calmly about this?"

Shayna looks at him, huffs, and walks away heading toward the main doors. Cliff follows her. Shayna rushes pass Sister Carlton and Sister Richardson never looking or even saying a word to them. As they see Cliff approaching, they smile and wave at him. Cliff waves back as he rushes pass. Shayna gets to the main doors and pushes one open. Cliff catches up to her. She looks at Cliff as she holds the door open.

"Fine, you want to talk," Shayna said. "How about the fact you--"

Shayna rushes through the door, with Cliff right on her heels and the main doors close behind them. Sister Carlton and Sister Richardson look around and see everyone has gone.

"My my." Sister Carlton said. "Seems there's trouble in the Greye family."

"I see." Sister Richardson said. "Guess their marriage is having some problems."

"Wonder what's going on."

"Ya got me."

They sit silently for a bit, Sister Carlton takes a small stem of grapes out of a zip lock bag, sitting on the table in front of her and eats a few. Sister Richardson picks up her Wendy's soda cup off the table and takes a few sips from the straw inside it. She puts the cup down and points to Sister Carlton.

"Maybe he's drinking again." Sister Richardson said. "Being married to her has got to surely be stressful."

Sister Carlton ponders her statement.

"Nah, that ain't it Carla." Sister Carlton said. "That man's been sober for eleven years and praises God for it too. "

"Well, maybe she started drinking." Sister Richardson said. She laughs. "Lord knows, she needs to loosen up." Sister Carlton laughs at her statement, "You're funny but no." She yawns and stretches for a moment. "Oh, excuse me."

"You were yawning all through service. Why you so tired?"

"Charlotte's cycle started yesterday." Sister Carlton said. "My baby girl kept me up all night."

"Wow so early." Sister Richardson said. "She's eleven."

"I started at the same age." Sister Carlton said.

They sit in silence for a few seconds, you can almost hear the grinding as their wheels turn.

"You know, I was thinking." Sister Carlton said. "Shayna wasn't always like that. She was sweeter when her whole family attended here."

"Her whole family..." Sister Richardson said. "What are you talking about?"

"I mean her oldest daughter Gisele, Regina's sister. She went here, a lovely girl too. She was a praise dancer and sang in the choir. She hasn't been here for about... nine years now.

"SHUT UP! I didn't even know they had another daughter."

"She doesn't talk about her much. Must be the black sheep. It's a shame, I thought they were a happy family."

"They were, years ago. Now it's so tense between them."

"I know a few folks burned by Shayna."

"Me too. First, everything is happy go lucky but when things don't go her way, she'll kick you to the curb."

"Yes she will." Sister Carlton eats a few grapes. "I know you caught that exchange between Shayna and Minister Pauls. That was interesting."

"What was interesting to me, was that moment between Cliff and Minister Pauls."

"I saw that too. Well, she's kinda cute. I'll give her that."

"My mom told me," Sister Richardson said. "Shayna and Minister Pauls were good friends years ago. Mom worked at Regina's elementary school. Said Minister Pauls picked Regina up frequently but now, it's like Shayna wouldn't dare be seen with her."

"Really?" Sister Carlton said. "What's that about?"

"Baby, I wish I knew."

"I've been trying to get a bead on Minister Pauls, she's

been here for two years now, but my church channels got nothing.

"So, you going to Lynbrook tonight."

"Oh yeah, we must open up new channels right."

"Of course, mom taught this girl well."

Sister Richardson gets up and starts to get her things together. Sister Carlton stands as well, she stretches a bit first and then gets her belongings together too. They slowly make their way to the main doors.

"I do know this," Sister Carlton said. "Shayna needs to tread lightly." She smooths out her form fitting dress. "Cause Cliff is a good man, he make pretty babies too. She better treat him right."

"Girl, I know that's right." Sister Richardson said. "That Minister Thomas is a fine one too. I'd love to run my fingers through that pretty hair of his."

"His hair! Baby, give me twenty-four hours with that; I'll gladly repent in the morning."

"You are terrible."

"I know, pray for me."

"I will."

"You know what's a shame? That half the men nowadays are either coked up or locked up."

"Child, they're either low down or on the down low."

"She better hold on to Cliff, because finding another one like him is like trying to find a needle in a haystack."

"Baby you got that right."

They high five each other, then leave out the dining hall main doors. The last sound heard are the doors closing behind them.

~CHAPTER 2~

~Free Will + Choices + Options = The Path~

~SOULS TAKEN~

It's the start of a brand new week and a few days from the beginning of Summer. The sun sits high in a clear blue sky, under the sunshine stands a condemned and dilapidated house. It was a beautiful home, purchased by a young family filled with expectations and excited about starting their journey on this road called life. Unfortunately, that family left, when their prime neighborhood took a turn and now life no longer flourishes in this place. Only death, despair and hopelessness looms here along with the rats and roaches.

The scent of potpourri and Glade air freshener was extinguished a long time ago. It's the fused stench and pungency of rotting garbage, burnt plastic and bodily waste that have taken over the air. Electricity hasn't flowed for quite some time and even natural light is barely allowed to come in through the broken windows; For it's kept out by wooden boards and grimy sheets. The time of day basically passes by unknown at least until someone opens the front door. The only flickers of light inside come from a few candles that have been placed about what use to be called the living room.

A single flame from a candle seems to be floating a few inches above the burnt and crud filled floor. As this fire flies across the floor, a tiny plastic baggie comes into its light and dirty fingers swiftly pick it up. The baggie is held in front of the flame and they both start to rise. Mario's face moves into the light coming from the candle's flame. His light olive skin is dull and smudged. When Mario was seventeen, he had a chiseled, athletic build, and it made up for him being under the average height for a guy. Now his addiction has caused him to be a scrawny twenty-seven year old. Mario moves his unkempt, chaotic hair back from his eyes so he can clearly see what the baggie contains.

"He'll Work It Out" Chapter 2. Taryn C. Atkins

He holds the tiny clear packet up with the candle burning behind it and with eager anticipation his eyes widen, filled with hope that a trace of what he's hurting for is inside. He throws the baggie to the floor irritated by seeing it's empty. Mario kneels on the grime covered floor, he scratches at the three day growth of hair on his face.

"There's gotta be some around." He said.

His eyes anxiously scan the room and again he starts his search. Mario mumbles to himself as he quickly moves about the muck covered floor. There's the sound of muffled voices coming from another room, but in his current state he hears nothing. As Mario continues with his quest; He holds the candle in one hand and with the other picks up bottle caps. He searches within them, dying to find any residue or scraps of cotton left to reuse. Mario forages through pieces of garbage, impatiently inspecting them to see if they contain any remnants of the strong potion he so hungrily yearns.

Mario stops his search for a moment, he turns and stares at a filthy twin mattress in the corner of the room; Where there lays a body wildly draped across it, wearing an old grubby camouflage jacket, a dingy oversized t-shirt which has the faded word peace on it, dirty black jeans and shoddy work boots.

"Reg, Reg!" Mario said. "What you got man? You got anything?"

Reggie stirs a bit repositioning himself on the layer of newspapers covering the cruddy mattress but he doesn't reply. Mario returns to his search; He rapidly rummages through the area under the candles flame. As he hunts through another flimsy fragment of garbage, he unwittingly puts it too close to the fire and the piece of paper bursts into flames. Mario swiftly drops the burning paper before it reaches the ground, it lands on his filthy gray sweat pants. He brushes it off, then rapidly pounds the blaze out with his hands but it leaves its mark.

Mario rushes to his feet, groaning with annoyance, the former Ivy Leaguer roughly unzips and pulls off his paint stained, grungy blue sweat hoodie. He throws it to the ground thoroughly frustrated that his search has yielded no results. His eyes go to Reggie once again and he hurries to him. Mario grabs the front of his wife beater, it was white at one time but now it's a dingy gray. He wipes the sweat from his face with it. Mario kneels down next to the twin mattress and starts to fervently go through Reggie's jacket pockets. The movement disturbs Reggie and he abruptly wakes up grabbing Mario by his wife beater.

"Yo man, what are you doing?!" Reggie said. He shoves Mario away. "Get off me!"

Mario falls back on the ground saying, "Well you got anything! Come on Reg. I'm hurting man."

"We did the last ones hours ago!" Reggie said.

Mario leans against the wall, he's anxious and on edge.

"I need a hit man," Mario said. "We need to do something." He rubs his head trying to erase the memories that haunt his mind. "Those images are coming back." He bangs the back of his head against the wall. "I don't want to see them..." He hits his head a few times with his hand. "Don't want to remember... I need a hit." He starts to rock, moving back and forth. "We... we got to do something."

"Yeah, yeah." Reggie said. Still half asleep he rubs his face. "I can use a hit too. D should be coming through soon."

Reggie gets up, Mario watches him as he tries to straighten out his rumpled clothes. Mario notices that Reggie's addiction hasn't fully taken its toll on him.

"Alright Mario, I'm gonna make a run and try to get something. I'll be back soon."

"Please Reg, hurry back. Those images are coming back." He rubs and hits his head again. "I don't want to remember-you promised to help me not remember."

Reggie goes to Mario and squats down beside him.

"I'll look out, like always."

"You... you do Reg...." Mario sniffs, and wipes his nose with his wife beater. "You always look out for me. Just... just hurry back."

Reggie stands, "I'll try and make it quick. Lata man."

"He'll Work It Out" Chapter 2. Taryn C. Atkins

Reggie leaves and the front door shuts behind him. Mario puts his hoodie back on. He scans the room once more as he zips it up. Mario scratches his head and mumbles to himself.

"Come on, something gotta be around."

Mario kneels on the floor starting another search. He scurries about the room, then back to the twin mattress. As he searches the newspapers on top of it, he unknowingly dozes off finally giving into the fatigue his body feels.

A few hours have passed by since Mario crashed and Reggie has yet to return. While Mario lays comatose, the front door opens and a thuggish figure looking to be in his thirties, about two hundred ten and six-two stands in the doorway. He sports a oversize black and white football jersey, it has a scorpion on the chest and the number eighteen on the sleeve. He wears it with black baggy jeans and black Tims. His gear includes a black and white paisley bandana tied around his forehead, so his fresh cornrow braids could show.

This brawny, intimidating goon comes in, as he takes a few steps inside, he raises his hand to his lips, takes a long pull from his Newport cigarette and as smoke discharges from his lips, his watchdog eyes investigates the area. He doesn't notice in the corner laying in the shadows is Mario curled up on the mattress.

The murmur of voices coming from another room propels this strong arm to inspect further. He moves forward kicking a broken plastic crate out of his way as he heads toward the voices. Moments later two seedy looking figures rush through the room and out the front door. Mario still knocked out lays there oblivious to what is going on. The ruffian walks back through and heads outside.

The seedy figures rush out going their separate ways. Sitting in front of the house is a jet black, 2013 Escalade with custom rims. As the thug approaches it, the back passenger door opens and out of the SUV steps a woman in her early thirties.

Her makeup is beautifully flawless, intensifying her deep set, upturned hazel-green eyes and classic cheekbones. Her silky brown hair with champagne highlights is up in a ponytail that flows down to the middle of her back. Her body of forty-twenty six-forty is an outstanding exhibit for her garments. She wears a white tuxedo shirt with its buttons opened up enough to see the black leather bra underneath. The shirt is tied up around her midsection revealing spectacular abs. Her black leather mini skirt holds onto her hips with every movement, while her five inch, ankle strapped, black patent leather platform heels, accents her well-defined legs and brings her to five-nine.

As she closes the door behind her, the front tinted passenger window slowly slides down. She goes to the window, bends over and looks inside the SUV, but keeps her eyes down, staring at the floor.

"Sir, what would you like your pet to fetch you?" She said.

The thug stands a few feet behind the woman, moving his head from side to side as he admires the erotic view in front of him. Not moving from his current position, the thug leans to the side and looks into the SUV front window. He gives a thumbs up to the man seated behind the wheel of the Escalade. The driver is in his late twenties and dressed like a Wall Street businessman on a casual Friday.

"We're good D." The thug said. "You can come in."

"Alright in a sec," D said. He takes out his wallet, pulls out two hundred's then looks over at the woman. "Look at me."

The woman lifts her head, her docile eyes meets his governing ones and D hands her the bills.

"Go down the block to the liquor store. Pick me up a large Hennessy Black, go to the bodega, buy me three Dutch's and then go to Wendy's. Get me a ten piece nugget, medium fries and a large chocolate frosty. Get yourself a bottle of water and a salad."

D leans over to the glove compartment, opens it, takes out a set of keys and instead of handing them to her. He stuffs the keys down into her cleavage and out of sight.

"Those are the extra keys to this ride and the spot. Don't lose them. When you get back, just wait in the car until I call for you. You can go."

"Yes sir,"

Before she can leave.

"Hold up," D said.

The woman stops, she returns to her bent over position with her eyes down and staring at the SUV floor. D motions to the thug trying to get his attention, but he continues to admire his rear view of the woman. The thug happens to notice words on the woman's lower back which her mini skirt barely covers. He reaches out and pulls down the back of her mini skirt. What's revealed to him, is that she was marked a long time ago. He sees at the base, in the middle of her lower back and within quotes. He reads the words *branded* into her skin and they said. *"To Be Used"* Lewd thoughts fill his mind and an impish grin comes across his face as he softly slides his fingers under the words. The woman feels his touch but does nothing. She doesn't even turn around to give him a dirty look.

"Mingo you want something from Wendy's?" D said.

Mingo doesn't hear D, clearly his thoughts have been taken over by the lecherous expression sitting on his face as he releases the back of the woman's mini skirt.

"Yo Mingo!" D said. "You want something or what?!"

Mingo said pointing to the woman, "Oh I want to use something again, believe that!"

The woman having heard his statement never becomes enraged, just holds her position and keeps her eyes down.

"We'll have fun with that again," D said. "A little lata man. Right now, you want some food?"

"Nah D," Mingo said. "I'll save my appetite, for lata."

D doesn't look at her just motions for her to go.

"Yes sir," she said.

The woman straightens up and turns to leave. Mingo sees the accessory that pulls her form fitting outfit together and hints more to her story. It's the black leather dog collar bound about her neck, and attached to the D-ring that lays on top of it is a lengthy chrome leash which hung down in front of her. The black leather hand strap at the end of the leash stops mid calf. Dangling from that same D-ring is an oval silver name tag, it shimmers from the rays of the sun and the glare from it catches Mingo's attention.

"Wait, come here," Mingo said.

The woman turns, faces Mingo but never makes eye contact. When Mingo reaches for the silver name tag, she turns her head to the side. While holding the tag, he steps into her personal space to get a better look, and sees it's engraved with the name "Ivy."

"So that's your name." Mingo said releasing the name tag. "I like it."

"Thank you sir," Ivy said.

D gets out the SUV, his lanky stature is clad in a black tailored suit with a white shirt and black wingtip oxfords. He wears his short locs in a mohawk style with a fade and has a goatee. He looks at Mingo as he leans on the front hood.

"Mingo, I've told you her name about five times since we got her."

"Man I don't care bout her name. I'm just here to follow the directions."

D smiles nodding his head replying in a Jamaican accent, "Me know dat's right broda."

Mingo chuckles as D walks around the SUV motioning to Ivy.

"Alright, go get my stuff."

"Yes sir,"

Ivy leaves. D comes over and stands by Mingo, there's about a three inch difference in their height. They watch Ivy's hips sway from side to side as she rushes down the block. D turns to Mingo and pats him on his chest.

"Let's go in," D said.

A few seconds later, Mingo and D walk into the house.

"Ahh, it stinks," D said. He motions to Mingo. "Yo grab them sheets. I need some air."

Mingo rips the grimy sheets away from the broken windows. Light and fresh air bombard the inside. The sunlight exposes Mario's presence in the corner curled up on the mattress. D sees Mario, motions to Mingo and points to where Mario is sleeping.

"If he's not buying, he gotta go." D said.

"He'll Work It Out" Chapter 2. Taryn C. Atkins

Mingo rushes over, grabs Mario, pulls him up off the mattress and to his feet. Mario wakes up confused by what's going on.

"Wake up," Mingo said shaking Mario. "You buying?!"

"What... what?" Mario said.

Mario being caught off guard tries to get his feet planted. Mingo shakes him again.

"Are you buying man?!"

"Well-"

"Too slow, time to go!!"

Mingo starts dragging Mario to the front door, as they pass by D.

"Wait!" Mario said. "Come on! Wait! I'm buying I'm buying!"

D motions to Mingo to wait, he halts which allows Mario to steady himself.

"Let me see him." D said.

Mingo shoves Mario over in D's direction, Mario stumbles a little, but gets his footing. D snickers a bit as Mario approaches him.

"Alright, you want to stay?" D said. "Ya have to pay. You know the rules man."

"I got you." Mario said. "I... I got you."

"Oh, you got me?" D said. "Fine let's do business."

D places his hand in his outside suit pocket, he pulls out a medium black plastic zip lock bag and looks Mario over.

"I've got what can scratch that itch," D said. "How much you got?"

Mario stares at the zip lock bag almost hypnotized by it.

"I... I'm a little low right now." Mario said. "I got you tomorrow. Please D, hit me off man. I got you, for real."

D laughs shaking his head.

"What you Blimpy or something?!" D said. "A vile today and I'll pay you Tuesday, don't think so!" He puts the zip lock bag away, then signals to Mingo. "Take him out."

"Time to go," Mingo said grabbing Mario.

D turns his back and moves away as Mingo pulls Mario to the door once again. Mario struggles in Mingo's grasp trying to stay.

"Eric it's me!! Mario! Come on, you know me!"

D turns around and motions to Mingo saying, "Bring that punk here."

Mingo drags Mario back over again and pushes him toward D. Once Mario is near him, D steps in closer to Mario.

"What'd you call me?" Eric D said.

"You're Eric Devin," Mario said. "Eric D, we went to school together. Remember?"

"Only person calls me Eric is my mama." Eric D said.

"Let me look at ya."

Mario tries to step back from Eric D but Mingo comes up behind him, halting his movement.

"Straighten up punk," Mingo said flexing on Mario.

Eric D walks around Mario looking him over, circling him like a shark stalking his prey and a smile comes to his face.

"Word!! Mario." Eric D said. "Yeah, I remember you!"

"See," Mario said. "So...so D can you hit me off? Please, I'm... I'm good for it D for real. I'm hurting here man."

"Mario, yeah we used to call you Mr. A+! You didn't want to be bothered with us. The nobodies who lived in the hood. Well look who's in the hood now. Who was that guy you hung out with? Rich, Ray, Reggie! Yeah, that's it, Reggie. Y'all were from the suburbs."

Mario grows anxious, to ease the ache within him.

"Come on, Please D... I'm hurting."

"I heard you got all ivy league on us. What happened to all that?"

"Things happen, can... can I get that D?"

"Heard how you went up to that fancy university and that family of yours. Got..." Eric D blows into his hand like he's doing a magic trick. "Snuffed out by some drunk driver. Heard they burnt up right in front of ya."

"Ooh!! That's messed up!" Mingo said.

Mario turns away, "Stop stop... I don't talk about that."

"Oh so sorry," Eric D said. "You have my condolences but now you need something from this hood rat." Eric D turns his back to Mario and walks away, brushing off the arms and front of his suit jacket. "Funny how things change." He looks over his shoulder at Mario. "I think they call that irony."

"D man, please. Please... I need it man!" Mario's on edge, shaking and almost tearful. "Let me get a hit D, please. I... I'm good for it. Hit me off D. Please."

"Credit!" Eric D doesn't even turn around. "Sorry, don't do credit. Mingo! Time for him to go!"

Mingo grabs Mario again and roughly pulls him toward the front door. Mario struggles against Mingo's grasp once again trying so desperately to stay as he gets dragged toward the front door. Mario frenzied from needing a hit allows desperation to take him over.

"No, please. No! Anything D!" Mario said. "Come on! Please D anything! I need it man! Please, I'll do anything!"

Mingo opens the door and just as he's about to throw Mario out.

"Wait! Bring him here." Eric D said.

Mingo closes the door and holds Mario in place. A devilish smirk forms on the lips of Eric D. Those words uttered by Mario, are sweet to him and he reveled in this opportunity. Mingo shoves Mario over towards Eric D.

"Get over there," Mingo said.

Mario looks back at Mingo for a second, walks over to Eric D stops a few feet from him because Eric D still has his back turned. As Eric D turns to Mario, his face goes callous. Eric D looks straight into Mario's eyes.

"Anything you say." Eric D said.

Mario hesitates, then nods his head sealing his fate.

Eric D nods too, "Alright."

Eric D looks Mario over from head to toe and back again. Mario still being on edge watches Eric D giving him the once-over. Eric D moves closer to Mario. He reaches out to Mario's face.

"You're a little dingy and everything." Eric D said. He caresses Mario's cheek. "You're still a pretty one though."

"Come on man," Mario responds.

He swiftly pushes Eric D's hand away and shoves him. Now riled up by Mario's actions Eric D throws his hands up as he steps back.

"He'll Work It Out" Chapter 2. Taryn C. Atkins

"Fine!" Eric D said. He looks over at Mingo. "I was trying to make this easy."

Eric D quickly looks at Mario and steps to him, as he points his finger in his face.

"Easy for you! There goes Mr. Uppity A+ though. So listen up cause it's simple."

Eric D steps back as he pulls out the black plastic baggie again and holds it up in one hand for Mario to see.

"You want this in your pipe." Eric D looks Mario up and down. "First." He slides his hand down the front of his pants and grabs his package. "You gonna take care of mine. Get me!?"

"Come on..." Mario said shaking his head no. "Please D."

Eric D shrugs his shoulders replying, "Guess you don't need that hit that bad." He holds the bag up and taps it. "This batch, would've taken you there too. Hit that spot right. Pff, oh well." He puts the bag away. "You know what? I've got a better idea."

In one fluid motion, Eric D steps back, he turns away from Mario, reaches behind his back and under his suit jacket. As he turns back to Mario, he pulls out a Nickel plated, Colt forty-five automatic and points it at Mario.

"See this?" Eric D shows the gun to Mario. "I don't normally do this but since I know you; I'm gonna help you out."

Mario backs away again. Eric D watching him cower, laughs.

"Come on now where you going?"

Mario's departure is again canceled by Mingo, who pushes him forward.

"I'm offering you a chance to help yourself." He shows Mario the gun again. "And this, can make everything better."

Eric D moves closer to Mario, he takes the gun and points it at him. While he talks, he places the muzzle of the weapon close to the precise area he speaks on.

"See, you can put it in your mouth, maybe to your temple but if you don't want things too get messy."

"He'll Work It Out" Chapter 2. Taryn C. Atkins

Eric D takes the gun, puts it against Mario's chest pointing it directly at his heart.

"You aim it right there. Then BAM!!!"

The sudden noise makes Mario flinch, on seeing it Mingo laughs out loud for a moment. Eric D continues on with an eerie compassion.

"No more worries or cravings, you can finally be with that family of yours. After all, that's what you want."

Mario's face reveals a part of him is seriously thinking about the offer. Eric D puts the gun away, strolls over to Mario and stands next to him. He drapes his arm around Mario's shoulders.

"I'm trying to be a good samaritan and help you get out of a bad situation."

Mario moves out of Eric D's grasp. He turns to him as he scratches saying, "Come on... why you teasing me like that D?"

Eric D seeing dirt on his pants leg brushes it off.

"No teasing." Eric D said. "I feel for you; I do." He looks at Mario. "I'm just giving you choices here; Life is filled with choices. Life, death, heaven, hell, the choice is yours man. That's called free will. God gave us that and what a beautiful thing it is."

"Yo D," Mingo said. "Give that punk the A or B choice, tell him how to hit us off."

Eric D glances at Mingo. "Yeah I'm getting to it," He does a double take. "Us?! How is this an "us" situation?!"

"He's a pretty boy." Mingo said. "Ya know how we do, treat'em to that special train ride."

Eric D shakes his head slowly for a moment, "You nasty man. Everyone thinks I'm sick, but you're twisted." He smiles and laughs a bit. "That's why you my dog, you know I'm gonna hook you up. Now can I handle this?"

"Do your thing man, handle it." Mingo said.

Eric D turns his attention back to Mario.

"So Mario, here's your choices." Eric D said. "A... You first hit us off and take that special train ride. After that, you'll get that hit. That will make you fly. OR" He takes the gun back out, loads the chamber, steps back and points it at Mario's head. "B... I hit you off and you don't ever fly again! What's it gonna be? I'm a busy man and time is money. So you got three seconds. Tic... tic... tic."

Mario confused stutters and mumbles to himself.

"Speak up!" Eric D said. "I can't hear you! A real man should be proud of the choices he makes. Now which is it, A or B?!"

Mario cleared his throat, then said, "A."

Eric D looks over at Mingo with a disturbing grin.

"Mingo, looks like we got an appetizer to use before I call for our main course."

Mario looks at Mingo, who nods his head and with a wicked grin he leers at Mario.

"Glad I'm hungry," Mingo said.

Eric D promptly puts the gun away, steps closer to Mario and again puts his arm around his shoulders.

"I'm gonna take real good care of you." Eric D said.

Mario cravingly said, "Can I get that hit now D. Please?!"

"Patience." Eric D steps in front of Mario, takes Mario's face in his hands. "First, you're gonna be a good boy. Our very good boy." He lets go of Mario and motions to Mingo. "Lock that front door."

Mingo swiftly locks the front door, comes back and grabs Mario by the arm. He pulls him around and they get ready to leave out the room, heading toward the back of the house.

"Wait a second." Eric D said.

He takes a set of keys out his suit jacket and throws them to Mingo.

"You'll need those," Eric D said. "And you, need this."

Eric D reaches inside his pants pocket, takes a small tube out and throws it to Mario. He barely catches it. Mario looks and sees its Vaseline, he looks at Eric D. Who's standing there with a smirk on his face, rubbing his hands together.

"Make them lips real smooth and moist for us."

Mingo said with a vile tone, "Yeah, we like that."

Eric D kisses at Mario and motions to Mingo.

"Take him up. I'm right behind you."

Mario murmured to himself, "Take me up?"

"Let's go."

Mingo pulls Mario, they leave out the so called living room and are followed by Eric D. They all head down the hallway toward a black door. Mario notices the door has two secure locks on it. Mingo takes the keys, unlocks them and pushes the door open. He reaches inside feeling the wall to the right and flicks the light switch. The lights come on revealing a few feet away a staircase leading to the next floor of the house.

Mingo and Mario head up the stairs. Eric D enters, closes the door behind him and heads up the staircase. Mario looks up the staircase and sees another black door. Mingo gets to it and opens it. He and Mario step inside the dark room. Eric D enters a few seconds behind them. He closes the door and turns on the lights.

"Mingo break out three Corona's for us." Eric D said.

"Coming right up." Mingo said.

When Mario's eyes adjust he sees that he's in a huge room, that's been completely painted red. Where other rooms of the house would be, the walls have been knocked out, creating this one vast space that's the size of the entire house.

Mario starts to scan this massive room full of black and red, except for the first thing Mario notices across the way. Over in the far upper right corner was an Alaskan white marble, fully open bathroom. Complete with Kohler toilet, sink, and vanity, in the corner stood a large Cardinal glass, frameless shower with a oversized square stainless steel shower head and next to it sat a large Atlantis Whirlpool tub.

That was the beginning of this vast area's unique decor. Now to the left of the bathroom and centered against the wall was a king size, four post bed which was covered by a black satin comforter. A glint of silver hanging from the ceiling in front of it caught Mario's attention. When he looked up, he saw a set of long metal chains with padded black leather cuffs at the end and below them attached to the floor was another set of chains with cuffs. Mario grew nervous, his body quivered and concern flooded his face realizing where his addiction has led him.

"He'll Work It Out" Chapter 2. Taryn C. Atkins

As Mario takes in the sights around the spacious room. He sees to the left of the bed are two black leather recliners, mounted on the far wall in front of the bed and several feet from the doorway was a sixty inch, HD flat screen TV. Under it was a floating glass media center which was about a foot off the floor. Within it was the usual, a Playstation game unit, the cable box and a Bose surround sound music system. A black leather sofa sat in front of the TV, in between them was a glass coffee table that matched the media center perfectly. In the bottom left corner of the room was a custom crafted Scottish pub style bar, made of African blackwood with hand forged iron footrests and custom bar stools.

Mario's eyes grew a bit wider when they take a gander at the other side of the room, for it held a bizarre collection of unconventional furniture. It was to the right of the bathroom area, a few feet away from the tub where Mario saw a black adjustable tattoo chair. A small black end table was next to it and on top of the table, sat three bundles of thick white cotton rope.

A few feet down was a lengthy black dresser with nine dresser draws. Mario could only imagine the assortment of items kept within them. Centered on top was a compilation of five round tinted glass jars, in varied sizes with silver lids on them. Each jar contained some type of paraphernalia for the owner's fetish predilection. Mario trembled again, seeing mounted on the wall, above the dresser was a black metal rack. It was used to display diverse types and textures of riding crops, paddles and floggers.

Mario's eyes grew wide again, when spotting a few feet from the dresser and in the lower right corner of the room. The final item that ended this exhibit of fetish furniture. It was a large black metal dog cage with a black padded mat on the floor of it. Eric D goes over to the cage, he ever so proudly glides his hand over the top of it. As he leans against it, Eric D looked at Mario.

"This is where I keep my pet, Ivy." He said.

Mario stared at Eric D with a curious expression trying to wrap his mind around his statement.

"Yeah, that's wild right. Well, you'd be surprised at the clientele this hood rat has." He folds his arms as he leans against the metal cage. "A few months ago a client of mine asked me to bring my pharmaceuticals upstate. He wanted me to supply some exclusive clubs week long event. Anyway, his friends enjoyed my supplies and as part of my payment. He said I could have his pet Ivy for a month. I couldn't believe that but I told him when and where. Get this-she shows up at my door, kneeling, head bowed and handing me my contract of temporary ownership. Wild right!? I got about a week left."

Eric D takes off his suit jacket and places it on top of the cage. Mingo comes over, hands Eric D a Corona and gives one to Mario. Eric D guzzles some down. Mario quickly gulps his drink down, only stopping once to catch his breath for a second and then continues on till his bottle is empty. Eric D takes a few more swallows and places the bottle on top of the cage. He points to Mingo.

"Me and Mingo," Eric D said. "We plan to make good use of the time left. Ain't that right."

"Word!" Mingo said heading over to Eric D. "We gonna use it again, like the directions say."

Eric D picks up his Corona, he and Mingo clink their bottles together in agreement. Mingo heads over to the sofa. Eric D downs a few gulps of his Corona, when he finishes he looks around the massive room. He spread his arms out and looked over at Mario.

"See this place," Eric D said. "This woman, I met at that event upstate. She's what they call a..." He snaps his fingers while he searches for the correct word. He looks at Mario. "A dominatrix, yeah, she was a fine older woman too. They called her Mistress Zett. She thought I was cute, so we played a little. I'm kinky like that; I didn't mind switching it up and being a sub. Anyway Mistress Zett, she's the one who helped put this room of mine together."

Mario scans over everything in the area once again. Eric D walks over to the dresser, admiring the wall display filled with his BDSM toys and tools.

"So Mario... how you like my little collection here?"

"He'll Work It Out" Chapter 2. Taryn C. Atkins

While Eric D waits for Mario's response, he takes his shirt out his pants. Mario says nothing as he takes in the wall display once more. The sound of machine gun fire comes out of the surround system. Mario flinches, he turns around and sees Mingo sitting on the sofa playing a video game. Eric D walks over to the tattoo chair, sits down and lays back.

"Ya know, I never thought about this Master-slave stuff but being at that party, watching these people and playing myself. Man... I gotta say, I'm into it now." As he sits up, he laughs. "My client Bryce, is this older dude. He's about sixty-five. That's Ivy's husband, she's no more than thirty-two. Now get this-they've been married since she was thirteen. Thirteen! Ain't that some craziness. He told me, she was a freak when he got her. So he started grooming her for this right after their honeymoon. No wonder she got no problem with all this stuff. It's all she knows. Yo, she be lovin it too."

"Yo D!" Mingo said.

"What you want man?!" Eric D said. "And turn the sound down on that thing."

Mingo stops playing the video game for a moment, he gets up, takes the remote and turns the volume down. He throws the remote down on the sofa and turns to Eric D.

"Now what you want?" Eric D said.

"What I was gonna say," Mingo said. "If your boy Bryce got Ivy like that at thirteen, somebody turned her out, at like ten. I mean she's hot and all, even got a high-class thing going on too but she's a freak. Especially once she's tuned up, that chick flips. She goes nympho."

"Yo! You right man. Somebody had to be hittin that when she was a kid. Well, whoever was tappin that, turned her into a straight up sex fiend."

"Word D, cause Ivy can Triple X with it all day."

Mingo goes back over to the sofa and continues playing the video game. Eric D looks over at Mario.

"So my client Bryce, dude got money. He's a doctor, got a practice somewhere in Connecticut. Ivy's a chef." He laughs a bit. "I met them at some megachurch down south. My cousin invited me down to her church's big Thanksgiving Family and Friends Day. She said, all their little churches were coming together for the holiday. So I figure, go down, see my family, have a good meal and get my one service in before the year ends." He chuckles again. "I meet this couple there, husband and wife at that. We exchange numbers, once I'm back in New York we talk and he invites me to their spot in Connecticut, that's when I learn they're into BDSM. I mean into it, got a dungeon in their basement man. They introduce me to this *kinky* flow and I met them at a *church fellowship*. Who'd of thought!?"

Eric D stands and stretches, letting out this loud sigh and looks over at Mario, who is filled with anxiety and on edge. Not because of his surroundings but more so as a result of his yearning habit. Eric D sees it all over him too.

"Well, I'm sure you'd love to hear more of Ivy's story.
We'll talk more about that later. We got our own business
to take care of, don't we?"

Mario hesitantly shakes his head in agreement. Eric D passes by Mario and heads across the room toward the recliners.

"Mingo! Turn that off! Let's do this!"

"Be right there." Mingo said.

Mingo gets up and in one swift swoop removes his jersey. He leaves on a his wife beater, jeans and Tims. Mingo turns off the video game and chugs down the rest of his Corona. Eric D takes a seat in the left recliner, leans back but stops pulling the gun out from behind him. Eric D places the gun on the table next to him, then leans back and relaxes in the recliner. Eric D looks at Mario and gestures to him.

"Come here." Eric D said.

Mario takes his time going over but Mingo comes up behind him. Instead of pushing Mario with his hand. Mingo uses his body and bumps into Mario to move him along.

"Speed it up," Mingo said. "You heard D, get over there."

"He'll Work It Out" Chapter 2. Taryn C. Atkins

Mingo shoves Mario forward and as Mario moves closer, Eric D stands up.

"Take a seat Mario," Eric D said. "This way it'll be easier for you. So come on, sit down and be a good boy."

Mario passes by Eric D and sits down in the recliner. Eric D and Mingo move in closer to him, one is to Mario's left and the other to his right.

"No need to rush either." Eric D said taking off his shirt. "Be a good boy and take your time. Now, get us ready for that train ride we're gonna take you on."

Mario watches as they unzip their pants, his mind recoils, a tsunami of emotions flood it and it starts to spin. He looks at Eric D and Mingo, impish grins appear on their faces. They're talking to Mario but all he hears is white noise. Mario's mind spirals and whirls as white noise amplifies. He starts blinking his eyes almost uncontrollably because to him the room is growing foggy. Mario feels a hand first on his shoulder and then on the back of his neck. The hand moves up to the back of his head, it pushes his head forward, Mario's mind hits full tilt and everything goes black.

Outside Ivy walks up to the Escalade. She's holding a large Wendy's cup in her right hand, Wendy's shopping bag is on her right arm and she carries a thin black liquor store bag in her left hand. All of a sudden the blaring sound of four gunshots resonate from within the house. Ivy lets out an ear-splitting shriek and everything she holds falls to the ground. Ivy knowing something terrible has happened inside becomes panicked and fearful.

Ivy scrambles to get the keys out of her shirt for the Escalade as she races over to the drivers side, in her mind off in the distance the roar of sirens can be heard. She jiggles the car key in the lock once more, turns it and the SUV unlocks. Ivy pulls open the door, rushes into the drivers seat, puts the key in the ignition and starts the SUV. The sirens she hears in her mind seem to be getting closer. Ivy swiftly put the Escalade in drive and she tears out from the abandoned house.

As Ivy sped off in the SUV, her mind played out scenarios of her being caught there, having to be detained and questioned by the authorities. Although the idea of all that did concern her a bit. Ivy's deep seeded anxiety was a result of her thoughts about displeasing the ones she called her Owner and Master.

Back inside the house, the darkness slowly faded from Mario's mind. He looks down and Eric D and Mingo are laying sprawled out on the floor. Mario notices a hole right at Mingo's heart and he sees his wife beater turn dark red from blood. When he looks at Eric D, he sees the blood seeping out from three holes in his chest. Mario looks at his clothes covered in blood. He gets ready to rub his face and realizes he's holding Eric D's gun. Mario starts to wail and runs out of what his mind believes to be a blood covered room. He heads down the stairs and the sound of his own screams are surreal to him.

Mario runs into the room where it all began, still holding the gun, he runs into the corner near the twin mattress and as he continues to cry his body slides down the wall. Mario slumps in the corner of the room, his thirst having never been quenched he's still anxious and in much need of a hit. Which now he feels is a craving he'll always be tormented by and will never, ever find any relief for or any peace from.

"All I needed was a taste ya know..." Mario hits his forehead with the gun several times causing blood to trickle down his face. "Have to stop seeing them... I need to stop seeing them. Need to stop smelling their flesh burning... it's everywhere!! Their flesh burning mixed with gasoline. I don't want to see them but it keeps playing, over and over and over. PLEASE!! Make it stop!! Please!"

Mario closes his eyes, he leans his head back against the wall and after a few seconds, the gun drops from his hand. Again Mario has given into his bodies weariness and he falls asleep. Mario slept in peace for a moment but without warning his head begins to thrash. As images of the past, mixed with those of his present flooded his dreams. Mario's body jerks, he wakes up lunging forward as if he was pushing someone away.

"NO!!!" Mario starts to weep again. "All I wanted was a little hit. It's the only thing that makes the memories go away. One hit... I would've paid him back later but he kept teasing me. Holding the bag in my face, asking me how bad did I want it..." Tears stream down his face. "I couldn't give them the only thing I had left." He looks at the blood all over his clothes and hands. "Now what do I do? Reggie!! Where are you?! You promised you'd be back. Have to stop seeing them... have to stop the pain. So tired of hurting..." He looks at the gun and wipes some of the tears from his face. "I miss them so much." He picks up the gun, sniffles a bit and wipes away his tears. "It's all about choices." Tears run down his face. "Will the pain go away... You promise... That's all I want... I want all the pain to go away... I don't want to hurt anymore... Okay... Okay." Mario places the muzzle of the gun to his heart and looks straight ahead. "I just want the pain to... Stop."

Two police cars and an ambulance pull up to the house. As EMS workers and Police jump out their cars, another gunshot rings out, the police draw their guns and rush inside. People start gathering outside the house as curiosity overtakes them regarding the events going on inside.

A few hours have passed and Reggie speedily walks toward the abandoned house carrying under his arm a MacBook Pro.

"D should give us a few hits for this," Reggie said. He sucks his teeth. "Man, it's all good, Dray's a personal trainer. He can get another one of these easy."

Reggie rushes to his destination, a few blocks ahead at an auto repair shop, he sees the shops marquee and the time scrolls pass.

"4:45, okay that's cool, I still made good time. D should still be sitting in his ride out front. Man, I didn't mean to be gone so long." He hurries up the block. "Hold on Mario, I'm coming."

When Reggie looks ahead, he sees a crowd has formed around the outskirts of the house. Reggie makes his way through the crowd of onlookers and tries to get close enough to see for himself what's going on. The police tape stops Reggie from going any further. As he looks to see what's going on, besides the two police cars out front, he sees the coroner's van in front of the house, spectators and bystanders have gathered on both sides of the house and across the street from it. They stand around talking amongst themselves sharing their assumptions about what happened. Reggie looks at the young dude next to him.

"Yo, you know what happen?" Reggie said.

"Some kid across the street heard gunshots and called the cops." The young dude said.

An old man standing on the other side of Reggie taps his arm.

"I heard some of the cops talking." The old man said. "Some drug dealer and a few others got shot."

Some neighborhood chic pushes her way through the crowd, she shoves herself between Reggie and the old guy.

"They bring bodies out?" The neighborhood chic said.

"Nah, not yet." The young dude said, "I'm waiting for that too."

The neighborhood chic said, "My cousin said some crack fiend shot D and his boy Mingo, then killed himself."

Reggie worries about Mario, he stands there attentively listening and watches as workers go in and out of the condemned house.

"For real gurl." The young dude said.

"Yeah." The neighborhood chic responds. "My cousin Ebony was with that kid Showtime when he heard the shots. Ebony had to tell the cops about how that freak, you know the one that's been hanging with D. How she just up and left, drove off with D's ride too. Cops took Ebony and Showtime down to the station to get their statements."

"Look here they come!" The old man said pointing to the house. "They're bringing the bodies out!"

The crowds focus returns to the house as workers start to exit. A few plainclothes detectives come out first, some people with CSI vests on and then the coroners come out. One is pulling the front of the gurney assisted by the other coroner at the end of it. The first body is inside a body bag on top of the stretcher. They put the first body in the van, then take the gurney and make their way back inside the house. A few moments later they bring the second body out and in like fashion the second body is in a body bag laying on top of the gurney. The second body is put in the van and they go back in again.

After a few moments, they bring the last body out. As they come out the house the first coroner in front of the gurney, miss steps and loses his balance, the gurney starts to tilt to the side, the coroner at the other end tries to stop it but the body bag begins to slide off. Reggie and the rest of the onlookers take a collective deep breath watching what's happening. The coroner at the end grabs for the body bag and it tears open. The face of the body inside is revealed to all. Reggie sees it's Mario and to Reggie, it's as if Mario stares right at him. Reggie drops the MacBook Pro, in a panic pushes his way through the crowd and rushes off.

~HAPPY HOUR~

Summer has come, it's the middle of the week and on this splendid June evening, in the midst of various conversations music plays in a bar downtown in the West Village. Back in the day on Thursday Nights it was Ladies Only at this location; it was the home of a sexy and sleek, two floor, two bar night club known as "2i's". Women would come to lounge, people watch, drink and hit the dance floor letting the music stylings of DJ Missy B or DJ Trini move them.

Now it's a sports bar and lounge called The Lay Up. A favored spot which is bringing together the sports lovers and tastemakers in an extraordinary and multifaceted way. It's the tail end of happy hour and the place is at half of its capacity.

After walking through the foyer, when you enter this place you're greeted by an antique cash register sitting at the beginning of the thirty-five foot hand carved bar. The wall behind it held all the attributes needed for the bartenders to create and serve drinks. There is a mirror on it too, running from the ceiling to floor of the full length of the bar. Those at the bar sit on custom bar chairs each with uniquely carved wooden backs. Patrons watch sports on three HD wide screen TV's hanging high above it. The opposite wall is also covered by a mirror that runs the length of the bar as well. In between the bar and this wall is enough room where patrons can stand having conversations, check out the TV's over the bar and even dance with a partner or two if they want.

Besides the sports being viewed on the screens all around, the atmosphere is also tempered by the live DJ mixing in the booth upstairs above it all. The DJ cranks out the music at the right pitch so it could be enjoyed without disturbing those focused on their games.

At the end of the lengthy bar patrons step into a massive rectangular room. Where there is several four to six patron booths positioned around the room, each with its own thirty-six inch HD TV mounted on the wall. The center of this rectangle holds a few tables for two to four patrons, above them two large HD TV's hung back to back. There is a corridor in the far upper left corner of the room. Where the kitchen area and two sets of rest rooms are located.

Not far from the register, on the curved end of the bar, sits Alexis Moore aka Lexi. She is a thirty, tall, fit and pretty tomboy, who's brainy and street smart with chic style and swagger. Lexi reaches out and takes a few pretzels out of the bowl sitting on the bar in front of her. After putting two in her mouth, she pushes up the sleeves to her summer suit. Lexi notices a few crumbs on the white mid drift top she wears underneath her jacket. It matches perfectly with the leather shoe boots she sported. Lexi is one bar stool away from her close friend Barbara Faison aka Bobbie.

Bobbie's a thirty-three year old Aggressive with a urban preppy fashion sense. Bobbie observes herself in the mirror behind the bar as she adjusted her black newsboy cap. After getting it positioned to her liking she smiles and gives herself a nod; She brushes off her powder blue Polo shirt, which she has on with a black vest, stone wash blue jeans and black leather slip on loafers.

Their just chilling and kicking it with each other. The male bartender comes over, serves each of them a bottle of Corona Extra and two shot glasses filled with a clear liquid. Bobbie hands him cash, he takes the money and glances at Bobbie.

"I'll be right back with your change." He said.

"Keep it." Bobbie said.

"Thank you," he said. "Enjoy ladies. You know I'm Ty, I'll be around if you need anything."

As Ty walks away, Lexi closes her eyes and slaps one hand on the bar countertop three times. Bobbie watches Lexi grab one of the shots and raises the glass in the air.

"To Hump Day!" Lexi said. "We made it and now we're closer to the weekend." She looks at Bobbie. "We work hard on our perspecti... perspecti..."

"Don't hurt yourself." Bobbie said.

"I'm saying," Lexi said, "We work hard. We deserve this."

"Here! Here!" Bobbie said.

They down their first shots, slam their glasses on the bar and swiftly repeat the process with their second shot glasses. The strength of the liquor causes their faces to contort.

"Mmmph, I needed that," Bobbie said.

"Me too," Lexi said.

Bobbie takes a swig of her Corona as she checks out Lexi's outfit, an impressed expression forms on her face.

"Lexi you are wearing that suit. That electric blue is hot."

"Thanks."

"CK?"

"You know it, when I saw it at Nordstrom's, I had to have it."

Lexi takes her suit jacket off and puts it on the back of her chair, as she turns back around, she extends her arms over her head stretching. Bobbie shakes her head as she looks at Lexi's well tone and cut arms. As Lexi finishes her stretch, she watches Bobbie bend her right arm, she flexes it and touches the outline of her extended bicep.

"Not bad, not bad. I'm getting there." Bobbie said.

Lexi grabs her Corona, drinks down some and places it back on the bar. She leans back in her bar chair relaxing, absorbing the atmosphere around her. Bobbie pushes her cap back a little on her head, reaches out and touches Lexi's eye-catching abs. Lexi looks at Bobbie when she feels the touch.

"Now that's impressive." Bobbie said. She pokes at Lexi's abs. "Goodness, you gotta live in the gym to keep that up."

Lexi points to her rock-hard abs saying, "Working out does a body good. I gotta keep the ladies happy."

Bobbie slides off her bar chair, plants her feet, stands erect and lifts up the lower half of her shirt.

"Oh now don't get it twisted, this stud keeps it tight and right too." Bobbie said.

Lexi slowly shakes her head and smiles seeing Bobbie's chiseled abs. She reaches out and pokes Bobbie's abs twice.

"Alright, I ain't mad at ya," Lexi said. "An AG (Aggressive) gotta do what an AG gotta do."

They both extend a fist and give each other a pound.

"That's what I'm saying," Bobbie said.

Lexi and Bobbie get excited, they look at each other with bright faces realizing the DJ started playing a classic late eighties house music anthem.

"That's my jam!" Lexi said.

Lexi and Bobbie jump to their feet getting their dance groove on as the music plays.

"Oh oh watch it now." Bobby breaks loose doing her best house music dance moves. "Watch it! Watch it!"

"What... check it out!" Lexi brings her own flair of house music moves to the table. "You can't handle this!"

As Bobbie and Lexi show off their dance stylings, the bar crowd looks on, some laugh, a few encourage them on but all enjoy the show. After a few moments Lexi and Bobbie stop, the bar customers, even the staff clap and cheer for them. They take their bows, look at each other smiling and laughing. They high five each other and take their seats.

"I love me some good ol house music."

"Nothing like it."

Bobbie and Lexi take a few gulps of their Coronas and kick back enjoying the bar's ambience.

"So... where's Dana? She's actually letting you fly solo?"

"Yeah right, no such luck."

"I know," Bobbie said. "I hear that ball and chain when you're walking."

"Ah ha funny," Lexi said. "Least I got something keeping me warm and cozy at night."

Bobbie begins to comment when a stunner catches her eye and renders her speechless. Not only Bobbie is mesmerized, scattered about the place both male and female check out this gorgeous, golden toffee vision entering the room. Each assuming this captivating woman is coming into their hunting grounds, when it's actually the opposite.

As she moves across the floor, time seems to slow for Bobbie who's attention she's taken. Diverse eyes watch her as she uses her hand to toss her long dark flowing tresses over her shoulder. They take their time scanning her from head to toe, taking inventory of her elegant and posh attire. Which exudes allure and highlighted her total being. This mid forties femme fatale's natural air of sensual assertiveness emanates like a beacon and her presence intoxicates the atmosphere around her.

This mesmerizing woman is dressed in: a cherry red, off the shoulder, one sleeve, double slit, fitted maxi dress accompanied by a fierce pair of black high heels. When her hair lands on the sexy black silk wrap around her shoulders, it causes the wrap to fall off exposing her bare shoulder.

The woman in red stops and stands at the center point of the bar, while patiently waiting for either bartender to finish dealing with their current customer. Her cell phone vibrates in her black Louis Vuitton shoulder bag. She huffs reaching inside and pulls out her iPhone. Before answering the call she checks the display seeing it's a call from Cassi.

Under her breath, she said, "I'm sorry, not tonight."

She huffs, rolls her eyes putting the phone back in her bag as the call goes to voicemail. A woman with a diamond lip ring standing next to the woman in red begins to give her the once-over. The pierced patron's eyes go to her heels and she studies them for a moment.

"Honey stay on the carpet," The pierced patron said.

"Don't let this floor mess up your Red Bottoms."

"Oh I do, believe me." The woman in red said. "No worries though, I have a few of these."

"Oh..." The pierced patron said.

She picks up her drink, giving the woman in red a half smile and walks away. Time is back to normal for Bobbie, she leans to the side in her seat, places her elbow on her leg, bringing her hand to her chin and slowly rubs it with a sly grin. Bobbie checks out this lovely creature in red and having finally recovered her words.

"You see Lexi," Bobbie said. "Personally, I love having options." She taps Lexi and motions with her head toward the woman in red. "Check that red out."

Lexi turns around, taking in the full view of the woman in red.

"Dang," Lexi said. "Ooh, she's fine."

"She sure nuff is," Bobbie said.

Bobbie stands and prepares herself to approach. When she gets ready to head over, Lexi swiftly gets up and steps in front of her.

"Hold up there speedy. Where you going?"

Bobbie motions to the woman in red. "Where you think?"

While Lexi and Bobbie talk for a moment, a guy with a aussie accent garishly lets his interest be known as he approaches the woman in red but after a few seconds he walks away. His attempt is futile. Bobbie and Lexi then happen to notice a studious, porcelain toned woman, with long gray dreads go over to the woman in red. This woman receives at least, a warm pearly white smile from the woman in red but she walks away too. Her attempt also a failed one.

"Lexi this is me, I got this."

"I don't doubt your mack skills, but..." Lexi turns around and points at the woman in red. "You're about to step to her." She turns back to Bobbie and motions to her clothes. "Dressed like that?"

"I don't know what you're talking about."

Bobbie checks herself in the mirror on the wall behind them. She smooths the sides of her cap, brushes off her clothes and buffs the tops of her Kenneth Cole's. Bobbie looks at Lexi.

"This outfit has pulled many a female in its day."

"Well, today's not the day. So please, don't embarrass

yourself or me for that matter." She points to the woman in red again. "It takes a special breed to step to that."

"Well." Bobbie walks around Lexi. "I'm about to join that breed."

As Bobbie goes to the woman in red. Lexi shakes her head watching Bobbie, but then nonchalantly follows Bobbie over. Lexi hangs a a few feet back so she can see and hear what's happening. Bobbie puts on her best smile and steps to the woman in red.

"Hello sweetness," Bobbie said. "May I have the pleasure of buying you a drink?"

Lexi overhearing covers her face with her hand, under her breath, she said to herself, "Oh... that was weak."

The woman in red looks at Bobbie, scans her head to toe in a millisecond, gives a courteous smile and with a sultry voice she addresses the matter.

"No thank you." The woman in red said.

"Come on now lovely," Bobbie said, stepping closer as she signals to the male bartender to come. She leans in a bit. "So tell me what you like? Let me get it for you."

Lexi sees the woman in red's expression turn to aggravation but it goes unnoticed by Bobbie, who moves closer invading her personal space.

"I'm just being the gentlewoman that I am."

The woman in red looks Bobbie up and down, gives a minimal smile and steps back. Bobbie continues her pursuit by moving closer once again. She doesn't waste a breath by saying another word. The woman in red simply looks in the opposite direction and moves away. Lexi comes over and hits Bobbie on her shoulder.

"Come on," Lexi said.

"What," Bobbie said.

Bobbie follows Lexi back to their seats. Lexi puts on her suit jacket as Bobbie sits down in the empty chair next to Lexi's.

"Sweetness? Are you for real." Lexi said. "And what happened to personal space? Have you not learned anything from me?"

"Whatever' man," Bobbie said. She sucks her teeth. "She ain't all that anyway."

"Yeah okay," Lexi said laughing. "You keep telling yourself that. While you do, watch and learn, cause school's in session... Again."

Bobbie leans back, looking on as Lexi fixes herself, making sure she looks right. Lexi heads over to the woman in red, slowly approaching the woman in red from the right, she watches and judges the right time to make her appearance. The female bartender finally comes over to the woman in red.

"What can I get for you?" The female bartender said.

The woman in red said. "Please bring me a Cosmopolitan." She points toward the end of the bar. "I'll be sitting over there."

Lexi sees the direction the woman in red pointed in, nonchalantly Lexi moves herself to the left side of the woman in red, and now she's positioned somewhat behind her. Lexi puts her hand in her pants pocket and times her entrance. The woman in red puts a twenty on the bar and the bartender picks it up.

"I'll bring that right over." The female bartender said.

"Thank you, keep the change." The woman in red said.

"Thank you." The female bartender said.

The door opens for Lexi to enter when the woman in red turns around to walk away. Lexi smoothly steps into her path as she leans on the bar. The woman in red glances up at Lexi and looks directly into her eyes. Lexi gazes at the woman in red giving her a sexy, confident smile.

"Why sit so far away? Lexi said. "I'm at the opposite end."

The woman in red moves her eyes leisurely up and down Lexi, contemplating her.

"Well, you know what they say." The woman in red said.

"They say a lot of things," Lexi said. She sits down in the bar chair right next to her. "Please, do tell. Enlighten me."

The woman in red looks at Lexi with a seductive and inviting smile.

"They say, distance makes the heart grow fonder."

A man wearing a Giant's jersey rushes pass as he signals to his friends across the room. He bumps into the woman in red, pushing her forward towards Lexi. She stops herself from falling into Lexi. Their eyes meet and they take in each other. Although their bodies never touch, they have penetrated personal space. The feverish energy that's begun to stir between them intensifies.

"Excuse me." The woman in red said.

"Not a problem," Lexi said. "It's a welcome invasion... but if you don't mind."

Lexi stands up, she softly touches her hair moving it away to expose the side of the woman's neck. Lexi leans in, inhaling the perfume exuding from her and a smile surfaces on Lexi's face.

"Mmm, don't you smell good," Lexi whispers in her ear.

"Oh I know..." The woman in red said.

She moves in a bit closer she to Lexi looking amorously into Lexi's eyes as she reaches across to pick up her bag on the bar counter. Their eyes hold on each other as she puts the strap on her shoulder.

"It's like that all over." The woman in red said.

The woman in red walks away going to her seat at the end of the bar. Lexi turns in her direction and a smile appears again on her face. The woman's walk was thought-provoking. Lexi stands for a moment to watch her walk away. Lexi begins to slowly back step to her own seat. She continues to admire the natural movement of the woman's hips under her dress. Lexi stops next to Bobbie, taps her and points toward the woman in red.

"Did you see that!?" Lexi said. "That's a beautiful walk!"

The woman takes her seat at the end of the bar. She doesn't look at Lexi but Lexi notices her smiling. Lexi continues to watch her, with her back to the bar entrance. Lexi tries to make eye contact with her. When a good-looking, high maintenance young woman in her mid twenties enters the bar, clad in a zebra print, drop waist mini dress and heels.

She yells out. "Hey there baby!"

Bobbie looks back and smiles. When Lexi hears the young woman's voice her demeanor changes. She shakes her head slightly, glances up, murmur's a few words to herself and turns around with a huge smile.

"Hey! There she is." Lexi said.

"He'll Work It Out" Chapter 2. Taryn C. Atkins

The young woman extends her arms and rushes over. The young lady passes by Bobbie and rushes into Lexi's arms. She puts her arms around Lexi's neck and pulls her close.

"Sorry I'm late." The young woman said. "You would not believe the day I had."

"Well I was wondering where my baby was."

"Aw," The young woman said. "You were worried about me."

The female bartender serves the woman in red her Cosmo. The woman in red takes a few sips of her drink, looking on as Lexi and the young woman share a close, cozy hug. She watches as the young woman caresses the back of Lexi's neck. Lexi slides her hands over the back of the young woman appreciating the soft texture of her dress.

"I'm always concerned about my lady," Lexi said.

To top off the hug and ward off any suspicion Lexi starts to nuzzle the neck of the young woman. She quickly pushes Lexi back releasing herself from her arms.

"Alright now," The young woman said pointing at Lexi. "Don't start nothing."

"Dana, come on now," Lexi responds wearing a sly smile. "Can't I be happy to see you?"

"Sure, but umm..." Dana said. "There's so many ways you can show me too."

Dana once again gets into close quarters with Lexi. She slowly pulls Lexi's head down to her and she whispers in her ear. As Dana gives Lexi secret instructions, a huge smile forms on Lexi's lips. Dana moves away going to her seat. Lexi looks at Dana as she continues to smile and nods her head.

"I'll do exactly that."

"I know you will." Dana looks at Lexi and smiles. "Cause you're so fresh."

"And when did that become a bad thing."

"You're terrible." Dana turns to Bobbie and gives her an innocent hug. "Hi, Bobbie."

"Hey there, Dana." Bobbie said returning the hug.

They separate and Dana motions for Bobbie to move over to the next bar chair.

"See Bobbie," Dana said. "You need to take lessons from Lexi. Maybe it will help you keep a woman."

Bobbie moves over and Dana and Lexi sit down.

"Well as a matter of fact," Bobbie said. Behind Dana's back, she points toward the woman in red. "She was schooling me with--"

Lexi takes one of her hands and with a quickness she slaps Bobbie's hand down. Lexi speedily turns in the bartender's direction, swiftly raising her other hand to signal him.

"Ty! Yo Ty!" Lexi said.

Ty looks in that direction and sees Lexi signaling to him.

"Another round."

Ty shakes his head okay and continues to handle his current customer. Lexi's voice and actions overshadow Bobbie's intentions and the brief interaction between them goes unnoticed by Dana. Ty finishes up with his customer, picks up a bottle of Tequila and heads over to Lexi and her friends.

"Pace yourself ladies." Ty said. "This here is one hundred ten proof."

Ty takes the bottle of Tequila and fills up the four shot glasses already in front of them.

"There you go, enjoy ladies."

"Here you go." Bobbie hands Ty the money. "Thank you."

Ty gets ready to walk away, Lexi quickly reaches out and taps his arm. He turns to her.

"Ty, please bring over a glass of White Zinfandel," Lexi said. "For whenever Gigi decides to return." She looks at Dana, smiles and puts her arm around her. "And bring a Long Island Ice Tea for my lady Dana here."

"Hello Ty," Dana said as she waves at him.

"Hi Dana." Ty said. "Okay, so a White Zinfandel and a Long Island Ice Tea. Be back in a few."

Ty grabs the top half of the Tequila bottle sitting on the bar and as he's about to walk away Bobbie grabs the bottom half. Ty turns to Bobbie and he sits the Tequila bottle back on the bar.

"Leave the bottle," Bobbie said. She slides a hundred dollar bill over to Ty. "That's for the bottle plus the other drinks, keep the change and thanks."

Lexi and Dana see the bill Bobbie gave Ty and their expressions are mixed with excitement and astonishment.

"Look at you busting out a C-note," Lexi said.

"Well alright, big spender," Dana responds.

"Well hold on now Ty," Lexi said. "Please bring me another Corona. Since my friend here is being so generous."

Ty looks at Bobbie before walking away.

"It's okay add it," Bobbie said. "You can bring two over."

"No problem." Ty said. He picks up the money and as he walks away. "Be back in a few and thanks."

Ty walks off. Lexi and Dana continue to look at Bobbie with fondness and amazement. Bobbie looks at them as she drinks down the rest of her Corona. She finishes it and sits the empty bottle on the bar. Dana and Lexi keep staring at her fondly.

"Stop looking at me like that," Bobbie said. "I wasn't working for a while and y'all always had me. Y'all never gave me slack about it either. My family on the other hand never seem to let me forget it. Anyway, now that I'm back on my feet; I want to show that I appreciate you guys looking out for me. I love y'all."

"Awwww pookie." Dana seriously and jokingly responds.

She briskly caresses Bobbie's arm. "We love you too."

Lexi crosses her hands over her heart and looks at Bobbie with an affectionate and thoughtful expression. She sniffles a few times as if she's tearing up, acting as if she's holding back her tears.

"Oh, I'm sorry..." Lexi said acting all choked up. "I... I think we're having a moment here."

Bobbie shakes her head and swings her hand towards them.

"Forget y'all," Bobbie said.

Lexi reaches over and pats Bobbie on her shoulder being all serious now.

"We playing," Lexi said. "You know we love you too. We family Bee."

"And family looks out for each other." Dana said.

"Yeah okay," Bobbie said. "Now let's lighten up this mushy mood."

"Yeah alright," Lexi said.

The live DJ does his thing making a great atmosphere with the music being played. They chill out and enjoy it. Unnoticed by Dana, Lexi slyly flirts with the woman in red across the room.

"We need to go to a club soon Lexi," Dana said.

"I can go for some dancing too," Lexi said.

They sit savoring the music and Ty returns with their drinks.

"Here you go." Ty said. He places the drinks down in front of them. "Call me if you need anything else."

"Thank you Ty," Lexi said with a smile.

"No problem enjoy ladies." Ty said.

Ty walks away to tend to other customers. As the woman in red enjoys her drink and the music, she keeps an eye on Lexi. When Lexi looks in her direction the woman in red seizes the moment, she winks and kisses at her. Lexi being excited by the advances put forth, she slaps the top of the bar counter a few times once again and raises one of her shot glasses in the air.

"A toast," Lexi said. "To good friends, good times," She points her glass in Dana's direction. "And good women."

"I hear that," Bobbie said.

Lexi and Bobbie knock back their third Tequila shots but Dana doesn't drink any of her Long Island Ice Tea. Bobbie raises her other shot glass and seeing Bobbie do that Lexi raises her other shot glass in the air too.

"I got one," Bobbie said. "To the women we loved." She puts her glass in the direction of the woman in red. "To the women we lost." She puts her glass next to Lexi's.

"And to the many women, I will love."

"I ain't mad at ya," Lexi said.

Dana watches them speedily gulp down their drinks. The DJ pumps up the music again and once again Bobbie and Lexi become excited hearing the intro music playing to one of MJ's classic tunes from 1982. Lexi and Bobbie jump to their feet preparing themselves for another free performance. Bobbie does a sweet MJ spin before the intro finishes and points to Lexi.

"Kick it off!" Bobbie said.

Lexi goes over to Dana and as she lips sync's she does her own creative spin of MJ steps. Lexi sings and dances through the first two verses and chorus. Although it appears that she's focused on Dana, she's also making eye contact and singing to the woman in red also. As the woman in red watches Lexi she reciprocates the eye contact and smiles as she is entertained by Lexi's performance. Along with the rest of the bar customers and staff who's watching Lexi. A group of three women walk through the entrance of the bar as Lexi finishes with a smooth spin. Lexi hands over the next verses and chorus to Bobbie.

"Do your thing Bee!" Lexi said.

The bar customers clap to the song as they continue to watch the impromptu show. Bobbie takes over and approaches the small group of women, she takes the first woman by the hand. The woman is clearly a bit nervous but as Bobbie dances around the woman, mouthing the lyrics and doing MJ dance moves. The woman's attitude and expressions toward Bobbie go from being tense to being charmed.

Bobbie slowly twirls the woman, when it stops Bobbie is behind her just as the chorus starts. Bobbie puts her hands on the woman's hips and they move together doing "The Rock". As the chorus ends Bobbie takes the woman's hand again. Bobbie turns the woman to her and softly kisses her hand. Bobbie smiles as she looks into the woman's eyes.

"Thank you for the dance," Bobbie said.

"It was *my* pleasure." The woman said returning the smile.

The woman's friends go and find a table but she stays behind. The bar staff and customers cheer and clap once again, having enjoyed another dance presentation by Lexi and Bobbie. They take their bows once again enjoying the love everyone is showing them. Lexi goes to her seat and Dana gives her a passionate hug, to let all those watching know that Lexi belongs to her. The woman in red is not a bit bothered by Dana's antics. After a few seconds, Dana releases Lexi and they sit down. As Bobbie returns to her seat, the woman she was dancing with taps her on the shoulder. Bobbie turns to her, as Lexi and Dana carefully watch their interaction.

"Hi, I'm Suzanne." The woman said. "If you need a partner again, to dance or..." She smiles looking away for a second, then looks at Bobbie and shrugs her shoulders. "For whatever, I'm available."

"Nice to meet you, Suzanne," Bobbie said returning the smile. "I'm Bobbie, and I'll remember that."

"Okay then," Suzanne said. She looks back at Bobbie as she walks away. "Hope we can get together later."

Suzanne walks away to catch up with her friends and a huge smile is on Bobbie's face. Bobbie looks at Lexi, who stands up wearing a big grin. Bobbie comes over to Lexi throwing her hands in the air.

"I'm back baby!!" Bobbie proclaims. She does a few fist pumps and even the running man. "Yes."

Dana laughs watching Bobbie. Bobbie looks at Lexi, who is standing there with her arms folded across her chest again. She shakes her head and as Lexi looks at Bobbie, she pretends to get all choked up once again.

"You've made me proud grasshopper," Lexi said.

Bobbie stands honorably before Lexi, puts her fist in her hand and bows to Lexi.

"Thank you Sensei," Bobbie said.

Lexi bows responding, "Ahh So."

Bobbie and Lexi stand up, glance at each other, smile and start to crack up they point at each other and in-stereo they exclaim.

"You Stupid!"

They continue to laugh as they take their seats. Bobbie picks up the Tequila bottle and fills two of the shot glasses. She hands one of the shots to Lexi and they swiftly down their drinks. Both of them follow the shot with a few sips of their Corona. The various Tequila shots they've been drinking begin to take its toll. Dana makes eye contact with Ty and signals for him to come over. Dana pushes her Long Island Ice Tea back from her as Ty comes over.

"Loved the show." Ty said.

"He'll Work It Out" Chapter 2. Taryn C. Atkins

"Thanks," Bobbie said. "Someone loved being part of it too."

Bobbie looks over at Suzanne and sees Suzanne is looking at her. They make eye contact and share a smile with each other too. Lexi looks at Bobbie, glances over at Suzanne and then looks at Ty.

"Bobbie has a groupie Ty," Lexi said. "I'm so proud."

"If I wasn't behind this bar." Ty said. "I would have been out there dancing too." He looks at Dana. "So what's up."

"Well Ty, I see I'm going to have to drive tonight," Dana said. "So bring me a cherry coke with extra cherries."

"Coming up." Ty said.

Bobbie picks up the glass of Long Island Ice Tea that's sitting a few inches from Dana and places it down in front of her. Dana looks at Bobbie and Bobbie looks over at her.

"What?" Bobbie said. "No need to waste it."

Ty walks away, Lexi gulps another shot of Tequila and Bobbie pours a shot in the Long Island Ice Tea. Bobbie raises the glass of so call tea in the air.

"Here we go," Bobbie said. "Over the lips and through the gums. Look out stomach here it comes."

Lexi watches Bobbie chug the tea. Dana shakes her head as she watches Bobbie too. Bobbie stops and looks at the glass. She sees that over half of it is gone. Bobbie shakes her head feeling the effects.

"Whoa, alright... okay," Bobbie said.

Bobbie holds up the glass with the rest of the tea. She looks over at Lexi.

"So Lexi, ya think you can hang with me or what?"

"Give that here," Lexi said. She reaches over and takes the glass from Bobbie. "You don't scare me."

Lexi puts the glass of tea on the bar, she picks up the bottle of Tequila and starts to pour it into the glass of tea. She pours it into the glass until its half way filled. She looks at Bobbie, then at the glass and back at Bobbie.

"See that." Lexi points to the glass of tea. "I did that so you see, I'm drinking the same amount as you-this way you can't say somebody cheated!"

"He'll Work It Out" Chapter 2. Taryn C. Atkins

"Whatever' man, go on," Bobbie said. "Do what you think you can do."

"Here we go," Lexi said.

Lexi raises the concoction to her lips and drinks up. Dana folds her arms, she watches annoyed with them and their little drinking competition. Bobbie watches Lexi swig the remaining drink straight down her throat. When Lexi is done, she puts the glass down, takes a deep breath, filling her cheeks up with air, tilts her head back a little and blows the air out. Lexi raises her hands in victory.

"I Win!" Lexi said looking at Bobbie. "What else you got."

"I... I got nothing" Bobbie responds looking at Lexi and shaking her head. "I'm done."

"You got that right!" Dana said. "That's it for both of you."

Dana shakes her head as she looks at Lexi and Bobbie like they have totally lost it.

"Both of you, give up the car keys," Dana said. "Come on you two, car keys. Let's go!"

"No problem," Bobbie said. She reaches into her pants pocket and takes her keys out. "Safety first, I get it." She takes the car keys off the ring and gives them to Dana. "I'm keeping the house keys, I'm gonna need them for later."

"Alright, somebody's on the prowl," Lexi said.

Dana puts Bobbie's car keys in her Fendi tote bag.

"Bobbie I'll leave your car keys at Lexi's," Dana said. She turns to Lexi and holds out her hand. "You too, give me your car keys Lexi."

Lexi goes in her suit jacket, takes her keys out and hands them to Dana. Lexi hungrily looks Dana up and down.

"You gonna tuck me in? You fine sexy thing," Lexi said.

"Of course." Dana said. She puts Lexi's keys in her bag. "Don't I always?"

"You sure do baby." Lexi said.

"I'll be back," Dana said standing up. "I'm going to the ladies room. Be back in a few. Hope there's no line."

"He'll Work It Out" Chapter 2. Taryn C. Atkins

Bobbie pulls Dana's bar chair back so she can get out. Dana picks up her tote bag and places it on her shoulders. Lexi continues to look at Dana with longing.

"Mmm, you looking all good too," Lexi said.

"All for you baby." Dana said.

Dana goes to walk pass Lexi, she reaches out grabs Dana's hand and tries to pull Dana to her.

"Come here sexy," Lexi said

"Stop," Dana said smacking Lexi's hand. "Be good."

Lexi quickly lets her go. As Dana walks away, Lexi rubs her hand and looks in Dana's direction.

"That hurt!" Lexi said.

Dana doesn't look back at Lexi, she heads to the back of the bar, her and the woman in red make eye contact. They even pleasantly smile at one another. Lexi keeps watching Dana walk away heading to the ladies room. When Dana turns the corner, Lexi swiftly turns to Bobbie with a smile on her face.

"She's got a nice walk too," Lexi said sitting back down.

"Yes, so true" Bobbie said.

"She's flexible at that," Lexi said.

"Is that a fact," Bobbie said. "Dancer's are too."

"You're talking about Gigi dude."

"Why the change in attitude?"

"Cause that right there, I don't want to know!"

"Oh... so, Dana's energy?"

"Whoa, it's through the roof.

"Got video proof."

"No, that one's all mine.

"For real. You sure?"

"She's not going anywhere. I got that locked."

"What you're doing is trying to block. Cause at the same time, you want Ms. Red too. So tell me. What ya gonna do?"

"First, I'm getting that number. This I know.

"You do realize Dana's crazy though."

"I got it worked out, but I don't want to boast."

"Well then, that deserves a toast."

"He'll Work It Out" Chapter 2. Taryn C. Atkins

The woman in red smiles as she watches Bobbie and Lexi lift their Corona's, clink their bottles together and drink some down. The woman in red feels her phone vibrating in her bag once again. She reaches in her bag and pulls out her cell once more. She looks at the display and once again sees it's Cassi calling. The woman in red takes a deep breath and shakes her head, this time, she completely turns off her phone and shoves it back in her bag. She drinks the rest of her Cosmo and signals to the bartender.

Gigi walks through the bar entrance and stops in the small foyer for a few seconds to compose herself. She looks up at the ceiling she takes a quick deep breath and as she exhales. A female patron overflowing with tattoos, glances over at Gigi on her way out but the woman changes her direction and heads over to Gigi.

"Sorry to disturb you," The tattooed patron said with a fading British accent, "Your dress is adorable. Jones New York right?"

"Yes, it is," Gigi said giving the woman a smile.

"Where did you find it?" The tattooed patron said.

Gigi takes a second to think about the woman's question, she looks down at her khaki, cap sleeve wrap dress and runs her hand down the side of it.

"I believe; I got it from TJ Maxx."

"Really?"

"Yeah, they have great things sometimes."

"Well, I must check them out." The woman starts to walk away. "Let me go. Oh, love your Burberry match up too. Have a good evening."

"Thanks, you too. Loving that infinity neck tattoo."

The tattooed patron smiles at Gigi as she heads out. Gigi smiles, fixes the strap of her Burberry tote bag on her shoulder and peeks down at her Burberry taupe and mocha leather wedge sandals. She heads on inside going over to Bobbie and Lexi. As Gigi sits down in the bar chair next to Lexi, Bobbie gets up.

"Let me get a chair for Dana," Bobbie said.

Bobbie retrieves an empty bar chair she saw, sits it on the other side of Lexi and sits back down. Gigi takes a sip from her glass of wine and tries to get comfortable.

"Sorry about that," Gigi said. "It was--"

"Your family," Lexi said. She shakes her head. "You're twenty-eight, they need to give you a break already?"

"Lexi it was my grandmother," Gigi said. "You know she calls to check on me, ask me to come to church with her."

"Ahh, come on Gigi, you're out with friends," Lexi said. She motions with her hands waving off the situation. "Forget them and that church stuff right now."

As Gigi and Lexi continue to talk, across the room, Bobbie notices Suzanne is checking her out. Bobbie smiles and flirts and Suzanne returns Bobbie's advances. Suzanne leans over to her friends, says a few words, stands, gets her things and heads over in Bobbie's direction. As she nears they watch each other intensely. When Suzanne passes by, she signals to Bobbie to follow her. Suzanne leaves out the bar with a quickness, Bobbie gets up, drinks down the rest of her Corona and steps between Gigi and Lexi.

"Sorry to interrupt," Bobbie said. "It's been fun but one of my options is waiting outside. So, I'm out."

"Alright handle yours," Lexi said.

Bobbie and Lexi shake hands doing their special handshake. When they finish, Gigi turns to Bobbie before she leaves out.

"Now Bobbie you know I know you," Gigi said. "So relax and pace yourself alright. I know how you can rush things... especially once you're excited. I'm just saying."

As Gigi takes a sip of her wine, Bobbie looks at her. Gigi puts down her wine glass. Lexi and Gigi look at each other and laugh. Bobbie shakes her head as she walks away leaving out.

Bobbie said to herself, "Why do I stay friends with my ex's."

Gigi enjoys the music as she nurses on her wine. Lexi and the woman in red are in their own flirtatious realm with each other. Gigi tries to continue the conversation with Lexi but right now Lexi has tunnel vision. All her attention is focused across the room on the woman in red.

"Lexi... Lexi..." Gigi said. She nudges Lexi to get her

attention. "Lexi!"

"WHAT!?!" Lexi said as she abruptly turns to Gigi.

"You know my grandmother's just concerned about me."

"Yeah but Gigi, you wanted to come to happy hour in the first place. We get here and you spend half the time outside on the phone with your family."

"Okay but Lexi."

"Ahh see, you're killing my buzz!"

Lexi reaches pass Gigi and over to where Bobbie was sitting. She grabs the bottle of Tequila, pours herself two shots and drinks them down one behind the other. After gulping down the liquor, her face contorts a little.

"Look, Gigi, I don't feel like talking about them."

"Fine."

Lexi annoyed by her conversation with Gigi has taken her focus off the woman in red. Lexi sips on her Corona and watches some of the US Open that's playing on the large flat screen tv, up above the bar in front of her. The female bartender brings the woman in red over another Cosmo as she nurses her drink she keeps an eye on Lexi.

Gigi enjoys the music playing as she savors her wine. She turns her chair somewhat sideways so she can see the people in the bar better. Gigi looks around the bar and checks out the people there. She happens to make eye contact with the woman in red for a moment. They smile at each other, casually look each other over and smile at one another again before changing their focus. The woman in red returns her attention to Lexi. Gigi notices the woman in red is watching Lexi. A few moments pass, as Gigi drinks her wine she glances over at the woman in red again and sees she has not taken her eyes off Lexi. Gigi leans over to Lexi.

"Hey look," Gigi said. "Someone at the end of the bar seriously has their eye on you."

Lexi looks down the bar and after a few of the customers move out the way, she looks into the eyes of the woman in red. Who smiles and winks at Lexi, in return Lexi smiles and winks back.

"Oh yeah, she's definitely interested." Lexi smiles as she looks at the woman in red. "And so am I."

"He'll Work It Out" Chapter 2. Taryn C. Atkins

Lexi and the woman keep their eyes locked on each other. Lexi takes a swig of her Corona and places the bottle on the bar.

Lexi said under her breath, "Mmmph, dang she's sexy."

She turns to Gigi. "Look at her, she's hot right?"

Gigi glances at the woman in red and looks at Lexi.

"She's pretty." Gigi said. "Wait, Dana get here yet?"

"Yeah, she's here," Lexi said sounding detached. She points toward the back of the bar. "She's in the bathroom."

Once again tunnel vision has taken over, Lexi and the woman in red are in their own zone. The woman in red is abruptly interrupted by a muscle bound guy, who's testosterone is in full force this evening. As he does his best to impress the stunner. The woman in red politely smiles and deals with him. Lexi turns to Gigi.

"So Gigi, think I can get that?"

Before Gigi can respond back, Lexi realizes the sound of doubt in her question. She shakes her head and puts her hands up, moving them in a matter of fact kind of way.

"What am I saying; I'm gonna get that."

At the other end of the bar, the Hercules wanna be smiles and walks away, after being let down easily. The female bartender comes over. She lifts up the woman in red's half filled martini glass and wipes down the counter in front of her.

"Hi, how's it going. I'm Rena." The female bartender said.

"Everything okay over here?"

"Yes, things are fine. Thank you." The woman in red said.

"Just checking," Rena said putting the martini glass back down. "We cater to a mixed crowd and things are usually cool but I know from experience. When some guys learn you're batting for the other team. They can get ugly."

"True." The woman in red said. "Believe me, I've had my share of experiences too but I've learned how to handle them. Tonight's been... a good night thus far."

"He'll Work It Out" Chapter 2. Taryn C. Atkins

The woman in red picks up her martini glass and finishes off the rest of her Cosmo. She looks across the room at Lexi, who's keeping her in full view. Smiling, she puts the martini glass on the bar counter.

"And it's getting even better." The woman in red said.
"Well enjoy," Rena said. She takes the empty martini glass. "Would you like another?"
"Not right now but I'll take a bottle of water."
"Coming right up."

Rena goes to get the bottle of water, finally moving away from the woman in red and out of Lexi's line of sight. Once again allowing Lexi and the woman in red to make eye contact. They continue on with their flirtatious advances. Gigi lets Lexi flirt for a bit but then she roughly nudges Lexi.

"Okay stop," Gigi said. "You know Dana's crazy. She'll go off in here."
"Look here," Lexi said looking over at Gigi. "There is nothing wrong with having options." Lexi reaches into her suit jackets inner pocket and takes out a pen.
"Options," She looks at Gigi. "Are the spice of life."

Lexi stands up, reaches over the bar, grabs a napkin from behind it and sits back down. She clicks her pen and starts to write on the napkin. Gigi moves closer, trying to look over Lexi's arm to see exactly what's being written. On seeing what Lexi has written, Gigi tries to snatch the napkin away but Lexi blocks her.

"I know you're not giving that woman your number."
"Watch me."

Lexi looks to see where Ty is, once she sees him and she's in his view, she signals for him to come over. Ty nods his head, mouthing the word "Okay" to Lexi. Ty finishes up making a frosty sweet drink and serves it to his current customer. The customer pays him, Ty gives him back the change and he heads over to Lexi.

"Need something ladies?" Ty asks.
"I need a favor," Lexi said. "See the woman sitting at the other end of the bar?"

Ty doesn't even bother to turn around, he looks at Lexi and crosses his arms.

"Oh, you mean that savory glass of wine, draped in red and black? I've been so busy I never noticed."

Gigi and Lexi look at each other, shake their heads and laugh.

"Yeah okay," Gigi said.

"Anyway Ty," Lexi said. "Can you please give her this?"

Lexi extends her hand out to Ty holding the folded up napkin. He looks at the napkin, then at Gigi, who shrugs her shoulders and leaves Ty to make his own decision. Ty looks at the folded napkin again for a few more seconds.

"Deliver it yourself Lexi." Ty quickly said. "Dana's here too. She's crazy you know. The ghetto will come out and she'll go off in here, again."

Gigi slaps her hand down on the bar counter top, she laughs out loud a bit and looks at Lexi.

"Ty, that's exactly what I said," Gigi said.

"Come on Ty," Lexi said holding the napkin out to him. "Give it to her. Please."

"Fine." Ty responds quickly snatching the napkin from Lexi. "I'll do it real quick."

Ty goes to walk away but he turns back to Lexi. He points at Lexi as he comes back over to her.

"Lexi if Dana finds out I gave her the note. My name is Bennett and I'm not in it. Understand."

"Okay okay. Now go on, please."

Ty walks to the other side of the bar to deliver the napkin to the woman in red. As Lexi watches Ty, Gigi leans over to her, she puts her mouth close to Lexi's ear and with a soft, subdued voice.

"Testing testing now hear this," Gigi said. She increases her volume. "You're gonna get in so much trouble!"

Lexi promptly turns to Gigi replying, "Quit it stop hating!"

"Yeah okay," Gigi said. She takes a sip of her wine then places the glass back on the bar. "I've said my piece."

Lexi turns around and puts her attention back on Ty, who's now talking to the woman in red. Lexi sees Ty show the woman in red the napkin and he points in Lexi's direction. The woman in red looks at Lexi, smiles and takes the piece of napkin from Ty. She gestures for Ty to come closer. Ty leans in, she whispers to him, he nods his head, walks away and starts to prepare a drink. Lexi smiles, she quickly turns around in her seat and faces Gigi. She taps Gigi on her leg.

"Okay, look behind me," Lexi said. "Tell me what's happening."

Gigi picks up her wine glass and nurses on her wine while covertly looking over Lexi's shoulder. Gigi tries to slyly watch the woman in red.

"You should be happy now she's reading your note." Gigi said. "She put it in her bag. She's grabbing a napkin. Now she's writing on it." Gigi puts her glass back down. "Okay, now she's standing up. She's putting her pocketbook on her shoulder and it looks like she's getting ready to leave. Oh alright, she's headed this way."

"What?" Lexi said. Did you say she's headed this way?"

As the woman in red starts to walk over to them. Gigi grabs her glass of wine and takes a sip. From the corner of Gigi's eye, she sees the woman in red approaching. The woman in red comes up behind Lexi. Gigi puts her glass down, pretends to cough, she covers her mouth and looks at Lexi.

"She's right behind you." Gigi quickly whispered.

Gigi looks over and smiles at the woman in red who in turn smiles back. When the woman looks at Gigi, Gigi notices the woman looks at her intensely for a moment. Just as quick, the woman's focus returns to Lexi as she walks up behind her. Lexi looks at Gigi.

"Gigi." Lexi whispers. "I know you didn't let her walk--"

The woman in red taps Lexi on the shoulder.

"Excuse me." The woman in red said. "Hello again."

Lexi puts a smile on and turns to the woman in red.

"Hello to you," Lexi said.

The woman in red moves in closer to Lexi. She holds up a piece of napkin that's clasped between her two fingers.

"This is for you." The woman in red said. She slides it into the upper inside pocket of Lexi's suit jacket. "I'm leaving but I'll definitely be calling."

"Well, I'll definitely be looking forward to it," Lexi said.

Gigi casually moves her chair closer to Lexi. As Gigi drinks her wine, she leans in toward Lexi and slyly listens in on their conversation. The woman in red gives Lexi an amorous stare, as she reaches out and softly brushes off the lapel of Lexi's suit jacket.

The woman in red said. "So, who will be receiving or taking my call?"

Gigi whispers to Lexi, "The emergency room is gonna be receiving you, after taking a beat down from Dana. Which is why you need to stop."

Lexi's eyes travel slowly from the woman in red's high heels and up her titillating frame. Lexi's loving the journey all the way. She stops at her dark, mysterious eyes and Lexi looks deeply into them.

"Well, I'm Lexi and I'm more than capable of handling whatever the case may be."

Gigi said under her breath to Lexi, "Hope you can handle your crazy girlfriend."

Lexi ignores Gigi's statements as she takes in the woman in red's appealing and devilish smile.

"Mmm, interesting." The woman in red responds. She moves in closer to Lexi, this time sliding between her legs and as she gives Lexi a come-hither look. "More than capable, you say, but that's good to know. My name is Cassandra, it means she who entangles. Tell me, would you like to be?"

Lexi slyly smiles looking down for a second, as she looks back up and into the eyes of the woman in red. They are thoroughly enjoying the erotic innuendos in their conversation, along with the sexual energy flowing between them.

"Mmmph well--"

"Shh, tell me in detail when I call." Cassandra leans in, getting close to Lexi's ear and whispers. "Better yet, show me when we get together."

As Cassandra moves back, she seducingly stares into Lexi's eyes and caresses Lexi's cheek with one finger. Lexi's eyes become fixed on Cassandra's desirable red painted full lips, being entranced by

"He'll Work It Out" Chapter 2. Taryn C. Atkins

them Lexi feels the sexual gravity they possess pulling her forward. She starts to move her lips closer to Cassandra's. When Lexi gets within reach of indulging in them, Cassandra teasingly smiles and steps back. Lexi slowly shakes her head and smiles loving the tantalizing game being played between them. Lexi looks at Cassandra and with a raised eyebrow she said,

"When we get together, now that does sound appealing." Cassandra points over to Ty. "I have the bartender brewing up a special drink for you."

Gigi hearing this leans over to Lexi again, she said, under her breath, "Mmmph, gurl don't drink it."

Lexi cracks a smile and glances over her shoulder at Gigi. Lexi laughs a bit but tries to ignore Gigi's funny and sarcastic comments. She puts her attention back on Cassandra.

"I have to leave, early day tomorrow." Cassandra said.
"This has been, quite intriguing."
"Yes it certainly has." Lexi said.
"That drink." Cassandra takes her finger and erotically traces Lexi's ear. "Is sure to..." She trails her finger from Lexi's ear and sensually along the outline of Lexi's cheek. "Keep you thinking of me." As she caresses Lexi's chin. "Good night now."
"Good night." Lexi said.

As Cassandra walks away, Lexi stands up, faces the bar's entrance and watches Cassandra's breathtaking walk as she heads out the bar. Gigi looks in Cassandra's direction to see what Lexi is so fascinated by, on seeing Cassandra's sexy stride, Gigi unexpectedly gets captivated by it too. She finds herself staring. When Gigi realizes what she's doing, she looks away. Before leaving out the bar, Cassandra stops to put her silk wrap around her shoulders. Gigi looks at herself in the mirror behind the bar and shakes her head. She picks up her wine glass and takes a drink.

What was that? Gigi thought.

Gigi looks over at Lexi and sees she's still watching Cassandra. Gigi picks up the Tequila bottle and pours some into her wine glass. She picks up her wine glass, twirls it around for a second mixing the Tequila with the remaining wine. She swiftly finishes off what's in the wine glass. After Cassandra leaves, Lexi retakes her seat, looks at Gigi and points in Cassandra's direction.

"Gigi, you see that?" Lexi said.

"Nope," Gigi said. "I was looking out for Dana."

"You missed it, she's got this hot walk. I love it."

"Yeah okay, don't say I didn't warn you."

"It's like I said, options are the spice of life."

Out of nowhere Dana steps in between them.

"What?" Dana said. "What about options?"

Dana has returned from her journey to the ladies room and catches them a bit off guard.

"The... option... to choose." Lexi said. "Nobody should dictate to another person, be it church or state. Right Gigi?"

"What?" Gigi said.

Gigi looks at Lexi a bit confused by her statement. Dana looks away for a moment seeing a open chair on the other side of Lexi.

"Options, you know," Lexi said. Seeing Dana's preoccupied Lexi makes a face at Gigi. "One should have the option to make their own decisions, right Gigi?"

Dana walks around Lexi and goes to the chair. Dana puts her handbag on the back of the chair and sits down.

"Right, exactly." Gigi said. "Pro or Con the option should be yours."

"Well, who are we to judge anyway." Dana said. "I say live and let live."

Ty comes over carrying an irresistible looking drink. He places the drink down in front of Lexi, Gigi and Dana's eyes go to the glass.

"Excuse me," Ty said. "The woman who left a moment ago sent you this."

"What? Say that again." Dana said. She looks toward the bar entrance. "What woman?"

Dana looks at Ty and seeing Dana's expression, he looks over at Gigi. Dana looks at the drink again and you can see her attitude start to change. Ty slowly shakes his head. Lexi looks at the glass, smiles a moment and looks at Ty.

"So what's this called?" Lexi asks.

"Yeah, what's that called?!" Dana said.

All their eyes are on Ty waiting for his answer. He takes a few steps back from the bar counter.

"Oh So Tasty. Good night ladies." Ty quickly said.

He rushes off and away from the outburst to come.

"Are you serious," Dana said. She looks at Lexi. "Lexi for real."

"Dana come on now," Lexi said.

When Dana's upset and angry, a transformation happens. She changes from a refine young lady, to straight up ghetto chick in a matter of seconds. Dana stands up and turns to Lexi.

"Are you kidding me. Lexi! Oh So Tasty!! Are you freakin kidding me Lexi!!! I am not gonna stand for this!!!

Gigi moves to the empty seat next to her.

"Calm down Dana. It's not like I did something. The woman probably thought I was alone."

"What?!"

"Well, you stayed in the bathroom forever. It's not like you were by my side. So how would anyone know."

"Excuse me."

"Listen," Lexi said. She stands and turns to Dana. "This is getting on my nerves alright."

Dana puts her hands on her hips as she looks at Lexi.

"Oh really now," Dana responds.

"Lexi," Gigi said, looking at Lexi surprised by her actions. "What are you doing?"

Dana hears Gigi and looks over at her.

"Nah, Gigi it's okay," Dana said, she looks at Lexi. "She grown, go head. Speak your peace."

"Dana look, it's not my fault if a woman sees me alone and likes what she sees. I can't help it if she flirts with me, slips me her number or even buys me a drink."

Gigi shakes her head as she watches Lexi and Dana.

"Not your fault huh? Tell me this, you take her number?

"He'll Work It Out" Chapter 2. Taryn C. Atkins

Well... did you?"

Gigi said under her breath to herself, "Oh boy."

Lexi looks up to the ceiling and closes her eyes for a second. Lexi realizes what she said to Dana.

"Oh don't look away now, answer the question."

Gigi shakes her head, as she continues to watch Dana and Lexi but she moves her chair over.

Gigi said to herself, "Here we go."

Gigi looks over at them, she watches as Lexi takes her hand, slides it into her outside suit pocket, pulls out a piece of paper and puts it on the bar counter top.

"Now calm down," Lexi said. "I know how this looks; I was gonna tear it up but I didn't get the chance."

Dana shakes her head and goes into full blown ghetto.

"Are you serious!?" Dana said. "Didn't get the chance to tear it up! You should of never took it!! Then you try to blame *me* because *you* have the nerve to take some tricks number!" She points at Lexi. "Ya lucky that heifer left, believe that?! Cause I'll turn this place OUT!!!"

"Don't do that boo, come on now relax." Lexi tears up the piece of paper on the bar. "See all torn up okay. Relax, I wasn't gonna call. For real."

"Like that's supposed to make it all better. Please, don't be playing with me Lexi. You should of never taken it!"

"You're right-okay? Come on now baby relax."

Dana moves toward the bars exit.

"We're leaving, NOW! Get my things!"

"Alright, I'm right behind you."

Dana rushes out. Lexi gets their things. Gigi gets up and gets her belongings also. Lexi taps Gigi. When Gigi looks at her, Lexi winks, opens her suit jacket and pats the upper inside pocket.

"That number's right here," Lexi said. "I'm gonna get that, watch and see."

Gigi shakes her head saying, "Curiosity killed the cat."

"Satisfaction brought it back."

Dana's voice bellows from the front door of the bar.

"Lexi! Let's Go! Don't make me come back in there!!"

Lexi and Gigi rush out the bar.

"He'll Work It Out" Chapter 2. Taryn C. Atkins

~COUPLES NIGHT OUT~

It's a lovely Friday night in a beautiful town in Connecticut. The front door of a waterfront restaurant opens and thru it walks a tall, handsome man, sporting a white straw fedora hat and even the band around it fit with his wardrobe, he wore a neon green t-shirt and plaid Bermuda shorts with the colors of blue, white and neon green within them. Everything matched in some way even the neon green ankle socks that peeked out of his Nike white and blue tennis shoes. His clothing fit his athletic build quite well. As he held the restaurant door open, Nola stepped into the door frame, their colors matched nicely; Her long spring dress looked great on her frame and their outfits complimented each other. Before she stepped through the door, Nola looked up at the man and smiled.

"Dray baby," Nola said. "We've got to come back here."

"Anytime you want to Mrs. Lavell," Dray said with a smile.

"Why thank you, Mr. Lavell." She takes him by his arm. "I tell you, it's been nine years and hearing you call me Mrs. Lavell hasn't gotten old yet."

"And sweetheart, I hope it never does."

They step outside into an enjoyable summer breeze. Dray and Nola placed their arms around each others waist. As they strolled down the sidewalk, they shared loving glances as they headed towards the restaurants parking lot.

A few moments later coming out of the restaurant behind them was Cliff and Shayna. Their outfits also complimented each other for they wore a color scheme of blue denim with red and white. Shayna was a few strides in front of Cliff as they walked down the sidewalk.

Dray and Nola walked with their arms around each other. They stopped at the end of the path and Dray gently pulled Nola to him. They affectionately gazed into each others eyes, their love and attraction for each other drew them closer. They cozy up to each other and share a few soft, sensual kisses. They stop kissing for a moment, each breathing quick and deep, as they looked intensely into each others eyes. One could easily see the love and passion they felt for each other, and how they struggled within themselves to contain it because they were outside.

Cliff smiled as he saw them. Although he and Shayna still loved one another, Cliff remembered a time when they shared a passion like that for each other, and he wanted that for them again. Cliff quickened his step and caught up to Shayna, he reached out and took Shayna's hand in his. As they continued down the sidewalk, Cliff smiled enjoying them pleasantly walking together hand in hand. The moment was soon over when Shayna wiggled her hand out of his. Cliff tried to put his arm around Shayna's waist but she moved away. Cliff looked down to the end of the sidewalk once again and this time, he saw Dray and Nola engaged in a soulful kiss.

Cliff cleared his throat loudly so they could be aware of them approaching. Dray slowly opened his eyes and saw that Shayna and Cliff were a few feet away. They separate from their passionate lip-lock. Dray draped his arm around Nola's shoulder and they both smiled somewhat bashfully as they looked at Cliff and Shayna.

"So, Cliff I told you," Dray said. "Great spot right."

"Honey," Nola said as she laid her hand softly on Dray's chest. "The food was to die for, oh my goodness. I never ate so much shrimp and crab legs. It was so good, you know we've gotta come back here."

Although they were all standing together, Shayna seems to keep a few feet between her and Cliff. Nola looked over at Shayna.

"Shayna, don't you want to come back?" Nola said.

"Hmm, I don't know," Shayna said.

Cliff casually comes over, he stands next to Shayna and places his arm around her waist.

"Dray I'll give it to you," Cliff said. "You found a great spot. The food was incredible, I loved the waterfront dining and where we sat the view was fantastic." He looks at Shayna. "We'll have to come back too?"

"We could even stay over," Nola said. "Find a cozy bed and breakfast, and have a romantic weekend." She looks at Dray. "How about it baby?"

"A romantic weekend, with you," Dray said with a smile

as he looked at Nola. "Sounds great to me."

"Sounds great to me too!" Cliff said. "Shay--"

"Wait Cliff," Dray said. He motions to himself and Nola. "You know, me and mines, we'll have our own room. We don't get down like that."

"Dray," Nola said shoving him.

"What!?" Dray said. "I'm just saying, you never know."

Nola, Cliff, and Shayna look at Dray with dumbfounded expressions. Shayna huffs, folds her arms, as she shakes her head and stares at him.

"Well, we don't roll like that either." Cliff said.

"Oh okay..." Dray said. He smiles and starts to laugh. "I'm playing." He puts his hand on his stomach as he laughs. "Y'all should know me by now." His laughter continues as he points to them. "Your faces were funny, oh man, that was good."

They all shake their heads as they look at Dray. Nola sucks her teeth, then smiles a bit as she softly shoves Dray again. Cliff looks at Shayna.

"Anyway," Cliff said. "A romantic weekend in Connecticut, sounds like a plan. Shayna?"

"Well, I heard some of those places aren't clean," Shayna said. "Nowadays, you can't sleep or do anything else just anywhere. And as far as the food here." She makes a face. "Everything was a bit too salty for my taste."

"Funny, I thought you were enjoying yourself," Dray said.

"Sometimes you have to make the best of a bad situation," Shayna said.

Dray gives Shayna a look as he nods his head.

"Look, let's do seafood again next month," Cliff said.

Unnoticed by Cliff and Shayna, Dray slyly looks over at Nola and makes a face, showing he's clearly not enthusiastic about getting together with the couple for their monthly outing.

"Couples night out." Dray said. "Can't wait."

Nola motions over to Shayna.

"Shayna you pick the restaurant next time," Nola said.

"He'll Work It Out" Chapter 2. Taryn C. Atkins

"Yeah," Dray said. He puts a smile on his face and motions to Shayna. "You pick the restaurant. This way we all can have the pleasure of complaining."
"Stop that," Nola said as she gently shoves Dray.
"I'm playing." Dray said. "You know me, always joking."

Shayna casually reaches into her purse, but starts to look around inside it with an urgency.

"Oh know. Oh my goodness." Shayna said. "I... I dropped my wallet. Oh my God. We'll be right back."

Shayna starts to walk back to the restaurant. Cliff stays at the end of the sidewalk with Dray and Nola. Shayna notices that Cliff isn't walking with her, she sucks her teeth and huffs. She turns around and sees Cliff talking to them.

"Clifford!!" Shayna said.
"Yes," Cliff said looking over at Shayna.
"Come help me look," Shayna said motioning to Cliff.
"Oh, okay," Cliff said. He looks at Dray and Nola as he swiftly walks away. "We'll be back."

Cliff heads over to Shayna as Nola moves out of Dray's arms.
"We'll be right here," Nola said.

Shayna turns and motions to Nola acknowledging that she heard her. Cliff and Shayna promptly walk up the sidewalk going back to the restaurant. Dray rapidly taps Nola on her shoulder as Shayna and Cliff enter the restaurant. Nola turns around to him.

"What are you doing?" Dray said. "We could have made a break for it, and been free from Evermean's clutches."
"I told you to stop calling her that." Nola said.
"She's mean! I don't know how y'all deal with her."
"She wasn't always like that. Something's going on with her, and whatever it is. It's caused this change."
"Yeah well, all I know is Pastor, Priest, Exorcist, whatever, maybe they can get that demon out of her!"
"Dray-She's my best friend."
"I know, but I'm sorry," Dray said. "I would have kicked that friendship to the curb a long time ago. It would have been a straight up field goal too. Check it out."

"He'll Work It Out" Chapter 2. Taryn C. Atkins

Dray moves Nola to the side. He pretends to put a football tee down on the sidewalk, he positions the fantasy football on top of the tee. He backs away from it, puts the tip of his pointer finger in his mouth to wet it and raises it in the air to test for wind direction. Dray looks at Nola and motions to her to wait one second. Dray does a few stretches to loosen himself up, and then gets into his kick position. He runs toward the pretend football and does a perfect kick.

"Look out!!" Dray said.

Dray watches the make-believe football heading toward the imaginary goal post. He raises his arm and points toward it.

"It's going, it's going, and it's through the goal post! Yes!!
That friendship is outta here!!"

Dray throws his arms up making the touchdown signal.

"It's a Touchdown!!! Oh my God!! It's a Touchdown!!!"

He jumps around and makes crowd cheering noises. As Nola watches Dray, her facial expression tightens and becoming more serious. Dray continues not seeing Nola's face.

"And the crowd goes wild!! The crowd goes wild!!"

Dray looks over at Nola and sees her feelings on her face. He stops all movement and goes to her.

"You know I'm playing right?"

"She's my best friend. I've known her longer than I've been with you, and if you were to leave. She'd still be there."

As Nola turns away from Dray, she crosses her arms and steps away from him. He watches her walk away realizing what his words and actions have done. Nola stops a few feet away from him. She looks down at the sidewalk for a moment, raises her head and stares straight ahead. Dray slowly approaches her. He places his hands on Nola's waist and turns her around to him. Dray takes her in his arms and holds her close.

"Baby, I'm sorry." Dray said. "I know that's your BFF and all but dang, she's so tight! Like cracking a smile every once and a while would kill her."

Nola pushes him away.

"She wasn't always like that Dray..." Nola said. "I'm

telling you, she has a sense of humor." She moves a few steps away and turns to him. "Plus she's warm and caring too."

"Well please show me the video tape, cause right now she puts the rigid in frigid. I can't believe they even have kids."

"Well they do, and they love each other deeply."

"Really?" Dray said. "Cause from what I see, *her* fire been went out." Dray goes to step away but turns back to Nola. "I know how Cliff can get her fire going again. He needs to get his *Magic Mike* on! Get him a Tarzan or Construction Worker outfit and get them hips moving like a jack hammer! That will sure nuff stoke her fire."

Nola cracks a smile.

"You are so silly."

"Am I?"

Dray starts to do some exotic dance moves as he makes his way over to Nola.

"You remember that night. I strutted thru the front door of the house, wearing that Fireman outfit and said how I got a 911 call about a fire that needed to be put out."

"Dray stop it."

"Yeah you say that now, but after I peeled off that uniform and you saw this glistening body-I got every last single you had."

Nola blushes as she giggles.

"We played Mtume all night long."

"When I was leaving for work in the morning, Mrs. DeLuca next door watched me going to my car. I said good morning, but all she could do, is shake her head as she prayed over her rosary."

Nola folds her arms as she shakes her head. Dray stands next to her and puts his arm around her.

"Well after you left, *Mr. DeLuca* came over and asked for a copy."

"No."

Dray moves in front of Nola.

"So," Dray starts to reprise his exotic dance routine. "Should I teach Cliff some moves? Show him how to get his sexy on?"

Nola chuckles as she watches Dray perform. She notices Cliff and Shayna come out of the restaurant and are headed towards them. Dray is facing Nola and is involved in his exotic routine, not seeing Cliff and Shayna approaching.

Nola said under her breath, "Dray, they're coming. Dray."

Nola tries to warn Dray but he's into his performance. As Cliff and Shayna near they watch as Dray does a few body rolls as he back steps, and bumps right into Cliff. He looks at Cliff and Shayna.

"And you're back," Dray said. He puts his hand on Cliff's shoulder and looks at the ladies. "Excuse us please." He turns to Cliff as he points off the side. "Cliff."

"Okay," Cliff said with hesitation.

They turn away from the ladies and take a few steps away. Dray puts his arm around Cliff's shoulders and leans his head a bit over in Cliff's direction.

"That umm, little dance routine you saw."

"Yeah..."

"Let's," Dray looks at Cliff. "Keep that between us."

"Sure."

"Good man." Dray pats Cliff twice on his shoulder.

They turn around and head back over to their ladies. Dray walks over to Nola and puts his arm around her. He looks at Shayna.

"So," Dray said. "Did you find your wallet?"

"Yes we did," Shayna said.

"Great," Dray said. "Well, this was lovely. Everybody ready to go," He takes Nola's hand and goes to walk away pulling her. "Good night we'll see ya."

"Dray no, wait," Nola said pulling her hand out of his. "I'll meet you at the car; I need to use the ladies room."

"Okay," Dray said. He looks at Cliff and Shayna. "Alrighty," He takes Cliff's hand and shakes it. "Good night Cliff."

"Yeah have a good evening." Cliff said.

As they shake, Dray pulls Cliff to him and whispers.

"Why her?!"

"Huh, what?" Cliff said.

Dray turns to Shayna and they hug each other.

"Shayna, its always," As Dray hugs Shayna. "Such a pain,"

Shayna pushes Dray away.

"See, why do I even bother." Shayna said.

"I meant to say pleasure." Dray said. "I did-I meant its always a pleasure. Okay, so anyway." He looks at Nola. "Nola, I'll be in the car."

"Okay," Nola said. "Cliff, Shayna you go ahead." She gets ready to walk away but stops and turns to them. "I won't be long so it's alright if you have to go."

Cliff and Shayna turn in Nola's direction and have their backs to Dray. Nola sees Dray playing around behind their backs, simulating having a pie in his hand that's he's going to hit Shayna with. As Nola watches him, she slightly laughs. Shayna motions to Nola.

"No, go ahead," Shayna said. "We'll wait."

"You sure." Nola said.

"Yeah," Cliff said. As he steps closer to Shayna. "No problem."

"Okay, I'll be right back," Nola said. She motions to Dray laughing. "Dray I'll see you at the car."

"Okay." Dray said.

Nola walks over to the restaurant. Dray stops what he's doing just as Shayna and Cliff turn around to him.

"It's been fun," Dray said. "I'm gonna head to the car."

"Good night." Cliff said.

"Bye," Shayna said.

"Get home safe," Dray said.

Dray heads to his car. As they wait for Nola to return, Shayna takes a few steps away from Cliff. He looks at Shayna, smiles and walks up behind her. Cliff puts his hands on Shayna's waist and pulls her to him. As Cliff puts his arms around her, he snuggles up to her and gets all cheek to cheek.

"It's a beautiful night," Cliff said. "You look so lovely."

"Thank you," Shayna said.

Cliff nuzzles Shayna's neck and she smiles.

"Mmmm, you smell so good. That perfume is what caught my attention three aisles over in the grocery store that day. I'm so glad it helped me find you."

"Me too, it's my own blend you know."

"I know. What's the mix of oils again?"

"It's CK1, Frankincense and--"

The sound of a wind gong blares out interrupting the moment. The sound is coming from Cliff's cell phone.

"Stay right there baby and hold that thought. I was expecting a call from a client; I guess they text me instead."

Cliff lifts his head from Shayna's neck, he takes one arm from around her and reaches into his pants pocket.

"They were supposed to contact me much earlier."

Cliff pulls out his cell and looks at the text message.

"Oh, okay," Cliff said. He takes his other arm from around her. "Shayna give me a second, please. Let me text them back real quick."

"Fine," Shayna said.

Shayna walks a few steps away from him. As Cliff texts the person back. Shayna looks at him, shakes her head and huffs under her breath. She takes a deep breath, as she exhales she folds her arms and turns away from him. When Cliff is finished, he puts his cell back in his pants pocket and walks over to Shayna. He puts his arms back around her and gets all cozy with her once again.

"Where were we," Cliff said. "This was a great spot, the food was good, a comfortable atmosphere. We need to come back, just us and have a romantic evening out."

"I said I didn't like the food," Shayna said taking Cliff's arms from around her. "I'm sure you heard me."

Shayna moves away but Cliff tries to get close to her again.

"Well, you can always try something else."

"I don't want to come back."

Shayna walks away, Cliff looks up at the sky, takes a deep breath and exhales. He walks to Shayna and stands in front of her.

"Okay, what's going on now?" Cliff said. "Things were going so well, and now you're back in this mood again."

Shayna looks at him and takes a step back, moving away from him, as she crosses her arms.

"Who was that?" Shayna said.

"A client."

"I thought James and Andy were handling customers."

"They are, but some of my older clients like to know I'm still involved. What's the matter?"

"Your cell phone went off before we left the house. You were upstairs, I usually don't bother, but I picked it up in case it was important. There was a text message from her again, saying how wonderful lunch was." She points at him. "I knew you wouldn't hold up."

Cliff places his hand on top of the hand Shayna's pointing with, and slowly pushes her hand down.

"Is that what this mood is for?"

"Yes." Shayna pushes his hand away. "That's what this mood is for."

"We could have talked about this before we left the house."

Shayna backs away from him and starts pacing angrily.

"We've talked about this Cliff. A few times since things took place." She continues to march back and forth. Her tone raises the more she gets upset. "I guess whatever decisions we make together mean nothing because you're still seeing her. Even after I specifically asked you not too!"

"Look..." Cliff said. "Can you please stand still a moment."

Shayna stops in front of him. Cliff notices a couple come out of the restaurant and is headed in their direction. Cliff goes to Shayna, he takes her hand in his. After holding her hand for a few seconds, Shayna snatches her hand from him and crosses her arms.

"Listen Cliff--," Shayna said.

"Look calm down, and let this couple pass.

As the couple passes by, the guy looks at Cliff and nods. Cliff doesn't respond just nods to the guy. Once the couple passed them and are a few feet away. Cliff moves closer to Shayna.

"Okay, yes... I saw her." Cliff said. "She was going through a tough time and needed to talk. I just... wanted to be there for her."

"So you're going to see her. Regardless of everything, regardless of my feelings?"

"Shayna..."

"Are you going to see her again?"

The sound of several voices is heard in close proximity to Cliff and Shayna. Before they know it a small group of four urban young adults, step up on the sidewalk. As the small group walks up the path heading to the seafood restaurant they pass by Cliff and Shayna. Cliff waits for them to get a few feet away.

"Shayna if you would only try to underst--"

"It's a simple question."

"Shayna come on."

"Are you going to see her again!?"

The group overhears the confusion, they look back at Cliff and Shayna to see what's happening. Cliff looks at them and waves.

"Everything's fine here, enjoy your night."

Shayna moves away from Cliff. The young adults go about their business heading to the restaurant. Cliff sees them go inside. He turns his attention back to Shayna, she swiftly turns to him as he walks over to her.

"So answer the question!"

"No okay... No! I won't see her again, alright?"

"Good. I should hope not!"

Shayna turns from Cliff and walks to the end of the sidewalk. Cliff walks over to her and puts his hand softly on the middle of her back.

"You know, she's our daughter, and she needed to talk to her father."

Shayna swiftly turns and points to Cliff.

"She made her choice Cliff! If she needs someone to talk to; She has those *friends* out there."

Cliff walks away from Shayna for a moment. He turns around and looks up into the sky. Nola comes out of the restaurant and walks down the sidewalk heading toward them. Nola sees Cliff looking up into the sky. As he looks, he takes a deep breath, then slowly exhales. Cliff turns around and goes to Shayna.

"Shayna, just listen--"

"Clifford, I don't want to hear another word!"

Nola slows her pace seeing Shayna and Cliff engaged in a heated discussion. Nola stops a distance away from them trying to figure out when she should come over.

"We're her parents, we can't--"

"She chose that life, and I'm not gonna be a part of it! Understand!? Now, I'm going to the car. Tell Nola I'll talk to her later."

Shayna walks away from Cliff. Both are unaware of Nola's presence. Nola shakes her head slowly having overheard Shayna's last furious rant. She watches as Shayna walks off. Cliff stands there nodding his head agreeing to do what Shayna asked of him. He starts to walk back and forth. Nola watches Cliff and his movements clearly show he's upset. After a few moments, Nola approaches Cliff. His back is to Nola as she walks over to him.

"Hey Cliff," Nola said.

Cliff stands there looking in Shayna's direction.

"I thought I saw you." Cliff said. He turns to Nola. "So how much of that did you get anyway?"

"Just the tail end, before she walked away."

"Nola." Cliff motions in Shayna's direction. "I just want to know what's happening to her? What's happening to us? I mean, a lot has happened but we've always talked. So much has changed between us, and I don't know how we got here."

"Listen, I don't like who my best friend is right now either. What we can't fix, God can."

"I want things to get better now. That's all."

"Well sometimes, things take time. Mama Mae would

say. God's time isn't our time. So we have to be patient."

"Yeah," Cliff said. He laughs. "She would say that too. It gets so hard sometimes, and Shayna doesn't make it easy."

"Let me ask you this," Nola said. "Are you still in love with her? I mean like you did when you first got together."

"Of course I'm still in love with her, that's not changing. I'm here regardless of everything we've been through, because I'm still in love with her."

"Well, that's good, because according to my Bible love is a powerful weapon. So keep fighting, for both of you."

"Yeah, I'm gonna go. You want me to walk you to the car?"

"No, Dray sees me."

"Alright, good night Nola."

"Don't worry Cliff." She points up to heaven. "He knows more than we do. He'll work it out."

They step off the sidewalk and go to their individual rides.

~RENDEZVOUS INTERRUPTED~

Late that same night, Leah wore silky burgundy pj's and matching fluffy heeled slippers. Her pajamas seem to shimmer but it's the reflection of light coming down from the slender glass cylinder, pendant lights that hung down from the ceiling above her. As she chatted on the phone, she sat in one of her three graystone, counter stools at the island in the center of her kitchen. She's had her cozy, one level home for about twelve years. Leah has taken much time and care to decorate each room, accenting them with her own unique flava and flair.

Her kitchen had a harmonious blend of contemporary style with classic and sophisticated elements. White dove was the prime color of her kitchen. It not only brightened the room but it made it feel more spacious and alive. The accenting color was graystone, what brought out the room was the cobalt blue color of her BlueStar range and hood. The backsplash behind it was a smooth white dove subway tile with a hand finish.

Almost everything in her kitchen was one of those three colors. Even the bottle of Harvey's Bristol Cream blended right in with everything else. It sat on top of her island's whitish gray marble countertop. She held the cordless phone between her cheek and shoulder as she picked up the bottle of sherry. Leah poured some of the sherry into the long stemmed glass sitting in front of her.

Leah held the glass of sherry in her hand as she listened to the caller on the phone, she started to lazily swing her leg back and forth. Leah took a healthy sip of the sherry and put the glass down on the island. After enjoying the taste, Leah started to engage the caller.

"What are you doing Mama?" Leah said. "Playing Candy Crush... On James's iPad!... Well please, don't break it... Yeah, every so often... I talked with Shayna last weekend... Well, we're on different time schedules remember... No, I'm working the late shift at the hospital now... We talk when we can Mama... Well, you should make sure James is home when you do that... I'm just saying Mama... I saw Reggie about two or three weeks ago... Mama, I can't baby him either... Yeah I know, and it is terrible, but he's a grown man now... It's not easy, but Mama I can't do it... No, I can't worry about it anymore... Mama, I'm just getting back on my feet... Yeah, Regina told me she saw Wes... I'm not thinking about that man... Mama, it's been months since I seen him... I never know when he's coming in town... Well, whenever that is he won't be staying here that's for sure... Please, he's not thinking about me either."

A man's voice yells from the living room.

"Leah! Where's the pickles?!" He said. "Lee! You forgot the pickles on my sandwich!!"

Leah yawns loudly into the phone receiver trying to drown out the sound of the man's voice.

"Mama I'm gonna go. Yeah okay, I'll give you a call tomorrow. Love ya."

"He'll Work It Out" Chapter 2. Taryn C. Atkins

Leah swiftly ends the call, she stands, takes the bottle of sherry, walks around to the other side of the island and puts the bottle in one of her kitchen cabinets. As she turns around through the kitchen door steps an attractive man, wearing an a-shirt with black silk pajama bottoms and leather slippers. As he holds the kitchen door open, he looks at Leah and holds the stare for a few seconds.

"You got any pickles?" He said.

Leah walks over and picks up her glass of sherry; She uses her head to motion over to the refrigerator.

"Look in the fridge." Leah said.

As she leans back against the kitchen counter top. The man lets go of the kitchen door, he walks over to the refrigerator, goes inside it and takes out the jar of pickles. He closes the refrigerator door, turns around and walks back out through the kitchen doors. Leah shakes her head, turns around and drinks down the rest of her sherry. The man quietly comes back into the kitchen, sneaks up behind Leah, cozies up to her and he kisses her on the cheek.

"Did ya have a good time baby?" He said. "Mmmm... Gurl,
I sure missed you."

Leah walks away from him and puts her sherry glass in the kitchen sink. She takes one of her cooking magazines out of the rack on the side of the island, walks around to the other side of the island and takes a seat once more. Leah starts to flip through the magazine. The man folds his arms as he leans against the kitchen counter, and watches Leah for a moment as she flips through the magazine. He walks over to the island and stands right next to her.

"I heard you rush off the phone. Why we sneaking around. We got a kid together. Your family knows that."
He takes her hand and softly kisses it. "You're my sexy wifey."

"See." Leah pulls her hand away. "That's just the point. Wifey. When am I going to be your wife? I'm the mother of your son Wes and I'm getting tired of all this."

Wes sighs, he walks to the other side of the island.

"All what? Wes said. "I thought we had a great time tonight."

Wes pulls out the end counter stool, he turns it in Leah's direction and sits down. Leah turns her seat in his direction.

"That's all it's been. A night here, a night there. It's time for whatever we have to change to something serious."

Wes lets out another loud sigh and places his foot on the foot rest of the stool between them.

"Come on Leah, we're gonna do this again?"

"Apparently we need too!"

"Why do we have to be like conventional couples. We don't need no label on things. I love how we flow."

"We've been flowing since we were teenagers."

"Leah, you know I'm trying to get my business to a particular status. Come on now."

"Come on nothing! You've been like this since high school. The only business you've ever taken seriously was your own. Everybody else comes second in your world."

"I'm just working at getting mine that's all. Thought you understood that."

"I do, but you forget you're a father! And I'm the mother of your son. Reggie wouldn't be all messed up had you been a father and taken managing him seriously."

Wes slaps his hand down on the islands countertop as he stands up.

"Listen, the music industry's a shark tank. It's his own fault he got caught up with the wrong people. What was I supposed to do, act like he was my only client?! I'm not his babysitter ya know!"

Leah stands up, points at Wes and moves toward him.

"No, you're not! You're his father! And you should have been his father when you had him out there with you." She points toward the ground. "This isn't high school, we're grown now Wes. I'm in my forties with real responsibilities." She points in the direction of the bedroom. "This little escapade, these last few day was it for us. I'm done and I mean it this time."

"He'll Work It Out" Chapter 2. Taryn C. Atkins

Leah abruptly walks away, rushing through the kitchen door and into the living room. The living room is decorated with Leah's unique flair. The track lighting that's in various places in the ceiling brought out the walls gray owl color. Most of the living room furniture was a creamy beige. Leah rushed over to the large three piece sectional; Her heeled slippers clicked across the floor, the sound disappeared once she stepped on the creamy beige area rug.

She plopped down on the sectional and her forty-eight inch HD TV was blaring as it sat in its beautiful TV cabinet. It was still tuned to one of Wes's action films. She reached for the universal remote which sat on the circular cocktail table in front of the sectional. Leah quickly pointed it toward the TV and turned it off. She flung the remote down beside her on the sectional. Wes came into the room and slowly came over to her. He picked up the remote, placed it on the cocktail table, sat down beside her and leaned back on the sectional. They sat there in silence for a few seconds. Wes placed his arm around her shoulder and gently pulled her toward him.

"Come here," Wes said.

He took his hand, took Leah's chin in it, he softly turned her face in his direction and looked into her eyes.

"You know you're the only one for me." Wes moved closer to her and leaned in to kiss her. "Sexy thing you."

"Wes stop!" Leah pushed him back. "I'm serious."

"Me too," Wes said. He tried to kiss her again.

"Stop it!" Leah said. Pushing him back again. "I'm the only one for you. Yeah right," She gets up from the sectional, walks a few feet away and turns to him. "I'm not stupid! I heard about all those groupies."

Wes gets up from the sectional and goes to Leah.

"Leah I love you, those groupies don't mean nothing. You're the mother of my son. Can't no other woman say that. You're special to me."

"Special huh. Please."

Wes pulls Leah close to him, he takes her left hand in his and as he softly kisses it, he looks into her eyes.

"Look Lee, as soon as I get a few more artist for my

management company. I'll be sliding that diamond on your finger."

"Platinum setting, princess cut?"

"Whatever you want. As long as you let me." He kisses her left hand sensually. "Make you." He kisses her sensually on her cheek. "Mrs. Wesley Jacobs." He kisses her softly on the lips. "Just like you've been wanting."

Wes kisses Leah, she gives in to him and they kiss each other passionately. Wes tries to slyly move their sensual embrace to the sectional. Leah realizes what he's attempting to do, she smiles and laughs a little as she pushes him away. She gets a bit playful with him.

"You're not slick," Leah said. "You're saying all that." She motions to her body. "Cause you want some more of this."

"Well, hmph," Wes said as he confidently grabs his package and moves closer to her. "You want some more of this too."

"Huh," Leah said as she backs away from him. "I can't believe how fresh you are."

"Come on now," Wes said as he moves toward her. "You know, the best stuff is the fresh stuff. Now come here."

Wes reaches out to grab Leah, she moves and he misses her. She points at him as he approaches her.

"Get away from me."

She gets playful with him and rushes around to the other side of the cocktail table. He looks at her with a big smile and carnal passion in his eyes.

"Ooh baby I love a chase. When I catch you; I'm gonna tear it up."

Wes charges after her and Leah teasingly runs away from him going around the sectional. They play this game of cat and mouse. Wes rushes around the large sofa trying to catch her. When Leah dashes in front of it, Wes cuts his chase in half and jumps over the sectional. He cuts her off and as Leah turns to double back he grabs her pajama robe.

"Got ya, once I get that robe off, you're mine."

"He'll Work It Out" Chapter 2. Taryn C. Atkins

Wes spins Leah around to him, pulls her close as they fall back on the sectional. Leah's now in his arms and on top of him. Wes tries to take off her robe, Leah pretends to prevent that from happening. They continue to playfully wrestle for a few seconds when Wes holds the robe up in triumph.

"Yes, got it!"

Wes tosses her robe to the rug, does a slick move positioning himself top. As they stare deeply into each others eyes, he gives her a charming smile.

"I believe somewhere it said, "To the victor goes the spoils."

Wes begins to place sensuous and stimulating kisses bit by bit on her neck. Leah is about ready to concede. Wes moves in to kiss her lips when all of a sudden, the back door bell in the kitchen rings out several times. Leah swiftly looks toward the kitchen door.

"Who in the world...?" Leah looks at him. "Let me up so I can answer the back door."

"No..." Wes doesn't let her get up. "It's not like they can see we're here, be quiet and they'll go away."

"The lights are on Wes. They know I got to be home."

Leah tries to get up but Wes still won't let her.

"Forget the door, you don't have to answer it."

"Wes stop. It might be important, now let me up."

"Come on Lee don't go, give me five minutes."

"Five minutes!" She shoves him off. "Get outta here."

"Fine go."

Wes lays back on the sectional. Leah stands, she picks up her robe from off the rug and as she puts it on she looks at him.

"Five minutes. Hmph, I might as well get up."

Leah walks off. She rushes thru the kitchen door, as the back-door bell rings out again. Leah fixes her clothes as she heads toward the back-door. There's several knocks at the back-door plus the bell rings out yet again.

"Hold on hold on," Leah said. "Goodness. I'm coming."

Leah unlocks the back door in the kitchen. When she opens it, there stands Reggie.

"Hey, mom! Reggie said." What's going on?! How you

doing?"

"Reggie, we're not doing this again," Leah said. She goes to close the door. "You can call me tomorr--"

Before she can close it, Reggie rushes in the house.

"Wait, Mom, please," Reggie said. "Please, I... I'll stay a few minutes okay. Please."

"Just a few minutes," Leah said. She closes the back door and locks it. "So what are you doing here?"

Reggie and Leah make their way to the kitchen. Leah walks into the kitchen first and Reggie's right behind her.

"I wanted to see you," Reggie said. "Glad I caught you."

Reggie looks around nervously, he scratches every so often but tries to control himself. Leah looks Reggie over and sees he looks tired, a bit high-strung and anxious. It's been a few days since Reggie's last hit and images of Mario are haunting him.

"I was just umm, walking through the neighborhood, and I... I saw the lights on. I really miss you ma."

It's clearly seen that Reggie has not washed or changed his clothes in a while. An odor coming off of him reaches Leah's nose, being disturbed by it she grabs the bottle of Febreze from the kitchen counter and sprays it around.

"Sorry about that ma. I was with Mario, but umm... He's..." He gets lost in his thoughts concerning Mario and talks to himself. "I was out running around. I told him I would be right back but... I was gone a long time."

Leah looks at Reggie, she watches as he stares off into space for a moment and rambles on.

"I guess he couldn't take it, so he..." Reggie realizes what he's doing and looks over at his mother. "I... I haven't seen him in a few days. That's all."

Reggie holds his head down embarrassed by how he looks and the smell coming off of him. Leah puts the bottle of air freshener down on the kitchen counter. She goes to Reggie, takes his face in her hands, she looks at him for a moment and tries to wipe his face some.

"My baby," Leah said. "Look, you know I can't let you stay, but I'll let you get cleaned up and I'll fix you something to eat."

"Thanks," Reggie said. "Ma I appreciate it, I do; I know you don't have to."

"Well, I'm your mom right? You only get one. When you finish, I think there's still some clothes of yours in that hall closet."

"Okay."

Leah goes to the fridge, opens it and looks around in it."

"I fried some chicken the other day, there should be a few pieces left-made some potato salad too. How's that sound?"

"Whatever you got. You know I love your cooking ma. So did you work late?" You're usually knocked out by now."

Leah takes two plastic bowls out the fridge, she shoves the refrigerator door closed with the side of her arm and heads over to the kitchen counter.

"Well, I've been working the late shift for a moment. So I'm used to it now.

"Sorry for all the ringing and knocking."

As Reggie continues to look around. Leah puts the bowls down on the kitchen counter, she gets a plate and cup out of the dishwasher and sits them next to the bowls of food. She proceeds to make him a plate.

"After seeing the lights were still on, I thought you did your usual and fell asleep on the sectional."

"No, I was up with..."

Leah's forgotten all about her house guest in the living room.

She said, to herself, "Wes." *Please stay in there*. Leah thought turning to Reggie. "So, what do you want to drink?"

"Ma, I'm not choosy, anything sweet would be good."

Leah walks back to the refrigerator, opens the fridge, while trying to get her thoughts together, she grabs the Tropical Punch out the fridge, closes it and brings the juice over to the counter. Leah opens the container, picks up the cup and as she pours turns to Reggie.

"Actually Reggie, I talked with Mama a few moments

ago, she's concerned about ya. I'll throw on something and we'll go see her."

Before Leah could even get the chance to rework her predicament. Wes walks through the kitchen door. When Wes sees Reggie, an obnoxious smirk comes on his face. Leah shakes her head and takes a deep breath. She turns back to the counter and puts the glass of juice down by the plate of food. Wes stands there for a few, looking Reggie over and then comes into the kitchen.

"Well well, look a here," Wes said.

Wes goes to the fruit bowl on the kitchen counter and takes an apple from it. He opens up one of the kitchen drawer's and takes out a steak knife. Wes turns around and leans on the kitchen counter top. As he cuts a slice from the apple, Reggie walks over to the island, moves a stool out and as he sits down he looks over at his mother.

"Pfff I get it," Reggie said. He looks over at Wes. "Now I see why you're up late."

Wes eats the slice of the apple. Leah takes her hands and rubs them over her face. She looks at Reggie and then Wes. She watches them for a few seconds, as they watch each other.

"Well, anybody want coffee? Leah said. "Cause I do."

Wes cuts himself another slice of apple, he looks at Reggie as he puts it in his mouth. Leah shakes her head slowly as she goes to her coffee maker, grabbing her coffee cup and reads the phrase "Best Mom Ever." Remembering, when Reggie was seven years old he scraped his money together and bought her that cup for her birthday. Leah's face saddens realizing Reggie's not that innocent and bright-eyed little boy she once knew.

As Leah makes her cup of coffee she peers out the kitchen window into the darkness of the night. She focuses on her reflection and stares at herself for a moment or two. Leah slowly shakes her head as she looks at herself.

He would have to stop by tonight. She thought.

The silence in the room feels equal to one of those old time westerns. Where a high noon, gunfight showdown is about to take place. Both desperadoes want to claim their territory. As they watch each other with eagle eyes and their hands tight on the handle of each gun on their side. They wait, feeling edgy and agitated, who will be the quicker draw and spill first blood. Reggie huffs as he stares at Wes with contempt.

"So ma, what's this?!" Reggie said. "Or should I say who's this stranger?! Why is he here anyway?! He shouldn't even be up in here!"

As Leah turns to Reggie. Wes abruptly points at him.

"Listen here," Wes said moving in Reggie's direction. "Your mom don't have to answer to you."

"And you!" Reggie said as he jumps to his feet, he points back at Wes. "You don't say anything to me alright!"

Leah walks over to the island saying, "Everybody just calm down!"

Leah hears the Keurig beep, and notices that her coffee is ready.

"Reggie, what's this visit for anyway?" Leah said.

As she made her way back over to the coffee maker, she slides her cup from the machine, places it on the counter, takes a spoon out of the drawer placing it next to the cup.

"Like I said, I wanted to see you," Reggie said. "What I can't drop by now? That's a problem." He motions to Wes. "Cause he's here."

Leah walks to the fridge, takes out her hazelnut creamer and returns to the kitchen counter and puts together her cup of coffee

"Well, as you can see I'm all right," Leah said. "If you came to get some money. I'm not giving you a dime."

Reggie said as he slaps his hand down on the island, "I didn't ask!!"

Leah turns to Reggie. "Excuse me, you know what." She sucks her teeth. "I'm not having it." She motions to Reggie. "You can take that outta my house right now!"

She goes over to Wes, stands by him and looks at Reggie.

"Cause whether you like it or not. I've gotta guest."

Reggie looks at his mother stunned, he realizes with all that he has put her through he doesn't want to make her upset. Especially when his primary goal is to get a couple of dollars from her with him hurting and on edge, he does his best to calm himself.

"My bad." Reggie said. "Excuse me ma, I'm sorry for

intruding" He sits back down on the stool he looks over at his mother. "I am beat, haven't slept much you know. Can I, at least, sit for a few moments ma. Umm maybe have a little something to eat still. Please."

"Fine, but don't start nothing." She looks at Wes. "And I'm talking to both of you."

Wes takes his hand, motions that he's locking his lips shut, he puts one hand up in the air and lays the other on top of his heart. Leah walks away, takes the plate of food over to the microwave and warms it up. She walks back to her cup of coffee and finishes fixing it. Wes heads over to Reggie. Reggie keeps his eyes on Wes as he takes a seat on one of the island counter stools. The only thing between them is the center counter stool.

"So, back in town huh player?" Reggie said.

Leah quickly looks at him saying, "Reggie."

"I'm just making conversation." Reggie said.

Reggie leans on the island countertop and looks over at Wes, who is cutting off another slice of apple.

"I'm here handling some business," Wes said. "Checking on a few things."

"What things?" Reggie said.

"One moment," Wes said. He looks over at Leah and smiles. "Sweetheart, can you please get me a paper towel or napkin. This apple is making my face all messy."

Leah goes to the sink, pulls a paper towel off the roll, brings it over to Wes and hands it to him.

"Here you go," Leah said.

"Oh baby, come on now," Wes said. "You see I got this apple in one hand and my other hand is all sticky from cutting it." Wes sticks his face out. "Wipe my mouth off, please."

Leah says nothing but she can feel Reggie's eyes on her, she reaches over with the paper towel and wipes Wes's mouth.

"Thank you baby," Wes said.

"Sure." Leah said.

She walks away going back over to the kitchen counter where

"He'll Work It Out" Chapter 2. Taryn C. Atkins

her hot cup of coffee awaits. Wes smiles as he looks over at Leah.

"My baby takes good care of me," Wes said.

Wes looks over at Reggie with an obnoxious smile on his face.

"So anyway, what were you saying."

The microwave sounds off with three beeps, Leah takes the plate out and puts it down by the bowl of potato salad. She gets a spoon out the drawer, opens the bowl of potato salad and puts three heaping spoon fulls beside three pieces of chicken. She leaves the spoon on the plate, pulls two paper towels off the roll, picks up the plate and juice and brings it to Reggie.

As Leah comes over, Wes sees she has a smile filled with contentment on her face as she puts everything down in front of Reggie. Unnoticed by Leah, Reggie clearly sees Wes shake his head, rolling his eyes as he looks away. Wes doesn't realize that Reggie sees his expressions. Wes looks back at them, Reggie smiles as he looks up at his mom and stands up.

"Thanks," Reggie kisses her on the cheek. "I love you ma."

"I love you too baby," Leah said.

Wes watches and listens to their interaction. He loudly sucks his teeth as if he has something stuck in them. Reggie wraps his arms around his mother giving her a hug.

"I know I've put you through a lot ma." Reggie said. "I know, but you're always there for me."

Wes rolls his eyes again, as he looks off to the side and huffs.

Huh, not if I have anything to do with it. Wes thought.

Reggie sits back down at the island. He has a smile on his face as he looks across at Wes. When Wes looks at Reggie, he see's his own obnoxious grin, smiling right back at him. Leah looks at Reggie before walking away.

"Want some dessert." Leah said. "There's some of that Louisiana Crunch Cake you love so much in the fridge."

"Great." Reggie said. He digs into the plate of food in front of him. "So, what things are you checking on exactly?" Reggie questions munching on a piece of chicken. "Oh please, let me guess. Is it a blond, brunette or maybe a red head. Are those the so call *things* you're checking on?"

Reggie makes sure his mother hears the conversation but Wes already knows Leah is listening. Leah turns to them, takes her cup of coffee and moves closer. She leans back on the kitchen counter, watching and listening as she sips on her coffee.

"I've got some new artist. This time, I'm focusing on those who actually got talent."

Reggie makes a face at Wes's snide remark.

I need some cake. Leah thought.

Leah walks over to the fridge. She takes the cake container out and closes the fridge with her foot. She grabs a small plate out of one of the cabinets and cuts herself a slice.

Wes and Reggie continue their talking but at the moment, its muffled sounds to Leah. Her back is turned, while she enjoys her coffee and cake, she's inattentive to Reggie and Wes's conversation heating up.

"Yeah I've seen how you focus on your artist. Especially the female ones. Ain't that right?"

"Boy." Wes leans over to Reggie. "You better tread lightly, you hear."

"Tread lightly?! Why?! Cause I've been out on the road with you. I know first hand how you focused on a different female artist each night, all up in your hotel room." He motions to Leah. "Unlike her, I know your clients list! Especially in this town!" He drops the chicken bone on his plate. "So who you laying up with next?"

Leah's pulled back into reality. Reggie looks at her as she puts her coffee cup down on the kitchen counter.

"I can't believe you're still letting him play you."

"Reggie! Didn't I say don't start nothing, and this is none of your business."

"None of my business?"

Wes has grown tired of Reggie's presence and his interfering with how he deals with Leah.

"You know what," Wes said. "It's time for you to go boy."

"He'll Work It Out" Chapter 2. Taryn C. Atkins

Reggie slams both hands down on the island countertop as he jumps to his feet. Reggie leans over and points in Wes' face.

"Boy!" Reggie said. "I'm sure no boy anymore! Just like you never was a father! So don't even think you got the right to say anything to me!"

"Reggie how dare you!?!" Leah said.

"No, how dare you!? Reggie said. He motions and moves toward Leah. "You're still falling for this." He moves back toward Wes. "I'm coked up and still smell him coming."

"Okay, I'm done with this," Wes said as he stands. "You've outstayed your welcome." He moves in Reggie's direction. "You need to go befo--"

"Before what?!" Reggie said rushing over to Wes. "I'm not going anywhere!" Reggie taps his finger on Wes's chest. "If any one's going it's you, player!!" He stares Wes in his eye. "See I know you dog, if this spot had a fell thru," He looks Wes up and down. "I'm sure you had some other tricks lined up! Probably those "Liquor Sisters" as you call them, right?"

"Look here."

"So which one was next? Merlo or Alize?"

Wes halls off and shoves Reggie. Reggie moves back a few steps, he rushes over and pushes Wes. Reggie throws a punch at Wes's face. Wes moves out of its way and grabs Reggie. They start to mix it up and struggle with one another. Leah rushes over to them.

"DON'T!! STOP IT!! She hits at them. "STOP THIS!! Get off each other!!"

Reggie does a quick move and slams Wes down on the island. Reggie's food and drink fall to the floor. Reggie swiftly grabs the steak knife laying on top of the island and puts the knife to Wes's throat. Leah is frantic watching what's taking place.

"NO REGGIE NO!! LORD JESUS!! DON'T DO THIS!!"

Wes lays still, Reggie is over him holding the knife right to his jugular. Leah rushes over to the counter and grabs the house phone.

"Reggie get off him now! Or I'll call the police!"

"I'll tell you this player." Reggie presses the knife against

Wes's throat as he leans. "If you hurt her again. I'll hurt you."

"Reggie stop it, get off him or I'll dial 911 NOW! Reggie!!"

Reggie and Wes keep their eyes peeled on each other.

"Calm down Ma, nobody's hurt... Isn't that right?"

Wes nods his head agreeing, Reggie lets Wes go and drops the knife to the ground. Reggie moves away from Wes as he slowly sits up, rubbing his throat as he gets to his feet. Leah rushes over and gets between them, she shoves Reggie toward the back-door.

"Get out of here!!" Leah points toward the back-door. "Get out of my house Reggie! RIGHT NOW!!"

Reggie looks at his mother, then at Wes, who's standing behind Leah and wearing that obnoxious grin. Wes takes a few steps back, so Leah can't see and he waves goodbye to Reggie. Reggie shakes his head, as he looks at his mother, he gets ready to say something but doesn't get the chance.

"Reggie, I don't want to hear it! Go!"

Leah points to the back door once again. Reggie starts to leave but turns around. He goes to the cake container. He raises the cover, gets a few paper towels off the roll and grabs the rest of the cake with them. Reggie puts the lid back on and wraps the cake up in the paper towels.

"I'm going... I'm sorry about all this mom."

"Yeah." Leah huffs. "Whatever."

Reggie leaves out the kitchen, seconds later they hear the back-door open and shut. Leah goes to the back-door, locks it and returns to the kitchen. Wes stands there holding out his arms for her. Leah comes close and slaps his hands out the way. She pushes him to the side and walks to the kitchen door. Wes turns around to her.

"Leah come on now."

She places her hand on the kitchen door and looks over her shoulder at Wes.

"I don't want to hear it from you either. Now get this place cleaned up."

Leah pushes through the door and leaves the kitchen.

~CHAPTER 3~

~Victimized in Spirit, in Soul & in Body~

~WAR WITHIN~

The next day, in the Lenox Hill neighborhood of the Upper East Side, we arrive at a twenty-five story, luxury loft, and condominium complex. In the early eighties this building was a well known Toy Factory. Behind the door of one of these suites, when you enter you step on to an espresso stained oak floor, walking down the quiet hallway, you pass artistic and trendy photos, held in black picture frames and spaced out nicely, on the textured beige painted walls they hung on. When you exit the hallway, on the right sat, a rectangular, brushed stainless steel umbrella stand, next to it stood an antique iron coat rack tree and off to the side on the wall a good size mirror.

The light quickly comes across this ample space, because it enters through seven windows, that are five feet wide and extend from the floor up to the twelve-foot ceiling. Six of the windows stand side by side and run the length of the living room up to the marble island. They are exposed right now but usually the windows are hidden behind linen and sheer light gray mist curtains. The last window stays uncovered, it sits between the marble island and the kitchen's range. The loft, offset with exposed piping is warmed up with a candle fireplace. Right now the central air conditioning is on and flowing through the building. The living room walls are painted a gray mist and the colors of nature are the scheme of this area.

The kitchen with its theme of chrome and white had three stainless steel track lights focused on the kitchen area. The artful backsplash being a mosaic of white, gray and black, brought out the kitchen cabinets of snowbound white and its matching appliances being a mix of stainless steel and black. There were golden brown glass cylinder light pendants hanging over the lengthy and full-size marble island. Which attractively separated

"He'll Work It Out" Chapter 3. Taryn C. Atkins

the living room from the kitchen, making both areas spacious and cozy. A unique piece hung over the kitchen cabinets and exceptionally set off the entire kitchen area. It was the six-foot propeller of golden wood with brown tips.

On this Saturday afternoon, Gigi sits at the end of the island, in one of the four white leather and chrome barstools. She's relaxing in an Old Navy tee and pajama pant. Gigi turns the barstool sideways, leans against the back of the barstool and crosses her legs. She held the cordless phone to her ear with one hand and with the other she reaches for the ice tea glass sitting in front of her. The glass was filled half way with a dark red concoction. Gigi picks up the glass and takes a few sips as she listens to the person on the phone. After nursing on the juice, she puts the glass back down on the island.

"It's been a few months now..." Gigi said. "Because when I've called she's hung up... I'm almost thirty, it doesn't matter like it used to! She doesn't want to be bothered... Well, mom's the deaconess, she should pray! I've tried... Why should it always be me... She kicked me out remember!"

Gigi takes another drink, gets up and walks over to the custom sized bone gray sectional sofa. As she walks around it and listens to the person on the other end of the receiver. Gigi puts her glass down on top of the large square brushed stainless steel coffee table. She sits down on the plush sandstone area rug, right in the corner of the sectional where all parts meet. Gigi takes one of the steel blue sofa pillows, puts it behind her back and leans back against the sectional. When she looks up, Gigi sees the stainless steel shade which is attached to the stainless steel floor lamp, the light is arched over the sectional and is right in her line of sight. Gigi scoots over a bit so she can look up at the ceiling.

"Grandma, I can't. Mom would lose it that's why... The last place my mother wants her dyke daughter is at her church... It's been a moment since I've even been there! Grandma, I can't promise that now."

Gigi hears a room door open and close in the hallway. A female voice croons out the chorus of Prince's song "Kiss". The voice gets louder as it travels down the hall and toward the living room. Gigi listens to the crooner coming down the hall, she shakes her head and cracks a slight smile. Seconds later her roommate slides in making her appearance in the living room.

"Whoshhhhh!" Lexi said.

Lexi is sporting basketball shorts, a tank top, and ankle socks. Gigi waves her hand over her head trying to get Lexi's attention but Lexi doesn't see her. Lexi dances and sings her way over to one of the kitchen cabinets, opens it, takes out an ice tea glass and closes it. Lexi dances and sings her way over to the large stainless steel refrigerator. She puts her glass under the ice maker on the fridge door, presses the crushed ice button; The ice burst forth and after her glass is somewhat filled, she pulls it away. She sits the glass on the kitchen counter.

Gigi again waves her hand over her head trying to get Lexi to see that's she's there and on a phone call. Lexi being in her own groove doesn't even notice Gigi, utterly lost for the moment jamming to the music in her mind. Gigi gets up off the floor, sits on the sectional turned in Lexi's direction, and waits for Lexi to turn around.

Lexi opens the fridge, takes out a tall, clear plastic jug filled with the dark red juice with a variety of chopped fruit. She fills her glass and returns the jug back to the fridge. Lexi bellows out the last line of the Kiss chorus and does the guitar solo. Lexi turns around on the last word of the song and finally sees Gigi sitting on the sectional. Lexi smiles at Gigi.

"Hey G," Lexi said. "Sorry if we kept you up."

Gigi holds up the cordless phone for Lexi to see. Now seeing the phone in Gigi's hand.

"Oh, my bad, sorry."

Gigi moves to the middle point of the sectional, grabbing the sofa pillow off the floor putting it behind her. She puts her legs up and lays back on the sectional continuing with her call.

"It gets hard to pray sometimes..." Gigi said. "Grandma you've got God on speed dial. You get through right away."

"He'll Work It Out" Chapter 3. Taryn C. Atkins

Lexi walks back over to the kitchen cabinets, opens one up, she looks inside and pulls out a bag of Honey Barbecue Potato Chips. She closes the cabinet back and gets her glass from the kitchen counter. Lexi makes her way over to the sectional and overhears some of Gigi's phone call.

"Yes, I know Jesus loves me... Yes, he's knocking...
Grandma, it's just not that simple to me right now."

Lexi shakes her head as she puts her glass down on the brushed stainless steel rectangular end table.

Man, it never stops. Lexi thought.

Comfortably lounged at the end of the sectional Lexi tears open the bag of chips and turns in Gigi's direction. Lexi nibbles on the chips listening to the phone conversation.

"I'm not ready to open that door again." Gigi said to
herself. "Not... not just yet."

Once again up the hallway, the sound of a door opening and closing is heard. There's no singing, only the click-clack of high heels, and from their sound the woman clearly has a pep in her step. After a few seconds, Dana traipses out of the hallway and comes into the living room. Gigi looks at Dana, smiles, and shakes her head a bit seeing the thoroughly satisfied smile on Dana's face. Gigi puts her hand over the receiver for a moment.

"Hey," Gigi said.

Lexi and Dana look over at Gigi, who's wearing a smile.

"Lexi look." Gigi motions to Dana. "Somebody's all aglow,
all happy and effervescent."

"Ha-ha, amusing Gigi." Dana said.

Lexi smiles as she looks at Dana.

"Well, she should," Lexi said. She looks over at Gigi. "I
put in some overtime for that glow."

"You're terrible," Dana said as she playfully shoves Lexi.

"Oh, Dana," Gigi said. "By the way, effervescent means
bubbly in case--"

"I know what it means smart aleck." Dana said.

Gigi smiles, she takes her hand off the receiver and returns to her call. Dana looks down at Lexi sitting on the sectional.

"Okay baby," Dana said. "I'm going. Did you call

downstairs for me? So Eric can bring my car around?"

"Eric's off today," Lexi said. "Mark's bringing it around and Cesar's the doorman at the desk."

Dana smiles saying, "A twenty-four concierge, valet, indoor parking lot, on site super, plus on the top floors a gym, pool and tennis court. I love this building."

"I love my parents," Lexi said. "I love them for moving to Florida and giving me this place. Fully paid too! The Best Graduation and Birthday Gift Ever!"

"Let me go, now remember. I'm going out with a few friends from Astoria. We're meeting at the Shark Bar for a late lunch, going shopping and later tonight checking out some jazz club in the village."

Lexi looks Dana over from head to toe. Dana's hair is done, make-up tight and she's working a fierce, fun and flirty violet skater dress with matching high heels.

"Looking like that, you better go before you don't get out of here at all."

"Well, you be good and get some sleep. I'll call you if I plan on coming back tonight."

"Gurl, I'm tired."

"What do you want me to do then? Let me know now."

Lexi puts the chips on the end table. She gets up from the sectional and once she's on her feet, she stands by Dana.

"Well, call me tomorrow," Lexi said. "We'll get together on Wednesday."

"Umm..." Dana said folding her arms. "That's almost five days."

"Yeah I know."

Lexi starts to stretch out her body, raising her arms over her head, she turns her upper body left and right. Lexi stretches out her back and bends over to stretch out her legs.

"I need a few days to recover Dana. You know you be trying to wear a sister out."

"Well sexy." Dana smiles as she moves closer to Lexi and touches her chest. "So do you."

Lexi smiles replying, "I can't lie, I do."

"He'll Work It Out" Chapter 3. Taryn C. Atkins

Lexi moves closer to Dana, she looks into her eyes, places her hands on Dana's waist and they softly put their foreheads together.

> Under her breath, Lexi said, "You love it."
> Dana smiles replying, "I do. Mmmph, child let me go."
> She walks away and kisses at Lexi. "Mwah, I'll see ya, love ya boo." She turns to leave and waves at Gigi. "Bye Gigi."

Gigi smiles and waves bye to Dana. As Dana leaves, you hear her high heels on the wood floor once again. Lexi walks over to the hallway and watches Dana as she walks to the front door. Lexi smiles tilting her head to the side, she softly sighs as she watches Dana switch up the hallway.

As their loft front door slides open there's a brief pause, Lexi wiggles her fingers waving bye to Dana and then the front door slides shut. Lexi goes back over to the sectional, she sits down and taps Gigi on the leg. Gigi looks over at her and Lexi points in Dana's direction as she looks at Gigi.

> "See that," Lexi said. "Now that's the way you do it."

Gigi looks at Lexi and shakes her head. She watches as Lexi leans back against the sectional, puts her legs up on the coffee table, crosses her feet and ever so confidently puts her hands behind her head. Lexi takes her glass off the end table, she drinks some of the dark-red juice and places the glass back on the end table. Lexi picks up the bag of chips and enjoys a few more of them. She looks over at Gigi, who's still on her call.

> "Well, you keep praying for me grandma... I've gotta go; I need to do a few things... I'll see you soon... Grandma not yet... I'll come by the house to see you... I will, and we'll go out... Anywhere, I'll take you to Georgia Diner, Bbq's, or how about Katz. I know you love all three. Your choice... Okay... I love you too, see ya."

Lexi closes up the chips, puts them on the end table and leans back on the sectional. After Gigi ends her call, there are a few seconds of silence. Gigi sits up and moves to the edge of the sectional. She picks up her glass on the coffee table. Lexi looks over at Gigi and sees her drink down the remaining juice in her glass in one motion. She looks at Lexi.

"Mmm." Gigi points to her empty glass. "Now this is the best batch of Sangria you've ever made."

"Why thank you. Hey, we need--"

"One sec."

Gigi swiftly gets up off the sectional, she heads in Lexi's direction, causing Lexi to quickly pull her legs up into her chest so Gigi can go by. She walks to kitchen and puts her glass in the sink. Lexi turns herself sideways on the sectional, scoots herself back a bit, grabs a sofa pillow, puts it behind her, she leans back against it and stretches her legs out on the sectional.

As Lexi gets comfortable on the sectional, she hears one of the kitchen drawers open and shut. Then one of the cabinets open and close as well. After a few seconds, Gigi returns wearing yellow dishwashing gloves, holding some paper towels in one hand and a bottle of Windex in the other. Lexi looks up at Gigi. Gigi looks down at the coffee table and then over at Lexi. Gigi cracks a smile shrugging her shoulders.

"It's so nice, I like to keep it clean," Gigi said. She kneels down by the coffee table. "We don't want to leave any glass rings on."

"I... I guess not." Lexi said.

Gigi takes the Windex, sprays the top of the coffee table and begins to briskly scrub away at the top of the coffee table. Lexi watches as Gigi vigorously rubs away at the coffee table with a criticalness. Lexi sits up on the sectional so she can see Gigi better. She watches Gigi for a moment cleaning away with an urgency.

"So... rough call?"

Gigi doesn't respond to Lexi right away. She just scrubs away at the coffee table.

"I'm all right, my grandmother said to tell you hello. Oh, Cassandra called too, said she's on her way."

"Okay, but..."

Lexi looks at Gigi as she cleans the coffee table. Lexi gets up, moves herself to the sectional's edge and leans over to Gigi.

"Gigi, you're not all right. Your people are stressing you again with all that church and Jesus stuff."

Lexi watches Gigi and sees her intensity grow as she scrubs at the coffee table.

"It's... it's hard sometimes."

Lexi watches Gigi spray the Windex on the coffee table again. She puts the Windex bottle on the carpet beside her. Then continues with her urgent need to scrub away all remnants of dirt on it. Lexi gets down on the carpet.

"Gigi, stop," Lexi said.

"I'm just cleaning it off," Gigi said.

"It's clean."

"No, it's not. There's stuff you can't see."

Gigi continues to scrub the coffee table with determination. Lexi moves closer to Gigi.

"Gigi stop it. Now!"

Gigi stops moving, she drops the pieces of paper towel in her hand and lifts her hands off the coffee table. Lexi comes over to Gigi and reaches her hands out to get the yellow dishwashing gloves Gigi wore. Before removing them, Lexi notices Gigi's hands are trembling.

"Give me all of this."

Gigi sits down on the carpet, she takes the dishwashing gloves off and gives them to Lexi. Lexi snatches the paper towels off the coffee table, grabs the bottle of Windex and places everything on the carpet by the side of the other end table. Lexi turns toward Gigi.

"Alright, now close your eyes."

"Lexi I'm fine-"

"Uh-uh." Lexi points at her. "I said close your eyes."

Gigi doesn't argue with Lexi she just closes her eyes.

"Okay, now what."

"Slowly, take a deep breath in, slowly breathe out, as you exhale relax your body. Do it a few times."

Gigi slowly breathes in and out several times. Lexi even does it with her. They sit there in silence for a moment.

"Okay, open your eyes. How you doing now?" Lexi said.

"I'm feeling better," Gigi said.

"Good," Lexi said.

"Thanks," Gigi said.

Gigi and Lexi get up off the carpet. Lexi gets her glass and the chips off the end table. Gigi takes a seat at the far end of the sectional. Lexi gets ready to move but looks over at Gigi as she gets comfy.

"I'm getting more Sangria want some?"

Gigi looks over at Lexi as she tries to get into a comfortable position on the sectional.

"Yeah thanks, my glass is in the sink. Hand me the chips please. Toss em."

Lexi throws the bag of chips to Gigi. After Gigi catches them, Lexi heads over to the kitchen. Gigi opens the bag of chips and starts to nibble on them.

"So... Cassandra's coming over huh. I thought you were tired."

Lexi turns to Gigi holding the jug of Sangria in her hands.

"Not that tired."

Gigi smiles and shakes her head a bit as she continues to nibble on the chips. Lexi returns to her task of pouring their glasses of Sangria in the kitchen.

"Gigi, I don't get it. Why do you even let them preach to you in the first place? You should've hung up."

"First of all. I'm not gonna hang up on my grandmother, and second you know she's not like my mother."

"Okay true, but even she needs to let it rest. You are who you are. Leave it alone already."

Lexi comes back to the living room carrying their glasses of Sangria. Before Lexi takes a seat, she hands Gigi her drink. Gigi takes her glass and takes a few sips of the Sangria. Lexi turns herself toward Gigi and as Lexi sits down at the other end of the sectional, she tucks one leg under her. Gigi puts her glass on the coffee table and places the bag of chips between Lexi and her.

"Lexi, you wouldn't understand anyway," Gigi said. "As you so proudly say, "You've never gone to church."

"Yes, and proud of it." Lexi said. "No organized religion for me, and it doesn't make a difference what it is either.

Be it faith, denomination, sect, group or coven. Whatever, I'm not going for it. Half of them are faking the funk anyway. If I'm going to hell," She raises her glass in the air. "I'm going on my terms."

Lexi drinks down some of her Sangria, she takes several swallows of it and thoroughly enjoys each one. When she's done, there's a little less than half a glass left. Gigi shakes her head as she watches Lexi.

"You're terrible you know that."

"Mmm, oh that's good." Lexi puts her glass on the coffee table and looks over at Gigi shaking her head. "No not terrible. I'm honest."

Lexi leans over and takes the bag of chips. She reaches inside the bag, returning to nibbling on them as her and Gigi talk.

"What amazes me, is how you can so easily say that. I don't want to go to hell."

"Well baby, according to the "Church" that's exactly where "WE" are going. All because we like women and not men. I thought God loved everybody. How stupid am I."

Lexi closes up the bag of chips and places it on the coffee table.

"Well, God does love the person." Gigi said. "He hates the sin."

"Hates the sin," Lexi said. "That's what you said? Well, is it a sin because your mom and grandmother say so. And if you mean because it's in the "Bible," you know how many translations exist. Who's to say what sin is."

Lexi picks up her glass, goes to take a drink, stops and looks over at Gigi.

"And you know what. Those born again bible thumpers sin too. So please! How dare they judge us!"

Lexi gets ready to take a drink of her Sangria again but stops once more; She looks at Gigi.

"You know what's terrible, the way you still let your family get in your head."

Lexi drinks down the rest of her Sangria. She gets up from the sectional, she holds her glass in one hand and grabs the bag of chips off the coffee table with the other. She heads over to the kitchen but half way she turns to Gigi.

"You want more chips? Cause I'm putting them up."

"No, I'm fine."

Lexi head to the kitchen. Gigi gets up from the sectional, picks up her glass of Sangria and walks over to one of the living room windows. While Gigi stands in front of the window, looking through it she nurses on her drink enjoying their gorgeous city view. Lexi puts her glass in the sink and the chips back in one of the cabinets. She starts looking in the other cabinets seeing what other snacks are around.

"Listen Lexi, you seem to forget that once upon a time, I was one of those born again bible thumpers too. And it wasn't bad at all."

Gigi goes to take a sip of Sangria. Lexi slams one of the kitchen cabinets shut, she turns around and walks over to the island. The sound having startled Gigi makes her turn toward Lexi. Lexi stands on the other side of the island looking at Gigi.

"Now you listen. What's amazing to me, is how you've been straddling the fence since high school." Lexi walks around to the side of the island. "Gigi from the gate, I've always said, if you're going to be down with this lifestyle, then do it, but you're stressing! And you're stressing me!"

Lexi leans on the side of the island as she looks at Gigi.

"I'm getting really tired of this same conversation. So choose. It's simple! Church or Chicks?!"

"Lexi we've been best friends since we were fifteen, and you've seen a lot of stuff go down, but this, you can't understand the struggle I go through."

The room is silent as Gigi walks away from the window and takes a seat back on the sectional. Lexi walks over to the kitchen sink, rinses her glass out and puts it on the kitchen counter. She heads over to the refrigerator where she takes out the pitcher of Sangria and fills her glass up once again. She puts the pitcher back in the fridge, gets her glass from the counter and as she takes a drink of the Sangria she makes her way back over to the sectional. Lexi puts her glass on the coffee table and sits down by Gigi

"Look, Gigi, you want to go to church. Fine. Some churches cater to the gay community, have gay pastors and even preach all that Jesus stuff. Try one of them."
Lexi picks up her glass and raises it in the air. "The best of both worlds. Hooray!"

Lexi takes a sip of her drink and puts the glass down on the end table. She lays back trying to get comfortable on the sectional. Gigi puts her glass down on the coffee table, she sits back and folds her arms. Lexi reaches over, picks her glass back up and as her drink Gigi turns to her.

"Listen," Gigi said. "I was in a church where the true and living word of God was being taught. I've felt the presence of God, been filled with the Holy Spirit and all. And I... I know its not like that now, but I..." She shakes her head. "I'm not gonna go and hear a lie preached either. Just to please myself. That's okay."

Gigi sits back. Lexi sits up, her facial expression changes being stunned and agitated by Gigi's statement. Lexi puts her glass down on the end table, she gets up from the sectional, takes a few steps and quickly turns to Gigi.

"Excuse me," Lexi said. "A Lie. What's a lie is so called Christians saying they love you in one breath and are hypocrites the next." She walks away and turns to Gigi. "A Lie, Please."

Lexi comes over to Gigi and stands by the coffee table.

"Okay Gigi, let's talk truth then. The truth is, I recall you at nineteen crying! Standing with your bags at the front door of my parents house. Because your so called born again, bible toting mother, had kicked your dyke ass out her house! After you were "real" with her! It's been a while since you even spoke to her. Why is that huh? It's surely not because you haven't called. So when will you realize she doesn't want to talk to you. I mean Gigi, don't you get it! The Truth is your mother can't stand the sight of you! How's that huh! Is that enough truth for you!"

"He'll Work It Out" Chapter 3. Taryn C. Atkins

Lexi plops down on the sectional. The room goes dead quiet for a moment. Gigi huffs as she moves to the edge of the sectional.

"Wow... Umm..." Gigi said. She looks over at Lexi and stares at her for a few seconds. "Wow, okay..."

Gigi looks away floored by Lexi's remarks. Gigi shakes her head, slightly laughs for a second as she looks over at Lexi again.

"I... I can't believe you just said that to me." Gigi stands up. "I should've never started this conversation with you, but I thought I could talk to my best friend about anything. How stupid am I."

Gigi heads over to the hallway but stops before she leaves out the living room she turns to Lexi.

"Here's a truth," Gigi said. "Nobody knows when it's their time, and believe it or not. The decisions we make do effect our lives both naturally and spiritually, but you know what, I'll save that topic for another time."

Gigi promptly turns and leaves out the living room, a few seconds later a door opens and slams shut. Lexi quickly gets up and rushes over to the hallway.

"Hey Gigi, don't bother!" Lexi said. "Because again, this conversation is getting real old! So how about this, how about you do us all a favor, and pick a side already!"

Lexi goes to the end table, gets her drink, and rushes over to one of the living room windows. Lexi stands there for a few moments, looking out on to the loft's lovely view of the city. Lexi takes a deep breath and as she exhales, she starts to replay everything that just happened in her mind.

About fifteen or twenty minutes has passed as Lexi continues to gaze through the window. She goes to take another sip of her Sangria and sees its all gone. Lexi turns away from the window, heads toward the hallway and as she passes by the kitchen island, she puts her glass down on top of it. Lexi walks up the hall and stops at Gigi's bedroom door. She knocks three times but Gigi doesn't answer or say anything. She leans against the wall across from it.

"Listen, Gigi, I'm sorry. I apologize alright. Hey, remember in high school, when I was applying for

"He'll Work It Out" Chapter 3. Taryn C. Atkins

colleges. My guidance counselor said I should try for Columbia. All my other so call friends at the time, kept telling me, I wasn't good enough, that my grades were just average and all. I never said this, cause I was too embarrassed, but, even my parents thought Columbia was out of my reach. I remember being too nervous to even fill out the application because of all that, but you filled out my application for me. You helped me put my essay together and everything." She laughs. "You even brought the stamp for the envelope. I even remember you prayed before we put the envelope in the mailbox. If it weren't for you, I would have never gotten that scholarship to Columbia. You're my best friend Gigi, and all that happened way before you decided to switch teams."

Lexi goes back over to Gigi's bedroom door, she turns to the side and leans against it.

"Gigi, you're my best friend and we've always been there for each other no matter what. I don't get all mushy often, but I do love you. You're my family. We may argue, but you're my family and that's never gonna change. I didn't mean to hurt you and I'm not trying to hurt you. Like I've always said, be true to yourself. Forget about everybody else's feelings. Do whatever you need to do. If you want to go back to church and all that, beautiful. If you don't, that's fine too. Just... do you, is all I'm saying. That's all I ever wanted you to do. Now, Gigi... I have been drinking a lot of Sangria. So I may not remember everything I said later, but please know it's all coming from my heart... okay."

Lexi walks away from Gigi's door and back down the hallway. Her cell phone rings, she takes her cell out the side pocket of her shorts and checks the display to see who's calling. As Lexi takes a seat on the barstool at the end of the island, a big smile appears on her face and she quickly answers the call.

"Hello there. Okay, well you're about fifteen minutes away, depending on city traffic. I got you covered with parking. Just pull up in front of the building. I'll have the valet come out and park it in one of our spaces in the garage. Yeah no problem, it's okay. Take the elevator up to the twenty-first floor, its suite three. Alright now, I'm looking forward to it as well. Wait, Cassandra, what kind of car are you driving? A what? Get outta here. You've gotta tell me the story behind that. And I've got to drive it. Oh really, I can do that no problem. So, once the doorman lets me know you're coming up. I'll leave the door cracked and you can come on in. Okay, see you soon."

Lexi gets up from the barstool, goes to the loft's intercom system and picks up the receiver.

"Hi Cesar, its suite three on twenty-one. I have a guest pulling in front in about fifteen to twenty minutes. Her name is Cassandra. Cesar, get this, she's driving a 2007, Silver, Shelby GT 500 Convertible. I know, that's exactly what I said. Oh, I'll be driving it. It's a shame Eric's off, but I'm sure Mark's gonna love to park it. One of our three spots should be open. So buzz me when she's coming up. Thanks."

Lexi gets all happy and excited that Cassandra will be arriving soon. She pretends like she's driving a car around.

"What did she say, I'll have to earn the chance to drive it! Gurl, you don't know. I'll be driving that tonight!"

Lexi freezes and makes a mad dash for the hall.

"Bathroom break, too much Sangria."

Lexi rushes up the hallway and into the toilet. A few minutes pass and a door opens and shuts again. Gigi comes out of the hallway holding a few items. She is prepared to go out, wearing all black and looking sexy, sophisticated and stylish. Gigi walks over to the coat rack and places a leather jacket on one of the hooks. Before Gigi walks away, she looks in the mirror by it, moves her head around a bit looking herself over, reviewing her hair and makeup. She stares at herself for a second or two and gives herself a little nod.

"Very nice," Gigi said.

"He'll Work It Out" Chapter 3. Taryn C. Atkins

She heads over to the sectional carrying a pair of sneakers in one hand and over her shoulder there's a messenger bag. Gigi takes a seat at the far end of the sectional, puts her messenger bag on the coffee table and sits her sneakers on the carpet beside her. A door opens and shuts again and after a few seconds, Lexi walks out of the hallway. She looks over, sees Gigi is sitting on the sectional and is dressed.

"My my, don't you look all steamy," Lexi said. "So, where you going?"

"Out apparently." Gigi sharply said.

Gigi starts to put on her sneakers. Lexi comes over, sits down at the other end of the sectional and turns toward Gigi.

"Well, let's see," Lexi said. "Your hair and make-up are looking fierce. You got your skinny leather pants on with a tight black tank top. Both show off your body, but you already know that." She looks over at the coat rack. "Your short black leather biker jacket is hanging on the coat rack, and you're putting on your low-top, black leather, Chuck Taylor's. Which means you're 50/50 about taking your car. Plus your black leather Gap messenger bag is out." She looks over at Gigi and nods her head a few times. "Okay, I know this outfit."

"Oh do you," Gigi said.

"Yeah, it means two or three things. One, you're either catching a meeting at the center, so you can vent and flirt. Two, you're going to hit a spot in the village and just flirt. Now for me, both have the possibility of bringing home a new toy to play with, but for you-It means you'll bring back two or three numbers of possible candidates for further consideration. Or three, if you really don't feel like being bothered, you'll put your iPad in the messenger bag, walk or drive to a creative, earthy location and write."

Gigi finishes putting on her shoes and looks at Lexi.

"What you're doing is profiling you know."

"No, it's me knowing my best friend, and how she acts when she's upset, stressed, angry pick an emotion. You know me like that too. We've been best friends since fifteen. We should, duh."

"Best friends, hmm."

Lexi leans back on the sectional, she puts her legs up on the coffee table and crosses them.

"Yes, best friends Gigi. I know you heard me at your door. Look, even best friends are going to argue at times."

Lexi lightens the mood by putting on a British accent.

"Sorry to say this love, but it's not going to always be champagne and giggles."

Lexi laughs a bit and smiles at Gigi. Gigi shakes her head and smiles back.

"Arguments are gonna happen," Lexi said. "Doesn't mean we throw away years of friendship. Even though, we've had that same heated discussion from time to time since you've come out."

"I know," Gigi said standing up. "I'll be back. I left my iPad in the room."

Lexi looks at Gigi, Gigi smiles as she leaves out the living room and heads to her bedroom. Lexi takes her cell out, checks the time and smiles.

Under her breath, Lexi said, "She should be here soon."

Gigi comes back from her bedroom carrying her iPad. She comes over to the sectional, sits down and puts the iPad in her messenger bag on the coffee table. As Lexi puts her cell back in her pocket.

"Gigi look," Lexi said. "I'm fine with the choices I've made. It's you that's trippin. You want to go back to church, fine with me. You want to be bi, gay, lesbian, dyke, butch, whatever. Then do that, but you have to live with all that comes with it! I feel there's a higher power in control but that's good enough for me."

Lexi gets up, takes her glass off the island, as she heads into the kitchen and puts it in the sink. Lexi goes to the fridge grabs a bottle of water and gets ready to walk away. Gigi waves to her.

"Grab me a bottle of water," Gigi said. "Thanks."

Lexi gets a bottle for Gigi and heads back over to the sectional, hands it to her and sits down. Gigi puts the water in her messenger bag.

> "Again, I do feel there's a higher power in control out there. I'm not doing a makeover on myself to make him, her, or it happy. I'm gonna make Alexis happy and that's what matters. No man can judge me."

The loft intercom buzzes. Lexi gets up to answer it.

> "Yes, okay Cesar, thanks." She hangs up the receiver.

Gigi gets up off the sectional and walks to the hallway.

> "I'm forgetting everything," Gigi said. She heads back to her bedroom again. "Left my cell phone on the dresser."
>
> "Gigi, crack the front door please, Cassandra's coming up."
>
> "Okay."

Lexi puts her bottle of water on the island. She quickly lays on the floor and starts doing crunches. Gigi comes out her bedroom holding her cell and a bottle of perfume oil. She goes and cracks the front door then heads down the hall. Gigi looks down the hall, she sees Lexi on the floor in front of the island. Gigi comes out the hallway and looks at Lexi.

> "What are you doing?"
>
> "A quick thirty. Making sure my abs look tight and sexy."
>
> Gigi shakes her head. "You are too much."
>
> Lexi jumps up and looks at Gigi. "I am."

Lexi grabs her water, opens it and drinks. Gigi watches her, after a few gulps Lexi stops and sits the bottle down on the island. Lexi leans against the island and looks at Gigi.

> "Lexi, I'm not worried about man judging me. It's "doing me" that just may take me somewhere, I don't want to go. *Hell*, it's real Lexi. Don't you ever worry about that? Going to Hell?"
>
> Lexi looks away for a moment, then looks at Gigi. "No."

Gigi shakes her head as she walks away and goes to the mirror again. Lexi looks at her.

> "Sorry Gigi, but I don't."

"He'll Work It Out" Chapter 3. Taryn C. Atkins

Gigi swiftly looks herself over once again. She opens the bottle of perfume oil, rubs a little on both sides of her neck, a little in her cleavage and on both wrists. Gigi heads back over to the sectional. Lexi takes a seat on one of the barstools at the island.

"I'll be gone in a few minutes." Gigi sits down on the sectional. "And leave you to your illicit liaison."

"Eww, that sounds so dirty." Lexi looks at Gigi and smiles. "I like it."

Gigi laughs and shakes her head, she examines her messenger bag to make sure she has everything. Lexi looks up the hallway hearing the front door slide open and a "I Love Kool-Aid" smile appears on her face. Cassandra has walked through the front door, as she closes it, Lexi sees her long dark hair is out and flowing down her back. Cassandra turns around and heads down the hall. Lexi's enjoying the image of Cassandra walking toward her. Cassandra smiles a devilish grin as she approaches. She steps out the hallway wearing a three-quarter length electric blue, spring trench coat, sheer black stockings and black patent leather heels. Gigi's still rifles through her messenger bag and is unaware that Cassandra has made her appearance.

"Well hello there," Cassandra said.

"Hello to you," Lexi said. "I am, loving that color."

"Mmm, I thought you would."

"Let me take your coat."

Lexi goes to get up but Cassandra raises her hand telling her to stop. Lexi sits back down.

"First."

Cassandra backs away as she unties the belt of her trench coat. She opens it and reveals the stimulating lingerie she has on underneath. Which stops a few inches above her thigh high black stockings. Cassandra brings her hands over her head, she places them on each side of the hallways frame and looks at Lexi.

"So, how do you like?"

Lexi's I love Kool-Aid smile is now a I hit the Lotto smile.

"I do love a woman in red."

Under her breath, Gigi said to herself, "Okay, let me go."

"He'll Work It Out" Chapter 3. Taryn C. Atkins

Gigi puts her bag back on the coffee table for a moment, she stands up and as she turns in Lexi's direction.
"So Lexi," Gigi said. She finally sees Cassandra standing there. "Oh, okay... I'm uh..."
Cassandra looks at Gigi, doesn't cover herself simply holds her pose and smiles. Gigi looks at Lexi and shakes her head.
"So umm... I'm gonna go."
Lexi stands as she looks at Gigi with her a smile.
"Okay, but that last question of yours," Lexi said. "All I can say, at this current moment," She looks at Cassandra, motions to what she's wearing and looks at Gigi. "I'm not worried about nothing."
Gigi shakes her head as she looks at Lexi. Lexi looks at Cassandra, Who changes her position and leans against the wall.
"I made a great pitcher of Sangria," Lexi said. "Want some?"
"Sure," Cassandra said.
Lexi heads over to the kitchen. Gigi turns, grabs her messenger bag, puts the strap on her shoulder and heads over to the coat rack.
"I'm about to leave, just let me get my jacket," Gigi said.
Gigi raced over to the coat rack passing by Cassandra. Gigi puts her messenger bag on the floor by the coat rack. Cassandra removes coat, walks over to the sectional and lays her coat across the back of it. Cassandra then moves to the island, sits on one of the barstools and crosses her legs. In her current position Cassandra's able to see Lexi and Gigi. She looks at Gigi as she puts on her jacket. Cassandra glances at Lexi in the kitchen. She sees that Lexi's back is turned as she prepares their drinks. Cassandra watches Gigi refresh her lipstick in the mirror. Unnoticed by both, Cassandra smiles as her eyes carefully give Gigi a once-over.

Hmm, impressive. Cassandra thought.

Cassandra still having her legs crossed, places her hands on both sides of the barstool and turns herself to the side. Now being able to see the whole loft, she looks around. Gigi picks her bag up off the floor and brings the strap over her head. She turns toward the hallway, as she fixes the straps position across her, Gigi

"He'll Work It Out" Chapter 3. Taryn C. Atkins

carefully surveys Cassandra, even raises an eyebrow taking inventory.

Hmm, impressive. Gigi thought.

Unlike Cassandra, Gigi needs to work on her timing.

"It's Gigi right?" Cassandra said. "We spoke when I called."

Gigi's eyes quickly shift and she looks into Cassandra's face.

"Right," Gigi said. "Sorry, I.. I was admiring your heels; I've got those too."

"Honey, when I saw them," Cassandra said. "I gave up my credit card, no hesitation what so ever."

Lexi shakes her head as she listens to them.

Lexi says to herself, "Girl stuff, yuck."

"Gurl, saying the name makes me swoon," Gigi said. "Okay wait, here we go, those are the Black, Christian Louboutin, Lady Peep Patent Red Sole Pumps."

"Excellent," Cassandra said with a smile.

"You look hot in them too," Gigi said. "Ooh, I... I meant."

"It's alright," Cassandra said laughing. "I remember you, you were at the sports bar with Lexi."

"Yeah, we haven't actually met," Gigi said. "Cassandra right."

Lexi still has her back turned as she works on their drinks.

"Yes," Cassandra said with a sexy smile included.

"Well, I'm Gi--"

"Gigi." Lexi said. "Cassandra, she's my roommate and best friend, right Gigi?"

"Yes Lexi," Gigi said looking over at her. "We're best friends."

"Just checking," Lexi said with her back still turned.

Gigi shakes her head as she looks back at Cassandra.

"Anyway," Gigi said as she motions to herself and Lexi. "Pay us no mind." She heads over to Cassandra. "Once again, I'm Gigi, it's a pleasure to meet you."

Gigi extends her hand as she approaches Cassandra.

"Yes," Cassandra said. "And I'm Cassandra."

"He'll Work It Out" Chapter 3. Taryn C. Atkins

When Gigi gets close, as Cassandra places her hand within Gigi's, she breathes in the scent of Gigi's perfume. When they shake, they look into each others eyes and all of a sudden. A connection ambushes Gigi's being and a familiar association awakens within Cassandra. The scent and touch induce a memory to be recalled in Cassandra's mind. After a second or two, they quickly pull their hands away from each other and then glance off in different directions for a moment.

A second or two later their eyes return with a sense of gravitation and tension. Gigi looks down at her bag and fidgets with the strap. Cassandra smiles when she notices Gigi covertly move back putting space between them. Their eyes lock again.

"So..." Gigi said, smiling and nodding her head.

"So..." Cassandra said with a sexy smile. "It's a pleasure to meet you too."

Cassandra and Gigi hold each others attention, feeling the energy building between them. Cassandra smiles looking into Gigi's eyes, as she folds her hands and relaxes them on her knee. Gigi glances at Cassandra's legs, as her eyes, go to her messenger bag strap. She messes with the strap once again and pretends to cough. Gigi shakes her head, as she turns herself toward the mirror, looking into it with a perplexed expression as she walked over to it.

"Okay..." Lexi said turning around with drinks in hand.

She looks over at Cassandra. "Drinks are ready."

Gigi takes her lipstick out her bag and touches herself up.

"Wonderful," Cassandra said with a smile as she looked at Lexi.

"My Sangria is good too," Lexi said. She glances at Gigi. "I thought you were leaving."

"Yeah," Gigi said. Checking herself in the mirror once again. "I'm going."

Gigi puts her lipstick back in her bag, losing her antsy disposition, she turns to them with an easy going demeanor. She walks back over toward Cassandra as Lexi comes over with their drinks. Cassandra turns herself to Lexi. Gigi glances at Lexi, then

Cassandra and taps on the island. Cassandra looks at Gigi as she motions over her shoulder to Lexi.

"She's had a lot of that," Gigi said. "Don't be surprised if she conks out, just warning you."

Cassandra laughs. Lexi places Cassandra's glass of Sangria by her on the island. Lexi holds her glass and looks at Gigi.

"You do know I heard that," Lexi said.

"Good." Gigi said.

"Did you call downstairs for your car."

"No, it's nice out. I think I'll walk."

"Boo-ya!" Lexi leans over to Gigi. "Number three! Told ya!"

"Whatever."

Gigi walks away, she turns around and back steps slowly down the hallway.

"See ya later." Cassandra said.

"Hopefully much later." Lexi said.

Gigi looks at Lexi.

"It might be much later. I may just do all three."

"Don't live so dangerously."

Lexi takes a swallow of her Sangria. Gigi sees Lexi drink and looks at Cassandra. As Lexi sets her glass down on the island.

"Cassandra, remember what I said?"

Cassandra looks at her, Gigi points over to Lexi and pretends to snore.

"I'll give her less than thirty minutes, watch."

Lexi moves to the side of the island and closer to Cassandra. Cassandra looks at Lexi smiles and looks at Gigi.

"Well, I'll let you know what happens." Cassandra said.

"Please do."

"Goodbye Gigi." Lexi waves to her.

"Okay, bye."

They watch Gigi go to the front door, she slides it open, leaves out and pushes it shut. Their eyes go to each other as Lexi picks up her glass.

"A toast."

"Well allow me." Cassandra picks up her glass. "To

orchestrated interludes."

"And illicit liaisons."

They clink their glasses and drink. Lexi puts her glass down on the island, she moves closer to Cassandra. Lexi takes her pointer finger, gently lays it on the top of Cassandra's knee and softly slides it down to her ankle.

"I have three words for the way you look."

"Hmmm, do tell?"

"Ooooh... So tasty."

Lexi appreciates Cassandra enticing, devilish grin.

About an hour or so has passed, Gigi finds herself over on Forty-Seventh Street and Second Avenue, in the calming atmosphere of a waterfall and flower garden. She sits in a wrought iron chair gazing into the large waterfall. Although it's a bright day, the clouds are blocking the sun. Gigi closes her eyes, swallows a deep breath and calmly exhales. She takes her iPad out of her bag, opens it and starts it up. Gigi places it on the table in front of her, clicks the pages application and begins to type. Tears stream down her face.

"Father have mercy, hear my cry and grant me grace.
Cause it's hard wanting to get back in the race.
I don't know what to do, it seems so hard to find my way back to you.
These feelings deep within, they toss me to and fro, it's not easy for me, but a struggle choosing which way I should go.
Yes, I know your word and all that it states; I've thought time and time again about returning to the race.
These feelings inside me Lord there so hard to dismiss. You see much has gone on in my life. I've experienced more than my share of hurt, pain and strife.
It's hard to ignore this anguish, distress, and heartbreak I feel. I'm doing my best oh Lord, day by day to deal.
So please dear Lord have mercy on me and give me your grace, cause Lord I don't know if I can win this race."

Gigi wipes the tears from her face with her hands. Studying the words on the page she saves it, putting the iPad away, she gets up and prepares to leave when the shaded area is absorbed by the sunlight. Gigi sits down again to enjoy the suns warmth.

~SCENT OF DECEPTION~

A few days later, as evening time approaches, we enter a home's tastefully decorated master bedroom which has its own unique touch of flair. The room is a mix of modern lines with classic style, which makes it a place boasting with timeless elegance. The walls are done in a barely beige with a white dove trim, and the warming colors added here and there, defined the peaceful mood in this place.

Entering the sleek and sheltering, black canopy queen bed can be seen, on each side a dark wood nightstand sits with a contemporary table lamp on top of it. A dark orange ultra suede bench was placed in front of the bed. They all rested on a coral red area rug, which had abstract patterns of dark orange. On the wall to the far left of the bed was a grand picture window. Sitting in front of it was a gorgeous chaise lounge, upholstered in a dark orange velvet. There was a Louis Vuitton suitcase opened up on top of it, on the floor by it the matching duffle and men's travel bag. There was also a comfy club chair sitting in the corner.

To the left of the bedroom door was a dark wood dresser and mirror, on top, a Burberry cosmetic bag rested on one side of the vanity tray and held a few select designer perfumes and lotions. The other side of the tray had a black suede jewelry box and by it was an assortment of picture frames with photos, capturing Leah with her son Reggie at various school activities, sporting events and family outings. There was photo's with family members during holiday gatherings and other special times in their lives.

To the right of the bedroom door, there was a small dark wood entertainment center and over it hung an attractive flat screen TV. In the corner there's a walk in closet and on the wall to the right was an elegant dark wood armoire. The master bathroom sat in the upper right corner, the bathroom door is open revealing a rather roomy full bathroom and its motif was in sync with the bedroom.

"He'll Work It Out" Chapter 3. Taryn C. Atkins

The shower is currently running, when all at once resonating from it was the jovial laughter of a man and woman.

"Girl let me take this shower," Wes said. "You trying to drain me of all my strength. Get on outta here, go get dressed and get yourself to work."

A hoochie saunters out the bathroom, her hair is damp, makeup washed off and she's wrapped in a tight, mini leopard freak-me dress. She's carrying gold platform heels in one hand and a man's dress shirt in the other. She chews on a piece of gum like its going out of style as she turns around at the bathroom door.

"Well, I'll see you lata Boo," she said.

"Merlo, go out the door in the kitchen," Wes said. "I don't need neighbors in my business."

"I know," Merlo said. "Let a sista put her shoes on first."

Merlo turns around, throws the shirt on the bed and walks over to the bench. As Merlo gets ready to sit, she hears keys at the front door of the house, with platforms still in hand, she swiftly grabs her purse off the dresser and races out the bedroom. The front door starts to slowly open, Merlo quickly runs across the living room and rushes through the kitchen door. Merlo promptly leaves out the back door, making sure it doesn't slam and draw attention in the process.

Leah walks through the front door, she stands in the door frame and releases a sigh of relief for having arrived home. She takes her keys out the lock, closes the front door, then locks the top and bottom. She leans up against the front door, closes her eyes, tilts her head back and rests her head against the front door for a moment. A few seconds later she opens her eyes, realizing the shower is running a smile beams from her face.

Leah walks into her bedroom, puts her Coach bag down on the entertainment center and slips her heels off. Leah goes over to the bed, moves Wes's shirt over and sits. She lays back on the bed relaxing, listening to the shower running for a few moments and then turns over on her side.

"Hi baby," Leah said raising her voice a bit.

"Oh.. Hey you're... you're home??" Wes said.

"What's the matter?" Leah said.

"I thought you were working late at the hospital?" Wes said.

"Yeah, I was supposed to, but I changed shifts with a friend of mine. Thought we could spend some quality time together. So how are you, how was your day?"

"It was horrible," Wes said. "I've been stuck in meetings with clients all day and it's just been draining."

"Awwww," Leah said.

"They got me all tense and stressed. I walked in heading straight for a hot shower."

Leah sits up, gets up from the bed. She goes to the open bathroom door and leans up against the door frame.

"I just want to wash away the stress." Wes said

"Well, let me come in and help you." Leah goes to walk into the bathroom.

"No!!" Wes lets out a long yawn. "I'm beat babe. I'll be out in a moment. Then we can spend the rest of the night together."

"Okay, I like that idea."

Leah goes back over to the bed, she sits down, reaches over and picks up Wes's shirt. She lifts the chest of his shirt to her nose and breathes in. As she took in the scent of his cologne it caused her mind to reminisce.

"Mmmm Bulgari for Men." Leah remembered how she love the way that smells on him." Leah sniffs the collar.

"Ooooh, Issey Miyake. Lord have mercy, I remember the night I gave that to him."

Leah takes a whiff of the arm of his shirt and a unfamiliar fragrance brought her romantic recall to a sudden halt. It caused her facial expression to switch from delight to suspicion.

"Hold on." Leah breathes in again. "I know that's not mine!" She swiftly gets up and rushes into the bathroom.

"Wes! Why does your shirt smell like some cheap knock off perfume!?"

Leah stands there holding his shirt, the shower stops and the water is turned off. Wes slides the shower door back half way and looks around it at Leah.

"What?" Wes said.

"You heard me!" Leah said. She moves closer to the shower door. "Why does your shirt smell like cheap perfume!?"

"I told you, I was in meetings with clients."

"I'm tired of this!" Leah storms out the bathroom.

"Come on now Leah!" Wes sucks his teeth.

Leah rushes over to the bench and throws his shirt on top of it. She puts her hands to her temples massaging them, she slowly sits down on the bench.

I need to just walk away. She thought.

After a few minutes, Wes steps out of the bathroom, he stands at the bathroom door drying his hair off with a striped red, white and blue towel. His long navy blue robe hangs open and under it, he's wearing burgundy Hanes boxer briefs. Wes looks at Leah as he puts the towel around his neck.

"I had a rough day, wasn't nothing going on but business."

"You know what."

Leah looks at Wes, she picks up his shirt, stands to her feet, she turns toward him and fiercely throws the shirt at his face.

"I'm not stupid!"

The shirt smacks Wes in the face, he takes the shirt and throws it to the ground. Leah points at him as she moves toward him,

"I remember everything Reggie said!"

"Reggie's just angry! All he's doing is trying to come between us!" He calms his tone as he moves toward her.

"You know what though, maybe I should go. Cause it sounds like you don't trust me." Wes pulls off his robe, throws it on the bed and walks over to the chaise. "And If you don't trust me, then I don't need to be here."

Leah folds her arms as she walks over to the side of the bed. His back is to Leah, he searches through his suitcase and pulls out a pair of slacks. As he puts them on, he slyly looks over his shoulder for a second. Wes grabs a silk t-shirt out his suitcase. Leah turns in his direction and watches him. He tries to linger, waiting for Leah to stop him from leaving. Leah gets ready to go to him but stops herself. He picks up the duffel bag, places it beside the suitcase on the chaise and continues his performance by searching through the duffel.

"I'll be outta here in a few minutes."

Leah dashes over to the armoire, opens one of its drawers, takes out something to sleep in and slams it shut. She rushes over to the bathroom, grabs the inside door knob and turns to Wes.

"You do whatever you need to do. I'm taking a shower."

Leah slams the bathroom door behind her. Wes turns around and charges over to the bathroom door. He puts his hand on the door knob, tries to open it but the door is locked. Wes hears the shower start to run and bangs on the bathroom door.

"ALRIGHT FINE! I'm gone; I don't need this you know!"

Wes plops down on the bed. He pulls the towel from around his neck and throws it at the bathroom door. Wes lays back and looks up at the ceiling. He takes a deep breath and exhales.

I need this... for a few more days anyway. Come on think...

flip the script. Wes thought.

Wes got up from the bed, pacing back and forth a few times. He stands still for a second or two, goes over and sits down on the edge of the bed, staring at the bathroom door listening to the shower run. Tucking one hand under his arm he puts the other to his chin. A sly obnoxious smile slowly forms on his lips.

Some time has passed; the bathroom door opens and Leah walks out with a towel around her head wearing an oversize t-shirt. She takes the towel off her head, walks over to the entertainment center and looks over at the chaise. Leah sees neither suitcase nor duffel bag. Only the towel he was using is folded and lays on top of it. Leah goes over to the chair in the corner, reaches down and gets a magazine out the rack beside it

"Guess you did what you needed to."

Leah gets into bed, she props up some pillows behind her, leans back and reads her magazine. After a minute or two, there's a knock on the open bedroom door. Leah looks over the magazine and sees Wes standing there holding two glasses of champagne.

"I come in peace," Wes said.

"I think it's best you leave." Leah said.

"My stuff's at the door," Wes said. "Can you share a drink with me before I go?"

"I'm not thirsty," Leah said.

"Leah come on, I'm trying here."

"You're trying and trifling and I'm done."

Wes places the glasses on the entertainment center.

"Going through all this makes no sense." Wes said. "I come to town, looking to spend time with you and all you want to do is stress a brother."

"Stress you?!"

"Yeah," Wes said.

"The nerve of you!" Leah said. She puts the magazine on the bed and gets up. "How do you think I feel?" She moves toward Wes. "You come into town every blue moon. God knows who or what you've been with."

"I haven't been with anybody!"

"Really, your shirt reeks of women's perfume."

"You know I manage a few women artists."

Leah steps close to Wes takes her finger and touches the right side of his neck.

"I know a hickey when I see one too!"

"What are you talking about?"

Leah roughly turns Wes around and pushes him over toward the dresser with the mirror. Standing in front of it Leah sharply points to the mirror.

"See for yourself."

Leah stands there as Wes looks at his neck in the mirror.

"I don't see any hick--"

Wes sees the hickey and looks at her in the mirror.

"Lee I can explain-"

"Whatever, I've had it with you and this! Just get out!"

Leah turns away from Wes, she tries her best to hold back so many years of hurt but tears flow anyway. Wes goes to the entertainment center and gets the two glasses of champagne. He comes to Leah and stands in front of her.

"We both can use a drink now. So take this, Please."

"He'll Work It Out" Chapter 3. Taryn C. Atkins

Wes holds out the glass to Leah, she looks at it for a few seconds, wipes her tears and takes the glass from him. Wes raises his glass to her.

"Salud."

Wes drinks his champagne straight down.

"Mmmm, that taste good." He said.

Wes watches Leah drink her champagne. His mind recalls his actions moments before reentering the bedroom. Standing at the kitchen island with two glasses of champagne he lays beside his small travel bag. Unzipping the travel bag, he searches through various pill and vitamin bottles. Wes pulls out a small glass dropper bottle with a clear fluid inside. He holds up the small bottle to see how much of the fluid is left. As he holds it up Leah's cat jumps up on the island, startling Wes. He almost drops the small bottle.

"Tigger! Damn cat always coming out of nowhere."

The rather healthy, orange with white striped tabby, looking like a tiger cub, sits down on the counter by Wes and stares him down. Wes unscrews the bottle, takes the dropper out, hovers it over one of the glasses of champagne and places three drops of the clear fluid in the champagne.

Good ol Liquid E. He thought.

He closes the bottle and puts it back into his travel bag. Wes looks over at Tigger.

"Sometimes Tigger, a player has to do what's needed to
keep his women in line. Feel me?"

Wes reaches out to pet Tigger but his ear's lay back, as his back arches and he gives Wes a menacing hiss. Wes quickly pulls his hand back.

"Whatever, I never liked you either."

Tigger jumps off the counter. Wes picks up the glasses of champagne.

"Now old friend, let's go flip the script."

His mind returns to the moment at hand, Wes notices Leah has drunk barely half of the champagne. Leah hands Wes the glass and he returns them to sit on the entertainment center.. Patiently waiting for his *good friend* to kick in, he goes to Leah, and turns her toward him.

"He'll Work It Out" Chapter 3. Taryn C. Atkins

"Okay, I should have been straight with you. One of the meetings I had, well, it got a little wild and one of the girls kissed me on my neck. I put her in check, then left. Nothing happened Lee, I didn't even know that was there."

Leah shakes her head refusing to give in once again and she pushes his hands off of her shoulders.

"You know what... no!" Leah said. She aggressively shoves Wes away. "You're not gonna treat me like this."

"Treat you like what?! I'm not clocking you or checking your clothes. I don't question you when your hospital friends call here! Do I!?"

"I'm not doing anything!"

Leah turns away from Wes, he rushes around and gets in front of her.

"Am I at some other woman's house right now!? No!! I'm here with you, right?!"

"I'm tired of all of this, just leave. Please."

"Lee, come on now. We need to talk, and I'm not going anywhere till we do."

"I don't wanna talk to you!"

Leah goes to rush pass Wes, she looses her balance and reaches out for the nearest post of her canopy bed. Wes quickly grabs her hand and puts his arm around her waist.

"See baby?" Wes said. He helps Leah to the bed. "You got yourself all worked up for nothing."

"I... I got a little dizzy that's all." Leah said. "I'll be okay. I just need to sit down for a moment."

"Well, all this arguing ain't good for either of us."

They sit on the bed. Leah's becoming more subdued, she places her hand over her eyes for a second. Wes smiles knowing his *ol friend* is taking hold as Leah removes her hand and gazes at him through dilated eyes. Now with her resistance down Wes takes full advantage of the moment and draws her closer.

"Here baby, lean on me. I'm not leaving you like this."

He looks at Leah. "I'm gonna look out for my wifey."

Wes plants a few soft, seductive kisses on her lips, but Leah tries to pull away.

"Wes..." Leah tries to push him away with force. "Stop it..."

"We were supposed to spend quality time together right?"

Her resistance lessens as she weakens and his kisses become more passionate. Wes looks into her eyes.

"I'll go if you want me... Do you want me?"

"Yes..."

Leah places her hands on the sides of his face and pulls him to her. As they share a soulful kiss, Wes lays Leah back and rolls his body on top of hers.

~HURTING LOVE ONES~

Late that night, Mama Mae relaxes sitting on the couch in her sun room. Her legs are up and casually crossed on the sizeable ottoman in front of her. She's humming an old-time gospel hymn, resting her elbow on the arm of the couch. Mama Mae's doing her weekly routine of clipping coupons out of the past Sunday's Newspaper. Reggie walks through the kitchen door drying his hair with a towel and wearing a burgundy A-shirt, dark blue Adidas tracksuit pants with the jacket thrown over his shoulder.

"Grandma that shower felt good," Reggie said. "Thanks for letting me get cleaned up, and for the fresh clothes too."

"No problem darling." Mama Mae said. "A hot shower is good for relaxing your body and clearing the mind. It's good to see ya too, been a moment. I've been praying that you come by, been so concerned about ya."

Reggie looks around the room, he walks pass the curtains covering the sliding doors which lead out to the backyard. He puts the track suit jacket down on the ottoman as he takes a seat in the chair by the window.

"Yeah, it's been a moment," Reggie said. "What happen to the kitchen? Everything's all modern and updated."

"Oh, it's not called a kitchen no more," Mama Mae said.

"Now it's my sun room."

"Alright, a sun room. Aunt Shayna did this, didn't she?"

"Baby you know it." Mama Mae laughs a bit. "After your mom took me to Hawaii last year for my birthday. Well, Shayna decided she wanted to give me a present that would last. So, she and Cliff had my kitchen remodeled."

She notices Reggie constantly shaking his right leg.

"Now grandma," Reggie said. "Don't get me wrong, I like it. It's nice, the white and silver work but... I'm gonna miss all the wood and the flowery wallpaper. That was a true grandma's house kitchen."

"Yeah, I kinda miss it too." Mama Mae said. "Not too much though. Now, I can knit, read, and clip out these coupons for Sis and me. I can even lay down and take a nap, right here on this couch. Couldn't do any of that comfortably on those hard chairs."

"Okay, but..." Reggie said. "I can't smell your sweet potato corn bread anymore. Plus, we had some great times sitting around that big kitchen table. I learned to walk and run around that thing."

"I know," Mama Mae said. "Gigi and Gina did too."

"I remember I was ten," Reggie said. "Nobody was around and I got a hold of grandad's soldering iron. I burned my name into not one, but all four legs." Reggie laughs a little. "Ooh whee, my mom beat my behind so bad."

"I remember, you got the brilliant idea to run yourself into the hall bathroom. Lord have mercy, I felt for ya too. Leah walked up in there and locked the door behind her. The next thing we all heard was, "Mama please! Mama please!" Leah only gave you that spanking cause she was scared, you could of hurt yourself so bad."

"Well, it did the trick that's for sure. I never touched any of grandad's tools again."

"See, I tell ya spanking ain't always a bad thing."

Reggie turns a bit and looks over his shoulder.

"Now I like the island and the wooden barstools, those are cool, but I know you didn't get rid of grandad's freezer, that thing could hold close to five months worth of meat."

"Well, don't worry I didn't get rid of it. I had them put it down in the basement. When I need anything, I ask James to go get it for me."

"That's good, I wouldn't want you to hurt yourself going down those stairs. Where's James anyway? He didn't get home from work yet?"

"Oh, he's been home. I had a taste for a corn beef sandwich and you know there's only one spot to go to."

"You had him drive into the city to go to Katz?"

"Yes I did," Mama Mae said laughing a bit. "Yes I did."

"And he just got in from work," Reggie said. "Grandma that's bad."

"Child, he only got the chance to take off his suit jacket. Katz is so worth it though."

Reggie glanced at the small digital clock sitting on the end table near the couch.

"It's going on eleven-thirty are they even open?"

"They're open till after two in the morning, and James left before ten. He called a moment ago, he'll be here soon."

Reggie is sweating, he leans back in the chair for a moment. He tries to relax, but the continuous shaking of his leg shows the hot shower did nothing for him. Reggie being anxious and fidgety causes Mama Mae more concern.

"You alright over there?" Mama Mae said.

"Yeah yeah, I'm... I'm okay." Reggie said.

Reggie sits up and wipes his face with the towel. He leans back again but sits right back up. He casually looks around the room as he rocks back and forth. He spots Mama Mae's pocketbook, it's sitting on the floor, under the small end table beside the couch. Reggie looks over at his grandmother and watches as she cuts out coupons from the newspaper.

"You're getting coupons together huh?" Reggie said.

"You and Mother Livingston going shopping?"

"Yeah well," Mama Mae said laughing. "You know we can't resist a sale."

Mama Mae glances over at Reggie, who's nervously rocking back and forth, and pats the cushion next to her.

"Come and sit over here."

"I'm... I'm okay here Grandma."

"Reggie, I said come over here and sit next to me now."

There's silence as Reggie gets up, he takes the towel and puts it on the back of the chair. He takes a seat next to her. Mama Mae stops cutting her coupons, sits up, leans in toward Reggie, looks him over touching his face and arms, then leans back and goes back to cutting her coupons.

"Mm-hmm, you still taking them drugs. I know a spirit when I see it, you're not fooling anybody."

Reggie sighs, irritated by his grandmother's truthful statement.

"Come on grandma," Reggie stands up. "I was getting comfortable until you go poking and prodding me!"

Mama Mae gives Reggie a stern glare, he takes the hint and sits back down.

"I'm just saying."

"Fine." Mama Mae goes back to cutting out her shopping coupons. "Reggie I'm not putting any money in your hands, just for it to go up your nose or in your veins. My money is God sent and it won't be a part of that."

Reggie swiftly stands to his feet agitated by his grandmother's keen insight.

"See?! I come visit and get accused. Can't your grandson just come by to see ya, maybe get something to eat too?"

"Well, there's the fridge."

"Okay." Reggie sits back down.

"Alright." She starts to hum a gospel hymn.

Reggie sits for a few seconds, jumps up, goes to the refrigerator, opens it and his eyes search for something sweet to snack on.

"I stopped by mom's a few days ago," Reggie said. "Dad was there."

"I know," Mama Mae said. "Leah told me when she dropped off those clothes for ya. She also told me how you two got into it. Throwing each other around and everything."

Reggie closes the fridge and walks back over to his grandmother.

"I can't stand how mom's still letting him get over on her. He doesn't care about her!" He sits in the chair. "He didn't care nothin about me when I was out there with him."

"I know baby, he should have looked out for you."

"All he cares about is himself. You always looked out grandma."

"You're my only grandson, somebody had too."

"Remember that bully who tried to take my new toy in kindergarten? You gave him a good talking to. Man! You put the fear of God in him."

"My Lord, I remember that day." Mama Mae laughs.

"There was this other time, I wasn't fully saved yet and I remember this woman tried to call me a name in front of my little girls. Well, I grabbed that woman, and told her she better mind who she was talking to."

"Mom told me about that, said she never seen you like that and never wanted to again." They both laugh.

"Grandma, you're this family's guardian angel."

"Well, I did what I could. Listen, Reggie, I know you have hurts from your past and we can't change it, but Jesus can. He can heal all those pains and change your future. All you got to do is call on Him. There's salvation, and deliverance from those drugs in Jesus. I looked out for you when you were a little boy and Grandma is looking out for you now. Call on Jesus, baby."

"Grandma I know," Reggie said.

"Son let me tell ya," Mama Mae said. "When Dr. Wilson was at Full Gospel and spoke to the youth, she told them how she was a backslidden evangelist; How she got strung out on drugs and was out there for a while. She's had guns put to her head. Almost went to jail too! You see the devil planned to kill her out there, but God said- Not so. Then one day, when she got sick and tired, of being sick and tired of being on them drugs, that's when she truly gave her life to the Lord and look at her. It was J-E-S-U-S, Jesus who set her free. Dr. Wilson's been a pastor for years now. Her church started out as Humble Heart, now it's Kingdom Ambassadors Global Ministries and God's presence rests in that place. Plus she's one of the first black women to purchase a synagogue for her church. A synagogue Reggie, look at what God can do when you give him a chance."

"Grandma,"

"I've been to a few services there, and one of her church daughters testified about being bound by pornography and perversion. I remember that child made me laugh when she called herself trisexual. Said she called herself that, cause she was out there trying everything. Looking for love in all the wrong places. She talked on how she turned her back on God, one of the reasons being, she got tired of saved brothers being just like the unsaved ones. Anyway, when she left the church, she said she got herself a girlfriend, got into swinging and even became one of those *whip-women*. She was out there for close to eight years. I forget her name, but she said, it was nobody but Jesus that set her free, and said there's no distance or depth that God can't reach."

"Okay," Reggie said. "Her life isn't mine either, I... I should go, its late."

"Reggie, I shared all that cause you need to give God a chance son, what you don't have the strength to do, God can be your strength. What you can't fix, God can. If you'd only let him."

"I hear you grandma,"

"Yeah, but you're not listening" Mama Mae gets up. "Excuse me a moment, I need to get something out the living room."

"You relax," Reggie said. "Tell me, I'll go get it."

"Thanks but," Mama Mae said. "It's okay baby. I needed to get this body up for a bit anyway. I'll be right back."

"He'll Work It Out" Chapter 3. Taryn C. Atkins

Mama Mae walks through the kitchen door carrying the scissors in her hand. When Mama Mae leaves, Reggie goes right for her pocketbook on the floor. He quickly grabs it, zips it open and rummages through it looking for Mama Mae's wallet. Reggie finds and sorts through the money inside, taking out a fifty and twenty before stuffing the bills in his pocket.

"That's all I need," Reggie gets ready to put the bag down but stops. "Well... just a few more dollars."

As Reggie goes back in the pocketbook Mama Mae walks in.

"So how's that boy Mario doing?"

Mama Mae's eyes discover Reggie's hand in her bag. She rushes to him, moving between the ottoman and the couch.

"Give me my bag Reggie!"

Mama Mae grabs her pocketbook, trying to pull it away from Reggie but he keeps a tight grip on it.

"Grandma, I... I just need a few dollars! Please!"

"Reggie let go! Now!"

They both strenuously pull the pocketbook back and forth.

"Grandma you can spare a few dollars! Please, grandma! You won't miss it!"

"I said NO before! The answer is still NO! Now let go!"

Their tug a war becomes more hostile.

"Just a few dollars! You won't miss it! Give it to me! Please, I need it alright! Come on! I need it!!"

Mama Mae uses all her strength to pull the bag out of Reggie's grip.

"REGGIE-I SAID NO!!"

Mama Mae lets out a ghastly scream. Her body goes limp, having passed out she falls against Reggie. He holds her up as best he can, carefully guiding his grandmother down to the floor on her side. Reggie kneels beside her, he wipes his face and his eyes grow wide seeing his hands covered in blood. He sits paralyzed watching as she lays motionless. His hands tremble as he reaches out to her, he places his hand on her shoulder and delicately shakes her.

"Grandma... Grandma!"

There's no response from Mama Mae, she lays clutching her pocketbook against her. Moving the bag away, Reggie notices the scissors his grandmother used to clip coupons is deeply embedded in her stomach.

"Oh my God!!"

Reggie watches the lemon chiffon color of the area rug go dark from the blood flowing from her. He quickly stands and as he looks into his grandmother's face, his breathing becomes rapid, his heartbeat quickens and his mind races.

"What did I do!"

Reggie grabs the track suit jacket off the ottoman, rushes out the side door of the house and runs away. James is driving up the street, as he pulls his car into Mama Mae's driveway he sees a familiar frame running down the block. He gets out the car grabbing the plastic bag from the Katz Deli. Minutes later.

"Aunt Mae," James said walking through the kitchen door. "Was Reggie just--" He sees her laying on the floor by the couch, he throws the bag down and rushes toward her. "Aunt Mae!" Dropping to his knees. "Aunt Mae!! Can you hear me!!"

James places his hands on the damp rug, and discovers its soaked with her blood.

"Oh God!!"

He quickly wipes his hands on his shirt, turns to grab the house phone on the end table by the couch, and immediately dials 911.

"Yes Please! Send an ambulance right away! She's bleeding! Oh God... There's so much blood! I... I think she's been stabbed!! No... No, she's not moving! She's barely breathing! Please! Send an ambulance! We're at--"

~CHAPTER 4~

~Our Actions Have Consequences~

~HOSPITAL~

It's early in the morning, a little bit after two o'clock, doctors are being paged, stat calls occur and various color codes go forth from the hospital intercom system. Mama Mae's family wait in one of the hospital's surgical waiting rooms. Some family members sit while others stand and impatiently pace the floor. They're all trying to hold it together and wait to hear news on Mama Mae's condition. Family members are spread out around this spacious waiting room consisting of two large sections. Both have the same furniture but are opposite to each other.

This waiting room isn't hidden behind flat walls but a glass one, and running the length of the room is a glass window, where those who wait can view the outside hospital parking lot. The room has a purple and green decor; the right side is purple defining its association with wisdom and the left is green because of its emotional correspondence with safety and peace. When you walk through the waiting room entrance, you see the hospital information desk in the center but at this time nobodies on duty. Cliff stands in the hallway, a few feet from the waiting room entrance speaking with Lady Gorham and Elder Rayner.

"Pastor Gorham is out of town right now, but he's praying." Lady Gorham said. "He want's you to call him whenever you get home. No matter what time."

"I'll be sure to call," Cliff said.

"How long has she been in surgery?" Lady Gorham said.

"About an hour now," Cliff said.

"Any hospital staff speak to you." Elder Rayner said.

"Yeah, about 30 minutes ago a nurse came by," Cliff said. "Told us there were complications but it's going better."

"Well, what happen?" Lady Gorham said.

"Did she trip on something or fall?" Elder Rayner said.

"We're not sure what happened," Cliff said. "All we know, is James found her on the floor. She wasn't responding, he said she had lost a lot of blood, he rushed and called 911."

"Well, the doctors should be able to determine what happened." Elder Rayner said.

"If not. Mama Mae will sure tell us." Cliff said.

"Well, right now let's pray." Lady Gorham said.

Minister Thomas looked over and saw Lady Gorham and Elder Rayner, lay their hands on Cliff's shoulder, as they bowed their heads. Minister Thomas brought his attention back to the conversation he was engaged in with Dray and James. Unfortunately, it wasn't peace but anger that stirred. They stood in the purple section of the waiting room by the end of the lengthy lounge window. James didn't have a chance to change out of his clothes. Minister Thomas stared at James's shirt, he shook his head saddened by seeing it stained with Mama Mae's blood. James took a sip from the Dunkin Donuts cup in his hand. Dray turned toward the window and sat his energy drink can on the ledge.

"Wait," Minister Thomas said. "You sure it was Reggie?"

"I know Reggie when I see him," James said. "He did this!"

Leah paces the floor, when she hears James's voice raise, she stops and looks over at the three men for a moment. Minister Thomas sees Leah look at them.

"Lower your voice." Minister Thomas said. "No need to make Leah even more upset than she already is. Not until you're sure anyway."

Leah looks away and continues her pacing.

"Now, are you sure James?" Dray said.

"I saw him running from the house," James said.

"He's that desperate he'd hurt his grandmother?" Minister Thomas said.

"He's on that stuff," James said. "He'll do anything."

"Well, it's a shame that it's gotten to this point," Dray said. "At the same time, I'm not surprised either. I left him in my car for two minutes, and he jetted with my Mac."

James goes to the garbage by them and throws his coffee cup away. He shakes his head as he comes back over and looks at Dray.

"I'll find him," James said. "And on my life-" He huffs and motions to Dray. "He's gonna pay for this."

Now in the green section of the waiting room, over in the three seater that's facing the window was Mother Livingston. She slowly rocked back and forth as she watched Leah pace.

"Darling," Mother Livingston said. "Sit down for a while."

"I will in a minute," Leah said.

"You said that fifteen minutes ago." Mother Livingston said.

Leah's nerves are getting the best of her, she paces, going from one end of the three seater to the plant in the corner and back. Her eyes are a bit red from crying, she sniffles and wipes her nose with the tissue in her hand. Leah heads toward the plant again, she balls up the tissue and throws it in the garbage sitting beside it. As Leah continues pacing, she anxiously wrings her hands and stretches the band of her wrist watch every time she checks it.

"God, it feels like she's been in there forever," Leah said.

"Your mama's a strong woman." Mother Livingston said.

"She'll pull through this Leah."

"I just wish they would tell us something already."

"Well, no news is good news too."

"I pray that's true."

Leah finally sits down, she takes a deep breath and exhales with a huff. She reaches over to the end table next to her and picks up her open packet of cashews. Leah pours some in her hand and eats them. She shows Mother Livingston the packet.

"Mother you want some nuts?"

"Oh no baby, I'm alright. Thank you though."

Leah puts the cashews back on the table and picks up her bottle of, red plum nectar that's sitting next to them. She opens the bottle, pulls out the straw inside and takes a few sips. Leah sighs a little putting the bottle down on the table. She turns, looks over her shoulder at Wes, who's in the hallway on his cell phone. Leah watches him for a few seconds and shakes her head as she gets up. She goes over to the window and leans on the ledge, gazing.

> Under her breath, Leah said to herself, "Okay, that's three calls since we got here."

Mother Livingston watches Leah for a moment, she closes her eyes and continues to rock back and forth.

> *Lord be that doctor in the sick room now, bring Mae on through this like I know you can. In Jesus name. Amen.*
> Mother Livingston thought.

Outside the waiting room in the hallway deceitfulness rises. Wes leans against the wall, he has his cell to his ear and dialogues with the caller. Unlike the others who have on casual stuff or lounge wear, he has on a fedora, a muscle shirt with dress slacks and designer shoes. He watches as Cliff walks down the hall toward the elevators with Lady Gorham and Elder Rayner.

"No news yet," Wes said. "Basically, we're waiting now."

Wes looks through the waiting room window, Leah is standing up and looking at him. Wes signals to Leah to give him ten minutes.

> "Listen," Wes said. "I'm not staying in some hospital all night. I'll handle this and call you once I'm outta of here.

Shayna and Elder Mays casually walk up the hallway toward the waiting room. They both carry a Starbucks cup in their hand.

> "Thank you for running me over to Starbucks," Shayna said. "I'll get through this a little easier."

"No problem." Elder Mays said.

"We could have taken my car you know," Shayna said.

> "It's okay," Elder Mays said. "It's best you don't drive. Especially with all this on your mind."

As they approach, Shayna takes a sip of her coffee and sees Wes go in the waiting room. They stop a few feet from the entrance.

"I overheard James say, he thinks Reggie did this."

"My Lord, really."

"I don't think Leah even know's that."

> "Well right now leave it alone. Let your mother get out of surgery first."

"Yes of course."

"He'll Work It Out" Chapter 4. Taryn C. Atkins

Minister Thomas and Mother Livingston come out the waiting room and come over to Elder Mays and Shayna.

"We're gonna get ready to go Deaconess Greye." Elder Mays said.

"Okay," Shayna said.

"Please keep us posted about Mother Babcock and we will be praying." Elder Mays said. She hands her car keys to Minister Thomas. "I got Mother, please bring the car around. I'm in the same spot."

"Alright Elder." Minister Thomas said. He looks at Shayna. "If you and Cliff need anything, don't hesitate to call."

"Okay, thank you," Shayna said.

"No problem." Minister Thomas said.

Minister Thomas heads down the hall to the hospital elevators.

"As soon as Mother Babcock"s out of surgery please let us know okay." Mother Livingston said.

"I'll have Regina call you," Shayna said. Thanks for dropping by."

"No problem, please keep us posted." Elder Mays said.

"I will. Here let me walk you to the elevators." Shayna said.

Shayna walks down the hall with Elder Mays and Mother Livingston.

About thirty minutes have passed. Cliff and Shayna sit in the cozy two seater sofa by the door in the green section. His arm is around Shayna, her head is resting on his shoulder and her eyes are closed as she tries to catch a quick nap. Cliff fidgets in his seat still trying not disturb Shayna. Cliff is looking at the flat screen TV that's hanging in the corner. He's not focused on the TV or the episode of Law & Order SVU playing on it. He looks at his watch, takes a deep breath and as he rest his elbow he lets it out. Cliff looks at the TV again.

Cliff said to himself, "It's going on three o'clock, she's been in surgery a while. Hope we hear something soon."

"He'll Work It Out" Chapter 4. Taryn C. Atkins

Leah comes over and takes a seat in the three seaters near Cliff and Shayna. She glances at the TV and looks over at Cliff.

> "My nerves have had it," Leah said. "I'm about to get me a drink... Sorry about that, no offense."
>
> "None taken." Cliff said. "I know it's hard for all of us."

Cliff does his best to look about the room without disturbing Shayna.

> "I see Wes," Cliff said. He looks over at Leah. "Is everybody else over in the other section?"

Leah stands up and looks over in the purple section.

> "James and Dray over there." Leah said. "Watching some movie." She sits down. "Nola and Regina went to get some food for everybody. They left before Lady Gorham did... They should be back soon."

Leah looks over at Wes, he sits in a seat by the window, he looks over at Leah, who's glares hard at him, he gets up, puts his cell phone to his chest and takes a few steps toward her.

> "I'll be finished with this call in a second, Okay Lee?" Wes said.

Wes turns around, puts his cell back to his ear and walks back over to the window.

> "Whatever," Leah said. She looks at Cliff. "I'm going back over to the window." She gets up and heads over. "Try to take me a nap too."
>
> "Okay," Cliff said. He softly rests his head on Shayna's.

Leah takes a seat on the three seater facing the window. Wes is in the corner leaning on the window ledge. He stays facing the window as he speaks under his breath to the caller.

> "Look, Merlo, I'll be outta here in a few. I'll call you back once I leave."

Wes ends his call and takes his seat next to Leah. Wes pats Leah on her leg and looks over his shoulder at the flat screen.

> "Let's sit on the other side. So I can watch TV." Wes said.

He sits at the end, Leah walks around and sits in the middle seat. Wes picks up her packet of cashews off the table by him, pours some into his hands and eats a few. Wes picks up her bottle of nectar and takes a swig. He puts the bottle back down on the table.

"SVU, I love this show," Wes said." I saw this one, it's where DA Alex Cabot comes back from witness protection."

Wes puts his arm around Leah's shoulder, she smiles a bit as she leans back against him, Wes leans over and gives her a peck on the cheek.

"How you doing?" He said

"My nerves are all shook up." Leah said. "I'll be glad when we hear something."

"Yeah, me too."

Wes watches the TV and leans into Leah's ear.

"I can relax those nerves," Wes whispers. "That's if you don't mind being ghost for about 20 minutes."

Leah quickly turns to him, she smiles and shakes her head.

Leah speaks softly replying, "It's a shame but I know you're too serious right now."

"What... I'm trying to help."

"You're a trip."

Leah turns away from him and gives her attention to the TV. Wes leans into her and whispers in her ear.

"There's a handicap bathroom down the hall."

Leah hits him on the leg, they both laugh and play around with each other a bit. Cliff slowly takes his arm from around Shayna, he stands up and gives his body a good stretch. He looks at Shayna and is relieved that he didn't wake her. Cliff starts to make his way over toward James and Dray. He looks at his watch, then over at Wes and Leah. Wes is massaging Leah's shoulders.

"Y'all alright over there?" Cliff said.

"I'm trying to help this one relax," Wes said.

"We're good." Leah laughs replying. "I still can't believe this though."

"Me either." Cliff said. "Well, the best thing we can all do is pray. Prayer can do wonders."

"You're right," Leah said. "That's the best way we can help Mama right now."

"Right right, I hear ya," Wes said. "I'm all for putting positive energy out there."

"He'll Work It Out" Chapter 4. Taryn C. Atkins

Wes's cell rings again. Cliff and Leah look at Wes as he looks at his phone to see who's calling. He gets up and answers it.

"Hold on," Wes said. He looks at Leah "I've gotta take this Lee. It's business."

Leah motions to Wes saying, "Of course you do."

Wes answers the call, Leah watches him walk away again and return to his same spot by the window ledge. She looks at Cliff and shakes her head.

"Well guess I'll try to take that nap again," Leah said.

Leah tries to get comfortable in her seat. Cliff's cell phone vibrates in his pocket. He takes it out and checks it. It's a text from Gigi saying, "Will be there soon." Cliff sighs a bit realizing he must now also prepare himself for Gigi's arrival. Cliff looks over at James and Dray as they talk and he can see James looks on edge about something. He walks over to them in the purple section.

Cliff said, "Hey, y'all doing alright?"

"Not at all," Dray said, "James saw Reggie run away from Mama Mae's right before he found her."

"For Reggie to do this," Cliff said. "He's worse than we thought."

"He's not getting away with it either." James said.

"Listen, I need some air." He abruptly walks away.

They watch James rush out the waiting room.

"Man is on a mission Cliff," Dray said.

"Well let him get some air," Cliff said. "For now, we don't mention this to Leah."

"I know, believe me." Dray said.

Dray stretches out and continues to watch TV. Cliff returns to his sit. He eases his arm around Shayna all nice and cozy laying on his shoulder. Leah gets up from the three seater, she looks over at Wes, who's still on the phone and walks to the small sofa in the purple section. She sits down, puts her legs up and lays her head on the arm of the small sofa. Leah moves a little trying to get comfortable and relaxes. James returns and plops down near Dray.

"I thought you were going to get some air," Dray said.

"I don't want to miss the doctors updating us," James

said.

"We should hear something soon." Dray said.

Another fifteen or so minutes have passed. Dray gets up to stretch a bit and sees Nola and Regina walk in, finally returning from their trip to find nourishment.

"Hey everybody," Nola said. "We drove to see what's around. Y'all know at this time but so much is open. So..."

They walk over to the round table in the purple section of the waiting room.

"We figured," Regina said. "Get something none of us have had for a long time. So..."

Nola places three bags of White Castle on the table. Regina sets out paper plates on the table and next to it she sits two, two-liter bottles of Sprite. Next to the soda she puts a package of plastic red Solo cups. Dray and James walk over to the table.

"We brought a decent variety," Nola said. "We got cheeseburgers, fries, onion rings, fried clams."

"We figure," Regina said. "There should be something here for everybody.

Regina and Nola start to take the food out the bags, placing it nicely on the table for all. As well as napkins and condiments. James picks up a plate and goes for it. Regina gets a plate and sets herself up. Nola does too. All the voices wake Leah up.

"Ooh, yummy," Dray said sarcastically. As he looks over everything. "All I can say is... this is not going to be pretty. The windows don't open either."

"You're hilarious," Regina said.

"I'm serious," Dray responds. "White Castle, this early in the morning, are you crazy! Some of us aren't twenty-five anymore." He looks over at James. "How far is the bathroom anyway?"

"A few feet away," James said.

"Okay okay, It's workable," Dray said. "We must take precautions."

Leah sits up on the little sofa and watches them over at the table. She looks over her shoulder and sees Wes still on the phone. She looks back over at the table where they are.

"Oh please! You and Paris ate two bags of White Castle's last month," Nola said. "While both of you sat in your man cave and played Playstation."

"Well, we were in a battle playing NFL Blitz." Dray said.

Nola looks at Dray and sucks her teeth.

"Whatever," Nola said. "It took three bottles of Febreze to get that room smelling human again."

Regina looks at Dray saying, "Eww, that's gross."

'Well," Dray said. He grabs a cheeseburger, puts the whole thing in his mouth and chews. "Thank God, we at a hospital."

Nola, Dray, Regina and James take their plates over to the round table in the green section. Leah gets up and heads over to the table to help herself to some food. As she makes a plate, they each take a seat at the table in the green section and start to eat. Nola looks over at Shayna and Cliff, who's asleep and look all cozy together. She points over to them.

"That looks like old times," Nola said. "I haven't seen them like that since--"

"Since dinosaurs roamed the earth." Dray said,

Regina slaps Dray's arm saying, "That's not nice."

Leah comes over to them with her plate and cup in hand.

"That's funny Dray and true," Leah said.

"I tell ya," Cliff said. He looks over at the table. "Family will talk about ya, with you right in the room too."

"Yep, they do it. I know I do." Leah said.

"Me too," Nola said.

They all laugh a little but the tension returns as Kisha dressed rather corporate chic, walks into the waiting room. As she walks over to them, all eyes are on her. Wes although he's still talking on his cell, has turned around to hear what Kisha has to say. All pay close attention to Kisha, accept Shayna, who's still asleep.

"Hey everybody! Sorry, it took so long." Kisha said. "It's been a busy night in admitting; I was able to do some checking. Mama Mae's finally out of surgery."

All listening release a big sigh of relief.

"I know, thank God. The surgeon was Dr. Sara Dacosta.

Prayerfully, everything went well. The doctor should be out soon to speak to the family."

"Thank you so much Kisha," Leah said.

"Yeah, thanks for the update," Cliff said.

"No problem," Kisha said. "I'm glad I could find out something for you." She goes to leave. "I've gotta get back."

"Kisha wait a sec," Leah said. She approaches Kisha. "If you hear from Reggie please let him know what's happened. Tell him to call me, please."

Kisha said, "Of course, I've gotta get back to work though but I'll try to come back as soon as I can."

"Alright, thanks again," Leah said.

Kisha leaves and after a couple of minutes, Shayna starts to wake up. She lifts her head and looks at Cliff.

"Any word yet?" Shayna said.

"Mama Mae's out of surgery." Cliff said.

"Oh, that's good."

"Go back to sleep, I'll wake you when the doctor comes."

Shayna lays her head back on Cliff's shoulder.

"Thanks baby,"

Shayna drifts back to sleep. Leah eyes Wes, who's still talking on his cell phone.

That's it! I'm tired of this. Leah thought as she walked toward him. "What's so important this early in the morning?"

"I got to go," Wes said to the caller. He turns to Leah. "There's trouble with a client." He goes to hug Leah. "How you holding up Lee?"

Leah pushes Wes back but moves close to him.

"There's trouble here too," Leah said. "And I need you right now. Kisha told us Mama's out of surgery."

"Well, that's good. I'm here Lee; I still have to handle business. Come on, let's sit down. The doctor should be out soon."

Cliff carefully pulls his arm from around Shayna and gets up to grab a bite to eat. Wes and Leah sit down, as he puts his arm

"He'll Work It Out" Chapter 4. Taryn C. Atkins

around her; Leah snuggles up close to him. Wes puts his other arm around her and for a moment, things are just right. Leah closes her eyes and when she finally allows her body to relax, Wes' cell phone rings again. He swiftly answers the call.

"Hello," Wes said to the caller. "Yeah... I told you man, sixty/forty. That's what the contract said." He puts his hands over the cell and turns to Leah. "I've got to take this."

Wes gets up and returns to his spot at the waiting room window. Wes's loud talking has stirred Shayna. She stretches as she surveys the room for Cliff; She sees Cliff at the table in the purple section.

"Cliff," Shayna said.

"Yeah." Cliff said. As he turns toward her.

"Baby pour me a little soda, please. My mouth's so dry."

"Oh sure."

Cliff promptly grabs a Solo cup, pours some Sprite into it and brings it over to Shayna.

"Here you go sweetheart."

"Thank you baby." She takes a few sips and peers up at Cliff. "Doctor come by yet?"

"Not yet, but we know Mama Mae is out of surgery."

Shayna checks her watch and immediately becomes agitated.

"We should've heard something," Shayna said.

She stands sucking her teeth as she puts her cup down.

"Must I handle everything?" Shayna brushes off her clothes and gazes at Nola. "Nola come with me, please."

"Sure," Nola said. She comes over to Shayna. "What's up?"

"Maybe the ER can tell us something," Shayna said

Shayna leers at Cliff, as she and Nola walk out the waiting room. Cliff walks over to the entrance, he slowly shakes his head and watches them walk down the hallway. Dray leans over to Regina.

"She was nice for exactly two point nine seconds." Dray said. "That's got to be a world's record for the quickest attitude change."

"Haha, you so funny," Regina said.

"Funny but true once again," James said.

"He'll Work It Out" Chapter 4. Taryn C. Atkins

Wes has his back turned to everybody. He's still in the corner by the waiting room window talking on his cell phone.

Wes whispers, "I'll be out of here in five minutes. Bye."

Wes leans on the window ledge, Leah moves toward him and from the corner of his eye he sees her approaching. He abruptly straightens up.

"What! Come on man..." Wes said. "I'll say it again. A full band is needed for the gig! We paid for that. Yeah! Fine! You'll see me... Soon!" He ends the call. "These stupid promoters."

Leah's touches his arm and turns him toward her.

"What's going on?" Leah said.

"Babe, there's a big situation at this gig. Only the manager can handle it in person."

She moves close to him. "I really need you here."

"Lee, at least, we know your mom came through the surgery. I wish I could stay, but it's my business."

The family has moved from the table and sit around in the green section. They try to watch the TV but covertly, each of them watches Wes and Leah. Regina leans over to her father.

"I bet he's gonna leave," Regina said.

"Well, that's Leah's relationship," Cliff said. "Only she can dictate how's she's treated."

"I know," Regina said, crossing her legs. "Doesn't mean I have to like it."

"You're not the only one that doesn't." Cliff said.

Regina and Cliff try to watch TV. Dray and James each sit in one of the three seaters. Both have pulled a small table over and have their legs stretched out on it. Back over by the waiting room window.

"When will you be back?" Leah said.

"As soon as I can Lee. I promise." Wes said. He takes her in his arms and hugs her tightly. "I'll see you later."

"Please be home tonight."

"You got it." Wes gives Leah a sensual kiss. "Later sexy."

"Bye."

"I'll see you at your place." Wes ready to make a break

for it gives a loose wave to the family. *I'm out.* He thought.

"Alright family, I've gotta go. Y'all take it easy."

Wes bolts before even hearing the good-byes of the family. They tolerate Wes for Leah's sake. Leah goes to the three seater where James is knocked out and takes a seat. As she crosses her legs, she looks at Cliff and Regina sitting on the small sofa.

"Hey," Leah said."

Regina and Cliff glance at Leah.

"I'm over here getting some rest," Leah said. "Wake me when the doctor comes."

"Okay." Cliff said.

Just as Leah is about to relax, Gigi, Lexi and Bobbie rush into the waiting room. They're all in dressy casual clothing. Gigi heads straight to her father as her friends follow her.

"Dad, what happened?!" Gigi said. "I was out when I got your message. How's Grandma?"

Cliff stands and they hug. "Honey calm down." He said.

"Well, what happened?" Gigi said.

Regina stands, she and Gigi embrace, as Regina waves at her friends.

"Hey Lexi, Bobbie," Regina said.

"Hey, Gina," Lexi said.

"Hi," Bobbie said.

"Now please, tell me what happened," Gigi said.

"Well, apparently scissors were in her hand," Regina said. "They think she tripped somehow and landed on them.

"Oh my God!" Gigi said. She starts to well up. "Is she still in surgery?!"

"Have you heard anything Mr. Greye?" Lexi said.

"We know she's out of surgery." Cliff said. "The doctor should be out soon. Listen, Gigi, it's late, you and your friends should go on home and get some rest. We're about done here. I'll keep you posted."

"Dad I'm not leaving, my place is here." Gigi said.

"Mr. Greye," Bobbie said. "We came along cause we didn't want Gigi to be alone."

"Well thanks," Cliff said. Ladies, y'all have a seat. We're just waiting for the doctor to come out."

"There's food and something to drink on the table over there. It might be cold though," Regina said.

Gigi and her friends walk over to the purple section.

"Cool, I can go for White Castles," Bobbie said. She looks back at Regina. "Thanks Gina."

"No problem," Regina said.

Gigi waves to Leah and James, seeing Dray's asleep, she heads over to the purple section. Lexi and Bobbie help themselves to something to eat. Gigi takes the middle seat in the three seater by the glass wall and Regina sits down next to her. Regina takes her sisters hand in her's, Gigi looks at Lexi and Bobbie.

"Lexi," Gigi said.

Lexi peeks over at Gigi.

"Pour me some soda please," Gigi asks.

"I got ya," Lexi said.

"Grandma will be okay," Regina said. "Watch and see."

"I don't think I could handle if grandma..." Gigi said. "If she... oh my God."

"That's not the case," Gina said. "God's got her."

Lexi pours Gigi her cup of soda, brings it to her and returns to the table to finish her plate. Bobbie and Lexi come over to Gigi, both carrying a plate and cup in hand. Lexi sits on the other side of Gigi on the three seater. Bobbie puts her food down on the small table by Lexi, she pulls the table out, then goes to the hospital information desk and takes the chair from behind it. She rolls the chair back over to her friends and sits it behind the small table. Bobbie gets ready to dig into her food and sees Lexi, Gigi and Regina are staring at her.

"What?" Bobbie said.

"All these seats and you go get that one." Lexi said

"I want to sit near y'all not across the room." Bobbie said.

"Whatever." Lexi said shaking her head.

"This food is on time though," Bobbie said. "I was starving."

Bobbie and Lexi dig into their plates. Gigi nurses on her soda while they all wait for the doctor. Lexi finishes off a cheeseburger and takes a few swallows of soda. She looks over in the green section at Gigi's family and looks at Regina.

"So, where's your mom?" Lexi said.

"Oh, I'm sure she's here," Gigi said.

"Mom and Aunt Nola went to the ER," Regina said. "They went to find out some news on grandma."

"She'll return soon enough though," Gigi said.

"Well, relax," Lexi said. "After all, it's your Grandmother."

"True, but it's not that easy," Gigi said. "Especially with my mother."

A few minutes later Shayna and Nola return, they walk up the hallway and when they reach the glass window of the waiting room. Shayna stops dead in her tracks, seeing Gigi and her friends seated inside.

"Lord have mercy," Shayna said. She locks eyes on Gigi.

"Haven't I got enough to deal with."

Nola scopes Gigi with her friends. She turns to Shayna.

"Shayna, leave Gigi alone," Nola said. "Her grandmother was just rushed to the hospital."

"She didn't have to come here," Shayna said. "And with those friends too."

"Gigi has a right to be here," Nola said. "Let the girl be."

"Look, it's bad enough she's in that life in the first place," Shayna said. "I refuse to have it in my face too.

Cliff happens to notice Shayna through the waiting room window, seeing her expression he knows she has spotted Gigi and her friends. Shayna heads toward the waiting room entrance, as Cliff rushes over to the door; He gets there before Shayna and tries to take control of the situation unfolding.

"I called her Shayna," Cliff said.

"Of course you did," Shayna said.

"All of us are here, Gigi should be too."

"Well, you made a big mistake didn't you?"

"He'll Work It Out" Chapter 4. Taryn C. Atkins

Shayna rushes pass Cliff and makes a beeline toward Gigi. Cliff and Nola follow her. Gigi studies her nails and just as she lifts her head she sees her mother coming.

"Ma, please. I didn't come to argue," Gigi said. "I'm not leaving either, that's my grandmother in there."

"You could be considerate…" Shayna said, as she glares over at Lexi and Bobbie, then focuses on Gigi. "And flaunt your ways somewhere else."

"Excuse me," Lexi said standing up. "What'd you say?!"

"You heard me," Shayna said.

Lexi moves toward Shayna.

Gigi grabs Lexi's hand pulling her back. "No, Lexi."

"Lex," Bobbie said standing up. "Come on now, Easy."

Shayna points to the waiting room entrance.

"Gigi, you and your friends need to go,"

"Ma, please," Regina said. "Don't do this."

"You know what," Lexi said snatching her hand from Gigi. "Why don't you make us."

Shayna huffs, "Not a problem."

Shayna and Lexi move toward each other, Cliff and Nola quickly intervene, Gigi and Regina get up in unison, Bobbie tries to hold Lexi back and even Leah and James rush over.

"Shayna," Nola said putting herself between them. "Stop."

"Lexi, hold on," Bobbie said.

"Okay now, everybody calm down," Cliff said.

"Ma, don't," Gigi said. She faces Lexi. "Lexi stop."

"Ma, please." Regina said going to her. "Calm down."

"Are you kidding me," Leah said.

"Here we go," James said.

Everyone accept Dray, who's knocked out from the *itis* in the green section is totally unaware of anything going on. While everyone is involved in stopping the altercation. It's at this heated moment when a female doctor wearing surgical scrubs stands at the entrance and sees what's going on.

"Hello all," The doctor said. "Hello."

"He'll Work It Out" Chapter 4. Taryn C. Atkins

No one hears her at first, all are involved the drama and as the doctor scans the situation Dray snores loudly.

"Excuse Me!!" The doctor said.

Hearing an unfamiliar voice, all eyes turn toward the doctor.

"Is there a problem here!?" The doctor said.

"No, no problem doctor." Cliff said as he came over to her. "Just concerned family, that's all."

"This is a hospital though!" The doctor said.

"Everyone's just a bit on edge," Cliff said. "We're all waiting to hear news about our love one."

"Are you the family of Mrs. Mae Babcock?" The doctor said.

"Yes doctor," Shayna said. She comes over to the physician. "Yes, we're her family. She's..." Shayna gestures to herself and Leah. "She's our mother... we're all her family though."

All confusion ceases and eyes are on the doctor.

"Okay, well I'm Dr. Dacosta." She said. She motions over to the green side of the waiting room. "Let's go over here and I'll fill you in on everything concerning Mrs. Babcock."

Lexi and Bobbie sit back down in the purple section, as everybody else goes over to the green section. Some family members sit while others stand but all keep their eyes locked on the doctor. The doctor heads to the TV, then faces the family. Nola takes a seat next to Dray, shaking him awake.

"I handled your mother's surgery; I do apologize for it taking so long for me to come down. I just wanted to make sure Mrs. Babcock was settled in ICU. You're already aware she came in with scissors lodged in her stomach. She lost a lot of blood, so we had to give her blood when she got here. Even though the surgery went well, the fluid released from her stomach caused an infection. The next 8-12 hours are critical. So we are monitoring her closely."

"Can we see her?" Leah asks.

"As I said, she's in the ICU recovering, and needs her

sleep. I'll allow her two daughters to go in for a brief moment. I prefer everyone else to wait until tomorrow night to see her. Right now she needs to rest. The hard part's over, now we let these hours pass."

"Will she be okay?" Shayna said.

"Your mother's doing well." Dr. Dacosta said. "I advise all of you, go home and get rest. Here's my card if you need to reach me."

The doctor hands out her business cards to the family.

"Doctor, how long will she be here?" Gigi said.

"Possibly two weeks, maybe longer." Dr. Dacosta said. "We want to make sure the infection is gone, her pressure is good, and there's no internal bleeding. So we'll continue to monitor her. You all have my card, feel free to contact me. Get home safe."

The doctor promptly leaves the waiting room. The family exhales after getting the update on Mama Mae. Family members go back to their seats. Cliff faces the family.

"Praise God, family," Cliff said. "God brought Mama Mae this far and he'll bring her home to us too. Let's all go get some rest. Look let's all visit Mama Mae in shifts, we don't want her to over-exert herself. Okay?"

Family members agree. Shayna turns to the family.

"Mama's going to be weak," Shayna said. She looks at Gigi. "So everybody doesn't necessarily need to visit." She looks at the family. So please be considerate. One and all."

Gigi shakes her head as she gets her bag.

"Let's go." Gigi said to her friends.

Leah gets her pocketbook, says her goodbyes to the family, giving Gigi and Regina a quick hug. She walks over to Shayna.

"I'll meet you at the ICU," Leah said.

"Okay, I'll be right there," Shayna said.

Leah leaves out. Shayna goes to her seat and Cliff follows her.

"You didn't need to say that," Cliff said.

"Yes I did," Shayna said.

"I'll meet you in the lobby." Cliff turns to Regina. "Are you taking James?"

"Yes," Regina said. She looks at Cliff. "And I'm staying over to help him clean up.

"Okay," Cliff said. He goes to Gigi and kisses her on the cheek. "Love ya, get home safe and call me."

Gigi nods her head okay. Shayna overhears Cliff and Gigi as she gets her things together, she shakes her head and huffs. Nola comes over to talk to Shayna for a moment. Cliff leaves out. Nola, Shayna and Dray exchange hugs.

"Call me," Nola said. "Get some sleep."

"I will." Shayna said.

"Alright," Dray said, waving to the family. "Take it easy, get home safe everyone."

"We'll see y'all soon." Nola said.

Nola and Dray, walk out. Gigi's friends wait in the hall for her. James and Regina clean up the leftover food. Before Gigi leaves she approaches her mother.

"Tell me Mom," Gigi said. "Was all that code, for don't come here Gigi?"

Gigi huffs, shaking her head as she looks at her mother. Shayna doesn't respond, just continues to get her things together. Gigi looks at James and Regina.

"I'll see ya James," Gigi said. "Gina call me."

"Alright Gigi, be safe," James said.

"I'll call you after twelve," Gina said. "Love ya."

"Okay, love you too," Gigi said.

Gigi and her friends depart, James and Regina walk to the waiting room entrance. Shayna puts her bag on her shoulder.

"James, I'll meet you at the car," Regina said. "I want to talk to my mom."

"Alright," James said.

As James leaves, Shayna approaches Regina with open arms.

"How you feeling?" Regina said as they hug one another.

"Better, knowing Mama got through the surgery," Shayna said, as they release each other. "She's strong, she'll pull through. I just pray I can."

"We'll get through this, so will Grandma. God's with her and all of us are too."
"I know baby."
"I mean all of us Mom. You can't expect Gigi not visit grandma. Just like her coming here tonight. How could you do that to her."
"Gina, Gisele knows how I feel about her in that life. I don't want to see it or have anything to do with it."
"Mom, we're her family, and Christians. What happened here, wasn't *Christ-like* that's for sure.
"Look, I've got to get to ICU."
Shayna walks into the hall followed by Regina.
"I know but ma--"
Shayna turns to Regina.
"We'll talk later, now drive safe and I'll see you tomorrow."
Shayna heads to ICU and Regina walks to the elevators.

~I KNOW YOU~

Summer hours are in effect, although its evening of the same day it feels like late afternoon. Reggie stands in a converted four hundred square foot garage at a home out in Manhasset Hills, NY. It's been transformed into a modern, artful and cozy studio apartment. There's not many windows in this space, just a burst of color in the accessories and decor, a few splashes and dashes of pattern around but its the white walls and cabinets that assist in visually enlarging the area and brightens up the place.

Reggie sits in one of the two modern dining chairs, at the seventies classic parson's table in the kitchen area. He drops the fork onto an empty plate after finishing off a man size bite to eat and pushes the plate away. He pulls a small plate over with a sizable slice of sweet potato pie. Reggie hears a slight whimper coming from across the room. He looks over and sees on the wicker chair by the bed, stands an all white toy Poodle. The poodle looks at Reggie, cocks his head to the side and whimpers again. Reggie breaks off a piece of the crust and throws it over to the dog. The dog leaps into the air, catches the piece of crust and easily lands back on the wicker chair. The dog gobbles it down and lays on the chair. Reggie smiles seeing the dogs talents.

Reggie leans back in the chair and stretches. He looks outside through the sliding doors, Kisha's on the other side of the pool talking to her parents. She's wearing a light blue tracksuit as if she's going to workout. While her parents are dressed for a formal black tie affair. Eating his pie, Reggie studies their interaction.

"He can not stay here," Mr. Carrington said. "This is my home and I forbid it."

"Dad, no disrespect," Kisha points to the studio. "I paid for that garage to be converted." She gestures to herself. "I don't live here free either; I pay rent, utilities, and everything else that's in there. I brought my own car, pay my car note and my insurance."

"Kisha he's nothing but a junkie!" Mr. Carrington said. "I don't understand why you don't see that!"

"I do see that, but I see my friend too," Kisha said. "I'm twenty-seven, and it's been years since I've been that girl in college. Why don't you see that!"

"Exactly honey." Mrs. Carrington said. "All we're saying is you've worked so hard to get where you're at, you're finally back on your feet and doing so well. Sweetheart, you don't need anything or anyone dragging you down."

"Mom, I'm Reggie's best friend, and he's a mess right now. Whether he knows it or not. He needs me to be his friend, now, more than ever."

Mr. Carrington points at Kisha and moves toward her.

"Kisha, I want him gone before we get back tonight." Walking away he gives her a stern look. "I'm serious Kisha."

"Dad!" Kisha said.

Kisha looks at her mother and motions toward her father. They both look at him as he heads to the side of the house.

"Moses!" Mrs. Carrington said. "Give the girl a chance to explain the situation."

"He'll Work It Out" Chapter 4. Taryn C. Atkins

As Moses Carrington places his hand on the door knob of their house's side door, he looks back at his wife before going in.

"I've heard enough. Pamela-I want him gone!" Moses Carrington said. "If she doesn't like it she can go with him! I'll be in the car, Pamela, you hurry up, it's a two-hour drive and you know how New York traffic is."

Pamela Carrington places her hands on her hips as she angrily stares at her husband.

"Moses, don't talk to me like that," Pamela Carrington said. "And I'll be right there."

He goes into the house. Kisha looks up into the sky and crosses her arms. Her mother turns to her.

"Baby you can't blame your father." Pamela Carrington said. She walks away looking back at Kisha. "I'll deal with him though." She smiles. "Talk to you later."

Kisha looks at her mother.

"Thanks mom," Kisha said. "You look beautiful."

"Thank you baby." Pamela Carrington said.

Pamela Carrington sends a kiss to her daughter and heads into her house. Kisha walks over to her studio. Reggie finishes the pie, picks up the glass of milk next to it and drinks it down. Kisha pulls open the sliding door, comes in and looks over at her dog.

"Come on Toy-Toy, go play," Kisha said.

Reggie puts the empty glass down on the table. He sees the toy poodle sprint outside. Kisha closes the sliding door behind Toy-Toy.

"Toy-Toy... Cute." Reggie said.

"It fits him," Kisha said. "That's my little buddy."

"You let him go outside alone," Reggie said.

"Please," Kisha said. "I got him when he was a puppy and we've been here for three years. Toy-Toy knows this neighborhood by heart. He couldn't get lost if he tried." She grabs the empty plates off the table. "All finish I see... so you want anymore lasagna or pie?"

"I'm good right now," Reggie said. "Thanks a lot, that hit the spot."

"No problem," Kisha said.

She puts the plates in the sink.

"He'll Work It Out" Chapter 4. Taryn C. Atkins

"You sure?" Reggie asks. "That looked like an intense conversation."

"You know how that is," Kisha said. "Parents will be parents."

Kisha finishes clearing the dirty dishes, She goes to one of the kitchen cabinets and gets a glass out.

"Not that I was being nosey..." Reggie said. He laughs.

"Well yeah, I guess I was being nosey. I couldn't hear anything that y'all said; I didn't even hear outside noises until you opened the sliding door."

Kisha goes to the refrigerator and helps herself to a glass of lemonade.

"Oh," Kisha laughs. "When I had this garage converted; I made it sound proof. This way I can blast my music and not disturb a soul."

"Cool," Reggie said. "You think I get another slice of pie and some milk."

"No problem," Kisha said.

Kisha gives Reggie another pie slice and plants a second glass of milk beside it.

"Thanks, this is a sweet spot Kisha." He looks around. "You're lucky."

"Reggie believe me, I give God all the glory. So, how long were you waiting for me at the railroad?"

"A while, but I figured I'd see you sooner or later."

"You're lucky I had to pick up something. Since I got my car, I don't take the railroad much anymore.

As they sit across from each other an awkward silence fills the room. Kisha watches Toy-Toy play outside as she nurses her lemonade. Reggie works on his second helping. He looks up at Kisha and tries his best to hide his guilt.

"So... umm, how's my grandmother doing? Do they know what happened?

Kisha puts her glass down on the table.

"Apparently Mama Mae had scissors in her hand, she must have tripped and landed on them."

"She get through the surgery okay?"

"He'll Work It Out" Chapter 4. Taryn C. Atkins

"The surgery went well but she'll be in the hospital for a moment."

"She'll get better, I know she will." *She's got too.* He thought.

As Reggie finishes off the rest of his pie. Kisha sips her lemonade, clearly knowing what has gotten a hold of him, and its grip has him bound tightly. She puts the glass down and glances outside. Kisha wants to help her best friend, but will he be honest with her. Kisha and Reggie's eyes meet with intent, she takes a deep breath and as she exhales.

Okay, here we go. She thought.

"So Reggie tell me," Kisha said. "How long you been using?"

"What are you talking about?!" Reggie said.

"You know exactly what I'm talking about."

"Hold on Kisha, thanks for feeding a brother. That doesn't invite you into my business."

"Really?"

He stands up, "Yes, really!" He paces around the place. "Get out of here with that stuff!"

She turns her chair toward him. "Still got that nobody can tell me nothin attitude! How dare you say that to me!"

"Whatever! You don't know nothing about me, Please! Ms. Magna Cum Laude, whachu know!?"

Reggie plops down in wicker chair. Kisha approaches him, but decides to sit down on her bed facing him.

"You're shooting or snorting?" Kisha pulls up the sleeve of her left arm and extends it to him. "I know cause-I've got my own track marks to prove it."

Shocked he scrutinizes her scar tissue realizing how she got it. *Damn, not you Kisha.* Reggie thought.

Kisha walks away going to her sizeable chaise lounge chair in her living room. She sits down tucking her legs under her. There's silence as Reggie moves himself to the edge of the wicker chair and looks over at Kisha.

"How'd you do it? I mean, you... you graduated. I never

even made it to college."

She looks at him. "Well, Ivy League schools have drug dealers too. Yeah, I graduated, barely, and that's just because I was a functioning addict. One thing I've learned people always try to dress things up to cover real truth. It doesn't make a difference if you're running the streets or in a big office with a city view. A drug addict is still a drug addict, be it upper class, middle class or poor."

Reggie comes over and sits down beside her on the chaise.

"What... what happen?"

Kisha shrugs her shoulders as she turns toward him.

"It's classic a teenage girl far from home in a new environment, and all I wanted to do was fit in. My roommate did coke. She always offered and I usually said no, but after a few late nights of studying eventually I tried it. All it took was one time and I was hooked. Next thing you know I'm part of the *in-crowd*. I started seeing this guy named Aidan, a handsome, pre-law student with wealthy parents." She laughs. "Pre-law, that's sounds funny now. I soon learned Aidan was the main dealer on campus. I tell ya, when the enemy wants to set you up, he knows how to do it. I went from sniffing to shooting up. My scholarship paid for school and Aidan happily took care of my thousand dollar habit."

"Well, you look great. Whatever it was, rehab or N.A, it worked for you and you got yourself together."

"It didn't just happen on my own strength Reggie; One day during a party at Aidan's family beach house, we left the gang downstairs, broke off and went upstairs to his bedroom. Aidan fixed a needle for us, tied me off, shot me up first and then himself. The last thing I remember before passing out was hearing myself say "Jesus help me." I should have died that night, that was the plan anyway."

"You OD'd, but he was with you, right? He didn't leave you alone?"

Kisha disagrees shaking her head.

"Let me finish. Eventually, I woke up and found Aidan balled up in the corner, banging his head against the wall. His head was pouring blood and there was a bloody bat next to him. He kept babbling about monsters being after him."

"Yo, y'all must of got a bad batch!"

"Bad enough for Aidan to trip out and see his friends as monsters, he used the bat to beat them to death. The cops couldn't believe I was still breathing."

"Well, you were knocked out. He probably thought you were already dead."

"I thought that too, but when the police questioned me, they asked about a tall guy in all white. Police said Aidan told them he went to hit me with the bat, and some tall guy in all white stopped the bat mid-swing. Aidan said the man said, touch not my anointed. The cops didn't understand, but I did. See I remember Mama Mae always said. Jesus may not come when you want him, but he's always right on time. Reggie, Jesus was on time for me that night. When I got back to my dorm, I got on my knees and accepted Jesus into my heart."

"Kisha, I'm not that Reggie from high school anymore; I lost him a long time ago."

Reggie gets up, walks over to the sliding doors and crosses his arms as he stands staring outside.

Under his breath, he said, "If you knew who I hurt." He glances at her. "Kisha, so much has happened. You just don't know-"

Reggie goes to the kitchen chair removes his tracksuit jacket and puts it on.

"If you did, you wouldn't look at me the same." He turns to Kisha. "Look I'm gonna go; I didn't mean to cause friction between you and your parents."

Kisha approaches him.

"The Reggie I know isn't lost, Jesus knows exactly where you are and *He's* there for you. He can bring you out. It was nobody but Jesus that cleaned me up and set me free. The rehab centers and programs can teach you to survive without drugs. Believe me, I'm not knocking them, they have their place-but true deliverance from drugs or whatever, can be found in Jesus Christ. Reggie, it's your choice. Jesus is waiting for you. Just call on *Him.*"

Kisha takes the remaining dishes on the table to the sink.

"You sound like Grandma. I really messed up though; I don't think it can be fixed either." *They'll never... she'll never forgive me.* He thought

Kisha comes back over to Reggie.

"Reggie, I know this-Jesus can fix whatever the problem, and it's never too late."

Kisha walks to the kitchen counter, opens a drawer and takes a small yellow pad out and a pen. She places them on the counter, writes something and puts the pen down. She tears the paper off and bring it to Reggie.

"Here's my cell and work number." She puts the paper in his hand. "Call me anytime, no matter what. Okay?!"

"Yeah, thanks Kisha... for everything."

They hug, Reggie holds Kisha tight not wanting to let her go, she's one of the few lifelines he has yet to sever. They slowly release each other, while looking into each others eyes emotions they haven't felt since high school start stir. They both smile as they take a step back from each other. Kisha crosses her arms, bashfully her eyes wonder else where.

"I'm gonna use your bathroom before I go." He stutters.

"No need to ask."

As he's closing the bathroom door behind him, he hears several urgent knocks at her front door.

"Hold on, I'm coming." Kisha said.

Kisha unlocks it, opens it up and there stands James.

"Hey, Kisha," James said.

"Oh, James," Kisha said. "What are you doing here?"

"Sorry to disturb you," James said. "Regina gave me your address, she said Reggie may be here? I need to speak with him."

"Sure, come in," Kisha said.

"Thanks," James said. As he steps inside, looking around. "Great place."

"Thanks, Reggie's in the bathroom. He was just about to leave. A few more minutes and you would've missed him."

"Oh, I would've caught him sooner or later."

"Well, he'll be right out. I'm gonna go get my mail from my parents house." She gets ready to leave but turns back to James. "Oh, you want something to drink?"

"Nah, I'm good."

"Alright, I'll be right back."

Kisha grabs a set of keys off the hook, walks out through the sliding doors, as Toy-Toy trots over to her. They walk over to her parents house. A few minutes later Reggie leaves the bathroom, as he adjusts his jacket walking into the living room. He's unaware of James presence. When he looks up, they make eye contact. They peer at each other for a few seconds, James bolts toward him and grabs Reggie by his jacket.

"You did it!" James said.

"What are you talking about?" Reggie said.

"I saw you-I saw you run outta Aunt Mae's house!"

"Get off me man!" He struggles, trying to pull away from James. "Get off me man! Get off me!"

"It's your fault!" James said, shaking Reggie. "It's all your fault!!"

James punches Reggie in the stomach forcing Reggie to fold. James knees him in the face; Reggie drops to the ground disoriented landing on Kisha's shag rug. James grabs him by the jacket once again.

"Why her... huh?!"

James stands over Reggie.

"Why Reggie? Tell me why?!"

James pulls Reggie up closer to him, glaring angrily into his eyes.

"Why did you have to hurt her?!"

"He'll Work It Out" Chapter 4. Taryn C. Atkins

James lets loose a sharp blow to the face but he doesn't let Reggie drop. He clenches his fist tighter, pulls his arm back further and lands another extreme shot to Reggie's face. Reggie pulls away and cowers into a fetal position trying to protect himself.

"I didn't mean it! I didn't mean for it to happen!"

James continues his assault Reggie.

"She's your grandmother and you go do this!" He grabs Reggie's jacket lifting him up and bounces him off the living wall. "She cared about you!"

"I didn't mean for her to get hurt!"

James takes all his aggression out on Reggie. His intention with every punch being more furious than the last, was to give Reggie what he felt he strongly deserves. Reggie drops to the ground like a dirty laundry bag. His eye swells, blood runs from his mouth and he cries out as he tries to crawl away from James.

"I didn't want it to happen." Reggie gets to the kitchen table. "I didn't mean for--"

"All she ever did was show concern for you!"

James stands over him and points.

"And you go and do that to her!" He bends over to Reggie. "You just left her!"

James kicks Reggie in the chest, then snatches him, pulling him up face to face. Tears roll down James' cheeks.

"You left her laying there bleeding! You almost killed her!"

Kisha makes her way back to her studio with Toy-Toy right beside her. She picks up Toy-Toy's ball and throws it into the grass, as he rushes to fetch it. Kisha smiles watching Toy-Toy. Her eyes then focus on the sliding doors in the background where she sees Reggie laying on the floor by the kitchen table. James is holding Reggie by his jacket when he abruptly hauls off and punches Reggie in the face.

"Oh My God!" Kisha said, sprinting over to her studio.

"That's for stealing her money." James punches Reggie once again. "That's for leaving her like that!"

Reggie barely able to get apologetic words out because of the damage James is doing. He pulls Reggie to his feet. Reggie somewhat limp still tries to protect himself. Kisha bangs on the sliding doors and pulls one open. James is holding Reggie up, his face is bloody and swelling from the beating.

"Oh my God!!" Kisha said. She rushes over to them.
James get off him!!" She tries to pull James away.

"It's all his fault!" James said, looking at Kisha. "Did Reggie tell you that?! Huh, Reggie!!"

"James! I said get off him!"

James lets Reggie go, he painfully falls to the ground moaning. Kisha steps in front of James and pushes him away from Reggie.

"He did that to Mama Mae Kisha! Her own grandson left her like that!!"

Kisha rushes to the sink and grabs the dish towel.

"All to get some damn drugs! He left her there bleeding!"

Kisha looks at James as she wets the dish towel.

"How do you know it was Reggie?!"

"I saw him that's how! I saw him running from the house!"

Kisha rushes back to Reggie, kneels next to him, she carefully puts his head in her lap and begins to tend to him.

"You're telling me, Reggie stabbed Mama Mae?"

Reggie tries to look at Kisha as he shakes his head no.

"Yes!" James said. "He's the one that put his own grandmother in the hospital! He tried to get money from her, when she wouldn't give it to him, he stabbed her with the scissors! *He* stabbed her Kisha, then just left her!"

"My God, Reggie."

Reggie struggles to talk, he mumbles forcing words out.

"Kisha... No... no."

"If I hadn't come home she would've died!!!"

James moves closer, he bends over Reggie pointing at him. Reggie struggling, too weak to cover himself his hands just fall to the ground.

"Consider this a warning." James said. "Steal somethin else! Or hurt somebody else in this family!"

James stomps down on Reggie's hand.

"My God James! Leave him alone!!"

"This ain't nothin compared to what you're gonna get."

"Get out of my house! Get out!"

James stops at the front door and turns to Reggie.

"Why don't you do us all a favor and just off yourself already, like your junkie friend Mario."

James exits as Kisha continues to care for Reggie's wounds looking at him confusion and concern.

~HOME RESTING~

It's the middle of July and Mama Mae's finally home from the hospital. After being home a few days, family, friends, neighbors and members of her church family at Full Gospel Temple have been visiting. It's early in the afternoon, Mama Mae enjoys spending time in her living room with her two best friends. She sits on the sofa next to Mother Livingston and laying across Mama Mae's lap is her cat. Minister McDaniels sits on the loveseat.

Mama Mae relaxes in her house coat while all the ladies there are dressed summer chic with a conservative style. Mama Mae takes a sip from the glass of ice tea in her hand. She places it down on the serving tray which is sitting on top of the coffee table. There are two cups of coffee, a plate of cookies and two glasses of ice tea on the serving tray.

"Somebody sure missed you, Mother Babcock." Minister McDaniels said.

Mama Mae looks over at Minister McDaniels and she points to the cat. Mama Mae's attention goes to the cat as she softly strokes its back. All hear the cat purr enjoying the love.

"You talking bout my baby Fluffy." Mama Mae said. "She hasn't left my side since I got home."

"Well, she's a beautiful cat." Minister McDaniels said. "Completely snow white, with two different color eyes, that's so rare. What kind of cat is she anyway?"

"Well, Gina got her for me." Mama Mae said. "Said she was a... wait a minute, Fluffy is a... a Turkish Angora."

"She's lovely."

"Thanks, Fluffy knows she's cute too."

Mama Mae laughs. Mother Livingston reaches over and pats Mama Mae on her hand.

"Mae, I know you're glad to finally be home." Mother Livingston said.

"Sis, it sure feels good to sleep in my own bed." Mama Mae said. "Lord I can't stand hospitals."

"I'm sure you don't miss the food either." Minister McDaniels said.

"Oh please, don't get me started." Mama Mae said.

Minister McDaniels reaches over to her cup of coffee.

"Love the trunk coffee table, Mother Babcock." Minister McDaniels said. "Mother Livingston has this antique armoire that's so trendy too. So where did you two get them, Pier 1?"

As Minister McDaniels takes a sip of her brew, Mama Mae, and Mother Livingston look at each other smiling. They glance back over at Minister McDaniels.

"Mine's a family heirloom." Mama Mae said.

"Mines too." Mother Livingston said. "See baby, Mae and I had Pier 1 style before a Pier 1 even existed."

"That's sure 'nuff right." Mama Mae said.

Mother Livingston and Mama Mae laugh with each other. Minister McDaniels, reaches over and picks up one of the butter cookies off the plate on the serving tray. She takes it, dunks it into her coffee and enjoys eating it. Mother Livingston picks up her glass of ice tea, nurses it and sets it back down.

"Now, what about that grandson of yours? Mother Livingston said. "Anyone saw or heard from him?"

"No, nothing yet." Mama Mae said.

"I never thought Reggie could do something like that."

"Now Sis, he's wrong for the stealing but what happen with the scissors was an accident."

"Mae you're my best friend. You can't be scaring me like that; I'm not as strong as I used to be now."

"No, you're stronger," Mama Mae said. "You old windbag."

They both laugh.

"I'm just glad you're home," Mother Livingston said. "Someone should be here with ya. Just in case, Reggie shows up here."

"My family's keeping a watch on me. James lives here and Regina comes by often, she had to go run a few errands but should be back soon."

"Mae, now that I think about it, maybe its best for Reggie to just stay away right now."

"Well, I pray he doesn't stay away; I don't want the devil tormenting him more than he already is."

"He needs some tormenting, it may help him get himself together."

Minister Pauls walks through the living room door rubbing lotion on her hands.

"Thanks for letting me use your ladies room Mother Babcock." Minister Pauls said. She comes over and stands by the side of the sofa. "You have such a lovely home. I know it feels good to be back in it."

"Yes, it sure does."

"I know you're happy to be home." Mother Livingston said. "Now, tell the truth. Have you even sat in that kitchen, after all that's happened?"

Minister Pauls walks over to the living room's grand bay window and looks outside.

"Of course I have; I'm not gonna let no devil make me feel uncomfortable in my own home."

Minister Paul sits at the bay window and admires the view.

"Amen! That's right Mother Babcock, good for you." Minister McDaniels said.

"Mother Babcock," Minister Pauls said. Looking over at her. "This bay window and the classic neighborhood view is just priceless. I had a bay window when I lived in Atlanta; I loved it too." She returns her attention to the outdoors. "It reminds me of where I grew up in

Jamestown, up in Rhode Island."

"My granddaughter Gisele loves that bay window too." Mama Mae said. "It's her favorite spot in the house."

"I love Atlanta, how long did you live there?" Minister McDaniels said.

Minister Pauls looks at Minister McDaniels. Mother Livingston and Mama Mae pay attention to the conversation.

"Six or seven years before moving back here." Minister Pauls said.

"So what brought you back to the Big Apple." Mother Livingston said.

Minister Pauls gets up and walks over to the fireplace.

"Well, Pastor Gorham actually." Minister Pauls said. "He preached twice at the church I attended in Atlanta." She admires the photo's sitting on top of the fireplace. "I liked the word he brought forth." She scans over the pictures, that are on the walls and on each side of the fireplace. "My pastor at the time was alright but it was different when I heard Pastor Gorham. So, I decided to move back and be under his leadership." She turns to Mama Mae. "So many family pictures Mother. My mom loved pictures too."

"Yeah, I can't help myself. Those moments up there are frozen in time forever, and they're precious to me."

Minister Pauls continues to appreciate the family photos. Mother Livingston's face brightens up.

"Mae I almost forgot; I've got good news." Mother Livingston said with a smile. "My granddaughter and your God daughter Justine, got saved a few weeks ago!"

"Well Praise God!" Mama Mae said."

"I'm not gonna get into all the details right now. I'll save that story for another time. Just know Mae, that journal you told me to get her, will not go to waste."

"I'm sure it won't."

While Mama Mae and Mother Livingston chat away, Minister McDaniels enjoys her coffee and cookies. Minister Pauls reviews Mama Mae's family pictures one catches her attention. She picks up the framed picture from off the fireplace mantel, staring at the photo for a second, Minister Pauls turns to Mama Mae.

"Umm... excuse me, Mother Babcock," Minister Pauls said. "Who's this with Deaconess Greye? She brings the picture closer to Mama Mae. "It looks like they're at a high school graduation."

"Oh, that's Shayna's daughter Gisele. I mean Gigi." She looks at Mother Livingston. "Lord, all these nicknames get ya' confused."

Mother Livingston shakes her head agreeing. Minister Pauls studies the picture again and as she heads back toward the fireplace.

"I know Regina, she attends Full Gospel. I didn't know Deaconess Greye had another daughter?"

Minister Pauls places the picture back on the mantle.

"Gigi's Shayna's oldest daughter. Gigi's twenty-eight now and Gina is twenty-five. Looking at them, makes me realize time has flown by so quick."

Minister Pauls focuses on the photo for a few more seconds then walks away. She goes back to the bay window and sits. Mother Livingston reaches over to the sofa end table next to her and picks up a picture frame sitting on it.

"I just love this photo of Gigi in her Girl Scout uniform." Mother Livingston said. "Lord, I must have brought one hundred Girl Scout cookies that year."

"You!" Mama Mae said. "For four years all I had up in this house was boxes and boxes of Girl Scout cookies."

"What do you mean?" Minister McDaniels said.

Minister Pauls listens to their conversation.

"Well," Mama Mae said. "When Cliff and Shayna first brought their house. Gigi was supposed to change schools, but that child didn't want to. All because that new school didn't have the Girl Scouts. So, they asked me and Luke could Gigi stay here with us for a while. She lived with us for about four or five years."

"I remember her Girl Scout phase." Mother Livingston said. "She went from being a Brownie to a Cadette. Well, she only did like two years as a Cadette. Then she was done with it."

"We loved having her, and it helped them out too. Shayna was able to go back to school during those years and finish up her Masters for Accounting."

"Gigi loved being a Girl Scout." Mother Livingston said.

"She sure did." Mama Mae said. "Shayna barely saw her sometimes. Gigi was always off on some scout trip, meeting or sleep over."

"You have a lovely family Mother." Minister Pauls said.

"Thank you." Mama Mae responds.

"Regina's so much like you." Minister McDaniels said.

"Yeah," Mama Mae said laughing. "The family calls Gina my Mini Me."

Everyone in the room laughs a bit.

"I could see why." Minister Pauls said.

"Me too." Minister McDaniels said.

"Mae I tell you," Mother Livingston said. "It's sad to see Gigi and her mother going through such a rough patch, for so long now too. We're sorry we showed up when we did. That argument they had was heated. Gigi rushed out of here so upset."

"Yeah," Mama Mae said. "I was hoping Regina would have been here, but she's still out running errands." She looks at the clock over the fireplace. "It's going on twelve thirty now, Gina said she'll be here around 1." She reaches over to the coffee table, picks up her ice tea and takes a few sips. "Saints the best thing you can do for my family is keep us in your prayers. Cause prayer changes things."

Minister Pauls looks at her watch and stands up.

"Yes of course." Minister Pauls said. "Mother Babcock, I still have a few errands to run myself. So I must go."

Minister Pauls walks over to the loveseat where Minister McDaniels is sitting and picks up her MK handbag from off the seat. She puts the bag on the arm of the loveseat, opens it up and begins to search through it.

"Mother Livingston," Minister Pauls said. "Minister McDaniels will drive you home as planned." She pulls her car keys out. "Mother Babcock, I'm glad you're home."

"Believe me, I am too." Mama Mae said.

Minister Pauls approaches Mama Mae.

"Okay Mother," Minister Pauls said. "Now make sure you get your rest."

"I will." Mama Mae said.

"Let me show you some love." Minister Pauls said.

Minister Pauls leans over to give Mama Mae a hug, when out of nowhere Fluffy hisses at her.

"Oh my God!" Minister Pauls said. Quickly backing up.

"Jesus!" Mama Mae said. She pulls Fluffy to her. "I am so sorry. She's normally not like that. Probably just a little nervous, you know, from being around new people."

"Yes... of course. Well, let me go." Minister Pauls walks to the living room door. "Take it easy Mother Babcock. Have a good afternoon saints."

They say their good-byes and Minister Pauls walks out. Mama Mae looks over at Mother Livingston.

"Sis... that's the first time I ever saw Fluffy do that."

A little time has gone by, visitors have left and Mama Mae stands outside by the front door of her house, listening to the sounds of summer go forth. She takes in a slow deep breath and smiles as she exhales. Mama Mae takes a seat on her cozy porch bench. This quaint southern style porch is Mama Mae's peaceful place, it's special to her because her husband built it just for her. He wanted her to have a place she could just sit, relax and talk to God. It was the last thing he had built for her before he passed away. Mama Mae closed her eyes as she sits enjoying the fresh air and the warmth of the sun on her skin.

"That sun feels good. Lord, I'm so glad to be home."

A few minutes pass, Mama Mae hears a car pull into her driveway, car doors open and shut. She opens her eyes, looks over and sees Regina and Minister Randall coming toward the porch.

They walk up on the porch, Regina's holding in each hand a large Carvel cup with a straw sticking out the top of each one.

"Hey, there mother. How are you feeling today?" Minister Randall said. "You look great."

He goes to Mama Mae and kisses her on the cheek.

"Well, I'm doing alright." Mama Mae said. "Still a little achy, but I'm here, praise God."

"We're glad that you are too." Minister Randall said.

"Grandma," Regina said. "What are you doing outside?"

"I'm just talking to the Lord." Mama Mae said. "While enjoying this beautiful summer day he made. What are you two doing here?"

"Since Andre was off today, when I finished running errands he picked me up." Regina said. "We had a late lunch together."

"That's sounds nice." Mama Mae said. "Now, Pastor and Lady Gorham know y'all are courting right?"

"Yes ma'am." Minister Randall said.

"Yes, they do grandma," Regina said. "We told you last year. We've been seeing each other almost two years now."

"Well, I was just checking." Mama Mae said. "Making sure things are legit, as James would say."

"They are Mother Babcock." Minister Randall said.

"Well, you ladies enjoy the rest of your day. I've got to go get my car inspected." He kisses Mama Mae on her cheek again. "Now mother, use wisdom and get your rest. Let the Lord do a complete healing okay."

"I will son, it's good to see you." Mama Mae said.

"Same here." Minister Randall said. He goes to Gina. "Okay now, I'll talk to you later."

"Alright," Regina said.

Mama Mae watches their interaction carefully. Minister Randall kisses Regina on the cheek as well. He walks down the porch steps but turns to Regina.

"James is giving you a ride home right?" Minister Randall said.

"Yeah, he's supposed too," Regina said. "I'll be okay. If he doesn't, I'll stay over."

"Call me if anything changes." Minister Randall said.

"Okay, but if not, I'll call when I get in," Regina said.

As Minister Randall heads over to his car. Regina looks over at her grandmother.

Under her breath, Regina said. "He can be a little over protective sometime."

"I see," Mama Mae said. "Take notice of that Regina."

"Oh, believe me." She looks at him as he closes the door of his car. "I know grandma."

"Okay." Minister Randall said. He starts up his car. "See ya Gina, take it easy mother."

"You too son." Mama Mae said. "And you better be treating my baby right. Don't let me have to get my rod out and use it on ya'."

"Yes ma'am." Minister Randall said with a smile, he waves to Regina. "Bye now."

"Goodbye, son." Mama Mae said.

"I'll talk to you later Andre," Regina said.

Regina smiles as she glances at her grandmother and shakes her head. She watch Minister Randall backing his car out. When he drives off he beeps his horn twice.

"I'm so glad your home Grandma," Regina said.

"Me too." Mama Mae said. "Lord knows that hospital got on my nerves." She moves down a bit on the bench. "Come on and sit down, relax out here with me. I umm... see those Carvel cups you got there."

"I'm sure you do." Regina comes over and sits next to her grandmother. "I got your favorite, a Pistachio shake with a lot of cherries." She hands the shake to Mama Mae.

"And for me, good ole Butter Pecan."

"Thank ya baby, been a while since I had one of these."

"I know, enjoy."

"I sure will."

Regina sits back and crosses her legs. They toast each other tapping their Carvel cups together. They both take a strong pull from their straws and sit in silence enjoying their shakes. Regina turns to her grandmother.

"Grandma, I've been so worried about the family. So much has happened. Usually, I'm the strong one, but I don't know this time."

"Baby, God won't put more on you than you can bare."

"I know, but look at us. Dad had to sneak Gigi in the hospital to see you. Just so mom didn't have a fit."

"I know, it's a shame how things have gotten."

They both nurse their shakes as they talk.

"I mean, look at the day you came home, for Mommy to argue just because Gigi was here, was terrible."

"Well, they got into it again today Gina, and It wasn't pretty. Gigi stormed out of here. I've got to give her a call before I lay down. I don't understand what's going on with Shayna. We all have our feelings about what's going on with Gigi."

"Yeah but, whatever's going on with mom," Regina said. "Has gotten worse over the years."

"I know," Mama Mae said. "I didn't even raise Shayna like that. This is something else and it runs deep. Something has a hold on her, and only God can fix it."

"You've always been there grandma." Regina gets up. "You're there for all of us." She walks to the fence on the porch. "Look where Reggie's problem got you." Folding her arms. "You could have died."

"I'm home now Gina. And baby, Jesus has this family in is hands." She takes a sip of her shake. "God promised me a long time ago, that he'd save my family, bring'em together and everybody would be everything He's called them to be. I know it's gonna happen, cause I have faith in God." She puts the shake down on the arm of the bench. "God spoke it baby, so it has to happen, and it will because nothing is impossible with God, but you got to do your part and trust Him."

Regina turns to her grandmother.

"I don't know Grandma..."

"Gina you're stronger than you think. Have faith in God like I do, and know." She casually grasps her stomach. "God will not allow the devil to keep this family all broken up." She coughs a little and tries hiding her pain. "The best thing we can do with Gisele is love her, all she needs is unconditional love. Just like God gives us. Then watch, God will do the rest."

Another sudden pain hits Mama Mae's body. Her facial expression shows it this time and Regina sees it.

"Think my body's trying to tell me; I over did it today."

Regina helps Mama Mae get up.

"Alright, let's get you upstairs, you need to lay down."

"Give me a minute, this summer sun feels so good."

Mama Mae composes herself before moving while Regina watches her carefully.

"Baby girl, I know God has heard my prayers and he's got this family. Cliff's a good man; I have no doubt he'll look out for y'all. God's gonna work that situation out with Shayna and Gigi, watch and see." She moans. "Let Leah know I love her, God loves her too and wants the best for her." She coughs. "Tell Leah don't settle for less and don't give up on Reggie either. You tell them for me alright. God is not through with this family, I know it."

"Okay, but right now." Regina stands. "Let's get you to bed Grandma."

"Alright."

"Now take your time and lean on me."

Regina holds out her hand, Mama Mae places her hand within Regina's and gets up from the bench.

"Gina, remember, no matter how bad things may look."

Regina slowly helps Mama Mae over to the front door.

"God is in control. What we must learn, is to let go and let God. Even when we can't see it, have the faith to know, he'll work it out."

"I know Grandma."

"Good." She looks over at the bench and points. "Now, don't forget my shake."

"He'll Work It Out" Chapter 4. Taryn C. Atkins

Gina shakes her head looking at Mama Mae and they smile.

~WEB OF SEDUCTION~

Several hours later, early in the evening around sixish Gigi arrives home. Gigi stands at her front door, mumbles under her breath as she struggles with her keys. Finally unlocking the door, she slides it open, walks in and pushes the door closed behind her. The door slams but it bounces back open, staying slightly cracked. Gigi doesn't look back just heads down the hallway. She stops mid way to kick off her heels. As they fly down the hall she screams out.

"I can't believe that woman!" Gigi said. "You think I would get some consideration!" She comes out the hallway. "My grandmother did just get home from the hospital!"

Gigi walks into the living room and throws her MK bag on the sectional.

"I still can't believe I had to actually sneak into the hospital to see my own grandmother! Why! All so Deaconess Greye wouldn't get upset!" She picks up a pillow from off the sofa. "I'm sick and tired of Deaconess Greye getting upset over every single thing about me!"

Gigi screams and throws the pillow across the room. It hits the corner of the hallway wall and lands on the floor. Outside the loft Cassandra gets off the elevator, holding keys in her hand, as she walks over to Lexi and Gigi's front door. She hears Gigi's ranting and sees that the door is cracked. Cassandra pulls her shades up, letting them rest on her head, slowly sliding back the front door and softly shut it. Cassandra heads down the hallway as Gigi continues her ranting.

"Child of God-Yeah... right! Child of the devil is more like it!" She looks up to heaven. "God, it's hard to believe you would even fill somebody like that with the Holy Spirit!"

Gigi's back is turned away from the hallway, she doesn't notice Cassandra walk in. Cassandra stands there watching as Gigi voices her feelings.

"I didn't ask to be this way you know!"

Cassandra smirks, listening to Gigi's rant realizing she's showed up right on time. Cassandra bends over and picks up the pillow on the floor; Slowly approaching Gigi, who's caught up in her anger and still unaware of Cassandra's presence.

"How 'bout you tell Deaconess Greye that! Can you possibly get that through her thick skull?!"

Cassandra reaches out to tap Gigi on the shoulder. Unsuccessfully Gigi abruptly turns around and is caught off guard.

"Jesus!" Gigi said, pulling her hands up to her heart.

"What are you doing here?"

"Sorry," Cassandra said, with a slight giggle. "I didn't mean to scare you. The door was cracked. I heard screaming and just came in. I think this is yours."

She hands Gigi the pillow. Gigi takes the pillow and tosses it on the sectional.

"Are you okay?" Cassandra said.

Gigi walks around picking up her belongings.

"It's just the usual," Gigi said. "I'll be right back."

Gigi goes to the hallway as Cassandra follows her. She watches Gigi switch in her straight, crop cuffed Hudson jeans as she walks down the hall. Cassandra smiles and raises a her brow watching Gigi enter her bedroom.

Gigi's voice bellows from her room. "Lexi's not home yet."

"Oh, I'm meeting her here." Cassandra said. "She left her keys in my car, said it was alright for me to wait inside. Guess I'm a bit early."

Gigi shouts from her bedroom. "Okay then, make yourself comfortable."

"Thank you," Cassandra said.

Cassandra takes her shades off her head as she goes to the island, putting them down on it. She places her Louis Vuitton bag on top of it too. Cassandra sees a ladybug, on the shoulder of her denim boyfriend shirt. She brushes it off, then looks down at where the shirt is tied about her midsection and tugs on the tie a bit. Cassandra turns around, twirling her rust maxi skirt with her movement leaning back on the island. Gigi comes out of her bedroom heading down the hallway. Cassandra slyly checks her out, noticing Gigi's chic' but modest, bat-wing belted top, unable to hide her ample cup size. Cassandra steers her attention to the propeller over the kitchen cabinets.

> "I like the propeller," Cassandra said. "It's a unique piece."
>
> "I think so too," Gigi said, walking out from the hallway. "Lexi's father was in the Air Force. I think that's actually from one of the planes he flew."
>
> "Wow," Cassandra said."

Cassandra looks over at Gigi as she approaches. Cassandra seems to tower over her but it's only because of the strappy, platform sandals she's wearing, while Gigi is bare footed.

> "Look," Gigi said. "Feel free to turn on the cable, have yourself something to eat or drink. I had a rough day. So, I'm not the best company. I need to go stretch out on my bed."
>
> "You don't have to do that," Cassandra said. She walks over to the sectional. "I firmly believe that all things happen for a reason." She sits down on the sectional, crossing her legs and looks at Gigi. "Apparently something is bothering you, and I showed up at the right time." She pats the sofa cushion beside her. "Come on over here and talk to me."

Gigi places her hand on the island, leans against it and looks at Cassandra.

> "I appreciate that-I do," Gigi said. "I don't want to bring down your mood talking about my crazy life issues."
>
> "Oh please, that's nonsense," Cassandra said. "You need to vent and I'm here. So have a seat and lets talk."

Gigi looks away considering the proposal; She looks at Cassandra and smiles.

> "Okay, but first," Gigi said. Taking a few steps backward heading to the kitchen. "I need something to take the edge off. I'm gonna have some wine, would you like some?"
>
> "Sure."

"Merlot okay."

"That's good."

Gigi grabs two wine glasses and places them on the kitchen counter. She walks to the fridge and pulls out a bottle of wine. Cassandra watches Gigi as she fills their glasses of wine. Her eyes travel Gigi's form, appreciating its appeal.

Hmmph, I could have taken the edge off. Cassandra thought.

Cassandra stands up, walks toward one of the living room windows and pulls back the light gray mist curtains. She stands underneath it, looking out admiring the city skyline. Gigi brings over their glasses, she stops at the island noticing Cassandra over by the window. She sits the glasses down on top of the island. While Cassandra enjoys the view from the loft's window. Gigi continues to visually inspect Cassandra.

Gigi takes in the Cassandra, she notices that even when Cassandra's dressed casual, it's put together with class, style, and sex appeal, it's captivating and inviting. Throughout Gigi's observance of Cassandra, Gigi realizes Cassandra is provoking unchartered feelings within her. Gigi takes a deep breath and as she exhales, she looks away and shakes her head a bit as she picks up their wine glasses.

"Here you go," Gigi said.

Cassandra turns around and sees Gigi holding the wine glasses by the island. Gigi moves toward the living room area. As Cassandra makes her way over. Her eyes cunningly look over Gigi. Cassandra takes pleasure in catching sight of the fact that Gigi's well equipped with her own attributes that are shapely, steamy and equally inviting.

Cassandra smiles recalling that unexpected moment exchanged between them. Although Cassandra's aware that their attraction to each other may just be a mere ember. She's confident that the right breeze can change that ember to a flame. Cassandra comes around the sectional and Gigi gives her the glass of wine.

"Thank you," Cassandra said.

As Gigi brushes by Cassandra, Gigi recalls that intense exchange of energy between them, and even now as Gigi moves by

Cassandra she feels a strong pull between them. Gigi tries to play it safe, making sure there's some distance between them and sits at the other end of the sectional.

When Gigi passes, Cassandra catches a whiff of her perfume once again. She closes her eyes as she inhales the scent and another memory flashes before her. Her body tingles and a soft moan escapes her lips. Cassandra shakes her head regaining her composure and concealing the affect of Gigi's fragrance. They take their seats, Cassandra sits near the middle of her side of the sectional. Gigi on the other hand, sits at the end of hers. There's silence for a few as they enjoy their wine. Gigi holds her glass of wine and nurses it. Cassandra places her glass down on the coffee table.

"So now," Cassandra said, turning toward Gigi. "Why all the screaming?"

"Well, my family is in the church," Gigi said. "Ya know, like that song... saved, sanctified, holy ghost filled, understand?"

"I get it."

"Do you believe in God? Or go to church?"

"Hmm, something like that."

"Well, I went to church, was saved; I did it all and enjoyed it too, but I couldn't stay there. Not like this. See I refuse to be a hypocrite, so I left. I backslid." Gigi takes a few sips of her wine. "I walked away from God, because... I'm struggling with this."

"This meaning the fact you like women?" Cassandra said.

"Yeah," Gigi said. "It's not that I don't like guys-I... I just, like women too."

"Oh honey, what's not to like." Cassandra stands and shows herself off a bit. "I love being a woman."

As Gigi watches Cassandra, the attraction grows, feeling herself staring, Gigi looks away and takes a sip of her wine, but Cassandra has already seen the flame in Gigi's eyes.

"I mean," Cassandra picks up her glass. "We're beautiful creatures... yes?"

"He'll Work It Out" Chapter 4. Taryn C. Atkins

"Yes, you are. I... I mean we are. We're beautiful creatures."

Gigi drinks down some of her wine as she watches Cassandra taking a few sip of hers. Cassandra sets her glass down on the coffee table, she moves a bit closer to Gigi.

"Yes but..." Cassandra said, as she sits back down. "Your family gives you a hard time."

As Gigi places her glass on the coffee table, she repositions herself. Cassandra smiles leaning back on the sectional noticing Gigi moving closer.

"Well, the majority of my family may not like or agree with what I'm doing, but they still love me. My grandmother loves me, and prays for me. Now, she'll tell me the truth about going to hell and all. Reminds me all I need to do is rededicate myself to God. She lets me know that Jesus can deliver me out of this. If... if I want to be delivered."

"So, do you *really want* to be delivered?"

"I think about it, do you ever think about it? You said you believe, do you go to church?"

"Gigi, I've done church, and I've seen and know too much of what happens behind the scenes of it." She picks her wine glass up. "So for me, life's too short to worry about what people think."

Cassandra takes a few sips of her wine, putting her glass down, she repositions herself on the sectional and while getting comfortable moves closer to Gigi. Gigi places her now empty wine glass down on the coffee table.

"I understand that, but I guess I'm not talking about people. Doesn't it bother you what the Bible says about homosexuality?"

"Well, let's be specific. The Bible doesn't have the word "homosexuality" in it."

"No, but..." Gigi said. "In 1st Corinthians 6:9."

Cassandra huffs, as she looks away for a second and then brings her attention back to Gigi as she reaches out picking up her wine glass.

"It says, "Know ye not that the unrighteous shall not inherit the kingdom of God? Be not deceived: neither fornicators, nor idolaters, nor adulterers, nor effeminate..." Effeminate practically means the same thing as homosexual."

"My my, aren't we the Bible scholar," Cassandra said. She finishes her wine and puts the glass down. "You're well aware then, that in the bible Jesus never said anything about it."

"Okay, you're talking about red writing." Gigi said." "The whole Bible is the word of God."

"Translated over and over again, by men mind you."

"So you don't believe the bible is true? You don't believe in heaven or hell? Because I do."

"Well, I wouldn't say that; I just feel some of it is... up for discussion. Like it states in Isaiah 1:18, "Come now, and let us reason together."

Gigi looks away for a second. Cassandra smirks as she watches Gigi contemplate her words. Gigi's eyes go to their empty wine glasses.

"More wine? Gigi said, looking at Cassandra.

"I'd love some," Cassandra said.

Gigi gets up, picks up their glasses and heads over to the kitchen, her smile widens, now intrigued with Cassandra. Cassandra watches Gigi, she smiles a devilish grin knowing she's caught Gigi's attention. After preparing their fresh glasses of wine, Gigi heads back to the living room making eye contact with Cassandra. As they look at each other, Gigi's aggressive nature rises and reveals itself more. Sensing something changing within her, Gigi looks away. Cassandra grins eyeing her watch as Gigi comes over with the wine.

Gigi's aware of the gravity of attraction that surrounds them. Trying her best to suppress these new feelings that keep attempting to draw her in. Gigi hands Cassandra her fresh glass, when Gigi passes by she turns her body toward Cassandra and sits much closer. Cassandra in turn moves closer also but makes it her objective not to touch Gigi in any way.

"Question," Gigi said. "So how long have you...?"

"Loved women? Cassandra said. "Since I was twenty-two. My mother applauded my boldness for coming out to her." She laughs. "It surprised me how well she handled it."

"I was nineteen when I came out to my parents." Gigi takes a healthy sip of wine and swallows. "My mother... Well, she couldn't handle it. She kicked me out." She shakes her head a bit. "Our relationship will never be the same." She takes another sip of wine. "My mother will never accept me. Please, I can barely accept me. I want to live right but then... I feel what I feel."

Cassandra takes Gigi's glass from her and puts their glasses down on the table. She takes Gigi's hands within hers and gently pulls Gigi toward her.

"Gigi," Cassandra said. "There's nothing wrong with those feelings. Attraction is natural. After all, God did create it. So why not explore what appeals to you. Why limit yourself."

"I've been struggling with this a long time. And..."

"And I can see how much you worry. Like I said, life's too short." Cassandra lets go of Gigi's hands and sits up. "Everybody has to make their own choices. See Gigi, I'm a bit different, cause I say, do what feels good now." Cassandra shrugs. "Worry about the rest later."

"How," Gigi's eyes start to well up. "I... I disgust my mother."

Gigi lowers her head and sniffles. Cassandra reaches out, puts her finger softly on Gigi's chin and lifts her head. Tears run down Gigi's face. Cassandra moves Gigi's hair away from her face and gently wipes the tears from her eyes.

"Well it's sad, and a shame that your mother doesn't see you, as I do."

Gigi takes Cassandra's hands within hers and gently pulls Cassandra closer.

"So tell me-what do you see?"

"I see a beautiful, caring, and passionate woman."

"Really?"

"I do."

They move toward each other in anticipation wanting to share a passionate kiss. When they hear the front door slide open.

"Hello!" Lexi said. "I'm finally home!"

As the door slides shut Gigi promptly gets up, grabbing her glass of wine and hurries over to the living room windows, wiping her tears. A few seconds later Lexi comes out the hallway, looking all voguish, in a white, Valencia fancy blouse, a Donna Karan parchment, crushed pencil skirt, siren high heels with an MK bag in hand. Gigi turns to her as Lexi gives a big wave.

"Hello to all," Lexi said.

"Hey, well it's about time," Gigi said. She points to Cassandra. "Your company's been waiting forever."

"Well look at you!" Cassandra said getting up. "Looking all girlish, and sexy, dressed all corporate chic."

Gigi, sounding like a guy from the hood, jokingly said, "Yo boo, let me get that number."

"Don't start," Lexi said. "Every so often I have to bust out in a skirt or dress. It was my turn to handle the monthly press conference for my job. So, as you see, I had to dress for it."

"You look so pretty," Cassandra said with a smile.

"Y'all could not imagine the day I had!" Lexi said.

"Same here," Gigi said.

Lexi rests her bag down on a barstool, takes off her heels and walks over to the sectional. As Lexi comes over Cassandra approaches her.

"Hello to you," Cassandra said.

"Hey," Lexi said. "I need a few minutes to relax. I'll change, then we'll head out."

Gigi watches Cassandra put her arms around Lexi.

"Okay, you're looking all types of sexy," Cassandra said."

They embrace, Cassandra squeezes Lexi tight.

"Now this is my type of greeting. You feel good."

"Well, I'm glad you're home."

"I'm glad I'm home too."

While they embrace, Cassandra seductively looks at Gigi and winks. Gigi shakes her head looking away as she heads over to the kitchen drinking down the rest of her wine.

"I need more wine," Gigi said. "Y'all want some."

Cassandra and Lexi separate. Lexi looks over at Gigi.

"No, I'm good," Lexi said.

Gigi goes to the kitchen, Lexi and Cassandra take a seat on the sectional.

"Work was crazy today," Lexi said. "Seeing your sexy self, makes me feel a whole lot better."

"I have that effect on people," Cassandra said.

"I bet you do."

"I do."

Gigi comes over to the sectional with her fresh glass of wine and takes a seat by Lexi. Cassandra looks at Gigi

"You're feeling better, right Gigi?" Cassandra said.

'Excuse me?' Gigi said

"Yeah-excuse me?" Lexi said with a perplexed tone as she glances back and forth at both women.

"Gigi was going through something earlier, I happened to be here for her to talk to. I do hope I was helpful."

Lexi looks over at Gigi. "Well?"

"Well what?"

"Did she help you?"

"Yeah! She was very helpful, a great listener."

I bet she was. Lexi thought. She looks at Cassandra.

"Well, I'm glad you were there for her."

"Me too," Cassandra said.

"Thanks a lot," Gigi said as she leaned a little forward and looked over at Cassandra. "It was great talking with you."

"Same here," Cassandra said.

As they all sit there for moment an awkward silence takes over the room. Gigi nurses her wine, Lexi glances at each of them again as Cassandra picks up her glass and takes a few sips.

"Well," Lexi said. "I'm glad you two bonded."

"Yes," Gigi said.

"Yes, I'm glad we did too," Cassandra said.

Gigi drinks the rest of her wine straight down, gets up and turns to the ladies.

"I'm getting another," Gigi said. "It's been that kind of day. Cassandra another refill? Lexi you sure, you don't want some?"

"No, I'm good."

"I'm good too."

Gigi quickly heads to the kitchen to refresh her glass.

"So," Lexi said looking at Cassandra. "I'm gonna put my things in my room, change, hit the bathroom real quick and then we can go."

"Okay, I'll be right here," Cassandra said.

"Be back in a few," Lexi said.

Lexi gets up, picks up her heels, takes her bag off the barstool and heads to her bedroom. A few seconds later they hear Lexi's bedroom door open and close. Cassandra studies Gigi heading over to the island with her renewed glass of wine. They make eye contact but Gigi looks away pulling out one of the barstools and sits down.

Cassandra stands, picks up her glass of wine and heads over to Gigi. Cassandra makes eye contact with Gigi again as she passes by her going to the kitchen. Gigi sits at the island nursing her wine while looking through the living room windows. Cassandra pours the rest of her wine out and places the glass in the sink. She goes to the island and stands beside Gigi.

"I'm always available," Cassandra said. She reaches out and caresses Gigi's arm. "If you should ever need my help again."

"Umm thanks," Gigi said. Her eyes narrowed as she glanced at Cassandra in response to her touch. "I appreciate it."

Cassandra smiles a little as she watches Gigi take another healthy sip of wine. Gigi swallows it and looks up the hallway as she puts her glass down.

"Why are you acting so nervous?" Cassandra said.

"He'll Work It Out" Chapter 4. Taryn C. Atkins

"Nothing happen. Unless, you wanted something to... Did you?"

"A few more seconds and... Well... You leaned in."

"You did too. It's called chemistry, I like it." Cassandra whispers in Gigi's ear. "Don't you."

"Stop it."

Gigi takes a sip of wine and regroups. While being so close to Gigi, Cassandra gets another whiff of her perfume and her body tingles once again.

"That perfume you're wearing," Cassandra said, walking around Gigi to the other side of the island. "It's very enticing. What is it anyway?"

"It's a unique blend of oils. Doesn't really have a name, maybe I'll call it... enticing, I like that," Gigi looks deep into Cassandra's eyes. "And from that soft moan you make every time you catch its essence, apparently you do too."

Gigi raises a eye brow and slightly nods as they look at each other. Cassandra huffs, slightly smiling as she looks away for a second slowly shaking her head. Her eyes go back to Gigi.

"Touche'." Cassandra said with a nod

They smile and partake in an amorous stare. Lexi exits her bedroom. Cassandra takes her bag off the island, turns and walks over to the mirror on the wall. She checks herself in the mirror. After a few seconds, Lexi comes out of the hallway dressed in her comfortable tomboy gear.

"Alright, so let's go," Lexi said. She goes to Cassandra by the mirror. "You ready sexy."

"Of course," Cassandra said.

Gigi glances over her shoulder at Lexi and Cassandra. While Lexi watches Cassandra fix her hair, she smiles checking out her attire.

"I'm feeling that outfit," Lexi said with a mischievous grin. "So umm, we won't be out long, right?"

Cassandra looks at Lexi shaking her head.

"You are so bad," Cassandra said with a smile.

"I've heard," Lexi said.

"He'll Work It Out" Chapter 4. Taryn C. Atkins

Lexi heads to the kitchen and grabs two bottles of water out the fridge and places them on the island behind her. Cassandra picks up her shades off the island, and turns toward the hallway, she looks at Gigi before leaving. Lexi grabs a few grapes out the bowl in the fridge and closes it. As Lexi eats the grapes, she grabs the waters from off the island, looks over at Gigi and Cassandra.

"I'll see you soon Gigi," Cassandra said with a smile.

"Lata," Gigi said with a nod and a smile.

Their eyes stay locked on each other for a few seconds. As Lexi walks over, she notices the look between them. They both quickly turn away. Cassandra puts on her shades as she strolls up the hallway. Gigi beings to nurse her wine once again. Lexi glances down the hall at Cassandra as she approaches Gigi.

"My car's out front." Lexi said. "Go on downstairs, I'll be right there."

Cassandra slides the front door open, walks out and slides it shut behind her. Lexi's attention goes to Gigi, she eyes her hard for a few seconds. Gigi feeling her gaze turns to Lexi.

"Why are you looking at me like that?" Gigi said.

"Okay-what's up?" Lexi said.

"What are you talking about?"

"I know you."

"What?" Gigi takes a sip of her wine. "Don't act silly."

"I saw that look between you two; I know attraction when I see it. You turning aggressive on me?"

"What?! Me, an aggressive. Yeah right, come on."

Gigi gets up, takes her wine glass and walks over to the sectional. Lexi turns in her direction.

"Look, I'm not mad, Cassandra's fine. Maybe, she kick-started that aggressive side in you. It happens, don't worry its not like you're gonna run out and start buying boxers."

"That's funny but stop. Go on downstairs, she's waiting for you."

"All I'm saying, it's possible for a femme to have an aggressive side too."

"Will you stop it."

"I know how you can get. So don't bug out about it."

"Lexi will you get out of here."

Gigi sits down on the sectional looking at Lexi.

"Gigi just say the word, I'll back up from Cassandra; I've got Dana remember."

"I remember Dana, do you? You're terrible! Just go."

Lexi walks up the hall, the front door slides open but before leaving out.

"Gigi, remember!" Lexi proclaims. "Options, they're the spice of life!"

Gigi hears the door close, she lays down on the sectional, grabs a sofa pillow and places it on her chest.

"Cassandra." Gigi smiles, shaking her head. "Lord have mercy." She places the pillow over her face.

~CALLED HOME~

A week later, Leah and Wes, are dressed like they're headed out to dinner and to spend a night out on the town. Instead, they find themselves sitting in the green section again of the same surgical waiting room, where they and the rest of the family were at over a month ago. Their not alone this time in the massive room, a family sits and waits for news as well over in the purple section. There's also an older woman sitting behind the hospital information desk. As the various hospital sounds go forth, Wes sits on the small sofa, watching Leah as she paces back and forth in front of him.

"Baby sit down," Wes said. "No need to get yourself all worked up."

"I don't understand what happen." Leah said. "She was fine. Talking and laughing with me."

"Lee it's not your fault."

"I... I shouldn't have brought you with me. She gets so upset when she sees us together."

"Leah stop. We didn't do anything. Now come sit down."

Leah goes over to Wes and sits down next to him. He puts his arm around her and pulls her close.

"I'm scared Wes; I'm so frightened."

"I know, your mom's strong. She'll get through this."

They sit there in silence for a few minutes and Wes sees Regina in the hall. Regina rushes over to Leah.

"Hey y'all," Regina said. "I was at an audition when Dad called me. Aunt Leah what happened?"

"Oh God, Gina," Leah said, standing up. "Mama was sitting there on the sofa talking, she coughs and all this blood came out. Oh my God! Gina, there was so much blood."

"Rather then call an ambulance" Wes said. "I carried her to Lee's car and we rushed her over."

"Well have you heard anything?" Regina said."

"Cliff and Shayna are checking now," Leah said.

"Alright... Come on, let's sit down," Regina said.

They all grab a seat by the waiting room entrance.

"Did you get in touch with Gigi?" Leah said.

"Not yet," Regina said. "I texted her, told her to call me. I didn't want to leave a message; I'd rather talk to her."

"Yeah, well I let James know. He was out of town handling a client for Cliff. He just got on a plane."

"Grandma will get through this. God brought her through before. He'll do it again. Let's pray."

"Pray?!" As much as Mama used to pray, has God even heard her prayers?!"

"Come on now Aunt Leah, of course he has. He's heard her prayers and ours. I know things don't look great right now but we've got to have faith."

"Faith?! Really? Have you looked at our family? If God is so real, where is he at!?" Leah stands. "Why are we right back here?! Oh my God, I... I need some air."

Leah rushes from the waiting room. Wes stands, he looks at Regina and motions toward Leah.

"I'm fine," Regina said. "Go, she needs you."

Wes rushes out of the room and runs down the hall after Leah. Regina sits there praying and patiently waiting. A few moments later Cliff and Shayna enter the waiting room. Regina rushes to them. Shayna's eyes well up.

"Regina, Mama... Mama." Shayna said.

Shayna breaks down in tears, she moves into Cliff's arms. Cliff holds Shayna close to him and comforts her.

"Okay," Cliff said. "I know baby, I know."

"No, not Grandma..." Regina said. She starts tear up.

"This isn't supposed to happen." She goes to her father.

"Not like this Dad. Not like this."

They huddle together gaining strength from each other. Cliff holds them close as his tears roll down his face. Leah and Wes rush into the waiting room.

"You're back, how's..." Leah said. She stops in her tracks hears them crying. "Oh, God, Please no..." Her tears flow from her eyes as she turns to Wes. "No!"

Wes holds her close.

"I'm sorry Lee," Wes said. "I'm so sorry."

~CHAPTER 5~

~One's Remorse, One's Loathing & One's Compliance~

~HOME GOING~

It has taken time for the family to get things together and to prepare themselves for this day. About two weeks have passed and now this Saturday morning in the sanctuary of Full Gospel Temple the church is packed with the church family, natural family, friends, neighbors and associates who have gathered together for the Home Going Service of Mother Mae Babcock. Mama Mae told her family a long time ago, whenever the Lord calls her home she doesn't want anybody wearing black because it's a celebration. It's a *Home Going*, because she finally went on Home to Heaven, to be with her Lord. Mama Mae said she wanted everybody to be in bright colors and fine clothes like it's Resurrection Sunday.

Pastor Gorham sits on the pulpit, and behind him is seated Elder Mays and Elder Rayner. Marsha and Gilbert are seated toward the back of the pulpit to tend to Pastor and Lady Gorham. A beautiful slide show plays above the pulpit on the screen, showing various pictures of Mama Mae with her family and friends. In front of the pulpit Minister Thomas stands at one side of the casket and Minister Randall is positioned on the other.

Mama Mae's family sits on the left side of the sanctuary in the first two pews; the only two family members missing are Gigi and Reggie. Cliff has his arm around Shayna but keeps looking back at the church doors every few minutes to see if Gigi has arrived. Wes sits beside Nola and Dray seated with family and Kisha joins them as well. She keeps checking the crowd also to see if Reggie shows up. Across from the family in the first row sits Mother Livingston and the rest of the mothers of Full Gospel Temple. James, Shayna, Leah, Regina and Lady Gorham retake their seats after singing a selection dedicated to Mama Mae. It's now time for the home going eulogy.

"He'll Work It Out" Chapter 5. Taryn C. Atkins

Pastor Gorham stands with his black leather-bound Bible in hand and steps up to the podium; He looks over at the family and then out into the congregation.

"Good Morning All." Pastor Gorham said. "I won't be before you too long. I just want to share with you this morning, that special ingredient that makes this a home going service and not a funeral. And that, special ingredient is Jesus." He looks over at Mama Mae's family. "Family, I know your hearts are heavy. Mother Babcock will truly be missed but you all have the opportunity to see her again." He looks at the congregation. "Everyone here can see her again. You see, Mother Babcock accepted Jesus into her heart, she lived it, walked it, talked it and now she's made it! I plan on seeing her again. What about you?" He moves to the side of the podium. "There's no more time to be playing church. HELL IS REAL! It's my job to let you know that! I've got to tell you about confessing your sins, believing and receiving the Lord Jesus Christ into your heart, guide you in having a relationship with Jesus and living a righteous life. See, by doing that, heaven can be your home too. Jesus is soon to come, the two things that are definite is life and death. Where do you plan to spend eternity, because don't get it twisted there are only two choices. Heaven or Hell. So choose wisely."

As he speaks people in the congregation, respond back to him. He walks around on the altar as he delivers the word.

"Believe it or not even in this day and time people are still empty and dying inside, but whatever the void, Jesus can fill it. Not Buddha, not Muhammad, not Moon and not Confucius either. Jesus Christ! Many try to get around it, but there's no other name except Jesus can one receive salvation. Jesus is the vehicle that can take you from deception to true deliverance. Oh, don't make me preach teach up in here, cause that's another sermon. Jesus died on the cross and rose again. He sacrificed himself so you can be free and obtain eternal life."

Cliff turns around and notices Gigi standing in the back. He makes eye contact with her for a moment but she looks away. Cliff whispers to Shayna and gets up, when Gigi sees him making his way back to her, she leaves.

"The word says, in 1st Peter 4:18, look it up when you get home. I'm paraphrasing, "if the righteous scarcely be saved, where shall the ungodly and the sinner appear?" He goes back behind the podium. "I'll leave you with this; If you don't know Jesus for yourself, get to know Him before it's too late. I'm a witness, he can make you a new creature. So I admonish you, no as a matter of fact I dare you. Give Jesus a try. I'll tell you this, it'll be the best decision you ever made in your life. Well, I'm done. Now here's my lovely wife, Lady Gorham."

When Cliff gets to the back Gigi is already gone. Lady Gorham stands up, Pastor Gorham turns and passes her the microphone. He sits down as Lady Gorham steps to the podium.

"Good Morning everyone." Lady Gorham said. "It would be a dishonor to the Lord and Mother Babcock would surely be upset if we went on and didn't give you the chance to let Jesus into your heart. Please, come up if you want to give Jesus your life today."

The church musicians play worship music and after a few moments Leah and Nola come to the altar. Cliff rejoins the family as Lady Gorham goes over to Leah and Nola.

"Sisters, it's not a hard thing to accept Jesus into your heart. Just repeat after--"

Dray walks up to the altar also, family and people in the congregation praise God.

"Well, Praise God, I tell you, there's nobody like my Jesus. I can see Mother Babcock now, just smiling and dancing. Rejoicing right along with the angels."

Dray takes Nola's hand and kiss it. She looks at him through tear filled eyes and smiles. Leah looks back at Wes, he stares at her for a second or two, then shakes his head as he gets up and leaves. Leah turns her attention back to Lady Gorham, who starts to recite the Sinner's Prayer.

"Please repeat after me. Dear Jesus, I confess that I am a sinner. I'm sorry for all my sins and I repent of them. I believe in my heart and now confess with my mouth, that I believe in Jesus Christ, that you lived, suffered, died and rose again so that I can be saved, and not perish and have everlasting life. Please come into my heart, Jesus. I receive your salvation, and I want to follow you the rest of my life. Thank you, Jesus. Amen."

They all say the words that will change their lives forever. Dray keeps his emotions restrained while Nola and Leah slowly shed tears of joy. They turn to each other and embrace. Lady Gorham comes off the pulpit and hugs each of them.

"The angels are rejoicing," Lady Gorham said, she heads back to the podium. "Praise God saints."

One of the ushers hands each of them some Kleenex for their tears. Leah, Nola, and Dray retake their seats with the family.

"We'll now proceed with the final viewing. After the burial, the repass will take place at the home of Deacon and Deaconess Greye. The address and directions will be available to you on the table in the vestibule. Thank you for being here today."

~LAMENT OF REMORSE~

It's a beautiful summer afternoon, the birds are chirping and a fresh wind is blowing. The burial ended an hour ago and Reggie was watching from a distance, hiding behind one of the large headstones nearby, not wanting the family or anyone else to see him. Reggie slowly walks over to Mama Mae's grave site. He's still somewhat busted up and bruised from the pounding he received from James. Mama Mae's casket has already been lowered into the ground but the men haven't covered it. Reggie approaches the open grave, he moves to the edge and looks down into it. His face contorts being filled with mixed emotions consisting of regret, sorrow, and disbelief.

"He'll Work It Out" Chapter 5. Taryn C. Atkins

His grandmother the one that always looked out for him is gone. Four tormenting words are whispered within him, *"Its all your fault"* is used by the enemy to taunt Reggie pushing him toward the edge. Reggie looks at his grandmother's casket, the sounds of summer seem to fade around him with silence. Reggie struggles to kneel down by the grave, his eyes don't leave the casket, as tears roll down his face. His feelings erupt and he releases a long resounding wail from the depths of his being. After everything in him is spent, he collapses to his side and after a few moments rolls on his back. He cries, struggling to catch breath looking up into the sky.

"Grandma, I'm sorry," Reggie said. "I didn't mean for this to happen! Please forgive me!" He gets on his knees. "I didn't want this to happen. Lord Please, I'm sorry! I'm so sorry!" Tears stream down his face. "Please fix me Lord, please fix my heart, I need you! Lord, I can't do this without you."

Kisha kneels beside him, placing her hand on his shoulder. His eyes go to her.

"Kisha I didn't mean for her to get hurt... I didn't!"

"I know," Kisha said. "And Mama Mae knows that too, it's gonna be alright."

Kisha stands, helping him to his feet. He looks at her and they embrace for a moment and then go to her car.

~A DANCER'S PRAYER~

Later that same day, Gigi rushes out the elevator onto the twenty-fourth floor of her building. She said her hello's to the staff at the gym desk, then ran across the gym floor and into the dance studio. Gigi stood in the doorway, the only one left inside was the fitness trainer for her hip-hop aerobics class, and he was just about to walk out. She looked at the digital clock on the studio wall and it was 3:05 PM. The fitness trainer picks up his gym bag, turns to leave and sees Gigi standing in the doorway.

"Hey there Gigi." He said.

"Hey, Paris."

"He'll Work It Out" Chapter 5. Taryn C. Atkins

She smiled as he headed over, although Gigi played for the other team, she enjoyed looking at him. Paris was thirty-eight, about six-three, a muscular and cut up basketball player type body. He was handsome and milk chocolate, with a sexy pearly white smile, seductive eyes and born with swagger. The gold star at the top of this checklist was the fact he was totally sugar-free. Gigi shook her head as she watched him come over because she already knew, this complete and premium package was already the property of a lucky lady and the wedding ring on his finger was proof of that. Gigi smiled as he approached her. Paris stops in front of her, he raises his arms and rest his hands at the top of the doorway.

"Sorry, I missed class," Gigi said.
"There's always next week," Paris said.
"Is there another class tonight?" Gigi said.
"There was supposed to be," Paris said. "It got canceled."
"Think I could use the studio?"
"I don't mind. You got about forty-five minutes. There's a kickboxing class scheduled for four."
"That's great. I just needed it to... you know–"
"Dance... right? Do your thing, I'll let the desk know you're in here."
"Thanks, Paris, I appreciate it."
"No problem, Lexi told me about your grandmother. I'm so sorry. You have my deepest condolences."
"Thank you."
"How you holding up?"
"It's still in my head, It hasn't gotten to my heart yet."

A guy approaches them and when Gigi looks up, she does a double take because she sees an exact duplicate of Paris.

"Yo, man you ready to go?" He said.
"I'm coming now, Gigi, this is my brother Presley."
"Nice to meet you," Gigi said.
"Hello," Presley said. He takes Gigi's hand and kisses it.
"Nice to meet you too gorgeous."

Gigi takes her hand from Presley and looks at Paris.

"Wow you're a twin, that's incredible," Gigi said.

Presley puts his arm around his brother.

"He'll Work It Out" Chapter 5. Taryn C. Atkins

"He gets his looks from me." Presley said. "I'm the firstborn, the original. This guy, is the carbon copy."

Presley laughs. Paris pushes his brother away from him.

"I'm also the nice one," Paris said. He points at Presley.

"While this guy Gigi, well... don't get me started."

Presley leans up against the door frame.

"He's just mad," Presley said. "I don't have any ring holding me down; I'm what you call a wild stallion. It's gonna take someone that knows *exactly what they're doing* to control me and all I offer."

Paris shakes his head and huffs as he looks at his brother. Gigi shakes her head laughing a bit.

"Oh really, it's like that huh," Gigi said.

"Oh yes," Presley said. "See Gigi, I'm an actor and a model, and I thoroughly love what I do. Sometimes I love it so much, I tend to do shoot's that my agent tells me not to. My current agent is a rookie. I'm sure this one will let me go soon enough. It's a bit upsetting, they don't have the slightest idea what they're doing with me. I'm in negotiations right now with a new agent."

"So is acting in movies different from tv?" Gigi said.

"I only do movies," Presley said. He gestures toward Paris. "While this one is sweating all day and getting absolutely no pleasure out of it, at all. When I break a sweat; I'm enjoying every moment and so are my co-stars. I've been in a few select videos, maybe you've seen them."

"Ah yeah, I don't think so," Paris said. "Let me get him out of here. I'll see ya Gigi.

"Later Paris, bye Presley."

"Good night Gigi," Presley said.

Presley goes to take Gigi's hand again, Paris pushes Gigi's hand out the way and pushes Presley away from her.

"Let's go," Paris said. He looks at Gigi as they walk off.

"See you at the next class."

"Alright," Gigi said with a smile.

"He'll Work It Out" Chapter 5. Taryn C. Atkins

Gigi heads to the ladies locker room, after a few moments, she's back having changed her clothes. Gigi walks into the mirrored dance studio, stepping onto the sprung wood floor, she closes the door behind her and turns on the lights. The room brightens up before her and a smile comes on her face.

Gigi goes to the CD player, she puts her gym bag down, goes inside it, takes out a CD and puts it in the player. Gigi walks to the mirrored wall and scrutinizes her appearance in it. She's wearing a long sleeve, purple, liturgical dress with black, footless tights underneath.

"Wow," Gigi said to herself. "You haven't worn this for a long time. I'm surprised it still fits." She takes a deep breath and slowly exhales. "Grandma, I haven't danced like this for years, but this is for you."

Gigi goes to the CD player and presses play. She moves to the middle of the floor. The worship song takes over and Gigi begins to dance and as the vocalist sings.

She's a little tight, but as the song plays she loosens up. Gigi finally lets herself go and her movements flow with the music. All that is within her begins to come out and it changes from being a mere dance, to a prayer being sent up to the Lord. She relays all that she's feeling inside, and all that she needs and desires God to do, for her and within her. As Gigi dances, she pours herself out before the Lord and her tears flow as easily as her movements.

Gigi's unaware that her father is on the outside of the studio, looking through the glass. As Cliff watches her in awe, a tear rolls down his cheek because he hasn't seen her dance since she was nineteen. Gigi dances about the studio expressing all her emotions to God. She falls to the floor at the end of it and looks up to heaven as she cries.

"I love you grandma," Gigi said.

Cliff opens the studio door, he picks up a chair, goes over to Gigi, puts the chair down by her and takes a seat.

"That was beautiful," Cliff said. "I'm sure Mama Mae loved seeing you dance again. She's tapping God on the shoulder and pointing to you, saying all proud, "That's my granddaughter." She loved you so much."

"I didn't even have a chance to say goodbye," Gigi said. "I'm gonna miss her so much."

"We all will baby. Come on, you go change and let's go be with the family."

"Okay."

Gigi gets up, takes the CD out the player and puts it in her gym bag. She puts her gym bag on her shoulder, and they walk out the studio. Gigi turns around, feels for the light switch on the wall inside, flicks the light off and closes the studio door.

~THE REPASS~

Later that evening, various people were stopping by Cliff and Shayna's home. Shayna wanted space, so they lived further out on the island. It's a clear evening, the temperature is comfortable and there's a lovely summer breeze. Shayna decided to have the repass take place in their backyard. Years ago, since they had a decent amount of land, when Cliff's business took off he decided to revamp it. Cliff hired contractor's and had the whole backyard transformed into a great outdoor living area. The whole family loved it and there was something added for everybody.

You could enter the backyard through the house or by way of the beautifully designed, wooden garden gate at the side of the house. As people arrived with food, they placed what they brought, on the counter in the area that was considered Cliff's second man cave. Which was the custom shaded, outdoor kitchen, equipped with sink, grill, side burners, ice compartment, storage space, and accessories. Family and visitors were seated in various places. Now on the first level of the deck, where the outdoor kitchen was, just a few steps away from it people were seated around the deck table. While a few feet away some sat around the fire pit. Others were a mere five stair steps down on the next level and seated around the pool.

Besides the sounds of nature, gospel music was softly playing tucked under the various conversations going forth between family, friends and a few of the Full Gospel Temple church members. Regina was at the gate saying goodbye to a few of Mama Mae's neighbors, that had stopped by to show their respect.

"Again, thank you so much for coming," Regina said.

Regina waved and closed the gate. As she turned around, Minister Randall was approaching her.

"So how are you holding up?" Minister Randall said."

"I'm doing okay right now," Regina said. "It's still so hard to believe."

Minister Randall takes Regina's hand in his and kisses the top of her hand.

"Well you know, I'm here for you." Minister Randall said.

"I know Andre, thank you."

Regina steps closer to Minister Randall and gently lays her hand on his chest. They look into each others eyes, he wraps his arms around her, he leans in and kisses Regina. She gets ready to move away but kisses him back. About a second or two into the kiss they both quickly back away from each other.

"Ooh Lord, I wanted to do that all day." Minister Randall said.

He bends over and places his hands on his knees.

"Me too, but you know we--" Regina said.

"I know I know." Minister Randall said. He stands up. "This isn't as easy as it looks."

"I know," Regina said. "It's tough for both of us."

"Alright." Minister Randall said. "If you say so."

"Excuse me," Regina said. She shoves him. "It is."

He laughs as he steps toward her and takes her hand.

"I'm just playing." Minister Randall said. "Oh, your mother's asking for you."

"Again?" She takes a deep breath and exhales." Alright, where is she now."

"She's sitting by the end of the pool."

They walk off holding hands and head back toward the backyard. Sister Richardson and Sister Carlton are sitting at the deck table, they enjoy their piled up plates of food and their glasses of ice cold lemonade, as they watch everybody there.

"They have a gorgeous home." Sister Carlton said. "You see they had this outside. I'm sure that was Ms. Shayna's idea."

"Well, use the bathroom at some point." Sister Richardson said.

"You're so right." Sister Carlton said.

"I don't blame her though," Sister Richardson said. "Can't trust everybody, that's family and church folks included. Everybody ain't saints like we are."

They continue to eat their food and nurse their glasses of lemonade. Sister Carlton takes a sip of her lemonade and looks around as she places her glass on the table.

"This is one of those swanky Long Island neighborhoods." Sister Carlton said. "You know, one of those exclusive communities, not gonna see too many of us around here. I bet it was her idea to move around here."

"Well, they didn't just move here." Sister Richardson said. "My mom told me, they've lived here for about twenty years, ever since the girls were small. I ain't mad at them either. If you got it, why not have it. Praise the Lord."

"Oh they got it too, their always getting in the tithe and offering lines."

"Well, if you paid your tithes and gave more than a five dollar offering sometimes. God could bless you too."

"Now listen here, don't be starting with me."

"I'm just saying, the truth is the truth anyhow." Sister Richardson takes a sip of her lemonade and puts the glass down. "Anyway, it was a beautiful service."

"Yes, it was. I didn't see Minister Pauls around."

"Me either, you think she would be there. Or at least, make an appearance here. She's part of the leadership."

"Well you know, some folks don't go to things like this."

"True, if that other daughter shows up... things may get mighty interesting."

"Well," Sister Carlton leans back in her chair. "I'm glad we're front row center."

"He'll Work It Out" Chapter 5. Taryn C. Atkins

Nola opened the backyard door and as she stepped out onto the deck Elder Mays and Elder Rayner approached.

"Dear, we're going to head out." Elder Mays said.

"Oh, okay," Nola said. "We appreciate all you've done."

"Look, that's no problem." Elder Rayner said. "We're glad to help out."

"Yes yes, Mother Babcock was one of the pillars of Full Gospel Temple. Elder Mays said.

"We all loved mother very much." Elder Rayner said.

"Well, I know Mama Mae loved her church and her church family a great deal," Nola said.

"She will be greatly missed." Elder Rayner said.

Elder Mays points over to Shayna.

"Please check on Shayna." Elder Mays said. "She keeps asking for Cliff. I saw him when we got back from the burial but I haven't seen him for a moment now."

"I'll go see about her," Nola said. She starts to walk away.

"Once again thank you so much for everything."

"You're welcome." Elder Mays said.

"Give us a call if ya need anything." Elder Rayner said.

"We'll do that," Nola said.

As Nola walked away, Elder May's went over and opened the backyard door. She and Elder Rayner went into the house and left. Nola walked across the deck before she could get to the steps Dray met up with her.

"Hey, come here you," Dray said.

Dray put his arm around Nola's waist and pulled her to him.

"Hi, baby," Nola said.

"Just wanted to check on ya," Dray said. "How you feeling?"

"I'm gonna miss Mama Mae," Nola said. "You never actually realize how much a person affects your life until their gone. I spent more time with her this year then any other and I learned a lot from her."

"Well, from the first time she met me, she treated me like one of her own. Me being adopted, I loved that. Yeah, I'll miss Mama Mae; I'm glad you learned a lot from her too. Especially how to make her sweet potato corn bread.

Man, I can shout on that alone."

"You so silly. Look, I'm gonna check on Shayna."

"Okay well, I'm sitting by the fire pit."

"Alright, I'll be over."

Nola goes to walk away but Dray doesn't let her go.

"Gimme a kiss first." Dray puckers up his lips.

"Dray you need to stop."

"What? Everyone here knows we're married, and I haven't kissed my wife all day; I want a kiss."

"We're in the middle of the deck."

"Well, I'm not talking about a down and dirty kiss. Just a nice long tap kiss, that's all."

"Everyone can see."

"Alright alright, I'll have a temper tantrum right now. You know I'll do it too. So it's either give me a kiss or I'll drop to the ground right now. I swear; I'll do it. It's up to you."

Nola takes note of whose around, and looks at Dray and slowly shakes her head.

"See your crazy self will do it."

"I will too. Just because I got saved doesn't mean I lost my sense of humor. So... what's it gonna be? Hmm."

Dray and Nola looked at each other smiling. Nola closed her eyes and leaned in, they shared a nice long tap kiss and when they separated Dray added sound to it.

"Mwah! Thank you, baby."

"Happy now?"

"Yes I am, I'm gonna go sit down now."

"I'll be over there after I check on Shayna."

"Alright."

Dray turns around with a big smile on his face and skips over to the fire pit. Nola laughs watching him. He gets to his seat by the fire pit, looks at Nola and waves at her energetically. Nola smiles, shakes her head a bit and walks down the steps to the pool. She looks across and sees Shayna sitting at the tail end. Nola leans against the railing before heading over to her. She takes a moment to think and gets lost in her thoughts. When Dray sits down, he notices everyone over at the fire pit is either smiling or laughing at his antics. Except for James, who's looking at him strange.

"What in the world was that?" James said.

"That was me, making my wife feel better," Dray said.

"By jumping around and looking foolish," James said.

"Yes, because it made her laugh and look at her, now she's smiling. Which means, I made her feel just a little bit better today."

"You looked silly to me."

"Well, it wasn't for you either."

"Yeah well, I don't get it."

"Which is why you're not married."

Regina and Minister Randall come around into the backyard. Regina observes Nola by the steps as she and Minister Randall approached. Regina could see Nola looked somewhat out of it.

"I'm gonna grab something to eat." Minister Randall said.

"Okay," Regina said.

Minister Randall goes up the steps and to the outdoor kitchen.

"Aunt Nola?" Regina said, tapping her. "Hey, you okay?"

"Oh, I'm sorry," Nola said. "I was just thinking; I've been best friends with your mom for a while but it's only been within this year, that I actually started to spend some time with Mama Mae. I was always so busy. I should've made more time."

"Well, hold onto the time you did spend with her. You know grandma loved you and Uncle Dray."

"Yeah I know, she was so happy for us when we got married."

"She's especially happy for you two today." Regina smiles and rubs Nola's arm. "I'm sure grandma shouted seeing y'all get saved today. I'm happy for all of you too."

"You know," Nola nods her head and smiles. "I am too."

Shayna sat alone at the end of the pool and stared at the mountainous backdrop of the swimming pool. Although it was an artificial rock formation, Cliff had the builders make it mimic one of nature's unique wonders. So, while Cliff's favorite spot was his indoor man cave and the outdoor kitchen. Shayna's was the custom waterfall and grotto Cliff had built just for her. It was her peaceful retreat and she smiled remembering how much her mother loved it.

A water slide was created for their girls, it started at the top of the mountainous structure, just above the waterfall. The slide was about five feet above the waterline, it came around and ended a few feet away from the waterfall. When you swim through the waterfall, you enter a grotto which had bench seating, fiber optic lighting, and speakers. This waterfall was a natural, safe haven for Shayna and a soothing gateway to their romantic hideaway. Shayna smiled and her face saddened a bit also as she remembered the good and bad times that have taken place around the pool. Shayna sighed as she looked over toward the house. Seeing Nola and Regina, she signaled to them to come over.

"Well, duty calls," Nola said, pointing to Shayna. "Guess your mom wants us to come over."

"You go, it's your turn anyway," Regina said. "I'm gonna check on Aunt Leah."

Regina walks away, she goes up the steps and over to the fire pit. There are six dark gray wicker deck chairs with burgundy back and seat cushions, plus a matching bench. They were in a square formation around the fire pit, and seated around the fire pit were Leah, James, Dray, Mother Livingston, Minister Thomas and Minister Randall was sitting on the bench. Regina went over and sat down next to Minister Randall. A conversation went on between Dray, Mother Livingston and Minister Thomas, James scooted his chair closer to Leah and leaned over to her.

"Leah, you've got to talk to me at some point," James said.

"No. I don't," Leah said. "At least not today and not now."

"Leah," James said. "I'm not saying what I did to Reggie was right. Yes, my anger took over. He's a grown man though, and he needed to learn there are consequences to your actions."

"That still doesn't excuse what you did," Leah said.

"I know that, but I came to you like a man should, and

told you myself. I've apologized several times too."

"I know you have; I even understand why you did it," Leah said. "I'm still angry that you did though."

"Well," James said. "I'm not gonna lie-I'm still mad at Reggie! I'm trying to let it go... right now, I just can't."

"Part of me is angry at him too, but that's still my child. I'm just worried about him. Nobody has seen or heard from him. Not even Kisha. I just pray he's alright."

Minister McDaniels and Sister Cantres were seated by the pool for a while, they stood up, got their things and headed over to the group seated around the fire pit.

"We're getting ready to leave." Minister McDaniels said."

"You all have my deepest condolences and are in my prayer's." Sister Cantres said. From the little time I got to know Mother Babcock, me being newly saved, she showed me so much love and imparted so much wisdom into my life. She was a true child of God and sweetly saved as Elder Mays would say."

"Thank you so much, darling," Leah said.

"I know I'm gonna miss having Mother Babcock around." Minister McDaniels said.

"Yes, Mama Mae was a beautiful person," Dray said.

"I look forward to seeing her again in glory." Minister McDaniels said.

"That's right, I do too." Minister Thomas said.

"Oh, I made a big pan of ox tails for you." Minister McDaniels said. "Plus a pot of peas and rice." She points over to the outdoor kitchen. "There over on the counter. I hope you like them."

"Oh, I tasted some already!" James said. "They are good! Thank you so much."

Minister Randall had a plate in his hand, he finishes eating the meat off of one of the oxtails and puts the bone down. He sucks the gravy off his fingers, points down to his plate as he looks over at Minister McDaniels.

"I got some right here!" Minister Randall said. "And as James said, they are good!" He looks over at James. "Can

I get an Amen Brother James."

"AMEN Brother!" James said.

Everyone around the fire pit laughs.

"Well thank you." Minister McDaniels said.

"My grandmother loved your cooking," Regina said.

"Well, I truly loved Mother Babcock." Minister McDaniels said. Alright then, we're gonna go."

Minister Thomas stands up saying. "Well let me walk you to your car."

"No need, it's right down the block." Minister McDaniels said. "So good night all, and we'll see you soon. God willing."

"Good night everybody." Sister Cantres said.

Minister Thomas retakes his seat. Everyone around the fire pit said good night to Minister McDaniels and Sister Cantres. The ladies went down the steps and around to the backyard gate. Those sitting around the fire pit continued talking among themselves. Regina glanced over at her mother. Shayna was seated and Nola was standing by her. As Shayna spoke to Nola, her eyes would gaze toward the house ever so often, watching for Cliff.

"Where in the world did Clifford go?" Shayna said.

"He probably needed some air," Nola said. "You know, just a moment to himself. It's been tough for all of us Shayna. I'm sure he'll be back soon."

"Well, not soon enough," Shayna said as she stood up.

"Let me check in the house."

Shayna marched toward the house. Nola watched her for a second, shook her head and huffed. *Take it down a notch.* Nola thought following Shayna inside the house. Leah and Regina are over at the outdoor kitchen. Leah fixes herself a plate of food.

"Gina, to tell the truth, I'm glad everyone is almost gone," Leah said. "The more people try to comfort me, the more I just want to be left alone." She puts some fried chicken on her plate. "I mean, the grief comes and goes, but these conversations." She puts a scoop of potato salad on her plate. "They are not helping." She gets a

Solo cup from the stack and pours herself some Sprite. "Anyway, how are you holding up?"

Regina leans back against the counter as Leah starts to eat.

"Alright thus far," Regina said. "It'll hit me later. Hey, I thought Wes would be here with you."

"Please," Leah said. "Don't get me started about that man."

Cliff arrives back home, pulls his car into the driveway and a few moments later Gigi pulls her car up behind his. They get out their cars. As Gigi walks over to her dad, she smooths out the loose, open back summer dress she wore. Gigi leans up against Cliff's car re-adjusting the straw fedora hat she wore.

"I'm really nervous," Gigi said. "Dad, maybe-Maybe I should just go."

"No," Cliff said. "We're your family, and at a time like this. The family should be together." He holds out his hand to Gigi. "Alright?"

Gigi looks away, takes a deep breath and exhales. She looks at her dad's hand and stares at it for a few seconds. Gigi looks up at her father as she places her hand in his.

"Alright," Gigi said.

Cliff glances over Gigi's outfit as he takes her hand.

"Dress is kinda short don't you think?"

"Dad."

"You look great, it's cute... just a little short is all."

"Dad stop it, I've got biker pants on under it."

"Oh... okay."

Gigi shook her head and smiled as Cliff pushed open the gate, they walk hand in hand and head back to the backyard. They walk around, step up on the deck and go over to the fire pit.

"Sorry for being gone so long," Cliff said.

"Hello all," Gigi said.

Family and church members rush over and greet Gigi. When Sister Carlton sees Cliff and Gigi, she reaches over and taps Sister Richardson. They both sit up in their chairs paying close attention to what's going on.

"Hey lady, " Leah said. They hug each other. "You

holding up okay?

"I'm trying," Gigi said. As they release each other. "Glad I'm here with the family ."

"I'm glad too," Regina said. She hugs her sister tightly.

Cliff comes over, puts his arms around Regina and Gigi.

"We're all glad." Cliff said.

Cliff hugs them both at the same time and as he releases them. He rests his hand on Gigi's shoulder.

"You hungry, I'll fix you a plate," Cliff said.

"Not right now," Gigi said.

"You okay?" Cliff said.

Gigi shakes her head, takes a deep breath and exhales, as she forces a smile.

"I'm getting there," Gigi said.

"Sis," Regina said, taking Gigi's hand in hers. "I'm right here with you."

"Okay, I'll be back," Cliff said. "I'm gonna go change."

Everyone goes back around the fire pit. This time, Gigi and Regina sit on the bench together. Sister Carlton and Sister Richardson watch so intently; that they might as well pop popcorn. Cliff goes to the backyard door and before he can grasp the door knob. Nola pushes the door open and steps out onto the deck. She looks right into Cliff's eyes as she heads over to the fire pit.

"Betta get ready, she's right behind me." Nola said.

Shayna comes out onto the deck, her eyes fall on Cliff and before he can get a word out she steps to him.

"Where did you disappear to?" Shayna said.

Before Cliff gets the chance to answer, laughter breaks out over at the fire pit. Shayna and Cliff look over and Shayna sees Gigi sitting there. Shayna swiftly turns to Cliff.

"What is she doing here?!" Shayna said.

Before Cliff can even form the words to reply, Shayna becomes irate because of Gigi's presence and rushes over to her. Cliff reaches out, grabs Shayna's arm and pulls her close.

"Stop this," Cliff said." She has a right to be here."

Shayna snatches her arm from his grip and promptly goes to Gigi. Cliff follows her over, stands at the side of the bench. Shayna realizing guest are still at the house tries to keep her emotions under control.

"What are you doing?" Shayna said. "You need to go."

"Don't do this." Cliff said.

"Ma," Gigi said. "At a time like this. I... I need to be with my family."

"Ma, what are you doing?!" Regina said.

"Gigi I want you to go now, please," Shayna said, trying to contain her emotions. "You can't be here."

"Ma come on. Gigi said. "Please."

You gotta be kiddin me. Leah thought as she watched Shayna go at Gigi.

"I don't want you here," Shayna said. "Can't you just understand that."

"Ma, you can't do this-" Gigi said.

"I want you out NOW!" Shayna points toward the gate. "GET OUT!"

The family and guest are shocked by Shayna's outburst. Sister Carlton and Sister Richardson in unison turn their chairs toward the confusion. Leah stands and moves toward Shayna.

"I don't believe you, Leah said. "Stop this."

"The family needs be together," Cliff said. "Especially right now."

"I want her to leave, now!" Shayna said pointing at Gigi.

"You are so wrong," Leah said.

"This is none of your business Leah!" Shayna said.

"Right now! It's all of our business!" Leah said.

The few Full Gospel Temple members left at the house are stunned by what's happening but two members are enjoying their front row seats. Regina's eyes well up.

"Why are you doing this?!" Regina said.

"Shayna this is ridiculous," Nola said, going over to comfort Regina. "She's your daughter!" Gesturing toward Gigi.

Gigi's own emotions overwhelm her.

"She hasn't been my daughter for a long time," Shayna

said.

"Fine!" Gigi said rushing to her feet.

Shayna caught off guard takes a few steps back. Gigi walks toward the steps, as she passes her father Cliff touches her arm.

"Gigi don't go, please," Cliff said.

"It's alright dad," Gigi said. "I shouldn't have come." She walks down the steps. "First I want to know why." She swiftly turns to Shayna. "Can you at least tell me that? What is so horrible about me?!"

"I said GET OUT!" Shayna said.

"NO!" Gigi said. She walks back up the steps, pointing at her mother. "You look me in my face and tell me why!"

"Why?! Because this is a Christian house, and I don't want you and that lifestyle in it..." Shayna turns away, taking a few steps toward the house. "So please, just leave!"

Gigi rushes over, stopping in front of her mother.

"Just say it then Ma! You want me to leave because I'm a... Butch!? Dyke!? Lesbian!? How about simply Homosexual?"

Shayna steps to Gigi, pointing at her saying, "Get Out!"

Shayna turns away, walks over to the steps grabbing the railing. Gigi turns toward her mother.

"You can't even say it, can you?"

Gigi goes to Shayna, "Look at me, Ma! Look At Me!"

Shayna doesn't turn around to Gigi at all. She just crosses her arms and looks straight ahead her.

"Can't even give me that much. Well, I'm done."

Gigi walks down the steps getting ready to leave. Regina quickly stands up, tears start to roll down her face.

"Gigi no! Come back... Please." Regina said.

Gigi stops moving, tears run down her face too. Gigi doesn't look back, she looks over her shoulder, shakes her head and proceeds to leave. Cliff runs down the steps and over to Gigi getting in her path. Shayna's eyes go to them.

"Gisele please," Cliff said. "Please, gummy bear, I'm asking you. Don't go."

Gigi lowers her head crying. She takes a deep breath and slowly exhales.

"Sorry papa bear."

Wiping her tears Gigi shakes her head and looks up at her father.

"Dad, I am done." Gigi looks over at Shayna. "Don't worry, you won't ever see me again."

Gigi promptly walks away, going around to the gate. She opens it, looks back toward the backyard and leaves. The wooden gate closes behind her. The family hears a car start up, followed by screeching tires as it speeds off. As Regina sits back down on the bench, Minister Randall sits by Regina, placing his arm around Regina consoling her. Leah walks over to where she was seated, picks up her purse and turns to Minister Thomas.

"Can you please drive me home? Leah said. "It is time for me to go."

"Sure, we should go too." Minister Thomas said. He stands up. "Mother Livingston, are you ready to go?"

"Yes, I am." Mother Livingston said as she stood up."

"Andre, you coming with us?" Minister Thomas said.

"No, of course not." Minister Randall said.

Regina looks at Minister Randall as she wipes her tears.

"It's okay Andre, I need to stay here." Regina said.

"You sure?" Minister Randall said.

"Yes, I'll be okay. You go." Regina said.

"I'll call you when I get home." Minister Randall said. He stands and looks at Minister Thomas. "I have to get my jacket, it's in the house. I'll meet you at your car."

"Okay." Minister Thomas said.

Minister Randall goes to the backyard door and into the house. Leah, Mother Livingston and Minister Thomas head over to the steps. Minister Thomas helps Mother Livingston down the steps. Leah huffs as she approaches Shayna.

"Baby, you never cease to amaze me," Leah said. "Do you really have the Holy Spirit?! Because one thing I do know, it doesn't do that." She walks down the steps, turns and looks at her sister. "You should be ashamed of yourself. I'll tell you this. If being saved, means I can get like you; I may rethink this whole thing."

Leah walks off, she goes over to Cliff and pats him on the shoulder. Mother Livingston turns to Shayna.

"I'm glad your mother wasn't here to see that." Mother Livingston said. "What happen here was atrocious! Today of all days." She points at Shayna. "Make it right with that girl. Before you don't get the opportunity to make it right." She turns to Minister Thomas. "I'm ready now."

"Yes ma'am," Minister Thomas said.

Leah walks around to the gate. Minister Thomas walks with Mother Livingston. They stop by Cliff, Minister Thomas reaches out and they shakes hands as he looks over at Shayna.

"Deacon Greye, Deaconess Greye," Minister Thomas said. "I'll be praying for you and with you. Remember, God is there for you. Please call me if you need anything."

"I will." Cliff said.

Cliff glances at Shayna and then toward the wooden gate watching as Leah, Mother Livingston, and Minister Thomas leave. He sees Minister Randall waiting for them on the other side of the gate. Minister Randall looks at Cliff and raises his hand to him, saying bye. Cliff raises his hand to him also and nods. There's tension in the air and silence for a few moments. Cliff walks up the steps staring hard at Shayna. He steps onto the deck and stands by her, before speaking he continues to glare at her.

"You know what," Cliff said. "I've put up with a lot of things you've done."

Shayna promptly turns to him.

"Cliff--" Shayna said.

"No! Let me finish." Cliff said. "For you to be so cruel, and at a time like this too. Well, that just takes the cake."

He huffs looking at her. "Congratulations."

Cliff goes to walk away and Shayna grabs his arm.

"Cliff please."

"Let go, Shayna."

"Cliff..." Shayna holds on to his arm.

"I said let go of me!"

Cliff yanks his arm away from her, rushes to the backyard door, snatches it open and goes inside. The family and guest who remain stare at Shayna. The tension in the atmosphere is thick. Shayna looks around and her eyes go to Sister Carlton and Sister Richardson.

"Please, forgive my family," Shayna said. "As you know, it's a terrible time for all of us."

"Us?! Nola said. "Is that what you just said? Us?!" She approaches Shayna. "Even before Mama Mae passed, the only person you've cared about is yourself!" She mocks her. "I'm so upset. I can't take this. Can't they see what I'm going through?" She gets in Shayna's face. "I'm sick of it!" She points at her. "If you don't get it together soon, all you're gonna be left with is you." She walks down the steps. "Dray I'll be in the car."

"I'm right behind you baby." Dray said.

Nola goes to their car. Dray gets up and steps to Shayna.

"You know, when I first met Nola," Dray said. "She always talked about you, you being her loving, caring and compassionate best friend." He motions toward Shayna. "She looks up to you." He stands by Shayna but looks forward. "See, I told her, that friend she talked so much about was dead and gone. I'm sure this, has opened her eyes." He looks at Shayna. "I hope you're happy cause now... She's grieving for two people." He looks over at James as he walks down the steps. "Later man."

"Man, I'm out too," James said. "I'll call you."

"Alright." Dray said. He looks at Regina. "See ya Gina."

"Bye," Regina said.

Dray leaves. James goes the backyard door, opens it but before he goes in he looks at Regina.

"Gina, come on," James said.

"No, it's alright," Regina said. "I'm gonna help clean up."

"You don't have to," James said.

"James stop... I'll be fine. I'll call you later."

"Alright." James looks over at Shayna at sucks his teeth.

"Well, you've done it again... as usual." He goes in the house.

There are only the sounds of nature to be heard. The only guest left are Sister Richardson and Sister Carlton. They stand, get their things and approach Shayna.

"So, we're gonna go." Sister Carlton said. "Have a good night."

"Good night now." Sister Richardson said.

They leave and the sound of the wooden gate closing behind them is heard. Shayna goes to Regina and sits beside her on the bench. They sit in silence for a few seconds, then Regina speaks.

"Ma, don't you see," Regina said. "You're in His way! God tries to move here, and you get in His way." She gets up, takes a few steps and turns to her mother. "He tries to move again and again you get in His way. Jesus will fix everything, but you have to get out of His way!"

"It's... it's not my fault Gigi is..." Shayna said. She stands up. "And I won't be blamed either, understand me?! It's not my fault Regina. It's Not!"

"Ma nobody said--"

"I didn't do that to her! " Shayna rushes pass, Regina. "I'm not responsible for her being... No! I can't be! I won't be!"

Shayna rushes in the house. Regina stands on the deck, she looks around and sees she's alone. She looks over at the outdoor kitchen, seeing all the pans and containers of food on the counter top. Regina looks over at the table where Sister Carlton and Sister Richardson was seated and sees dirty plates as well.

"Well, let me get these dishes, and get the food inside."

Regina goes over to the table, picks up the dishes and cups left on it. She brings the dishes over to the sink in the outdoor kitchen and her emotions overtake her. She throws the dishes in the sink and falls to the floor with tears stream down her face.

~CHAPTER 6~

~Uncovered Lies, Relinquished Desires

& Revealed Truths~

~BETRAYAL'S REVELATION~

Leaving from the repass Minister Thomas drove Leah straight home. She hoped Wes would be back and waiting there to comfort her. Especially after such an emotional time of laying her mother to rest, but of course, when she enters she finds herself alone. All Leah did at that point was go into her bedroom. She didn't even change out of her clothes, for the day had taken its toll. Leah laid across her bed, she reached around, grabbed her body pillow at the head of the be and pulled it to her. Closing her eyes he held it close.

Leah slept for a few hours because of the mental and emotional overload that the past two weeks have took her through. She woke up late that night to the sound of her house phone ringing. Leah reaches over to her nightstand and picks up the cordless phone, still half asleep as she answers the call.

"Hello... Hey... Where are you? I thought you would be here... I needed you with me Wes and you leave..." She rolls onto her back. "Oh my goodness... Are you serious right now... .Wes, I can't do this." She abruptly sits up. "Wes, come on really? It's a travel bag!. Just get another one." She moves to the edge of the bed. "Fine, I'll send it!"

Leah ends the call. She sits on the side of her bed and stretches. She sees Wes's travel bag on the corner of her dresser, sucking her teeth she huffs and climbs off the bed. Leah goes to her dresser, she grabs the strap on the bag, snatching it off the dresser and strides out her bedroom. Seconds later Leah walks into her kitchen carrying the travel bag.

"Now I'm Fed Ex sending packages."

Leah throws the travel bag on the kitchen island, pulls one of the chairs out and sits down.

"What's so important?"

Leah zips open the bag, she starts to look through the contents and sees its filled with various plastic pill bottles.

"Can he take any more vitamins? What's this? Bactrim DS? Wait... that's for HIV. Oh my God!"

Leah's face goes almost white realizing the magnitude of the situation Wes has placed her in.

"This can't be happening."

Leah leans back in the chair, looks up and repeatedly pounds her fist on the island.

"No... God no. This can't be happening to me."

~DARK COMFORT~

When Gigi left the repass, after such a volatile scene with her mother and the day just being one filled with a gamut of emotions. Gigi stopped in at her and Lexi's favorite bar in Chelsea. Her single purpose was to drown her feelings in several glasses Jack Daniel's.

Several hours have passed into the night, the sound of the front door is heard sliding open and then locks shut. As Gigi comes down the hallway, she passes by Lexi's bedroom door, there's jazz music softly playing, but it goes unnoticed. She staggers out the hallway still looking attractive in her loose, open back summer dress. She carries her MK totebag and straw fedora in one hand and her keys and heels in the other. Without the heels, the length of her dress still showed off her well-defined dancer's legs. Gigi went to the coat rack and dropped everything on the floor beside it.

"I'm done." Gigi said in a slurred tone. "I don't need you."

Gigi slightly stumbled heading over to the living room making her way to the sectional.

"You don't want me! Then I am done with you too,

Deaconess Greye!" She sits on the sectional. "So, so long!"

Gigi quickly stands up, turns around and points toward the living room windows.

"You hear that Deaconess Greye?! I don't need you!" Her body starts to sway back and forth. "Oh boy, I... I think I need to sit down." She sits down on the sofa. Her body starts to rock from side to side. "Guess I... need to lay down. Nap time for me."

Gigi lays on the sectional, grabbing the light summer blanket that's folded in the corner, she opens it and covers herself.

"Deaconess Greye, you don't have to worry about me-no more!"

Gigi puts a sofa pillows under her head and covers herself from head to toe. She's asleep in seconds. A few moments pass, a door opens and the silky voice of Cassandra resonates from the back of the loft.

"Hey, Lexi!" Cassandra said. "I thought you had to work.
Well, I'm glad you're home. Look I'm still getting ready.
Stay out there for a moment. I've got a surprise for you."

More time passes and Gigi remains asleep on the sectional. Cassandra walks out of the hallway, prepped for a sensual and stimulating evening. The long sexy nightgown she wears captures and accentuates her essence. As Cassandra walks over to the living room, seeing a lump laying under the blanket on the sectional she approaches.

"Aww, she fell asleep," Cassandra said. She goes over to the sectional and glides her fingers over the figure under the blanket. "Sweetheart, oh, Lexi." She shakes the figure. "Come on baby wake up!"

Cassandra watches as the silhouette under the blanket turns over. Gigi pulls the blanket from over her head and glances up.

"Hey there Cassandra," Gigi said with a yawn.

Cassandra, surprised to see its Gigi backs up a bit and smiles. Gigi still basically asleep, just turns over and goes back to her nap. Two or three seconds pass, all at once reality takes hold and Gigi abruptly sits up.

"Ca... Cassandra?! What are you doing here?!"

Cassandra laughs a little seeing Gigi's reaction.

"I thought you were Lexi," Cassandra said. "Since Dana's out of town, we planned to get together. Lexi thought you would be staying with your family tonight. Heard about your grandmother, my condolences."

"Thanks," Gigi said. She pulls the blanket off, stands and glances at Cassandra. "Well, I'm sorry for showing up."

Gigi carefully walks across the room to the kitchen. Cassandra watches her and sees Gigi is somewhat unsteady on her feet. Gigi opens one of the kitchen cabinets, grabs a glass and goes to the fridge. After getting a few ice cubes, Gigi takes out a bottle of bourbon from another cabinet. She brings the glass and whiskey over to the island and pours herself a drink. She gulps it down and pours another. After downing the second glass she looks at Cassandra.

"I'm sorry to be an inconvenience." Gigi said, pouring herself yet another glass of whiskey. "I didn't mean to mess up any bodies plans, like I apparently did earlier."

Gigi swallows her fresh glass.

"Please, stop apologizing," Cassandra said. She gets up and heads to the kitchen. "You're not an inconvenience." She goes to the fridge. "I saw Lexi for a late lunch, she gave me the keys, told me to make myself comfortable and she'd see me after work." She gets a bottle of water out and opens it as she approaches Gigi. "At the last minute Lexi's company sent her to handle some project in their Jersey office."

As Gigi goes to drink her next glass of bourbon, Cassandra takes the glass and hands her the bottle of water.

"Drink this," Cassandra said. "You've had enough of that."

Gigi drinks some water. Cassandra turns and leans against the island. Gigi backs up and leans against the kitchen counter.

"Anyway, Lexi was just suppose to work late," Cassandra said. She ended up having to stay over in Jersey, said I could stay here and she'll see me tomorrow afternoon. When I heard the door, I thought it was her and as you see," She opens her robe, and model's her nightgown to Gigi. "I was going to surprise her."

Gigi drinks more water as she watches Cassandra show off her lingerie. Gigi's inhibitions having been loosened, her newly revealed aggressive side keeps exerting itself and her attempts to control it keep failing.

"Mmm... nice surprise." Gigi said.

Gigi's unaware of the fact that she's staring at Cassandra, and that her eyes are carefully taking inventory of Cassandra's physique. A seducing smile comes upon Cassandra's face because she's well aware of what Gigi is doing. Cassandra being one who knows how to adapt swiftly, views this moment as a delicious opportunity. She closes her robe and leans back against the island once again.

"So, enough about me," Cassandra said. "How are you holding up?"

Gigi somewhat comes to herself shaking her head a bit. She huffs as she walks away, going to the living room and Cassandra follows her over.

"Well, I couldn't even grieve with my family," Gigi said.
"Cause my mother and I got into it again; I couldn't believe how she was acting, and at a time like this."
"Goodness, sounds like it got bad," Cassandra said.
"It was terrible!" Gigi said.

Gigi plops down on the sectional as she drinks more water. Cassandra sits down on the sectional tucking one leg under her and turns herself toward Gigi.

"I mean, come on mom," Gigi said. "We just buried your mother-my grandmother! And you really want me to deal with this all alone." She gets choked up. "You... you don't even want me to be with my family. Is she kidding me?! I... I can't even be with my family!"

Gigi's eyes start to well up but she forces back her tears.

"I'm so sorry," Cassandra said.

"I'm just so tired of being pushed away by her."

"Sounds to me like you have a right to feel that way."

"I mean, I try and try with her, but nothing changes." Gigi drinks more water. "Well, I've had it this time; I am so done!" She turns to Cassandra. "You know, I've had a few relationships with guys and they start out great, but..." She huffs shaking her head. "They never seem to work out. I end up getting hurt again and again and again. Which is another reason why I'm with women; I'm so tired of being the one getting hurt all the time. I refuse to take it from men, and I'm done taking it from mom too."

"When I was a teenager; I saw my father constantly cheat on my mother." Cassandra said. "They'd argue, he'd stop for a day or two but he'd do it again. My mom came from a very affluent family, it's not like she needed my father. When I turned seventeen, I told my mom to leave him," She shakes her head. "She wouldn't though, she was that doting, faithful and loving wife. He ended up leaving her, for some younger woman. My mom went into a deep depression. It landed her in the hospital too. You think he'd care right? Hmph, not at all. Instead, he took custody of my younger sister Cassidy, and took her with him."

Gigi shakes her head, "Now that's messed up."

Gigi nurses her bottle of water as she listens to Cassandra.

"After seeing my mom stay and take all that, I decided I'll never need or be involved with any man. So believe me, I understand where you're coming from."

"Which is why-" Gigi said.

Gigi gets up placing the water bottle on the coffee table. She goes to the kitchen, gets her glass of bourbon from the counter, comes back and sits down on the sectional. She moves over a bit putting a little distance between her and Cassandra.

"I need this." Gigi takes a sip from her glass.

"I see, so I guess no wine for you tonight?"

"Nope. I appreciate you giving me the water but tonight, I need something much stronger. I don't want to think or feel anything. I just want to move on pure impulse."

That's good to know. Cassandra thought.

Gigi finishes off her whiskey, stands with glass in hand and looks at Cassandra.

"I'm getting another and that's it for me."

Gigi heads over to the kitchen once again.

"Can you pour me some wine, please?" Cassandra said.

"Sure."

Gigi pours herself another and prepares wine for Cassandra.

"See... after tonight," Gigi said, getting a wine glass out the cabinet. "I've decided, I'm tired of playing by the rules." She takes a bottle of Merlot from the fridge. "Nobody else is playing by them anyway, so why should I?"

After pouring their drinks Gigi brings them over. Cassandra mouths thank you as she takes her glass.

"It's about having options, right?" Gigi said sitting on the sectional. "I hear having options is the spice of life."

Gigi takes a healthy sip of her drink.

"Well," Cassandra said.

Cassandra takes her wine, getting up from the sectional and walks over to one of the living room windows.

"Personally," Cassandra peers out the window at the beautiful view of the city. "I think its all about your preference. After all, it's a big city. Would you rather any flavor out there?" She turns and goes to the island, sits on a barstool and turns toward Gigi. "Or are your taste's more particular and refined?" As she crosses her legs, her robe falls open. "For... let's say a special delicacy, that's here."

Cassandra takes a sip of her wine. As Gigi nurses her drink her eyes trail up Cassandra's body, what Gigi doesn't realize Cassandra's eyes are also wondering intently.

"Goodness, you're fine." Gigi said.

Their eyes make contact and Cassandra smiles.

"See something you have a taste for?" Cassandra said.

"He'll Work It Out" Chapter 6. Taryn C. Atkins

Gigi shakes her head realizing her private thought was not that at all but her aggressive side making itself boldly known.

"I said more wine. I... I thought you were finished. So I was just asking... You know, if you wanted more wine?"

Gigi fans herself. "Is... is it getting hot in here?"

"It feels just right to me,"

Cassandra smiles seducingly nursing her glass. Gigi looks away, trying to regroup and dispel the sexual tension that is evident in the atmosphere. Gigi leans back, puts her legs up on the coffeetable and gulps down the rest of her glass of whiskey.

"Umm... again," Gigi looks over at Cassandra. "I'm sorry for messing up you and Lexi's plans, but you really wouldn't believe how my mother acted."

Cassandra gets up, comes back over to the sectional and takes a seat by Gigi.

"I'm sorry things are so bad between you two. Especially after your loss. You should have someone caring for you."

"Exactly! How about what I need?"

"You know what," Cassandra puts her glass on the coffeetable. "You're upset," She motions to the loft. "And this is your place. I'm sure you need some time to yourself. So clearly, I'm the inconvenience." Cassandra stands. "I'll just get dressed and go."

Cassandra goes to walk away, moving toward the hallway.

"No, wait!" Gigi reaches out and grabs Cassandra's hand. "I don't mind if you stay." She slowly releases her hand. "I... I like talking to you. Besides, Lexi's expecting you to be here when she gets in tomorrow."

"Right..." Cassandra nods a few times as she takes a deep breath and exhales. "Lexi... needs me to be here for her. I'm sure Dana would disagree with you." She moves closer and sits down next to Gigi. "Well, nevertheless, as you see I'm not dressed for girl talk tonight. I wouldn't want all this to bother you. I would go change, but I'm comfortable."

"Well, I wouldn't want you to be uncomfortable."

As Gigi turns to put her empty glass on the table by her, she goes to look at Cassandra when a sharp pain shoots through her neck and shoulder. Gigi grabs the side of her neck, wincing in pain she drops her glass onto the sectional.

"With all that's going on, I'm not surprised you're stressed." Cassandra walks behind the sectional and proceeds to massage Gigi's neck and shoulders. "Poor baby, you're all in knots. Let's see what I can do about that." Cassandra works on her. "My goodness, your body is so tense. Relax."

"Just take it easy, it hurts."

Cassandra massages Gigi, trying to relieve her anxiety.

"So, I have a question-" Cassandra said. "It's only been since you came out, that you and your mom's relationship has been like this?"

"Well, things changed when I moved back home."

"Moved back home? Okay, you lost me."

"The short version, when I was just a kid. I didn't want to change schools when my parents brought their house. I was crazy about the Girl Scouts. The school I was in had the Girl Scouts and the one I was supposed to transfer to didn't. So, I lived with my grandparents from like the third to seventh grade. I was twelve when I moved back home."

"Oh okay, so how's your neck feeling?"

"It's starting to loosen up."

"Good, continue."

"Well, after moving back, my first so call experience was at my friend Nicole's house, she lived a few houses down from us. Nicole wanted to play house and she wanted me to be the husband."

"Really? Now that is interesting."

"Anyway, as we were playing, Nicole said it was time for the husband to go to work. Nicole said for me to kiss her goodbye. I went to kiss her on the cheek, she turned her face and we kissed on the lips. I don't know what happened but something changed. I felt so different.

"He'll Work It Out" Chapter 6. Taryn C. Atkins

When the husband left for work. I left for real, and ran my behind home."

Cassandra laughs. "You got outta there huh."

"Yes I did; I couldn't stand Nicole for a while, but we became friends again when we were fifteen or sixteen. She's actually the first girl I had a real experience with. It wasn't long after that me and my mom's relationship started feeling strained. It got worse over the years and when I came out. Well, I guess for my mom, that was the breaking point."

"I can see it's rough on you; I'm here for you though."

"Thanks a lot."

Gigi enjoys Cassandra's massage, as she relaxes, Gigi inhales Cassandra's perfume.

"Mmm, you smell good."

"Thanks, it's a habit. Whenever I slip into something silky; I place a dab of perfume in just the right areas. This outfit is comfy too, feels so soft on my skin."

Gigi's stress decreases with Cassandra's massage. She relaxes, tilts her head down composed and pleased with Cassandra's touch. Gigi being at ease, her aggressive side surfaces.

"I'm sure you're soft too." Gigi realizing she's spoken her thoughts aloud swiftly lifts her head. "The massage, it really feels good. Thanks, you do that so well."

Cassandra leans in and enticingly whispers in Gigi's ear.

"That's not all I do well."

Cassandra softly plants a kiss on Gigi's neck. Startled by her touch Gigi quickly moves away.

"I... I think my neck is feeling much better." Gigi moves over. "Thanks..."

"Glad to help, but trust me," Cassandra leans on the sectional looking at Gigi. "I know stress, with your grandmother's passing, and everything going on between you and your mom." She reaches out and softly glides her finger down Gigi's arm. "Your body is screaming."

"He'll Work It Out" Chapter 6. Taryn C. Atkins

Gigi swiftly gets up off the sectional, promptly moving herself away from Cassandra and over to one of the living room windows.

"I'm good.. It's just been a long and emotional day. I'll be fine though. Things are rough right now but its okay. I'll... I'll get through this; I always do."

Gigi's hurt runs deep, she tries her best to find the strength to control her own feelings and needs.

"Cassandra, it's late, go on to bed. I'll be okay."

Gigi's back is to Cassandra, as her emotions get the best of her, she struggles to hold her tears at bay.

"It's just the same old family stuff. While this *is* a little worse. I'll... I'll get through this too."

Gigi can no longer hold her tears and they flow. Cassandra can't see her face but hears Gigi's soft whimpers.

"You're not by yourself, and I see how you're hurting."

Gigi glances over her shoulder, seeing Cassandra coming over she looks away and tries to wipe her tears, they keep on flowing.

"Baby, the pain in your body is not just from stress. It's responding to all that pain in your heart too."

"What doesn't kill you makes you stronger, right?"

"So, you want to live with constant pain?"

"No I don't, but my mother's feelings about me and this lifestyle are not changing anytime soon."

Cassandra reaches out, caressing Gigi's back and shoulders.

"Forget about how she feels," Cassandra said. "You're hurting to much, and you deserve to feel more than pain." She softly kneads Gigi's shoulders. "Gigi you deserve to be happy, be pleased and loved. Don't you know that?" She tenderly lays her head on Gigi's shoulder and strokes her arm. "I want you to know; I'm here for you."

Cassandra feels Gigi's body tremble enjoying her attentive and warm touch. Gigi turns her head, she looks over her shoulder at Cassandra and they share this intimate moment. Gigi closes her eyes and draws in a breath, she wipes her tears exhaling and swallows as she musters up a slither of strength.

"You know what," Gigi wipes her tears from her cheek. "You should..."

Gigi takes a few steps away as Cassandra looks at her.

"You should go home."

"Really?" Cassandra said.

Under her breath, Gigi said to herself, "Please let her go." She brought her hands to the sides of her head, closing her eyes she massaged her temples for a moment. *Please go, cause if she stays... I don't want to talk.* Gigi thought.

Cassandra looks at Gigi hard for a few seconds backing away from her and slowly shaking her head.

"Alright... I'll go."

Cassandra turns and walks away. After a few seconds, Gigi turns around, she moves to the island watching Cassandra walk up the hallway heading to Lexi's bedroom. Gigi's defenses fall.

I won't go through this again. Cassandra thought.

Gigi's runs up the hallway and before Cassandra gets to Lexi's bedroom, Gigi grabs her hand.

"Don't go." Gigi said.

"Why not," Cassandra said. "You told me to."

"Well don't." Gigi said.

Cassandra shakes her head and laughs.

"Gigi I don't have time for games."

"Neither do I."

"It sure seems like it,"

"Look, I'm sorry."

"I am too."

Cassandra tries to walk away but Gigi doesn't let her hand go.

"Don't do this."

"Why not."

Cassandra doesn't look at Gigi, her back is turned.

"Cassandra don't go." Gigi gets close to her. "Stay."

Cassandra looks over her shoulder toward Gigi.

"Why should I?"

Gigi slides Cassandra's robe off, it drops to the floor as she sensually caresses Cassandra's back.

"He'll Work It Out" Chapter 6. Taryn C. Atkins

"Just stay with me," Gigi gently glides her hands down Cassandra's arms. "Please."

Gigi's fingers comb Cassandra's hair to the side, exposing her neck, as Gigi leans in their temperatures rise and she hears Cassandra take in a quick breath as her head tilts.

"Why?"

Gigi sensually kisses Cassandra's neck. Gigi's breath quickens, her body moves closer to Cassandra. Cassandra inhales Gigi's perfume, it once again incites her being, causing a gasps to leave from her lips. As Cassandra closes her eyes Gigi whispers amorously into her ear.

"Cause I need you."

Cassandra softly moans as she turns to Gigi.

~THE EXPLOSION~

It's been a week since the repass, on this Saturday morning, late in the month of August and in the kitchen of the Greye family home. Shayna has on a great pair of Bloomie's pajamas as she stands at the end of their stunning white marble island. She breaks off a piece of the croissant sitting on the plate in front of her. As she chews, she flips the pages of the newspaper that's laying on the island countertop. Shayna picks up the glass of orange juice by the plate and takes a few sips. An inch over is another plate with a bagel on it, to the left of that plate is a glass of orange juice and to the right an empty coffee cup with the name Cliff written across it.

Shayna looks up hearing footsteps and wheels on their red oak finished floors. Cliff walks into the kitchen, carrying his briefcase, his suit jacket is across his arm and he rolls a medium size suitcase in behind him. Shayna looks over and when Cliff sees her there, the atmosphere is immediately filled with tension. Cliff says nothing, he sits the briefcase and suitcase by the wall and drapes his suit jacket across the suitcase.

Cliff looked stylish in his Stacy Adams, Mike Vested Suit, the dark burgundy tone looked so handsome on him. He wore a crisp white dress shirt under the open burgundy vest and the pair of burgundy Dolce Gabbana shoes matched his suit perfectly. Cliff takes the tie draped over his shoulder and puts it around his neck. He tucks it under the collar of his shirt but doesn't tie it. Cliff goes to the end of the island and reaches for his coffee cup. Shayna leans in, attempting to kiss him on the cheek but he moves away. She looks at Cliff bewildered by his actions.

Cliff takes his coffee cup over to the coffee maker on the kitchen counter, pours himself some and heads over to their kitchen table. He glances at Shayna, passing by her he huffs and shakes his head. Cliff puts his coffee cup down on the kitchen table before he sits down. Cliff turns toward the island, picks up the plate with the bagel and the glass of orange juice from it. He puts them down on the kitchen table and sits. He stretches over and grabs the sports section from off the end of the island. Shayna looks at him floored that he hasn't said anything to her.

"Well, good morning," Shayna said.

"Yeah," Cliff said.

Shayna goes to the kitchen table and takes a seat across from Cliff.

"I haven't seen you," Shayna said. "Where have yo--"

"I've been working late," Cliff said.

"You went back to work already? Shayna said. "I thought you took extra time because of mama."

"Well, I went back," Cliff said.

He glances over the sports section and eats breakfast. The kitchen is quiet for a moment but the tension in the air continues to thicken. Shayna gets up and goes back over to where she was standing at the end of the island. She takes a sip of her orange juice and as she puts the glass down she looks over at Cliff.

"Well, where have you been sleeping? Cause--"

"I've been sleeping in the guest room and staying over at my office, alright."

The tension between them is gets thicker.

"No it isn't alright, this isn't good. We need to talk."

Cliff closes the newspaper, puts it down on the table and turns toward her.

"Talk about what exactly?"

"This-this distance between us. I don't need this now."

"He'll Work It Out" Chapter 6. Taryn C. Atkins

"You? You don't need this right now? Incredible! It's incredible how you have tunnel vision no matter what. Making everything always about you."

"I've had a lot to deal with the last few weeks."

"It's what we've had to deal with!"

"Well, you know what I mean! I don't need this distance between us. Feels like we're a thousand miles apart."

"We are a thousand miles apart." He stands up. "The only reason you feel it, is because the bridge is actually broken this time!"

"Now Cliff, you know *the word* says don't let the sun go down on your wrath."

"Well, pray the Lord has mercy on my soul. You never seem to have problems sleeping though."

Cliff walks away from the kitchen table, he goes over to the kitchen window and stares out onto their backyard. Placing his hand on the window frame, he leans against it as he looks outside. Shayna looks over at him, his back is to Shayna and the room goes quiet once again. After a few moments, Shayna goes to Cliff.

"Look, I'm sorry okay? She reaches out and touches his back. "I'm sorry about what happened with Gigi." She takes Cliff's arm and turns him around to her. "You know it's hard for me to see her in that lifestyle."

"Yeah I know," Cliff puts his arms around her waist.

"Baby, she's our daughter."

"I know."

"We're the only parents Gigi's got."

"Yeah I know but..."

"So you could at least try to--"

"No, I can't!" Shayna pulls away from him. "I can't help it!"

She walks away from him and goes back over to the island.

"Yeah but Shayna, c'mon."

Shayna abruptly turns to him. "Clifford, please! I don't want to talk about this any further! You can, at least, be more understanding!"

Cliff focuses on Shayna. "What did you just say to me?"

"He'll Work It Out" Chapter 6. Taryn C. Atkins

He looks away, walks over to the exposed brick wall where the small fireplace is and leans against the wall for a moment. He huffs then turns to Shayna as he shakes his head.

"You just said be more understanding? Cliff slowly approaches her. "That is what you said right." He stands in front of Shayna, on the other side of the island and huffs again. "You just told me..." He slams his fist down on the countertop. "*Be more understanding!*"

Shayna caught off guard by the sudden change in Cliff's voice and actions becomes unbalanced and takes a few steps back.

"Cliff."

"I was understanding nine years ago, when I allowed you to put our daughter in the street!"

"Come on now."

Shayna takes her glass of orange juice, along with the newspaper and goes over to the kitchen table and sits down.

"I was understanding when I snuck around, just to keep a relationship with our daughter!"

"Please..."

"I was understanding, when I had to sneak our daughter into the hospital, just to visit her own grandmother. All so you wouldn't get upset."

"Cliff stop this."

"Remember when this *super understanding* part of me came to be? I sure do." He paces around the kitchen. "I was traveling for my business, Gigi was staying with Mama Mae, Gina just turned nine and you were finishing up your masters in accounting. On this particular night, Gina was over Mama Mae's too."

Shayna looks at Cliff as she slowly starts to stand up.

"Cliff... don't."

"One of your classes was difficult, at least that's what you said. So, you got this excellent tutor. Studying hard too. Or so I thought."

Shayna shakes her head, "I won't listen to this."

She attempts to leave out of the kitchen.

"Oh, you're gonna listen!!"

"He'll Work It Out" Chapter 6. Taryn C. Atkins

Cliff rushes over to Shayna and before she can walk into the living room, he grabs her arm.

"You're gonna listen." Cliff brings her back over to the kitchen table. "Because I've got a few things to say!"

As Cliff releases her arm, Shayna snatches her arm away from him. Cliff points over to the kitchen table.

"Now sit down!"

Cliff and Shayna look fiercely at each other. At first, Shayna doesn't move but seeing the seriousness in her husband's eyes. She goes to the kitchen table and sits back down.

"Fine." Shayna said.

Shayna folds her arms as Cliff walks over and leans against the end of the island.

"Here I am feeling guilty for traveling so much." Cliff said looking over at her. "So I plan to surprise you. I call, pretending to be in Chicago when I was actually still at JFK. I pick up a dozen of long stem red roses and drive home. You already told me it was your weekly study session and that you two were studying by the pool. So I knew your "tutor" would be here."

Shayna slowly stands pointing at him, "Cliff don't do this."

"I walk around to the backyard, go to the pool and I didn't see anybody. I do hear a little talking and some laughter, but then, I hear other interesting noises."

Cliff walks over to the kitchen window, he looks out into the backyard and looks at the pool.

"And these noises, are coming from behind the waterfall." He looks back at Shayna and points toward the window. "From inside the romantic grotto, that I had built for me and my wife!"

He walks back over to the island, puts his hands on the countertop and leans on it.

"I dropped the roses because I couldn't believe what I was hearing." He shakes his head a bit. "Nah, not my wife, I said to myself. So with my three piece on, I dive into the pool. What I saw when I came up out the water...

Wow!" He looks over at Shayna. "I'm sure you remember what I saw."

"Cliff stop this."

"Tell me what I saw Shayna? He turns toward her. "Tell me."

Shayna tries to leave again, Cliff speedily moves in front of her and cuts off her way of escape.

"Tell me what I saw Shayna!"

"No! I won't." Shayna shakes her head. "I can't. You stop this!" She points at him. "Stop this right now!!"

"Why, because you can't bear to say it or even hear it."

Cliff huffs and walks away. He goes back over to the island, turns around, leans against it and looks at Shayna.

"Well allow me, cause I remember exactly what I saw. I saw you with your tutor. Wasn't any tutoring though! From what I saw you clearly enjoyed her going dow-"

Shayna rushes over and slaps Cliff.

"Shut up! Don't say it!! She goes to hit him again. "Don't you dare say it!!"

Cliff grabs her hand before she connects again. Shayna snatches her hand away from him, she rushes to the kitchen table and sits down. The kitchen is dead quiet for a few moments.

"It was... 93." Cliff said. "Yeah, in 93 you went back to finish your Masters. Gigi was living with your parents. You didn't actually finish your Masters until 98. That was a year after the pool thing. So, tell me this?" He goes to the kitchen table and sits across from Shayna. "How long were you two together?"

Shayna looks at Cliff. "What?"

"You heard me! C'mon, be honest for a change. My business took off and I was traveling all the time. Even though you were in school. We used to argue about how much I traveled, but that stopped. I thought you were glad to be back in school. That wasn't it though, was it? So, how long were you two together?"

Shayna shakes her head. "I... I don't want to talk about this. Please!"

Cliff slams his hand down on the table, "Tell me!"

Shayna looks at him, "It was a long time ago and it's over." She reaches across the table and takes his hand in hers. "Why does it even matter?"

Cliff snatches his hand away.

"It matters to me that's why. Now tell me!"

Shayna stands, picks up her glass of orange juice, takes a sip and walks to the kitchen sink. Cliff turns in Shayna's direction. She pours out the orange juice and sits the glass in the sink. Cliff watches Shayna, as she turns around, her head is down, she leans against the kitchen counter and folds her arms. Shayna closes her eyes, takes in a deep breath and exhales.

"Shayna."

She quickly raises her head and opens her eyes staring at Cliff.

"Okay... Okay." Shayna said.

"So then tell me Shayna! Cliff said."

"I wasn't in a good place," Shayna said. "I didn't feel good about myself and you were always gone. I felt like I lost myself. I was, just your wife and their mother. And that was it, I lost me. I didn't... *We* didn't plan it, it just happened." She walks over to the end of the island. "I didn't feel important or beautiful anymore." Her eyes well up. "You're my best friend," She starts to cry. "And you weren't there for me anymore. I had no one to talk to, vent to, you weren't there, not even for me to laugh with anymore. And she... she was there for me."

"Alright, I get all that, and I'm sorry I wasn't there, but you still haven't told me how long."

Shayna looks at the ground, takes in a quick deep breath, blows it out and looks at Cliff.

Underneath her breath, Shayna said, "Five years."

"Stop playing games Shayna." Cliff stands up. "Say it."

"Five years, alright. We were together five years. It ended after the pool incident. She left New York after that."

Cliff goes over to the island.

"Five years is a long time. So, I've got another question."

"Oh my God Cliff," She walks away and turns to him. "It's

over. Why do you want to do this?!"

"Cause I need to know, that's why."

"Fine, what?"

"The grotto is one thing, I'm sure you've been together in this house, right?"

"Cliff... come on."

Cliff points at Shayna. "Listen," He points to himself. "If I was with somebody else." He huffs. "I know you would want to know, where, when, date and time. So please, now where?"

Shayna looks at Cliff, she glances up at the ceiling, then turns away taking in a deep breath and exhales as she walks to the kitchen table. She takes a seat. The room is quiet. Cliff turns toward Shayna, he leans against the island and studies her closely. As his eyes are focused on her, he nods his head.

"In our bed?" He comes and sits down at the kitchen table.

"Yes."

"On our couch? How about in our den?"

"Yes, Cliff stop this."

Cliff stands up and moves about the kitchen.

"How about on the carpet in front of the fireplace in our bedroom?" He goes over and slaps the top of the island.

"How about here on the island? There too?!"

"Yes... okay, yes!" She stands up. "Are you satisfied! Are you happy that you know all the intricate little details now?!"

"Actually, I am." He approaches Shayna. "For the first time, in a very long time, you're being honest with me."

"Well, this is over now."

Shayna goes to leave the kitchen but Cliff gets in front of her once again.

"Sorry, not just yet. I have a few more questions."

"Damn." She turns away from him and heads over to the kitchen table. "What now?!"

Shayna sits once again as Cliff leans against the island.

"I said I'd never ask you but... I want to know now."

"He'll Work It Out" Chapter 6. Taryn C. Atkins

"Cliff you promised me."
"Well, you've broken a few promises haven't you?"
"Fine... ask."
"When you left here, for your so-called "business trip" to Texas. Did you really go to be with her?"
"You were drinking all the time, we were arguing, it was a lot to deal with and then you hit me."
"I know, I wish I could take that moment back, I do. That's why I said sorry, got into AA, sobered up, got saved and with God I haven't had a drink in eleven years."
"I know but..." Shayna said as tears started to flow down her cheek. "After you hit me-I just couldn't take any more, and I couldn't take if it happened again."
"So when you left... you went to be with her?!"
"Yes... she didn't know that though. Still doesn't."

Cliff comes over and sits down at the kitchen table.

"You... you left us."
"Cliff."
"So, if Gina wasn't hit by that car, you would have stayed with her. You wouldn't even be here would you."
"You're over-thinking this."
"No, I'm not. So was she in love with you?"
"Cliff please."
"It's a yes or no answer. Did she fall in love with you?"
"Yes, she did."

Cliff moves his chair around the table closer to Shayna. There is silence for a moment as he stares at her, Shayna hears him take in a deep breath and slowly exhale.

"Are you still in love with me?"

Her eyes quickly go to his, she takes his face in her hands.

"Of course I am, I've never stopped being in love with you.
"Okay," Cliff said taking her hands in his. "Tell me this."
"Don't..." Shayna looks at Cliff shaking her head. "Please don't do this."
"Shayna I need to know."

"He'll Work It Out" Chapter 6. Taryn C. Atkins

Cliff looks away inhaling another deep breath, his heart pounds in his chest as he exhales. *Do I really want know the answer?* He thought. Cliff's eyes go to Shayna as he clears his throat.

"Were you... in love with her?"

"Cliff." She stands up. "I can't do this anymore." She rushes pass him. "Please, I can't."

Shayna goes to the exposed brick wall. Cliff stands up and turns in her direction.

"Just tell me, did you fall in love with her?"

Shayna abruptly turns toward Cliff.

"I don't know alright! I... I just don't..." She looks away as she shakes her head and looks at Cliff again. "I don't know."

Cliff stares at Shayna for a few moments, he huffs, shakes his head and laughs.

"Wow... and you have the nerve, to have so much to say to Gigi don't you?"

Shayna shakes her head and points at Cliff.

"Stop it."

"You know what's the highlight to all this." He walks over to Shayna. "I've got to look into her face, every time I go to church. So I see what you did all the time. And you know what. God forgive me, but..," He points at Shayna. "I'm glad you see her face too."

Shayna pushes pass Cliff, rushing over to the kitchen table and as she leans on one of the chairs, she breaks down.

"No more! Please!" She raises her head and cries out. "Why are you being so cruel?!"

"Cruel?! I've been understanding Shayna. More than understanding." He walks toward the living room but then turns back. "I forgave you, remember?" He heads over to her. "And it wasn't easy either. God had to deal with my heart. I never showed you or her any resentment or anger. I've never even brought it up. Until today."

Shayna wipes her tears pulling herself together. Cliff sits at the kitchen table. Silence takes over the kitchen for a few moments once again. Cliff turns to Shayna.

"Don't you see Shayna? You've been cruel. Too cruel in fact. The guilt from your own past has caused you to reject our daughter. Instead of allowing the compassion and love of Jesus to pull our daughter toward Him, you continually pushed her further and further away. The way I see it, you're the one that should start being understanding!" He shakes his head and stands to his feet. "Look, I'm tired of living under all this deception. I'm going out of town to take care of some business. I'll be gone for two weeks. When I get back; I'll be staying at a hotel."

"Cliff please."

Shayna stands as Cliff goes to his suitcase, he picks up his suit jacket and puts it on. Shayna watches him grab his briefcase. Cliff takes the handle of his suitcase and leaves out the kitchen.

"Cliff wait, please."

Shayna watches Cliff walk out the front door. She stands in the kitchen frozen until she hears the sound of his car skid off. Shayna rushes to the front door, she turns around and leans against it. She tilts her head back, placing her hands over her face as her tears flow once again.

"Cliff don't go..."

"I think it's a bit too late for that."

Hearing the voice Shayna snatches her hands away from her face and sees Regina sitting on the sofa in the living room. Regina doesn't look her way.

"Regina we were just..."

"Please don't," Regina said. "I just got here a minute ago, but all things happen for a reason. All I heard, was the last thing Daddy said. That's all I needed to hear too." She huffs and shakes her head. "You kicked Gigi out, cut her off and all this time. You've had your own skeletons in the closet."

"Regina, it's... it's not what you think. Your father and I were just-"

"How dare you?" Regina looks at her mother. "All this time, you've been punishing Gigi for your own sins."

"Regina," Shayna moves toward her. "It's not like that."
"I can't believe you! You're still trying to cover stuff up."
"Regina you don't under-"
"Understand? That's your next word, right? I understand Matthew 7:5. "Hypocrite. First cast out the beam out of thine own eye; and then shalt thou see clearly to cast out the mote out of thy brother's eye." She stands up. "In this case, your daughter's eye, but *Deaconess Greye* could never admit she's wrong. Right mother?"

Shayna watches as Regina walks out the front door. Shayna drops to the floor, she opens up her mouth but no words come out. As Shayna rocks back and forth with tears running down her face she wails.

"No!"

~FACING TRUTH~

The seasons have changed, and we're now in the midst of Fall; its late in the month of September and on this early Saturday afternoon, inside one of the rehab center rooms, a small group is seated in a circle waiting for their group meeting to begin. Just outside the circle, standing with her arms crossed is a five-ten, exotic and intriguing looking woman in her late forties. She's provocatively alluring, dressed in her stylish business apparel. Those seated within the circle are Reggie's rehab counselor, Reggie, Kisha, Leah, James and Pamela Carrington. Everybody had on casual wear except for Pamela Carrington. She looked elegant in her classic black and white Chanel suit. The woman approached the circle, all those within put their attention on her.

"Good afternoon everyone." The woman said. "My name is Suzette Scarsboro, I'm the head director here; I stopped in before you started because I just wanted to thank you family members for coming out. It's important to us that our client's family be involved. So prayerfully all relationships involved can make a full recovery along with our client. I'm going to leave you with Reggie's rehab counselor, Ronald Pemberton. Have a great session all."

"Thank you, Suzette." Ronald Pemberton said.

Suzette smiles, nods her head at Ronald and exits the room closing the door behind her. Ronald Pemberton cleared his throat as he stood up.

"Hello, this session is called-*Facing Truth*." My name is Ronald Pemberton, feel free to call me Ron. I'm forty-five and a recovering heroin addict, clean for twenty years. When I was using, I did anything to use, lie, cheat, steal. I even hurt quite a few people. I'll start out by telling you the truth about myself because "Facing Truth" is all about having the client face the truth about the hurts and pains brought on by their addiction. So the client and others can face it, deal with it, hopefully reconcile, heal and prayerfully move on in their lives. Now this is your first family session. We all know everything can't be fixed in the first session but this is a start. Can we all just go around real quick and introduce yourselves and who you are to Reggie." He puts his hand on his chest. "I'm Ron and I'm Reggie's counselor here." He sits down.

"Well, I'm Reggie and I'm the client."

"I'm Kisha and I'm Reggie's best friend. We've been best friends since the fifth grade and I'm here to support him through this."

"I'm Leah and I'm Reggie's mother. That's my baby boy and my only child. I may not like what's happened to him or what he's done. I'm still his mother and I'm here no matter what."

"I'm James and I'm Reggie's cousin." He points at Reggie. "I haven't forgotten what you've done and I don't want to be here either. I'm only here, cause Leah asked me to come with her. And believe me, I could care less about what you have to say."

"I'm Pamela Carrington, you can call me Pam. I'm Kisha's mother. My husband was supposed to be here too. He wants no part of this, and he wants no part of Reggie. My husband loves his daughter though. Kisha is

"He'll Work It Out" Chapter 6. Taryn C. Atkins

his heart, which is why, he disapproves of her being involved with Reggie. I, on the other hand, not only love but support my daughter. I remember Reggie before all this happened, and I believe Reggie can pull himself up and get through this. I think it's wonderful and beautiful that Kisha can see through all that too, and can be there for Reggie. That's how real friendship is after all. So, I'm here for both of them." She stands up. "Now, unfortunately, I can't stay this time. My husband is waiting for me in the car. We have a fundraiser to attend. Please let me know when you're having the next session. Have a great afternoon everyone."

Leah looks over at Pam.

"Pam," Leah said. "What you said about my son was beautiful, thank you. And I know it's been years since we've seen each other. So, it's nice to meet you again and I hope we can get together sometime."

"It's also nice to meet you again." Pamela Carrington said. And yes, it would be great to get together with you as well."

Kisha looks over at her mom and smiles.

"Thanks for coming Mom, I love you," Kisha said.

"I love you too darling," Pamela Carrington said.

Pamela Carrington waves and blows a kiss to Kisha. She waves to everybody and leaves.

"Well, I'm glad you're all here," Ron said. "What can I say now? Reggie's a great guy. He came to us six or seven weeks ago. Well, Kisha brought him in and he was all busted up. Once his body felt better, all Reggie wanted to do was get clean and get his life back on track. So here's how it works. Reggie is going to talk first, then the family. Reggie you're up, you have the floor."

Everybody watches Reggie and waits for him to say something. Reggie sits there quiet for a few moments staring at the floor. Ron puts his hand on Reggie's back.

"Reggie it's okay," Ron said.

Reggie glances at Ron nodding his head a few times.

"Well, I know you didn't have to come," Reggie said. "So thanks for being here. I know you haven't seen me for weeks. After everything that happened, it was better for me to get to a place where I could get help."

"So you've been here for weeks? Leah said. "And you couldn't call and tell me anything?"

"Mom," Reggie said. "It was Kisha that knew about this place and she got me in."

"I'm glad she's there for you too," Leah said. "I'm your mother though; I've been worried sick about you."

"You're right Ms. Leah," Kisha said. "I should have told you; I just thought it would be best for Reggie to get into some place first. Let him get started on his recovery before seeing anyone from the family. That's all."

"Ma, I just..." Reggie said. "I just wanted to get my mind free of drugs first."

"Be a man and say what you mean!" James said. "You thought it best for you to hide out here. That's the truth."

"Alright, everyone calm down," Ron said. He looks over at James. "Again-let Reggie speak first."

James glares at Reggie and huffs.

"While I've been here," Reggie said. "I had to face the fact that, I hurt my family and my friends while I've been strung out. I had to face the fact that-" He takes a deep breath and looks at Leah. "Ma, I'm the one that hurt Grandma."

"You mean you stabbed her!" James said. "Then took her money and left her for dead!"

"It was an accident, I swear!" Reggie said. "I was going through grandma's handbag, she walked in, grabbed it, we pulled back and forth; I didn't know she had scissors in her hand. Before I knew it, she was laying there. I saw the blood... and, all I could do was run. I stole the money, yes, and that was wrong and I'm sorry for that but I didn't stab her! And I never intended to hurt grandma either." He turns to Leah. "Ma, you have to believe me! I didn't mean to hurt her... I didn't!"

James jumps up out of his seat.

"Yeah, well you did hurt her!" James said, pointing at Reggie. "And then you left her just laying there!"

James rushes across the room going for Reggie as Ron reaches for James stopping him before he does.

"Hey, come on James! Take it easy!" Ron said. "Calm it down man, Chill!"

James pushes Ron away from him.

"Get off me man!" James said, he gestures across the room to Reggie. "You know what!? Accident or not Mama Mae is gone and it's because of YOU! Deal with that TRUTH!"

Kisha stands up, she points at James moving toward him.

"Fine, speaking of truth!" Kisha said. "You tell Leah how you beat Reggie until he could barely move?! Did you tell her, how you said it was better for everyone that he kill himself?! Did you James? What about that TRUTH James."

"Kisha don't." Reggie said.

"No Reggie," Kisha said, sitting back down crossing her legs. "We're all here to talk truth, right?"

"I did, as a matter of fact." James said. He points over to Kisha. "I told Leah cause I felt bad about what I did. See, I didn't run away-I stood up like a man and faced what I did. I didn't run off and hide either." He looks at Reggie. "You just don't know how much Mama Mae loved you and this family. She told the family what happened and asked all of us to forgive you. That it wasn't your fault, but as far as I'm concerned, it's all your fault!!" He stands and looks at Leah. "Look, Leah, I'm sorry; I can't do this yet. I get angry just looking at him. I gotta get out of here!"

James rushes out the meeting slamming the door behind him. The room gets quiet for a moment.

"He's right," Reggie said. "It's my fault, no matter how many times I say sorry... I can never forgive myself for Mama Mae dying."

"Reggie..." Kisha said.

"This is "Facing Truth," Reggie said. "I have to face the fact that because of me being an addict," His eyes well up trying to hold back his tears. "I hurt my own grandmother, she's dead because of me and because I didn't look out for my best friend, he's gone too." He looks at Kisha. "Mario killed himself because he couldn't take being strung out any longer. I was supposed to look out for him. Instead, I'm the one who got him started-I got him strung out." Tears run down his face. "They're dead because of me! I wish I were never born."

"Now hold it right there!" Leah said. "I'm the one that went through twenty-one hours of labor to get you here. I knew from the first moment I saw your face, and every moment to come, be it good or bad. Will never change me knowing that you're the best thing in my life." She sits by Reggie. "I love you, always have and always will. I know you're hurting, and you've got a lot to get through but you're not alone."

Leah reaches out and takes Reggie's hand in hers.

"We're here for you," Kisha said.

Kisha reaches out and takes Reggie's other hand. Reggie looks at Kisha, as she holds his hand and they look deeply into each others eyes.

"Always." Kisha said.

"So, we're going to get through this together," Leah said. "As a family." She looks at Ron and then Reggie. "Like Ron said, everything can't be fixed in the first session but this is a start."

"That's right," Ron said.

Leah smiles as she makes eye contact with Ron.

"So let's set up that next session," Leah said. She looks at Reggie. "Okay, Reggie?"

Reggie wipes his face and shakes his head in agreement.

"Okay," Reggie said. "I love you mom."

"You betta," Leah said laughing a bit. "Especially after twenty-one hours of labor. Now when's our next session."

"Great!" Ron said. He picks up his clipboard from underneath his seat. "Let me look at the schedule."

As Ron checks out the schedule on his clipboard. Reggie hugs Leah for a moment and as they release each other Leah kisses Reggie on the cheek. He reaches over and hugs Kisha too. As they embrace each other holding each other tight for a moment or two longer.

"Thanks for being here," Reggie said. "I love you."

"I love you too," Kisha said.

~CRY FOR RESTORATION~

The skies are still filled with overcast clouds as heavy rain the rain tapered to a light drizzle. On this late afternoon in the middle of the week during the final week of September. Car's honk, public transportation rushes by, a dog barks at someone and a few teenagers laugh with one another as they run pass. Nola and Shayna with their umbrella's over head walk up to the doors of the Full Gospel Temple Ministries. Nola trendy as always in a pair of blue skinny jeans, a graphic tee shirt with a black blazer and flats. While Shayna's dressed business casual with black slacks, a black top, gray blazer, with a long gold necklace and black gold toed, pointed pumps.

"So are you going to be okay?" Nola said.

"I... I don't know." Shayna said. "I've destroyed my family. Cliff's been staying at a hotel for weeks. Gina's gone before I even get up, or she stays over at mama's with James."

"Have you tried to call Gigi again?" Nola said.

"Yes," Shayna said. "I've left messages but she hasn't returned any of my calls."

"Well, you can't blame her Shayna," Nola said.

"I know," Shayna said. "After all I've done, it's what I deserve."

"I should agree with you but I won't. We've all made mistakes. I just pray you've learned from yours."

"He'll Work It Out" Chapter 6. Taryn C. Atkins

Shayna takes a deep breath and exhales as she closes up her umbrella.

"Even if I have Nola, it doesn't mean that everything is gonna be an easy to fix."

"As long as you feel your family's worth fighting for, God will move on your behalf. It all starts with you."

"Yeah, I know."

"So I'm gonna let you go on in. Call me later."

Shayna nods her head, Nola walks to her car as Shayna goes in the church. Minutes later, in the corridor of church offices, Shayna sits in the middle pew. Down the hall to Shayna's left, she see's Aisha come out of Lady Gorham's office. Aisha is a mid thirties, studiously pleasant and graceful woman, she smiles as she approaches Shayna.

"Good afternoon Deaconess Greye," Aisha said.

"Good afternoon Aisha," Shayna said.

"Someone just went in to see Lady Gorham. As soon as they're done, I'll come get you."

"Okay, I'll be right here.

Aisha smiles at Shayna as she turns and heads back to the office. Shayna watches Aisha go in and hears the door close behind her. Shayna sits back and waits to see Lady Gorham.

After about ten minutes or so, Shayna hears another office door open down the hall to her right. When Shayna looks in that direction, she spots Minister Pauls enter the corridor. As Minister Pauls walks to the water cooler in the corner. Shayna looks in the opposite direction.

Minister Pauls fills her cup and drinks. As she brings the cup down, Minister Pauls notices Shayna sitting there. She throws the cup in the garbage and walks over to Shayna. Minister Pauls waits till she's closer to make her presence known.

"Hello Deaconess Greye," Minister Pauls said.

Shayna looks in her direction.

"Hi Minister Pauls," Shayna said. "Why are you here?"

"Well, I just finished a counseling session." Minister Pauls said. "So how are you doing?"

"I guess... as well as expected."

"Why are you here?"

"I'm waiting to see Lady Gorham."

Minister Pauls watches Shayna runs her hands over her face. Shayna looks away, taking in a quick deep breath, she blows it out and looks at Minister Pauls as she takes a seat beside her.

"You... You've been crying. What's going on?"

Shayna shakes her head. "Nothing."

Minister Pauls studies Shayna as she sits back and crosses her legs.

"Is he drinking? Minister Pauls swiftly sits up. "Did he put his hands on you again?"

"What? No! I'm not doing this with you. I'm here to speak with Lady Gorham."

"Shayna we were best friends, we talked about everything."

"Well, best friends don't up and run when things get hard, rearranging their whole life in a few hours, and then catch a plane to California the next day. After that day at the airport. I put all of it behind me. So..."

"I did too, until I got a call six years later. You sounded distraught. Tell me, was I suppose to just hang-up?"

Shayna looks at Minister Pauls, she glances down at the ground shaking her head as her eyes return to Minister Pauls.

"I guess not."

"So I did what was needed, we talked for a while and you sounded much better. I never thought you would've show up on my doorstep a few hours later."

"Why invite me if you didn't want me to come."

Minister Pauls huffs and shakes her head a bit.

"Really Shayna, I was all the way in Texas; I never thought you would actually come."

"If I was such an inconvenience you should've just told me. I would have caught the next flight back."

"Oh my goodness, do you really think, with everything going on back in New York, that I would actually turn you away. You were stressed out, which was why I took off and got that private villa in St. Martin." She brushes off her skirt. After all, wasn't I more your inconvenience. I was always there for you. The two times I needed you to just make a decision. You bailed on me."

Under her breath, Shayna said, "I don't want to talk about this now."

"When I proposed to you in St. Martin, I thought you looked happy; I even gave you a few days to answer, like you asked. Instead of talking to me when we got back. You repeat your actions at the airport that day, and bail on me once again. I wake up to find, the ring and a note telling me what happened to Gina. I didn't deserve that."

"I'm not talking about this, and I don't have time for this."

"Yeah, that's nothing new." Minister Pauls rises from her seat, turning to Shayna as she points at her. "It was so easy for you to go back to him. You know, you've gotten second chances from both of us haven't you?"

Shayna watches as Minister Pauls shakes her head while smoothing out her fishtail business suit.

I'm getting my second chance. Minister Pauls thought.

"I never meant for things to turn out like they did." Shayna said.

"You never did anything to prevent them either."

Shayna reaches out, taking Minister Pauls hand in hers.

"I never meant to hurt you."

Minister Pauls snatches her hand away.

"Oh please, don't you dare try that with me! When this was starting, maybe that would've worked. It's been twenty years. So I don't think so."

Shayna rises to her feet turning towards Minister Pauls.

"You wanted me to leave my husband and my daughters."

"Shayna you had already left them. We were together for close to two week and you weren't returning his calls or anything. You can say whatever you want now but you were happy with us being together. I loved you and you loved me too. You won't every admit it to yourself or to me for that matter but I know it, you knew it at the airport that day; you knew it while you were in Texas and deep inside you know it now. All I wanted, was for you to finally show me you loved me, just as much as I loved you."

"Please, I can't deal with this right now."

"Hey, no worries. We both moved on."

They hear the office door to Shayna's left open. Aisha comes out and as she heads over to Shayna and Minister Pauls, their expressions show tension between them. They both quickly turn towards Aisha disguising their feelings with a smile as she approaches them.

"Is everything alright?" Aisha said.

"Everything's fine." Minister Pauls said. "How are you?"

"I'm fine Minister Pauls," Aisha said with a smile. "Thank you for asking." She looks at Shayna. "Deaconess Greye, Lady Gorham's ready for you. She's going to meet with you in the sanctuary."

"Okay Aisha, thanks." Shayna said "I'll head right there."

Aisha smiles and walks away. Shayna and Minister Pauls watch Aisha goes back to the office and hear the door close behind her. Shayna turns to Minister Pauls once again.

"Cassandra," Shayna said.

"Lady Gorham is waiting for you Deaconess Greye." Minister Pauls said.

Shayna moves toward her but Minister Pauls steps back as she checks her watch.

"I gotta go, I have a session in a few minutes. You take care."

"You too."

When Minister Pauls turns away from Shayna her eyes begin to well up. Shayna's eyes fill with tears too watching her walk away. As Minister Pauls heads back to her office, her tears start to fall. Unable to hold her tears off any longer she quickens her steps and rushes into her office so no one is the wiser. When Shayna hears her office door close, she forces her own tears back as she walks out the corridor of offices. A few moments later Shayna walks into the sanctuary. Lady Gorham is straightening up humming a gospel tune, when she notices Shayna approaching from the corner of her eye.

"Grace and peace Deaconess Gray." Lady Gorham said.

Shayna attempts to hold off her tears, avoiding eye contact with Lady Gorham she takes a seat in one of the pews.

"I wanted to speak with you," Shayna said. "Now I just want to sit here."

"Everything alright?" Lady Gorham said.

Shayna tries to answer, but struggles to hold back her tears.

"I..." She finally breaks. "I've destroyed everything, everything I care about is lost; I've lost them all."

Lady Gorham rushes over to the alter searching for a box of tissues. She returns to Shayna and sits beside her.

"Okay, calm down." She gives Shayna a few tissues. "You're giving the devil too much glory. Alright, things may be all broken up and wounded but they're fixable, and able to be healed."

"I've hurt them all so much."

"Okay, you've made serious mistakes. That's wonderful, the Lord can truly work on you now because your heart is finally in the right place. Now he can move."

"I don't know if God can fix all that I've done."

"Well, I know one thing, God can do anything but fail," Lady Gorham stands. "You'll never know He can fix it until you talk to Him and ask. So, I'm gonna go so you can do that."

Lady Gorham leaves the sanctuary and Shayna's left alone.

Shayna laughs saying, "Funny, Mama always told us just pray what's in our heart." She takes a deep breath and exhales. "Okay Mama, here it goes."

Shayna stands, she walks about as she talks to God.

"Lord I come to you because I've lost my way. I... I pray you have mercy on me. I was so blind but now I see, and all the hurt and pain I've caused stands right before me. Lord, I've caused so much pain and strife. I can't believe I've done so much evil in your sight."

"He'll Work It Out" Chapter 6. Taryn C. Atkins

As Shayna talks to God, her sobs over take her, realizing the undeniable drama that she's brought upon others.

"Create in me a clean heart; renew a right spirit within me. Cast me not away Lord, restore my soul, please deliver and set me free. For it's in your presence I want to be. Lord, I'm crying out; I'm so sorry. Please hear me and don't hide your face from me."

Shayna's knees buckle as she cries out to the Lord.

"Please forgive me Lord and wash me from my sins. This is your child crying out to you, don't let the enemy win. Father hear my cries, my spirit is broken, my heart's aching; I'm so sorry. Please deliver me from all guilt and shame. Restore my soul Lord and I'll forever praise thy name."

~CHAPTER 7~

~Unconditional Love Can Recover & Make Whole~

~BROTHERLY COUNSEL~

A few days later during the first week of October, New Yorkers get the chance to enjoy a beautiful Indian Summer day. It's on this Saturday afternoon in the city that Dray and Paris walk up to the corner of East Houston and Ludlow. Dray sports a red Superman tank, blue shorts, and red Converse. Paris is looking suave in black shades, a black polo shirt, beige Bermudas, and sandals. No matter what these two wear their athletic, cut up and muscular builds make it look even more appealing. They walk up and stop on the corner right outside the Katz Deli.

"I love this weather," Paris said. "So glad to get another summer day before it gets cold."

"I know that's right," Dray said. "We're supposed to get a few days like this."

"Well, that's great," Paris said. "I can't stand being cold."

Dray's cell off, he pulls it out his pants pocket and checks it.

"They found parking," Dray said. "They're walking over."

"Okay," Paris said.

"So, you've never been here?" Dray said.

"Never, I never got the chance to."

"Well, you're gonna love it. Watch and see."

"I'm sure, I hear everybody comes through here."

"They do, just check the pictures on the wall."

"I'm trying to figure out what to order."

"I'm getting a hot corn beef sandwich on rye." Dray said. "That's my usual. Everything here tastes great though."

"That corned beef does sounds good." Paris said.

While they wait outside a group of women exit the deli. The two of them wearing New York Yankee gear stop in their tracks a few feet away from the guys.

"Mmm." The Asian woman wearing the Yankee cap said

as she looked at Paris. "I do love me a steaming cup of hot chocolate."

"Hey, Superman." The other woman in the Yankee jersey scanning Dray up and down said with a thick Caribbean accent. "You can come rescue me anytime."

Dray and Paris smile back and almost seem to move in unison as they both pointed to the wedding rings on their fingers. A sad expression paints over the face of both women.

"Aww, now that's a shame." The jersey-clad woman said.

"Yes, it is." The woman under the baseball cap agreed.

"Well, you two are a cute couple."

The ladies walk away. Dray and Paris stare at each other with perplexed looks and their eyes shoot back to the women.

"NO!!" Paris said.

"We're married to WOMEN!!" Dray said."

Cliff and company walk up. Cliff dons a light blue v-neck t-shirt, gray shorts, black sunglasses and gray canvas boat shoes. The two women never look back, they keep walking down the block to catch up with their friends.

"What was that about?" Cliff said looking at Dray.

Dray motions to himself and Paris.

"Do we look like we're gay?" Dray said.

"Well..." Cliff said. "You do show a lot of skin sometime."

"So what! It's hot!" Dray said. "What's wrong with a brother staying in shape? When did that become a bad thing?"

"Well, you live in the gym too," Paris said.

Dray rolls his eyes at Paris "Said the other personal trainer, who works in a gym, please..."

"Unfortunately, it's just the way the world is now man." Minister Thomas said. "People see a guy who takes care of his body. Sometimes they automatically think he's gay or on the down low. That's why it's important for people to see God on you. It's an inside work but it will show on the outside too."

"Well, I just got saved." Dray said. "They don't see nothing yet?"

"Give it time." Minister Randall said. "They will."

"Alright," Cliff said. "Y'all finally got me out here, let's go inside and eat."

"I hear that," Dray points to Paris. "First Cliff and company. This is my best friend, Paris Beaumont. I've known this knucklehead since college. We played ball together and he still can't beat me.

"Whatever man. Nice to meet y'all." Paris said.

"Same here," Cliff said. "Paris these are my close friends." He points to Minister Thomas. "This is Minister Casey Thomas, but you can call him Casey."

Minister Thomas wears great sunglasses, a thin blue cardigan, underneath it a striped blue and white t-shirt, blue jeans and loafers. He and Paris greet each other and shake hands. Cliff points at Brother Hamlin.

'This is Brother Marcus Hamlin."

Paris and Brother Hamlin, who has on an olive crewneck t-shirt, tan shorts, a tan straw hat and tan boat shoes. They all greet and shake hands. Cliff puts his arm around the shoulder of Minister Randall. Who has a bohemian look today, wearing a gray fedora hat, white t-shirt, navy trousers and navy loafers.

"This is Minister Andre Randall. I brought this fella because he's dating my baby girl. So, I keep him real close. You know what I'm saying?"

"I feel you," Paris said. "He's dating your baby girl too, keep him close, just in case you gotta take him out."

"That's right," Cliff said. He takes his arm from around Andre and does some boxing moves. "Don't sleep boy." He pretends to punch him. "I got moves."

"I ain't scared." Minister Randall said snickering. "God got my back."

"Well looking at Cliff's size. He better." Paris said.

Paris laughs, Minister Randall smiles shaking his head as they greet each other shaking hands.

"Alright, now that all formalities are out the way," Dray said. "Let's go get our grub on."

"Amen to that!" Minister Thomas responds.

"He'll Work It Out" Chapter 7. Taryn C. Atkins

Cliff opens the deli's door and the guys follow him inside.

About an hour passes, the men are sitting in the serving area, at a table by the wall near the picture of Clinton. The group burst out into laughter as their waitress comes over.

"Well alright." The waitress said. "I love seeing buddies out and enjoying themselves. Need anything else guys?"

"Nah, we're good right now," Dray said. "Come back in about fifteen minutes. Just in case."

"Okay." The waitress said walking away. "Be back in a few."

"So... before we leave to play pool." Minister Thomas said. "Cliff we want to talk with you."

Dray puts his hand on Cliff's shoulder.

"Yes, the time has come," Dray said. "We got you out that hotel because we're all concerned about you and Shayna."

"I know," Cliff said.

As they get ready to have a serious conversation. Some of the guys nurse on their sodas or nibble on their leftover dessert.

"So what's going on with you two?" Dray said. "Now I get how things could be rough. Especially after that repass."

"Right, and we're not here to get into you and your wife's business either." Minister Thomas said.

"We're all just concerned about you and Deaconess Greye." Minister Randall said.

"I mean, you've been staying at a hotel for weeks." Minister Thomas said. "We haven't seen you in service either. So we're here because we all love you and Shayna and like Andre said we're concerned. So we're all here just to offer you some brotherly counsel. That's all."

"I know, and I appreciate you all being concerned too." Cliff said. "After the repass, well, we're going through this hard patch. I'm not getting into specifics. That's between my wife and me, and regardless I respect her. So just keep us in your prayers. God has to deal with her and me."

Dray takes his arm from around Cliff. He reaches for his glass of soda and takes it in his hand.

"Well, so you know," Dray said. "Shayna came over the other day; She came in the house crying like crazy. She told us you sent her divorce papers."

Dray nurses on his soda.

"I did," Cliff said. "We got into it after the repass and a lot came out. Some stuff I knew-but a lot I didn't. And right now, I can't even look at her the same way."

"Shayna does get on my nerves and I have no problem saying that either," Dray said. "Nola loves you two though and I've grown to love y'all too. And Cliff I know this. You love that woman with all your heart. And you know, she loves you too. So think long and hard before you file those papers. None of us are perfect."

"I know that's right." Minister Thomas said. "We all have our issues and have made mistakes. I know I've made mistakes; I've been dealing with the fallout from some, for years. I'm sure, whatever it is, you and Deaconess Greye can get through this. If you do it together."

"I know one thing," Minister Randall said. "It would devastate Regina if you two got divorced."

"Cliff, you've been there for my wife and me when we went through our stuff." Brother Hamlin said. "Through all those hard moments, you kept asking did we still love each other and were we worth fighting for? So, I'm asking you those same questions. Do you still love her?"

"Yeah... I do." Cliff said with a nonchalant nod. "I wish I could say I didn't but I am still in love with her."

"So then what are you going to do?" Brother Hamlin said. "Are you going to fight for your marriage? Or just allow the devil to break you two up?"

"Marcus," Cliff said. "She let the devil do this to us, not me. I've taken a lot from Shayna, and... I'm tired of it now."

"Haven't you made mistakes too." Minister Thomas said. When you used to drink, you did. I remember you telling me, how messed up you would get. She still stood by you, didn't she."

"Yeah, but she left too."

"Okay true, she came back though."

Cliff huffs and laughs a bit as he shakes his head.

"Casey you just don't know the half of it," Cliff said.

"Cliff look, I'm the odd man out here," Paris said. "I'm not deep in the church like you all. I do recall a line in the marriage vows though. It said what God has joined together let no man put asunder. I believe asunder means separate. So, before you throw away some twenty plus years, like Dray said, you need to think about it. Especially if things can be fixed between you two."

"Guys I appreciate the concern, I do." Cliff said. "I'm tired of her lies, and I've grown real tired of helping her keep up appearances. While knowing all the deception that goes with it. Yes, I sent those papers. Will she sign them? I don't know."

"Deacon Greye." Minister Randall said. "Regina said, umm, you two were starting counseling with Pastor next week."

"And we are," Cliff said. "Right now though, I don't know if I even want to go to counseling. Cause we been there done that already. Did it work? Nope."

The waitress comes back over to their table.

"Hi guys," The waitress said. "You want anything else?"

"We're all done here," Dray said. He reaches over and gives the waitress two hundred dollar bills. "Here you go and keep the change. You were great."

The waitress looks at the money Dray handed her and smiles.

"Thank you so much." The waitress said.

"No problem," Dray said

"Come back soon fella's." The waitress said. "Take care."

As the waitress walks away from the table. Cliff huffs.

"Listen guys," Cliff said. "I don't know what's gonna

happen between Shayna and me. I know this, I've taken my hands off. It's up to God now."

"Really." Brother Hamlin said with a huff. "That's a real easy way out. So remember this brother, how can we expect God to forgive us? If we can't forgive others."

"Yeah... I know..." Cliff said.

"Do you?" Brother Hamlin said.

"I do." Cliff said. "This isn't easy for me either."

"Good." Brother Hamlin said.

"It shouldn't be." Minister Thomas said.

"Alright then," Dray said. "This counseling session is over, lets hit the pool hall."

All the guys get up and make their way over to the door to leave out. Minister Thomas pats Cliff on the back.

"Look Cliff," Minister Thomas said. "We all know you're upset and you have all the right to be. Just don't rush to make any decisions while you're angry. Some of my biggest mistakes happened, because I made quick decisions without thinking first. So, don't make any decisions right now, calm down, think things thru and most of all talk to God first. Okay."

Cliff nods his head a few times.

"Alright." Cliff said.

He and the guys leave out the deli.

~LET US REASON~

It's mid October and early in the evening as everyone works to get over the hump of the week. Shayna paces on the dark red plush carpet, walking the length of Pastor Gorham's office from one end to the other. Every time she checks her watch, she changes directions trekking from the picture window to the door and back again. Pastor Gorham sits behind his custom dark mahogany desk scanning over a document in his hand. Lady Gorham stands at his side with her hand laying on top of the back of his oversize black leather office chair. She's also reviewing the document he holds.

Shayna stops dead center in the front of Pastor Gorham's desk and peers at them with deep concern in her eyes.

"Did he text or call either one of you?" Shayna said. She glances at her watch once again. "It's going on five-thirty and he knows our appointment was for four."

Pastor Gorham lays the document on his desk as he looks up at Shayna. Lady Gorham proceeds to walk around the desk.

"I haven't heard from Cliff." Pastor Gorham said. "The last time we spoke, was when Aisha got him on the phone to setup this appointment."

"Oh my God," Shayna said as she started her pacing again. "He's not coming."

Lady Gorham approaches Shayna.

"Come on now," Lady Gorham said. "I'm sure he wouldn't setup this appointment and then not show."

"I'm not so sure," Shayna said. "It was easy for him to have," Shayna motions to the documents on Pastor Gorham's desk. "Someone else serve me those divorce papers. Him not showing up, maybe that's to show me he's really done with us." She sits down on the dark brown leather sofa. "Maybe... I should sign, why prolong things."

Lady Gorham folds her arms as she leans against the front of the desk.

"Look here," Lady Gorham said. "Are you just gonna throw in the towel after twenty something years together."

Shayna looks up at Lady Gorham.

"I don't want to, but... I hurt him so much, and... I don't think he can forgive me this time. The last time he was at service, he could barely look at me. He even rushed out when he saw me coming toward him."

"Well, he's upset." Pastor Gorham said. "Allow him some space and let God deal with his heart."

"It's been weeks though."

"It took a few weeks last time you two were in this position." Lady Gorham said. "This time, it may take a few more."

"He won't even answer my calls." Shayna said.

"Give him time," Lady Gorham said. "Do you know if he's been keeping in touch with your daughters."

"I'm sure he has but..."

Cliff opens the office door and walks inside. Shayna's eyes study him as he walks toward Pastor Gorham.

"I'm here," Cliff said. "I apologize for being late Pastor Gorham, Lady Gorham."

Pastor Gorham stands.

"Well," Pastor Gorham said. "I'm just glad you made it."

He extends his hand to Cliff and they shake.

"Yes," Lady Gorham said. "Now lets get started."

Lady Gorham rolls the extra oversize office chair to the side of the desk. Shayna jumps to her feet and dashes over to Cliff.

"Where have you been?!" Shayna said. "It's after five-thirty, you we're suppose to be here by four."

"Listen," Cliff said. "I've been sitting in the car for the last forty-five minutes. You lucky I came in at all, so don't you dare get in my face!"

Cliff plops down in one of the burgundy leather chairs in front of Pastor Gorham's desk.

"Why agree to do this, then send me divorce papers?"

Cliff rises to his feet.

"I got one-why treat our daughter like she's got the plague, when you've been with a woman too?" Cliff goes to walk away but turns back to Shayna. "Or how about this... Why even bring your behind back to New York when your heart really wanted to stay in Texas with that bit--"

"Whoa... whoa!" Pastor Gorham said as he rushed from behind his desk and over to Cliff. "Calm down now!"

"You know what," Cliff said. "I'm sorry Pastor, it was a mistake for me to even come. I'm still way too angry."

"Cliff please," Shayna said. "Please don't leave. You're here now, that's what's important."

"You don't get it!" Cliff heads over to Shayna. "I can't

even look at you! All I see right now, is all your lies and deception. Plus, all the pain you've caused our daughter cause of you own selfishness. I... I can't deal right now! Maybe... not at all."

Cliff strides to the office door, before leaving he looks back at Pastor and Lady Gorham.

"Look, call me in a week. Maybe we can reschedule then..." He turns and grabs the door knob but looks back at them once again. "I can't promise it though."

They all watch as Cliff opens the door and exits the office.

~HE WHO FINDS~

It's a brisk Saturday afternoon in early November. Reggie took in a deep breath, exhaled and surveyed the resting place of his grandmother. He's become a different man from the last time he was there. Reggie was handsome and looking rather dapper in his business casual attire, like a man with a prosperous future ahead of him; He sported a navy beanie, a camel coat, blue scarf, navy cardigan over a crisp white collard shirt, dark blue jeans and brown shoes. Reggie closed his eyes for a moment and his lips started to move. He stood there praying for a few minutes. A moment later Kisha and her parents walked up. Kisha came up behind Reggie, reached out and touched him on his shoulder.

"Hey there," Kisha said.

Reggie quickly turns.

"Hey," Reggie said.

He put his arms around Kisha and they embrace for a few seconds. When they release each other Reggie reaches out to her mother.

"Thank you so much for coming out here," Reggie said.

Reggie and Pamela Carrington hug.

"No problem." Pamela Carrington said. "I'm just curious to know what's this about."

"I know," Reggie said. As they released each other. "I'll clear all that up in just a moment."

Reggie extends his hand to Kisha's father.

"Sir, I appreciate you and your wife coming," Reggie said.

Moses Carrington scrutinizes Reggie for a moment, then extends his hand and they shake.

"So, why are we all here Reggie?" Moses Carrington said.

Reggie points over to his grandmother's resting place.

"The last time I was here," Reggie said. "I was lost, strung out, broken, beaten and giving up on everything. God found me." He turns to them. "Not only God found me."

Reggie takes Kisha's hands in his and looks into her eyes. Kisha stares back into his and they smile.

"Kisha found me that day too. She's seen me at my worst and was still yet able to see the best in me. Besides God being with me helping me to get myself together. Kisha's been there with me too. Every step of the way. She's my best friend and I love her."

Reggie releases Kisha's hands, approaches her father standing in front of him.

"Sir, I don't just love your daughter; I'm in love with her. I've been in love with Kisha since the first time I saw her in the fifth grade. I know its only been a few months but things are better than they've ever been and getting better. I rededicated my life to the Lord. I attend my weekly meetings at the rehab. Plus, I have weekly sessions with Pastor Gorham and Mr. Pemberton, my rehab counselor. I make it a point to be in service on Tuesdays and Sundays. I'm also getting prepared to start college in the spring; I'll be taking Business Management and I plan to get my Bachelors. A few weeks ago-Praise God, my Uncle Cliff hired me, its entry level right now but I expect to excel."

Reggie motions toward an SUV parked near the seating area for the section. They look over and see Cliff leaning up against a silver Lincoln Navigator. Their eyes then return to Reggie.

"I'm going with my uncle on a business trip actually.

Our flight leaves in two hours but I wanted to do this first."

Reggie puts his attention back on the moment at hand. He looks at Kisha's father once again.

"Mr. Carrington, I've said all that because." He glances at Kisha and smiles. "Like I told you I'm in love with Kisha." He focuses on Mr. Carrington. "And Mr. Carrington..." He swallows hard. "I would be honored to make her my wife but I won't ask her unless it's alright with you and Mrs. Carrington."

Pamela Carrington smiles gawking at Reggie.

"Reggie," Pamela Carrington said. "I've seen the change in you over these last few months. I know it's been a struggle. I know you love my daughter and she surely loves you. So, you have my blessing."

Reggie smiles and quickly hugs Pamela Carrington.

"Thank you ma'am."

Reggie releases Mrs. Carrington and smiles peering over at Kisha, who's smiling too. He then stands in front of Mr. Carrington once again, eye to eye, Reggie stands straight and firm. Kisha looks at her father with a concerned expression. Pamela holds her husband's arm and looks up at him with equal concern. They all wait for his response.

"Sir."

Moses Carrington contemplates the expressions of his wife and daughter for a few seconds. He eyeballs Reggie.

"Kisha's never fought me on anything." Moses Carrington said. "Except with you. So, I know my daughter must love you. I know it's been a hard road Reggie, I know I didn't make it any easier either, and you still got ways to go. You look good though, I can tell you're putting your best foot forward and I'm not blind. I can see you love my daughter too. I figure, if she was able to see through the mess you were then and see who you are now, standing here. I can give you a chance too. So, you have my permission to ask."

"He'll Work It Out" Chapter 7. Taryn C. Atkins

Moses Carrington reaches out to shake Reggie's hand, Reggie gets ready to shake too but instead he grabs Moses Carrington and hugs him tightly.

"Thank you, sir, thank you so much."

When they release each other, Reggie turns to Kisha wearing a big smile. Reggie goes to Kisha, he gets down on one knee in front of her, clearing his throat as he looks up at her smiling.

"Kisha, most people think of a cemetery as the end of someone's natural life and the beginning of their eternal one. For me, a few months ago, this spot could have of been the end of both. That's changed because of God and you. So, it's here I want us to begin our life together."

Cliff stands off in the distance, leaning against a tree and watching as Reggie takes a small royal blue velvet box out of the side pocket of his coat. Reggie opens it and holds it up for Kisha to see. Her eyes go to a captivating two heart diamond ring. One heart consist of several tightly nestled round diamonds surrounding, a brilliant heart-shaped diamond in the center, gracefully resting on a white gold band. Her eyes open wider as she covers her mouth with her hands and starts to cry.

"I got a few weeks pay in advance." Reggie smiles. "One of Uncle Cliff's loyal clients is a jeweler, so he hooked me up. It's just a half carat, I got a diamond heart because my grandmother always said that God's love for his church and for us is unconditional and unbreakable. Kisha, that's how my love is for you. You're not only my best friend, you're the love of my life and my soulmate. I would be honored to call you my wife. So... Ms. Kisha Carrington." He looks away, takes in a deep breath, blows it out, looks up at her once again and smiles. "Will you marry me?"

"Yes... yes," Kisha said with tears rolling down her face.

"Oh my God, of course I will."

Kisha leans over, takes Reggie's face in her hands and kisses him. Reggie stands up, he takes Kisha in his arms and they share a scintillating kiss. Moses Carrington puts his arm around his wife's shoulder. They stand there with big smiles on their face watching

Kisha and Reggie. Cliff has a smile on his face too as he watches them. When they continue in their steamy lip lock Moses Carrington begins to loudly clear his throat. Reggie and Kisha then separate smiling as they gaze into each other's eyes.

"Kisha I love you so much."

"I love you too."

"Hey!" Cliff said. "Sorry to ruin the moment but we have a flight to catch."

Reggie looks over at Cliff.

"I'm coming now," Reggie said. His eyes return to Kisha.

"I'll be gone a week but I'll call every day."

"You better," Kisha said.

Reggie turns to Kisha's parents.

"Thank you, thank you both so much."

"No problem son." Moses Carrington said.

"We'll talk arrangements when you get back." Pamela Carrington said.

Reggie looks at Kisha as he starts to walk away.

"I love you and I'll see you soon," Reggie said.

Kisha rushes into his arms and they kiss passionately again.

"Love you," Kisha said.

Reggie walks with Cliff to the car.

"Uncle Cliff, I know you love Aunt Shayna, just like I love Kisha. Don't lose her, alright."

Cliff nods his head, they get in the SUV and drive off.

~GAME NIGHT~

The holiday season has come and gone, its two weeks into 2014 and on this Saturday afternoon, jazz music softly plays, tucked under laughter and conversation. The coffee table has been moved to the far left corner of the living room for this event, it has been replaced with a card table and two chairs.

Every month Gigi and Lexi have a game night at their place, where their close friends come over and they play, Backgammon, Uno, Spades, they even test their skills playing Pool and Madden on Lexi's Playstation. It's all couples this time and those in attendance include Gigi and Cassandra, Lexi and Dana and also Bobbie and Suzanne. All the ladies are dressed casually but each of their styles have a rather steamy and appealing uniqueness: Gigi chic artist, Cassandra sexy and sophisticated, Lexi hot and sporty tomboy, Dana ultra glam rocker, Bobbie bohemian tomboy and Suzanne western glam.

The seating arrangement around the card table was as follows: Gigi and Cassandra were seated on the sectional with the living room windows behind them. Lexi sat on the sectional too across from Dana who was seated in one of the chairs on the other side of the table. Suzanne was sitting at the end of the sectional near Bobbie, who was seated in the other chair at the card table across from Gigi.

"I love that Sangria," Suzanne said, she stood up. "I'm
getting me more. Anybody else want some?"

All the ladies raised their Solo cups. Cassandra shook her head as she put her cup on the card table and rose to her feet.

"Lushes," Cassandra said. "She only has two hands." She
looks at Suzanne. "I'll help you."

"Thanks," Suzanne said.

Suzanne took her cup along with Bobbie's and Lexi's. While Cassandra took her cup along with Gigi's and Dana's. They both head to the kitchen as Bobbie looks over at Suzanne.

"Baby," Bobbie said. "Can you please bring me some
wings and macaroni salad?"

"Sure baby," Suzanne said.

Suzanne and Cassandra walk over to the island. Suzanne reviews everything displayed on it, there was a large punch bowl filled with Sangria. Also a pan of lasagna, a pan of honey barbecue wings, a bowl of macaroni salad and a plate of deviled eggs. There was a tray of shrimp cocktail and a bowl of ambrosia too. Plus, the standard plate of crackers with squares of cheddar cheese, a bag of chips and a bowl of dip.

"So who cooked all this anyway?" Suzanne said.

"Everybody did something," Gigi said. "Lexi did the
Sangria."

"Of course," Lexi said.

"I did the lasagna and the deviled eggs," Cassandra said. "Gigi the wings, Dana the macaroni salad and Bobbie the shrimp cocktail and ambrosia. Lexi also did the incredibly hard task of taking the crackers out of the box, putting them on a plate and all after she risked danger, by taking a knife and cutting the cheddar cheese into squares."

"Oh let us not forget," Dana said. "All the energy Lexi exerted by opening up the bag of Lays potato chips and spooning the French onion dip out into a bowl."

"Hardy-har-har," Lexi said. "Aren't you two funny."

They all laugh. Cassandra grabs the silver ladle that's sitting in the punch bowl and starts refilling everyone's glass.

"Well, Bobbie should have told me," Suzanne said. "I would have cooked something."

"You're a guest this time," Bobbie said. "So no worries."

"Now next month," Lexi said. "By all means, you can cook your heart out."

"Behind you," Cassandra said. "On the kitchen counter are the plates and everything,"

"Okay," Suzanne said.

Suzanne turned around and laid out on the kitchen counter were royal blue Solo dinner and dessert plastic plates, bowls, cups, eating utensils and napkins. Suzanne makes Bobbie's plate. Thus far, it's the usual spade partners, Lexi and Dana going up against Gigi and Bobbie. Gigi stands to her feet and slaps a few cards down on the table.

"Give up those books!" Gigi said. "Look at that... Big joker, little joker and deuce of diamonds. We win, again!"

"Yes!" Bobbie said, jumping to her feet. "That's what I'm talking about G, do that!"

Bobbie and Gigi high five each other. Cassandra brings two of the refilled cups over to the ladies.

"Dana! What are you doing!" Lexi said. "Come on man! You're killing me here!"

"Here you go ladies," Cassandra said.

"He'll Work It Out" Chapter 7. Taryn C. Atkins

Cassandra hands Gigi and Dana their cups.

"Thank you, sweetie," Gigi said.

"Thanks," Dana said.

Cassandra goes back the kitchen. Gigi sits back down and goes over the score on the writing pad. Bobbie sits down too, gathers up the playing cards and starts to shuffle them.

"The score is," Gigi said. "Ouch, -150 to 390. That's bad!"

"Gigi we're spade partners for LIFE!" Bobbie said. "They SUCK!"

Cassandra grabs two more of the refilled cups off the island and brings them over.

"It's not me!" Lexi said. She motions to Dana. "She keeps cutting me! Dana this is Spades. There's no cutting in Spades! No Cutting!"

"I know you're not yelling at me." Dana said. She sucks her teeth. "You need to calm down." She takes a sip from her cup. "It's just a game anyway."

"Here you are," Cassandra said.

She hands Lexi and Bobbie their refilled cups.

"Thank ya," Bobbie said

"Thanks," Lexi said. "Dana spades is not just a game. It's a way of life."

"That's it," Dana said getting up from the table. "I'm done."

"Come on Dana," Lexi said.

"Nope, I'm done Lexi." Dana said.

Dana sits down on the other end of the sectional by Gigi and nurses on her cup of Sangria. Cassandra looks over at Gigi.

"Honey, want anything while I'm here," Cassandra said.

"I'll take some ambrosia," Gigi said. "Thank you, baby."

"No problem," Cassandra said.

"Oh please G," Bobbie said as she chuckled. "Trying to be all proper. Ambrosia... That's just a fancy word for fruit salad soup'd up with some yogurt and mini marshmallows."

"He'll Work It Out" Chapter 7. Taryn C. Atkins

Dana sees Cassandra kiss at Gigi. She watches as they gaze and smile at each other. Cassandra looks away and goes to the kitchen counter. Dana leans over to Gigi.

"Look at you with the hot cougar," Dana said. "How's that going?"

Gigi smiles, "I must say it's going great."

"Alright, Gigi's got a girlfriend." Dana said.

Cassandra gets one of the plastic bowls off the kitchen counter and comes back to the island.

"Yes I do," Gigi said with a smile as she leans over to Lexi. "A fine one too I must say."

Cassandra looks at Gigi as she scoops up the ambrosia and puts it in a bowl.

"I can hear you," Cassandra said.

"Good," Gigi said.

Smiling Cassandra shakes her head.

"Think I'll get me a little something too," Dana said. She stands and looks at Lexi. "You want something pookie."

"No," Lexi said.

"Grouch," Dana said.

Dana heads over to the kitchen as Gigi taps Lexi.

"Excuse me, did you hear me?" Gigi said with a smile. "I said my girlfriend is fine."

"Yeah... yeah, I heard you." Lexi said.

"I've also driven her car," Gigi said with a smile. "Several times. Have you, ever driven, a 2007, Shelby GT 500 Convertible? Hmm?"

Lexi looked over at Gigi with a stern expression. Gigi smiled at Lexi as she started to shake her head.

"No, I haven't," Lexi said. "Now move back."

Bobbie leans over to Lexi too.

Under her breath, Bobbie said, "Hater." She looks at Gigi.

"I'm happy for you two Gigi."

"Thanks, Bobbie," Gigi said. She glances at Cassandra, smiles and then looks back at Bobbie. "I am too."

Bobbie sees Gigi glance over at Lexi and sticks out her tongue. Bobbie laughs leaning back in her chair.

"Whatever," Lexi said.. "Alright, I need a partner for the

next round." She turns around and looks at the ladies over in the kitchen. "Dana..."

"Don't even ask me," Dana said.

"Cassandra," Lexi said.

"Sorry Lex," Cassandra said. "I don't do cards,"

"Suzanne how about it," Lexi said.

"I'll give it a shot," Suzanne said. "I think I still remember how to play. We played spades all the time in college."

The ladies occupying the kitchen finish fixing their plates and every one else's. They all head back to the living room. Suzanne sits at the card table across from Lexi. Dana puts her cup down on the end table and sits by Lexi. Cassandra hands Gigi a spoon and her bowl of ambrosia and takes a her seat by Gigi, she crosses her legs and nurses on her cup of Sangria.

"Alright, new game," Lexi said.

Lexi reaches over and gets the writing pad sitting on the card table by Gigi. She roughly rips off the top page. Everybody watches Lexi as she crumbles it up and throws it down on the sectional beside her. Gigi shakes her head as she looks at Lexi.

"Anger issues," Gigi said.

"Mm-hmm." Dana said.

"Sore loser issues if you ask me," Bobbie said.

"Sounds about right to me too." Cassandra said.

Lexi looks around at those who commented about her.

"Excuse me," Lexi said. "Can we play the game, please."

"Fine with me sore loser," Bobbie said.

Some ladies nurse on their drinks others enjoy their plate or bowl of food. Lexi takes the pad and puts it back down on the card table next to Gigi.

"Now... New game." Lexi said motioning to Bobbie.

"Deal."

Bobbie shuffles the cards three times and deals them out. They all sit there in silence for a moment and all that is heard is the melodious, sultry voice of Nancy Wilson playing. Suzanne throws out the first card of the new game.

"So Gigi," Dana said. "How you been doing?"

"I'm okay," Gigi said. "Lord knows, I miss my grandmother and I've had my days that's for sure." She smiles glancing at Cassandra. "But... I'm glad to have someone to help me with that."

Cassandra looks at Gigi, smiles and winks. Gigi smiles back as she checks the cards in her hand.

"Have you talked to your sister since then?" Dana said.

"No, I haven't seen or talked to anyone," Gigi said.

"They've been calling her though," Lexi said putting down a card. "They've left several voice mails and some emails. When we caught that bad weather over the holidays. They even tried to Skype with her. Gigi won't return their calls or anything. I don't blame her either."

"Your mom has serious issues," Bobbie said.

Bobbie throws out a card and Gigi picks up the book. The ladies continue to play cards as all of them continue to talk.

"My mom has an issue with my lifestyle," Gigi said.

"Those church folks tell you what not to do." Bobbie said. She puts her cards down on the table. "While in the Pastor's office," She goes over to the coffee table, with her back to the ladies', she pretends to have someone bent over in front of her and starts to grind. "They're getting their freak on."

They all laugh, Gigi shakes her head as she watches Bobbie come back to the card table and take her seat.

"You so wrong," Gigi said.

"Sorry, but she's so right," Suzanne said. "They tell you don't do this, that and the other. When all the while they're lying to you and doing all those things; And because they go to church every Sunday, they're going to heaven? Yet, I'm honest about whatever I do, be it with myself, others and especially God, but yet I'm going to hell because I don't go to church! I don't get that at all."

"I know that's right," Bobbie said.

"Well, you ain't gonna find a perfect church out there." Gigi said. "It doesn't exist, because we're not perfect. That's why you're not supposed to just look to people, you're supposed to look and follow God. Jesus is the only perfect one I know. Jesus lived in this flesh, suffered through everything we do, and yet lived a sinless life. Which is why God sent him. So he could sacrifice himself for us, so regardless of everything, I believe there's salvation and true deliverance from this, that and the other, through Jesus."

"Okay preacher, I've got some questions," Suzanne said. "If Jesus is so perfect, then why are you here? Why are you sitting here with a girlfriend and not a boyfriend? Why are you here with us and not in a church somewhere? So are you still going to heaven too, or are you going to hell with the rest of us?"

"Here we go-" Lexi said putting down her cards. "Forget it." She leans back on the sectional. "Just put down the cards and let's just continue with this discussion."

"For real!" Bobbie said. "Well, we probably would of beat y'all with this hand anyway."

Everybody playing, puts their cards down on the table. Suzanne turns her chair towards Gigi, Bobbie leans back in her chair as everyone gets comfortable too.

"So..." Suzanne said.

"Well, I was a Christian and went to church," Gigi said. "I've got no problem saying I was a tongue talking, saved, sanctified, Holy Ghost filled, fire baptized servant of the true and living God. And I'm not sitting here hiding my own issues and hurts. There not with God though, there with people. I love God, and I left the church because I refuse to be a hypocrite. Oh and don't get it twisted. I know what my sins are and I don't call wrong right either. If I died right now; I know I'm going to hell. So for me, every second, minute and so on, I know it's nothing but the grace and mercy of God."

The room gets eerily quiet as they take in Gig's statement.

"Okay, fine..." Suzanne said. "You chose to leave the church because of your own issues and whatever. Sounds to me like you even chose to be gay. Which means, you also have the luxury to go back to being straight."

"Wait a minute-" Gigi said sitting up. "What makes you think that would be a luxury? For me, anyway."

"Hold on... let me finish." Suzanne said. She quickly takes a drink of her Sangria and puts the cup down. "Now, there's some of us, who didn't choose to be the way we are at all, and we get no compassion or any empathy from those in the church either. Well, I'll say from so called "*Christians*..." Please, they, show love to us? They can barely show love to each other. So we can forget about any type of love coming our way."

"She's right Gigi," Lexi said folding her arms. "We've been friends since high school. Your mom never tried to get to know me. She didn't like me from the gate, and once she learned I was gay, she really hated me then! Yet she calls herself a Christian."

"See-I for one," Suzanne said. "I've never experienced any type of trauma, drama or abuse in my life. I was introduced to sex early though. I was about nine when I first found my brother's porn stash. He had magazines of women with men, women with women, and even men with men. I never told him or my parents what I found. Now, as I got older, every so often, I would go see what was new. As my brother got older, his porn collection grew and he added tapes. I was about thirteen when he left for college. So before my parents would get in from work. I'd watch them. He had tapes with all types of things, straight, gay, lesbian, orgies, gang bangs, bondage, various fetishes and even animals."

"Animals?!" Bobbie said.

"Baby, you have no idea!" Suzanne said. "I'll say this though... Sometimes man's best friend is their lover too."

The room erupts as all the ladies burst forth with exclamatory expressions in reaction to Suzanne's statement.

"Oh yeah!" Suzanne said. "I'm not going there, cause y'all ain't ready!"

The ladies shocked expressions don't change as they continue to comment on the matter.

"Alright, hold on!" Gigi said. "Wait y'all!"

The ladies calm themselves and listen once again.

"Now Suzanne, even that," Gigi said. "Some, not all, but some people, choose to do that because they've been hurt so much, be it mentally, physically or emotionally. So instead of dealing with another human, with the possibility of them being hurt once again. They would rather, be with an animal."

"That's deep!" Lexi said getting up. "I need another drank."

"Yeah me too," Dana said. "Cause that messed me up."

"For real," Bobbie said.

"It's sad, but..." Suzanne said. "What Gigi said, is true."

Lexi takes her cup, grabs Dana and Bobbie's and heads over to the island.

"While that is sad for some," Cassandra said. "There are also those, who have just become insatiable in their sexual desires too."

Lexi puts the cups down on the island but just stands there for a moment listening to the conversation.

"Insatiable," Dana said. "Okay, what do you mean by that?"

"Basically, it means," Cassandra said. "They're not sexually satisfied by being with a man or woman. It just doesn't do it for them anymore. So now, they look to animals for their sexual pleasure."

"Whoa!" Lexi said. "I have officially heard it all now."

"I know that's right." Bobbie said. "I have officially learned more that I wanted to, today. Thank you. Can we please go back to playing spades now?"

"That's why." Gigi said.

I guess not. Bobbie thought.

"The bottom line," Gigi said. "No matter the issue, problem, disorder, lifestyle, perversion or sin, there's salvation, deliverance and true freedom in Jesus, And

not just some people need Jesus." She huffs. "We all do."
"Well, I know one thing." Dana said. "That word insatiable, although it sounds sexy, especially they way Cassandra says it. That is one thing, I don't want to ever be, for anything for that matter."
Lexi gets the ladle out the bowl and refills their cups.
"Aww, not even for me boo." Lexi said.
"Sorry, but not even for you baby." Dana said.
"I don't know." Suzanne said. "I'm twenty-nine now and I didn't go crazy watching those tapes. My brother started going to church a few years ago. Every so often he'll try to talk to me about God and all that. I'm just so surprised at how much he's changed. He even threw out his collection, tapes and all. He even apologized to me. Told me, he knew I was going into his stash when I was young, and at the time he thought it was funny. He was just happy I wasn't bothering him. He said the reason he apologized to me and keeps me in his prayers. Is because he feels he played apart in how my attitude is toward sex. I told him no worries, I'm okay. Even let him know I have my own collection now."
"I'm sure he didn't take that well." Lexi said.
"Of course not." Suzanne said. "I held my ground and told him how I felt. I told him, as far as I'm concerned. All he did for me, was make me a more open person. I don't put any type of label on myself and I never say never. I keep it real and honest, especially with myself. Is that a bad thing? I don't think so, because there's a whole lot of people, lying to themselves and everybody else. Professing one thing on Sunday, then living and doing the exact opposite every other day of the week. Yet, those are the ones that have the nerve to tell me, I'm the one going to hell. Every so often, my brother invites me to his church or some thing centering around God. I have nothing but love for my brother, so maybe I'll go one day. Right now, I don't think so, but hey you never

know" She shrugs her shoulders. "Who knows what the future holds."

Lexi brings their drinks over to the card table.

"Well, you're right about some of us not having a choice." Bobbie said. "I don't think I did. My parents always wanted a boy. The doctor even told them they were having one. So, they pretty much thought they were having a boy. They told all their friends they were too. When it was baby shower time, they got all the boy stuff they would ever need. When a girl popped out instead, what could they do? I know they didn't put all that stuff to waste. As I grew up, when people gave me girl stuff, it just didn't feel right. I've always been one of the guys. So, when I came out to my parents. They didn't even get upset, their happy. As far as their concerned they still ended up with their boy."

The room is silent as they wait to see who will speak next.

"Umm..." Dana said. "Sometimes it's still hard for me to talk about..." She takes a sip of Sangria. "I'm amongst friends. So..." She takes a deep breath, exhales and clears her throat. "When I was about eleven, my mother used to worked nights. Her sister and her husband use to watch me. I was in the bathroom, my aunt was washing me up, her husband came in and said he would do it. When she said no, he slapped her and pushed her out the bathroom. My aunt was Muslim, she would be in the next room praying to Allah." Dana scoots down to the edge of the sectional. "I remember because I could hear her asking Allah to make it stop. That never happened."

Dana gets up, takes her cup of Sangria and walks to the island. The ladies watch her closely. She pulls out one of the barstools, sits down and as she crosses her legs takes a sip of her Sangria.

"Well," Dana said. "It started with my uncle just washing me up when I came over. I was young and too scared to say anything to my mother." She drinks down some of her Sangria. "That went on for about a year, when I turned twelve and puberty started. He decided he was

"He'll Work It Out" Chapter 7. Taryn C. Atkins

gonna make me a woman. I did tell my mom, she never said anything to them. She was more caught up with her own problems then worrying about mine. I remember my aunt and uncle use to help my mom out when money ran low. So... guess she didn't want to stir up stuff." She drinks more of her Sangria. "I think... I don't do any type of church, cause with all that praying my aunt did, God never showed up for me. Then when I was sixteen, my mom got married and moved to Miami. Said it was time for her to enjoy her life, and time for me to take care of myself. She left and never looked back. We talk on holidays still but that's it. Anyway, after all that, I never really felt anything for guys. Just seemed natural for me to be with a woman."

"Well, since we're all being so open with each other." Lexi said. "No traumatic experience or any abuse here. I've got aunts, uncles and a few cousins on both my parents side that are gay. I've always been tall and a tomboy at heart. I was fourteen and my parents asked this college student they knew, to watch me one weekend while they went away. She invited over one of her female friends and they thought I was cute. Make a long story short. My first experience was a threesome. No damage was done here that's for sure. I would've ended up a lesbian anyway."

"Suzanne, I agree with you," Dana said. "There are plenty of Christians professing one thing and living another. That's real and they keep getting away with it."

"I'm not sure about that." Lexi said. "A lot of preachers have been getting exposed lately."

"True," Gigi said. "That doesn't mean everybody's doing wrong either. I believe that there's a remnant of people who are truly living right before God."

"That's sweet Gigi," Cassandra said. "And also naive... I use to have a minister friend like you, she only saw the good in the church but it wasn't long before she got an up close and personal rude awakening." She takes a healthy sip from her cup. "I remember when my friend got saved, she loved God and totally left this lifestyle. She became a minister and even fell in love with a man. They were about to get married too." She nurses on her drink. "My friend lived in California at the time this happened. Anyway, where she attended church at the time, the Pastor's wife also known as "*The First Lady*". Well, the First Lady called her out in service one day. She told her, the Lord said for her to travel with her for a season. You know, when she went out of town for preaching engagements. Anyway, my friend wanted to be obedient to the Lord so she went."

Cassandra's voice and the jazz music playing was the only thing heard. Nobody else said anything, they just listened. Cassandra took a sip from her cup once again.

"My friend was so excited for the Lord to open up this opportunity for her. She would be walking right beside leadership and not just any leader either. I mean come on its the First Lady after all. So my friend told me about this one time on the road. The First Lady told her to stay in the room with her. She had a suite with an open out couch. So to save on expenses, she decided to stay in the suite with the First Lady."

"Big mistake." Suzanne said.

"Let me finish," Cassandra said. "Well, they got in late after a powerful service. The First Lady preached up a storm, my friend said God moved in a mighty way, people got saved, healed, delivered. You know the usual church spiel. Well, they went to bed, the First Lady went off to her bedroom and my friend slept on the open out couch. A few hours had passed and my friend told me she woke up having an orgasm. When she looked down, the First Lady was between her legs."

A collective gasp is heard, while a few of the ladies sit with their mouth gaped open as Cassandra continues.

"My friend pulled away from her, covered herself up and asked the First Lady, with tears running down her face.

Why would she even do something like that. The First Lady said to my friend and I quote... "Why should she deny herself what appeals to her." End quote."
"Wow." Bobbie said.
"Oh, I'm not finished yet," Cassandra said. "My friend then told the First Lady, she was going to let the pastor who's her husband mind you, she was going to tell him about what happened." She huffs. "The First Lady said, Oh, he knows. We have an understanding. My husband lets me enjoy my appetite for women, as I allow him his boy toys."
"Say what?!" Gigi said.
"I am so done right now!" Dana said.
"Yeah, my friend was too." Cassandra said. "She left that church and California, moved around for a bit and didn't go back to church right away. She ended up in Chicago, got into a church there and it happened again, with another female leader. Once again she left, this time to Atlanta, joined another church and things were actually going well too, until... It happened a third time with yet another female leader. My friend was through at that point. She figured hey, she loved church and women so why not do both. After all, those leaders were and God was still using them." She takes in a deep breath as she gets up from the sectional. "Anyway, after that, we lost contact."

Cassandra takes her cup and heads to the kitchen. Lexi sits up, she moves closer to the card table and pulls all the playing cards over to her.

Under her breath, Lexi said, "Watch this everybody." She clears her throat as she puts the cards together. "Hey, Cassandra, you can be honest. Is that minister friend of yours really you?"

Lexi begins to shuffle the cards. Cassandra puts her cup down on the island, turns around and comes back to the sectional. She stands by the side of it where everyone can see her.

"Now darling," Cassandra said eyeing Lexi. "Look at this

body well, does it actually look like a package that a minister would be wrapped in?"

Lexi views Cassandra, putting her hand on her chin as she carefully studies Cassandra's body. Lexi then huffs.

"I don't think so." Lexi said.

"Exactly." Cassandra said.

Cassandra returns to island, takes her cup to the fridge while refilling it with ice she silently sucks her teeth.

I don't think so... That's what those church leaders said to me too. Cassandra thought.

"Well," Bobbie said. "I think it's a shame what happened to your friend, and in the church, of all places."

Cassandra grabs a dessert plate and returns to the island.

"That's happening all over," Dana said. "I remember reading this post. I forget where I saw it but it talked about this pastor committing homosexual bestiality."

"What?" Lexi said.

They all look at each other puzzled by Dana's statement and then return their attention to Dana. Cassandra peeks back and forth at the ladies, listening as she refills her glass with Sangria adding snacks to her small plate.

"Alright Dana," Bobbie said. "What does that mean?!"

"I think I know where she's going ." Cassandra said.

"But I don't want to go there again." Bobbie said.

They all snicker.

"Well," Gigi said. "You lost me."

"Me too," Suzanne said.

"Okay look," Dana said. "The pastor is the shepherd right?"

"Right." Lexi and Suzanne said in stereo.

"The people in the congregation are the sheep?" Dana said.

Cassandra comes over carrying her cup and a small plate.

"Right." Bobbie and Gigi said in unison.

"Well," Dana said. "This pastor was sleeping with one of his male sheep."

"Okay, I get it." Suzanne said.

Lexi puts the deck of cards down in front of Bobbie, they stare at one another nodding their heads as Bobbie cuts the cards. Cassandra sits down by Gigi once again.

>Lexi and Bobbie say in harmony. "Ohh, homosexual bestiality!"
>"That's it-bathroom break for me." Gigi said
>"Alright," Lexi said dealing out the cards. "New game!"

Gigi gets up, she turns to Cassandra smiling.

>"Want to join me?" Gigi said grinning flirtatiously. "It's universal for women to go to the bathroom together."

The other ladies in the room nonchalantly listen as they start a fresh spades game. Cassandra smiles gazing up at Gigi.

>"Mm hmm, No thank you."
>"What? Don't trust me?"
>"Nope."

Cassandra puts a cracker in her mouth as she crosses her legs. She takes a drink from her cup while watching Gigi head toward the hallway. While the ladies play cards and talk amongst themselves. Cassandra hears a phone vibrate on the end table by her. She sees its Gigi's cell. Cassandra doesn't pick up Gigi's cell, she reaches over and checks it. She sees a text saying "Hey its Auntie, Regina and I miss u, so coming by. Be there in thirty. Like it or Not." Cassandra turns off the phone and sits there for a moment. She leans over and picks up her LV bag on the carpet by her. The ladies continue playing cards but get a little boisterous for a bit. Cassandra takes her cell out her bag and reviews her text messages. She quickly sits up and makes a call.

>"Hello." Cassandra said. "Is Mr. Or Mrs. Balkcon available? Oh... okay, thank you, I'll try their cells."
>Cassandra ends the call, she stands grabbing her cup and plate, and heads to the kitchen. "Goodness, I hope I can catch them."

The ladies over hear Cassandra. She throws her plate in the garbage, dumps her cup out in the sink and goes back to the living room. Cassandra doesn't sit, she grabs her bag off the sectional and makes another call as she heads over to the island. When Cassandra gets to the hallway, Gigi walks out and on seeing

Cassandra tries to place her arms around her waist. Cassandra gestures for Gigi to wait as she proceeds over to the island, Gigi follows her.

"Hello, Mrs. Balkcon." Cassandra said. "Cassandra Pauls here. Oh, no problem. I'll hold on."

"Cassandra Pauls huh." Gigi said. She looks at Cassandra and smiles. "It suits you."

Cassandra glances at Gigi and puts her finger to her lips.

"Shh," Cassandra said going back her call. "Yes, I'm here, I do apologize; I thought our appointment was for next Saturday. Yes, both houses are still available. As I told you and your husband both owners are interested in your proposal." She puts her bag on one of the barstools. "Yes, we can. I'm currently in the city. I can meet you at the town house in a hour. Great, see you then."

Cassandra ends the call, puts her cell in her bag, takes out her shades and car keys.

"What's going on?" Gigi said.

"Sweetheart, I've got to go." Cassandra said. "I have an appointment with a client. I thought it was next Saturday but its today."

"Can't you just reschedule with them?"

"They're ready to buy, I do that and another realtor will get the sale."

"Right..."

Gigi looks away sucking her teeth. Cassandra turns Gigi's face to her and puts her arms around her neck.

"Baby, I'll be back early tomorrow. I'll even cook breakfast."

"I want pancakes and turkey sausage." Bobbie said.

"Scrambled eggs and bacon here." Lexi said.

"Chicken and waffles for me." Dana said.

"Half a grapefruit and toast please." Suzanne said.

Everyone's attention shoots to Suzanne.

"A half of grapefruit," Dana said.

"And toast," Bobbie said.

"Really..." Lexi said.

"Please forgive her," Bobbie said glancing at Lexi and Dana She looks at Gigi and Cassandra snickering.

"She's still learning to order ethnically correct."

"Very funny." Suzanne said shoving Bobbie.

The ladies go back to their card game. Gigi and Cassandra look at them shaking their heads, then return their focus to each other. Gigi grins putting her arms around Cassandra's waist holding her close.

"How about," Gigi said. "I throw some clothes in a bag and just stay with you for the weekend."

Cassandra smiles shaking her head, "I don't think so."

"Why not? You got some other woman at your place?"

"Of course not, but I don't relax at my place either. It's more like my office really. I work when I'm there and calls come in consistently. We wouldn't have any peace. Which is why I come here, darling. So I can thoroughly enjoy relaxing with you."

"Well, okay, I was looking forward to us spooning though, and being all cuddled up together all weekend."

"I know, I was too. I'll make it up to you."

"I'm listening."

Cassandra whispers in Gigi's ear for a moment, Gigi smiles as Cassandra moves away from her ear.

"Oh, I don't mind that at all." Gigi said.

"I bet you don't." Cassandra smiles releasing Gigi.

"I've got plans for you too." Gigi smiles. "So rest up."

"Hmph." Cassandra smiles seductively. "You too."

Gigi smiles going to the intercom, she calls downstairs to have Cassandra's car brought around. Cassandra takes her beige cashmere shawl with mink trim off the coat rack and puts it around her shoulders. Then gets her LV bag off the island and turns to the ladies in the living room.

"Ladies, it's been lovely but..." Cassandra said. "Business calls."

"Aww, it was nice meeting you." Suzanne said.

"You too." Cassandra said. "Lexi, Dana, Bobbie see you

soon."

"Take it easy." Dana said.

"Drive safe." Bobbie said.

"Later." Lexi said.

Cassandra turns to Gigi as she approaches, Cassandra extends her hand, Gigi accepts and their hands join.

"Walk me to the door." Cassandra said.

The hallway being slightly narrow, Cassandra walks in front of Gigi. Cassandra slides the front door open and walks out into the hall. Gigi leans against the door frame, her head tilts slightly to the side for a second watching Cassandra's lovely walk as she goes to the elevators. After pressing for an elevator, Cassandra checks what floor each elevator is on then turns toward Gigi. When their eyes meet Gigi smiles and winks at her. Cassandra smiles and even blushes a tad.

"I'll miss you." Gigi said.

"Same here." Cassandra said.

"Call me when you get home."

"I will."

The elevator door opens, Cassandra looks at Gigi again and waves as she gets in. Cassandra leans up against the wall, her eyes stare at the ceiling for a moment and then she closes them. She shakes her head a little, takes a breath and exhales.

No, don't do it. Not yet. Cassandra thought.

Cassandra keeps her eyes close and tilts her head down. Gigi stands there watching the elevator.

Don't, it's too early. Gigi thought.

When Gigi sees the elevator doors start to close, she jets over and stops them from shutting.

"Wait!" Gigi said.

Cassandra eyes quickly open, they fall upon Gigi and she moves toward her.

"I love you," Gigi said.

"I love you too," Cassandra said.

Gigi releases the elevator, as it closes they both smile. Cassandra leans against the wall as it travels downstairs.

"She, said it." Cassandra lays her hand on her chest. "I

"He'll Work It Out" Chapter 7. Taryn C. Atkins

said it." Her cell rings catching her off guard. She quickly takes it out her bag. "Hey Cassi," Cassandra said. "Sorry for my calls... Oh, everything's fine... Needed to make a quick departure..." *Not ready to meet the family, that's all.* Cassandra thought. "Oh, sure... You go on... I didn't mean to disturb you on set. Later sis."

As Cassandra's elevator approaches the lobby. Regina and Leah wait for one of the elevators to come. Regina's style for today is rather corporate chic, yet her attire has a trendy feel to it. Leah's in casual winter wear, sporting her own fierce fashion sense as usual. A elevator arrives, it opens and Regina and Leah step inside. Leah presses the twenty first floor and as their elevator doors close, Cassandra's elevator opens. She steps out tossing her cashmere shawl over her shoulder. She walks out the building putting on her shades, gets into her Shelby and drives off with a content and confident smile.

Gigi walks up the hallway in the loft wearing a smile brimming with delight. When she comes out the hallway, she notices Lexi standing over at the intercom with a sour expression.

"What's wrong with you?" Gigi said.

"Thanks for letting us know Cesar," Lexi said, she hangs up the receiver staring at Gigi. "Regina and Leah are on their way up."

"Are you kidding me?" Gigi said.

"Not at all," Lexi said.

Seconds later their front doorbell rings.

"And there they go," Lexi said. She huffs shaking her head. "I'll let you get that."

Lexi walks away heading to the living room. Gigi shakes her head a bit as reality makes its impact. She takes a deep breath and exhales going to the front door, as the doorbell rings again.

"Hold on, I'm coming!" Gigi said.

Lexi takes her seat next to Dana.

"And so it begins," Lexi said.

"What's going on?" Dana said.

"You'll see in a moment,"

"He'll Work It Out" Chapter 7. Taryn C. Atkins

After a few moments Gigi walks out of the hallway followed by Leah and Regina. Dana seeing Gigi's family shoots a look at Lexi.

"Hi everybody," Regina said.

"Hello, ladies," Leah said.

"Oh, here we go," Dana said.

Dana and Lexi stand and approach Leah and Regina. Bobbie and Suzanne eyeball each other and watch the group standing by the hallway.

"Look, don't bother," Dana said. "We know what happen after the funeral."

"And it's not going down like that today" Lexi said.

"Lexi, we're just here to talk to Gigi." Regina said.

"She hasn't returned your calls for a reason," Lexi said.

"Cause apparently," Dana said. "She don't want to be bothered. So, y'all can leave now."

Leah's eyes go to Gigi, she watches Gigi say nothing, just shrugs her shoulders and folds her arms.

"Really," Leah said. She looks at Dana. "I don't know who you are but I'm here to see my niece. That's all."

Bobbie gets up from the card table, sits on the arm of the sectional and watches the group.

"I know exactly who y'all are," Dana said moving toward Leah. Y'all are the family, that's been putting my friend through hell!"

"And what happen at her mom'!," Lexi said. "Will not happen here."

"I know that's right!" Dana said. "Believe that!"

"You know what!" Leah said.

Dana and Leah go for each other but Bobbie rushes over and gets in between them.

"Okay, everyone calm down!" Bobbie said.

"They're not welcome Bobbie!" Lexi said.

"Well, that's Gigi's family Lex." Bobbie said.

Suzanne gets up seeing the commotion but watches from the living room. Gigi's friends are near the island and her family in front of the hallway. While Bobbie stands in the center of the situation, making sure things don't get out of hand. Gigi walks away, she leans against the kitchen counter and stands there with her arms folded.

"Bobbie, we're not here to start trouble." Regina said.

"Well, that's what you found!" Dana said.

"Look, I get it," Regina said. "You're her friends and y'all want to protect her. All I want to do, is talk to my sister."

"Well, nobody asked you to come here," Dana said. She motions toward Gigi. "Especially Gigi, so y'all need to go!"

"Excuse me!" Leah said. "Listen here! Let me tell you something!"

Leah swiftly raises her hand, pointing at Dana as she moves toward her.

"What!" Dana moves toward Leah. "You don't know me!"

Suzanne moves closer, stopping where the living room begins, she stands by the end table watching and listening.

"Baby don't get it twisted." Leah said. "You don't know me!"

Alright, Dana needs to back up. Suzanne thought.

Dana and Leah go toward each other but Gigi steps in and doesn't allow them to get to each other. Regina keeps Leah back while Bobbie holds back Dana.

"Y'all don't live here," Dana said. "How you just gonna show up?!"

"Say that again!" Lexi said.

Bobbie sees Lexi step back and sit on one of the barstools.

"Cause I'm Gigi's aunt." Leah said. "And we're family, that's how."

"I don't care who you are!" Dana said.

"Little girl!" Leah said moving toward Dana again. "You better stay in your grade."

"Or What!" Dana said moving toward Leah. "You feeling froggy, leap then!"

"Dana come on now!" Bobbie said.

"Oh, I can leap!" Leah said.

Leah moves forward, trying to get pass Gigi and Regina as she reaches for Dana.

"Aunt Leah, stop it!" Regina said.

"Alright everybody just calm down!" Gigi said.

Leah and Dana go toward each other again. Gigi, Regina, and Bobbie do their best to keep them apart. Bobbie looks at Lexi.

"Lexi get your girl!" Bobbie said

Lexi grabs Dana by her arm. Dana looks at Lexi, as she pulls her over to the living room windows.

"Lexi!" Dana said. "What are you doing?!"

Lexi grabs a barstools, brings it over and sits it by Dana.

"Sit down." Lexi said pointing to the barstool.

"No!" Dana said motions toward Leah. "I'm telling you, she don't know who's she's dealing with!"

Lexi moves closer to Dana and points in her face.

"Nah, you don't know!" Lexi said. "Now sit down!"

"What?!" Dana said. "Please."

Dana sucks her teeth and attempts to walk pass. Lexi grabs her by the arm pulling her to the barstool. Dana bumps into the barstool, Lexi plops her down in it and gets in her face.

"Stop it!" Lexi said though clenched teeth. "Gigi's still my best friend and that's not her mother. That's her sister and aunt. So, calm it down!"

"Fine." Dana said through gritted teeth as well.

Dana sucks her teeth again as she folds her arms and looks toward Leah and Regina. Lexi grabs a barstool for herself and sits by Dana.

"Listen Bobbie," Regina said. "We didn't come to argue."

"No, we didn't, "Leah said. "We're not gonna stand here and be disrespected either." She looks at Dana. "You can best believe that!"

Dana gets up, "Well neither are we!"

"Dana," Lexi said.

Dana rolls her eyes sitting back down on the barstool. Gigi walks to the kitchen counter, leans against it again looking down at the floor and folds her arms.

"Lexi look," Regina said. "We're not just showing up. Leah text Gigi about thirty minutes ago."

Lexi eyes go to Gigi.

"You get a text?" Lexi said.

Gigi looks at her shrugging her shoulders.

"I don't know," Gigi said. "I might of, I haven't checked."

"Check it," Leah said. "Cause I did text you."

Gigi's eyes return their attention to the floor.

"Regardless of that," Regina said. "It's been months since we seen or talked to Gigi."

"That's not our fault," Lexi said. "That's not Gigi's fault either for that matter."

"Yeah," Dana said. "Your own mother made it clear. She doesn't want to be bothered with Gigi. So, why should she be bothered with any of you?!"

"Cause we're still her family." Leah said. "That's why!"

"So what!" Dana said. "Like being family is actually supposed to mean something. Please, 99.9% of the time its family that hurts you the most!"

Dana gets up, dashing forward. Before she can jet pass, Lexi sticks out her arm and stops her.

"Look you," Leah said.

Leah moves forward but Regina reaches across her as well, stopping her. Dana loudly sucks her teeth, taking her seat on the barstool.

"Look, ladies," Regina said. "We came here cause we're concerned about Gigi." She looks over at Gigi. "And Gigi, Hello." Gigi raises her head and looks at Regina. "We're not leaving until we talk."

Gigi takes a deep breath as she glances up at the ceiling and exhales. She lowers her head and focuses on Regina and Leah.

"I understand," Bobbie said. "So, we're gonna go." She turns to Lexi "Lex, let Gigi get a moment with her people."

Lexi and Dana stay seated. Bobbie shakes her head and looks at Suzanne.

"Pick up the intercom," Bobbie said. "Tell them, three on twenty-one wants the Jeep brought around."

"Okay." Suzanne said.

Suzanne picks her bag up off the floor by the sectional, goes to the intercom and calls downstairs. Bobbie looks at Lexi.

"Lexi, you and Dana come on," Bobbie said.

"We don't have to leave," Lexi said. "I live here too. We can go in my room."

Bobbie shakes her head as she walks over to the coat rack. Bobbie gets her vintage military jacket and Suzanne's western peacoat. She hands Suzanne her coat and they prepare to leave. Bobbie stares at Lexi.

"Hey you know I get it," Bobbie said. "Either way, that's Gigi's sister and aunt. We both know Lexi, their not like her mother. So, whether you two leave or go in the room. Give them time alone to talk. Alright Lex."

"Yeah," Lexi said.

"Alright, we'll see ya," Bobbie said turning to Gigi "Lata G."

"Bye," Gigi said.

As Bobbie and Suzanne move toward the hallway. Bobbie looks at Leah and Regina.

"Alright now," Bobbie said. "Y'all take it easy."

"See ya everybody," Suzanne said.

Leah and Regina wave bye to Bobbie and Suzanne and they leave out. Lexi looks in Leah and Regina's direction as she stands. Gigi turns around to the kitchen counter. Regina and Leah watch Gigi gets a Solo cup and goes to the island.

"It's game day after all," Lexi said. "And I need the new Madden game anyway." She motions to Dana. "So, let's go, lets take a drive to Best Buy."

"We shouldn't go anywhere," Dana said. "They're the ones that need to leave Lexi."

"Dana!" Lexi said motioning toward the hallway. "Go get your coat out the room and go to the elevator."

"Fine." Dana said.

Dana sucks her teeth again and walks off in a huff stomping down the hallway. Lexi stops by Leah and Regina, she looks down the hall at Dana.

"I'll be right there," Lexi said.

"Whatever," Dana said.

"He'll Work It Out" Chapter 7. Taryn C. Atkins

Gigi pours herself a cup of Sangria. Dana goes into Lexi's room slamming the door behind her. After a few seconds, Dana comes out, slides the front door open and exits. Lexi goes to the intercom, picks up the receiver and calls downstairs.

"Hey Cesar," Lexi said. "Yeah, this is Lexi, you know three on twenty-one. Bring Dana's car around please. Thanks."

Lexi hangs up, gets her leather bomber off the coat rack and puts it on as she approaches Gigi. Leah takes her coat off and drapes it over the arm of the sectional.

"You want me to stay?" Lexi said.

Gigi looks at Leah and Regina, then Lexi.

"It's okay," Gigi said. "I'll be fine."

Regina goes to the island, taking a seat on a barstool. Leah comes over and stands by her. Regina turns her seat toward Gigi.

"Alright," Lexi said. "Call me if you need to." She looks at Regina and Leah. "Bye."

"Thank you," Regina said.

"Sure," Lexi said. She motions bye to Leah. "See ya."

"See ya," Leah said.

Lexi enters the hallway and exits the loft. Gigi clears her throat as she looks toward the living room windows. She picks up her cup and takes a healthy sip of Sangria. Although Gigi's friends have left the loft, an awkward tension still looms. Gigi clears her throat once again, puts her cup down on the island and looks at her sister and aunt.

"So, why the visit?" Gigi said. "Oh, if you were worried. No thoughts of suicide. Well, not today anyway." She takes a sip from her cup. "Besides, I don't like guns and I can't swallow pills."

Gigi's eyes go to the living room windows again.

"Now, when I was nineteen after mom kicked me out. I did try cutting my wrist; I even made sure I did it the right way."

Gigi takes another sip from her cup of Sangria.

"What?!" Regina said.

"Oh my God!" Leah said.

"I... I never knew that!" Regina said.

"Neither did I!" Leah said.

"Calm down," Gigi said looking at them. "Nobody in the family knows." She puts her cup down. "And I want to keep it like that, okay!"

"Gigi," Regina said. "Mom and dad should--"

"Nobody Gina!" Gigi said. "Aunt Leah nobody."

Leah huffs, looks off to the side and folds her arms.

"Alright fine." Leah said. She looks at Gigi motioning toward the hallway. "Any of your friends know?"

"Only Lexi does," Gigi said. "She happened to walk into the bathroom a few moments later. Lexi pulled off her favorite Looney Tune socks and tied them around my wrist. I remember trying to stop her but I was too weak."

Gigi takes a sip from her cup as she observes Regina and Leah stunned expressions. The room is dead silent as they eyeball Gigi.

"Oh, come on," Gigi said. "No reason to look like that. She huffs moving to the side of the island. "As you can see it didn't work. I guess that's supposed to be a good thing. I'm not sure," She takes a sip from her cup as she walks away but turns back to them. "I know, let's ask mom."

Gigi rolls her eyes as she strolls to the living room, Regina and Leah keep their attention on Gigi and turn themselves in her direction.

"Anyway, as you see I'm all right." Gigi moves toward the sectional. "Thanks for coming by, appreciate it, love you both and give dad my love."

Gigi goes to the far end of the sectional, she looks at them before sitting.

"Oh-Tell mom I said I'm still here, sorry" She raises her cup. "Cheers."

Gigi drinks from her cup as she sits. Regina and Leah look at each other, then stare at Gigi for a moment processing all that's been stated before they speak. Gigi sits back on the sectional, crossing her legs, she takes another mouthful of Sangria and places her glass on the end table by her.

"Gigi you don't have to be like that," Regina said.

"Sorry sis," Gigi said. "My house, my rules for a change,"
"You know what," Leah said. "I don't appreciate the tone in your voice, and I don't care how old you are either. I'm still your aunt and fifteen years your senior. So, shut it down."

"We've been concerned about you," Regina said. "Its been a while since we've seen or heard anything from you."

Regina navigates over to Gigi, placing her Coach bag on the end table, she walks around the card table and sits by Gigi on the sectional.

"We're not here to give you a hard time either," Leah said. She comes over and sits at the card table. "We're here because we love you."

"Believe me, I get not returning mom's calls." Regina said. "Everybody has been trying to reach you since the repass. It's been months Gigi and you could've at least returned..." She gestures to herself and Leah "Our phone calls."

"Look, I've kept away for a reason," Gigi said. "So, excuse me if I'm not bubbling over to see you. After what happened that day, it was easier for me to make that the last time I saw or even talked to anyone in my family."

Gigi picks up her cup and nurses her drink as they talk.

"That's messed up, Gigi," Regina said.

"Well, I'm tired of getting hurt too Gina," Gigi said.

"Daddy and I never changed toward you," Regina said. "Neither did Aunt Leah, none of us ever treated you funny."

"Mama never changed toward you," Leah said. "Mama was raw with it, always told us the truth, straight out Heaven or Hell! She still loved us with all her heart. Yes, your mom has been terrible but... Baby, like it or not only God can change her."

"I've always been straight with you," Regina said. "I don't agree with your lifestyle, but you know I love you. And whether you want to believe it or not. God is gonna get the glory out of your life Gigi. God is there for you."

Gigi huffs, getting up from the sectional she glances at Regina as she heads toward the kitchen.

"I'm a backslider, remember." Gigi said. "I know who God is. That doesn't change the pain I feel, does it!?"

Gigi gets choked up with emotion, as she does her best to hold back her tears. Regina watches her go to the kitchen.

"It doesn't change that my own mother can't stand the sight of me, and consistently shoved me away all my life!"

Gigi hurries to the kitchen counter, puts her cup down on it, places her hands on the counter and leans against it for strength as her tears flow. Regina and Leah look at each other when they hear Gigi's whimpers. Regina stands, as she walks over to the island. Leah turns herself toward them and leans on the card table in front of her.

"Gina, Aunt Leah," Gigi said. "I'm tired of hurting, and so tired of fighting. Mom has made it abundantly clear. She wants nothing to do with me. So, why should I bother." She wipes her face turning around to them. "I'd rather have no family and have peace." She comes over to the island. "At least," She points down the hallway. "I'll have those friends, and they care about me with no questions asked. Plus, I've finally allowed myself to fall in love with someone, and she loves me too." She goes back to the kitchen counter and picks up her cup. "I'm tired of my heart being in pain." She goes to the punch bowl and refills her cup. "I've got a right to be happy for a change."

After preparing her glass of Sangria, Gigi takes it, passes by Regina going to the other side of the island and takes a seat in the barstool by the sectional. Regina turns to Gigi as Leah gets up from the card table.

"Gisele," Leah said going to Gigi. "I know about hurt, baby. Lord knows, Wes has put me through enough of it." She leans against the back of the sectional. "I'll tell you this though, rededicating my life to Jesus was the best thing I've ever done. The Lord is healing my hurts and believe me, they run deep." She stands and places her hand on Gigi's shoulder and points down the hallway. "I'm glad you got those friends but... Gigi, nobody, no man or woman can be a true and real friend like Jesus."

Gigi glances at her aunt as Leah returns to leaning against the back of the sectional. Gigi's eyes then go to her sister and Gigi realizes she's seated between them. Her sister Regina is standing on her right by the side of the island and her Aunt Leah is on her left by the sectional. Regina moves a bit closer to Gigi.

"When you look up happiness in the bible," Regina said.

"The references you get deal with worldly pleasures. Ecclesiastes 2:1 comes up, to paraphrase, it basically talks about pleasure and satisfaction. It says, so enjoy yourself and have a good time, but that it was all vanity, futile and pointless."

"So what are you telling me?" Gigi said.

Gigi finishes her drink and sits the cup on the island.

"I'm saying," Regina said. "That peace, you'll give up everything for, that love, you say you've finally found, and that happiness, you say you deserve so much. When you're in the world and not in God. All of it, is temporary Gigi." Regina walks around a bit as she talks to Gigi. "The enemy... The devil-is the father of lies, he'll give you all that and patiently wait; He'll let you get a false sense of security and then, when you least expect it, he'll snatch it all away, just to destroy you... That's what the devil does. That's his end game, all the devil wants to do is steal, kill and destroy." Regina begins to walk about again, turning to Gigi every so often as she talks to her. "Where as those who are righteous, those in God. Philippians 4:7 says, "the peace of God, which passeth all understanding, shall keep your hearts and minds through Christ Jesus. Gigi, God's love is unconditional, it's always with us. He's not a *wishy-washy* God, Gigi. His love is sure, it's true and nothing can take it away."

As Leah listens and watches Regina her expression is one of astonishment.

"My Lord," Leah said under her breath. "She sounds exactly like Mama."

"I know," Gigi said hearing Leah, she nods her head in agreement "That's why she's Grandma's Mini Me."

"Sure nuff." Leah said.

Regina returns to the side of the island as she approaches Gigi. "Romans 8:38-39 states," Regina said. "For I am persuaded, that neither death, nor life, nor angels, nor principalities, nor powers, nor things present, nor things to come, Nor height, nor depth, nor any other creature, shall be able to separate us from the love of God, which is in Christ Jesus our Lord." Gigi, why settle for temporary happiness, when God gives everlasting joy, in Isaiah 51:11 it says: "everlasting joy shall be upon their head: they shall obtain gladness and joy; and sorrow and mourning shall flee away." Regina moves closer to Gigi. "Yeah I know you're a backslider, and God may be quiet right now, but he hasn't left you either." Regina goes to the sectional and stands by Leah. "The word says, He's married to the backslider." She leans against the back of the sectional. "The way mom has been hurts me too. I've learned to take all my pains and hurts to Jesus. He's the only one who can heal them."

"Gina," Leah said motioning to Regina. "Tell Gigi about that counselor at the church,"

"Well, there's a minister at the church," Regina said. "She and Mom were friends back in the day. She came around a lot but you never met her. You were staying with grandma at the time. I have her business card." Regina goes to her bag sitting on the end table and begins to search around inside it. "She councils people regarding homosexuality, and other alternative lifestyles." She continues to search her bag. "I know its in here."

"I'm not speaking with any minister," Gigi said.

"He'll Work It Out" Chapter 7. Taryn C. Atkins

"Especially one that knows my mom. I'm sure mom has already talked to her about me anyway. Which means she's already biased." Gigi stands picking up her cup off the island. "So, no thank you."

As Regina searches her bag for the business card. Gigi goes over to the fridge and puts ice in her cup.

"Their just acquaintances now Gigi." Regina said. "They barely talk. Besides, her sessions are confidential. Trust me."

"Gigi, at least, think about it," Leah said.

Gigi looks at Leah as she goes to the punch bowl of Sangria, she grabs the ladle and as she fills up her cup again, takes a deep breath and exhales.

"I don't know," Gigi said shaking her head a bit. She takes a sip from her cup. "When did FGT get a counselor anyway. I thought Pastor, Lady Gorham or the Elders did that."

"They still do," Regina said. "I'm sure it lightens the load with her being a board certified psychologist."

Gigi moves to the side of the island.

"Still," Gigi said shaking her head. "She knows mom."

Gigi heads into the living room, she passes Regina, goes over to the sectional and sits down. Gigi enjoys another cup of Sangria as she gets comfortable. Leah stands, she moves closer to the island and contemplates the food sitting on it. Gigi places her cup down on the card table.

"Look, I'm positive she knows nothing about you," Regina said. "When I spoke to her; I just told her, I had a friend that may want to talk to her."

"Gigi are those your wings?" Leah said.

"Yes," Gigi said.

"Can I have some?

"Help yourself, the blue cheese is in the fridge, there's some juice in there too."

"Well, what's in the punch bowl? It looks good, you've had about three cups since we've been here."

"It's Sangria,"

"Okay... Juice it is," Leah said.

Leah prepares herself a plate. Regina pulls the card out.

"Finally, here it is," Regina said. "Gigi, no pressure but you should set up a session with her. What harm could it do?"

Regina hands Gigi the card as she sits down by her. Gigi takes it and inspects the information.

"Her name is Minister Cassandra Pauls." Regina said.

As Gigi hears the name, every sound in the room muffles as it echoes in her mind. When it all clicks Gigi releases a slight gasp realizing exactly who she is. Gigi reveals no change in emotion or expression placing the card on the card table. She picks up her cup of Sangria looking off to the side taking a healthy sip. Gigi studies the card, swallowing she turns her attention to Regina.

"Thanks Gina," Gigi said. "I would've never known."

"Call her," Regina said.

Gigi looks at Regina, then back at the card taking in the name printed upon it again.

"She's very easy to talk to."

Gigi nods, her eyes go to Regina and she nonchalantly smiles.

"I'm sure she is,"

~MENDING LOVE~

About a week later, on this early Friday evening, Shayna stood near the oven range checking on the meal she prepared. Nola was looking comfy relaxing in a turquoise green zip-up hoodie, a navy washed tank top, boot cut jeans and navy Chuck Taylor's. Nola sits at the kitchen table drinking a cup of tea, she finishes taking a sip and places the cup on the table.

"What did you cook?" Nola said. "Cause everything smells wonderful."

"I made a few of Cliff's favorites," Shayna said.

"That's good," Nola said. "My mom always quoted that saying, the way to a man's heart is through his stomach."

"I figure it couldn't hurt either," Shayna said.

Shayna comes over and stands by the side of the island.

"So what's on the menu?" Nola said.

"Well," Shayna said. "I cooked a pot roast, mash potatoes, french cut string beans and my homemade dinner rolls. I got a Tiramisu Cheesecake in the fridge. Plus, a bottle of sparkling red grape juice." She leans against the island and folds her arms. "I'm so nervous; I've only seen Cliff at our counseling sessions and church services. At church, he won't even sit with me." She takes a deep breath and exhales. "Cliff's supposed to come back home tonight. He hasn't been home for about five months now." She smooths out her dress. "I just want tonight to go well that's all; I want it to be special for us."

"I know." Nola said.

"When I peeked out the front window," Shayna said. "I didn't see any suitcase or bags with him. Maybe he's just here to get those divorce papers."

"Well, you've been in counseling for three months now," Nola said. "If he really wanted a divorce, he would of asked for those papers two months ago."

"I'm not sure Nola. "Shayna said. "All I know is that I hurt him. I hurt him and our family so much. Not just for a few months either but for years. So I... I couldn't blame him if he wanted to walk away."

"You said your sessions were going well," Nola said. "Did it seem like he wanted to walk away?.

"No, but..." Shayna said.

Shayna goes to the kitchen table and sits down.

"What?" Nola said.

"He said he was tired," Shayna said. "He said how we're going through this again. He didn't want to go through all this counseling, just to end up right back here again."

"Okay well, he does have a right to say that Shayna, at the same time, he's still showing up for sessions. Nobody's forcing him to be there. So, he's coming to counseling because he wants y'all to work things out. You have to have faith in your love for each other too."

"And I do, its just... I was the reason why we needed counseling the first time. When we finished it, we walked away thinking everything was fine between us. Now look at what's happened, once again I'm the reason why we need counseling. So maybe, because he's tired of it. He just went along with the sessions to get back at me."

"Cliff's not that type of person."

"I know he's not. Things can make you change though. Lord knows, I never planned to become the person that I've been for the past seventeen years. And, I surely never thought, I would be that person who'd not only kick their own daughter out but disown her too. So, if he wants me to sign those divorce papers, after all that I've done to him, I'll sign them. I don't want to, cause I still love him so much, but I've hurt him just as much."

"Well, one step at a time. Let's see how tonight goes."

"Yeah well, I just pray things go well."

Nola looks over at Shayna and smiles. She checks out Shayna's so-call casual evening wear. Which consisted of a beautiful fuchsia Diane Von Furstenberg classic wrap dress, dangly earrings, elegant bracelet and fuchsia high strappy heels with exposed painted toes included.

"Well, God is on your side, because what God has joined together, no devil can separate, Amen!"

"Amen, my sister."

"Now I know you love Cliff, and I'm 99.9% sure that man still loves you too. God is on your side, the food smells delicious, you're hair and makeup are fierce and you're looking pretty hot in that pink. Plus, with all the love you two have for each other. That sounds like a recipe for a pleasant evening to me. Don't you think so?"

Nola smiles and Shayna smiles too nodding her head in agreement. Cliff is outside his house talking with Dray and Minister Thomas. They each look rather handsome and sport their own winter style. Cliff all rough and rugged, in his tweed wool driver cap, black sheep button-front cardigan, blue jeans and Jack

Jones classic leather boots. Dray kept it simple with a baggy gray beanie, gray sweater, black jeans and gray Tims. While Minister Thomas was rather trendy in his chocolate beanie, chocolate pea coat with a navy scarf, underneath a mint shirt, navy jeans and burgundy leather boots.

"Where's your stuff?" Dray said.

"You didn't keep it at the hotel." Minister Thomas said.

"No, I didn't," Cliff said. "My stuffs in the car. I'm just not taking it out yet that's all."

"Well... Umm," Dray said. "I thought you were moving back in tonight,"

"Yeah, I'm suppose too, but..." Cliff said.

Cliff looks at the house, takes a deep breath and as he blows it out, they see his breath leave his mouth on this cold evening. Cliff shakes his head, messes with his hat and he looks at the guys.

"Okay..." Minister Thomas said. "What do mean by that?"

"It means, I'm not sure if I want to stay," Cliff said.

"I thought the counseling sessions were going well." Minister Thomas said. "At least, that's what you said."

"Yeah," Dray said. "Shayna told us things were going well too, so what's up?"

"We've been to counseling before." Cliff said. "And look what happen. I don't feel like going through this again."

"Well," Minister Thomas said. "Did you say that in any of your sessions?"

"Yeah I did," Cliff said. "And her answers seemed genuine, but they did last time too. I don't know fella's, what would y'all do?"

"Look we can't tell you what to do," Dray said. "And it's not our place to tell you either."

"You both agreed to do counseling." Minister Thomas said. "Nobody forced you to go, right?"

"No," Cliff said. "I went because I wanted to."

"Which means both of you want to work out." Minister Thomas said. "Look, when you decided to marry Shayna, you didn't know what would happen, but you took a chance because you loved her. God took a chance on you before you were even born. He took a chance with all of us for that matter. And He knew every good and bad thing about us. He yet loved us enough to sacrifice Jesus for us. Just so we would have a way to escape the devil's plan for us. When you put that ring on Shayna's finger, you decided that she's worth taken a chance on. So, you can decide if you still feel that way."

"When you first met Shayna," Dray said. "Was there anybody else trying to hook up with her?"

"Yeah, there were a few guys," Cliff said.

"Okay, did they run you off?" Minister Thomas said.

"Not at all," Cliff said. "I didn't giv'em a chance."

"Right." Dray said. "Cause you loved her, and even though you weren't married yet, as far as you were concerned she was already your wife. So tell me, do you still love her?"

"Yeah I do." Cliff said.

"Do you think she's a gift from God?" Minister Thomas said. "One He created for you and vise versa."

"I know, I feel like that about Nola." Dray said.

"When I get married," Minister Thomas said. "I'll feel that way about my wife too. Now, do you feel like that about Shayna?"

"I do," Cliff said. "A prophet even told us that years ago,"

"Well, the enemy's trying to steal your gift," Dray said.

"Are you just gonna let him take it from you like that?!"

"I know," Minister Thomas said. "I wouldn't let nobody take what God's given me, will you?!"

"I don't think so!" Cliff said. "The devil is a liar!"

"That's right!" Minister Thomas said. "So, go in there and reclaim your gift! Reclaim the gift God has personally given you! Yes!"

They all say in unison, "YEAH!"

They all chest bump each other and Cliff swiftly walks over to his house. Dray and Minister Thomas look at each other.

"Okay, that whole umm, chest bump thing," Dray said.

"Will never be spoken of again, right?!"

"Right." Minister Thomas said.

Dray and Minister Thomas shake hands and walk off in opposite directions, going to their cars. Cliff goes into the house and closes the door behind him. When Shayna and Nola hear the front door close, they realize Cliff has come in, Shayna stands up, Nola takes another quick sip of her tea and stands up too. They hug, kissing the air on each side of the other. Nola grabs two of Shayna's homemade dinner rolls out the bowl on the island as she goes to the back door to make her exit.

"Call me tomorrow." Nola softly said.

"Alright," Shayna said. "I'll see ya."

Nola leaves as Shayna walks over to the island, she closes her eyes, takes a deep breath and as she exhales she opens her eyes. Shayna wrings her hands as she paces back and forth a few times. She walks over to the kitchen table and sits down.

Cliff stands in their living room by the fireplace, looking at the pictures of his family sitting on the mantle. He picks up their wedding photo and stares at it for a moment. As he clears his throat he carefully places it down.

Well, Father, its up to you now. Cliff thought.

He glances up at the ceiling over the fireplace as he rubs the back of his neck. Cliff focuses on four markings upon it, slightly smiles and walks away. He goes over to his dark rust armchair, takes off his cardigan and drapes it over the back of it. Under it, he wore a long sleeve, black v-henley neck t-shirt which complimented his muscular build.

"I'm in the kitchen," Shayna said. "Be out in a moment,

I'm checking on dinner."

Cliff sits down in his armchair, breathing in the delicious aroma of the meal prepared for evening.

He said under his breath, "She made my favorites, pot roast, potatoes, string beans and her homemade dinner rolls."

Cliff smiles as he leans back in his chair. Shayna steps out the kitchen, before going into the living room she checks herself over in the full length mirror on the wall. She closes her eyes and slowly inhales, as she exhales.

Lord, your will be done, in Jesus name. Shayna thought.

Shayna walks into the living room, on seeing Cliff sitting in his armchair again, she tilts her head and a smile beams forth. He's unaware of her presence, until the unique scent of her perfume catches his attention. Cliff looks over his shoulder, when his eyes fall upon Shayna; He's awestruck. She smooths out her dress once again as Cliff stares at her and slowly stands. When their eyes finally meet, locking onto one another, in harmony a fresh love for each other is birthed.

"Hi," Shayna said wearing a nervous smile.

"Hi..." Cliff said. "Wow, you are so beautiful."

"Thank you," Shayna said. "I'm glad you're here."

"Me too." Cliff said. "I love that perfume of yours. After all these years it's still so enticing."

As they approach each other, Cliff looks at his clothes, he rubs his hands over his jeans.

"Man, look at you," Cliff said. "You look stunning. I feel sloppy."

When they get closer to each other, they both reach out taking each other's hands.

"Well, you're looking ever so handsome," Shayna said. She nestles his neck. "And mmm... You smell good too. You're wearing the cologne I brought you for Christmas."

"Yeah, I like it." Cliff said. "You know, I wasn't sure if I was coming back... It feels good to be home though."

"I'm glad you're here," Shayna said.

They embrace, while holding each other, almost in unison they both close their eyes, take in a deep breath and with one accord they exhale. They softly squeeze each other a little tighter and pull each other a bit closer.

"I want to show you something," Cliff said.

They hold on to one another for a second or two longer before releasing each other. Cliff takes Shayna by the hand. He brings her over to the fireplace, positions her in front of him and points up at the high ceiling above their fireplace.

"Look there," Cliff said. "You see that?"

"You mean those four burn marks?" Shayna said.

Cliff places his hands on the sides of her waist.

"Yeah, remember when we first bought this house? I took the small torch, climbed that old ladder and burned all our initials up there."

"I remember, you scared me to death watching you stand on top of that thing."

"I did though." Cliff turns her to him. "You remember why?"

"Of course I do," Shayna smiles putting her arms around his neck. "You burned our initials there, to symbolize our families love for each other. That our love was so high, it was above any problem that came our way."

"I still believe that," Cliff puts his arms around her. "Shayna, I love you. I never wanted a divorce; I sent those papers cause I was angry. My intentions were to hurt you and I apologize for that. Regardless of all that's happened, I'm still deeply in love with you."

"I'm still deeply in love with you too." Shayna softly touches his face. "I'm in love with you just as much now, as when we first got married. I'm sorry for hurting you and our girls the way I did." Turning and walking away from Cliff for a moment. "I'm sorry for everything I've put you all through." Her eyes being to water. "You three, mean the world to me." Her tears flow. "I don't want to lose you, and I pray God can restore our family." She urns to him. "Cliff, I'm sorry, I'm so sorry for everything."

Cliff approaches Shayna and softly wipes her tears.

"Baby, I know you are, and God is restoring our family. It's starting right here-with us."

Cliff pulls Shayna to him, they wrap their arms around each other as they hold each other close, a warm and content smile appears on each of them.

"I love you Cliff, I've missed you so much."

"I love you too, and baby, I've missed you even more. We've got some serious catching up to do."

"He'll Work It Out" Chapter 7. Taryn C. Atkins

"We've got several years actually. Can you handle that?"

Cliff huffs, "Watch me."

Cliff softly kisses Shayna on the lips and she reciprocates. They gaze deeply into each others eyes and kiss each other ever so sensually. Cliff breaks from the kiss.

"Let's move this, to a much better location." Cliff said.

"If you insist..." Shayna said. "Either way, we've got a lot of ground to cover." She seductively smiles. "Right?"

Cliff pulls off his shirt throwing it to the ground.

"Oh, yes."

Cliff pulls Shayna to him and they passionately kiss. Shayna breaks from the kiss. She takes him by the hand leading him out of the living room toward their bedroom.

"Let's go get reacquainted, again and again, and again."

"Now that's the plan, come here!"

Cliff scoops Shayna up and he heads to their bedroom.

A few hours have passed, Regina walks through the front door and sees the fireplace going and a blanket on the sofa.

"Guess mom fell asleep on the couch again," Regina said.

Regina hears muffled sounds coming from the kitchen. She rushes in, turning on the lights and sees her parents getting reacquainted.

"OH GOD! SORRY! MY EYES! MY EYES!"

Regina turns off the lights and rushes out. She goes to the end table by the lengthy custom sofa and turns on the lamp. Regina tosses the blanket off the sofa, she goes to sit down on the sofa but stops. Regina stands their for a moment thinking, she makes a face and shakes her head. She moves to the armchair, she gets ready to take a seat but stops herself once again. Regina goes to the other side of the living room and sits in the brand new recliner. After a few minutes, Shayna and Cliff come out the kitchen, wearing their bathrobes with their arms around each other's waist, and smiling. Regina watches them joyfully plop down on the sofa together.

"Hi sweetheart," Shayna said.

"Hey, there baby girl," Cliff said.

"I thought you were at mama's tonight," Shayna said.

"Apparently," Regina said with a embarrassed blush."

"We were going to surprise you," Shayna said. "You know we've been going to counseling, and, as you can see we're back together."

"Yeah... I noticed."

"No divorce baby girl," Cliff said. "I'm home to stay."

"Well, that's a blessing,"

"God's restoring our family Gina," Shayna said. "I've been calling Gigi, left several messages for her. She hasn't called yet, but I don't blame her. I'm gonna go there."

"That's a good idea," Cliff said. "It's probably better for you to talk to Gigi in person."

"Yeah, that's what I thought," Shayna said.

"That would be the best mom," Regina said. "Aunt Leah and I did, it was tense, but it lightened up as we talked."

"Alright, I'll do that soon," Shayna said.

Cliff clears his throat, Shayna looks at him and he nonchalantly motions his head in the direction of their bedroom.

"Okay, so good night sweetheart," Shayna said. "See you in the morning."

"Night baby girl." Cliff said.

"Good night," Regina said.

Shayna and Cliff leave out the living room whispering, giggling and playing around with one another. Regina slowly shakes her head as she watches them exit, she finally hears their bedroom door close.

"I'm never eating on that kitchen table again."

~GOING ON~

Late in the month of January on this Monday afternoon. The melodious sound of up beat pop music is heard coming out the mall speakers. People hustle and bustle about inside the Queens Center Mall as they always do. The food court was moderately active. Leah relaxes in her stylish dress down gear. She sat at one of the food court tables reading her Bible while nursing a cup of coffee. Lexi and a male friend cut through the food court, Lexi's dressed in winter tomboy chic and the guy wears classic urban style. As they take the short cut Lexi does a double take when she notices Leah.

Lexi stops walking, her friend passes by her but soon notices that Lexi has stopped. He turns around and walks back to her. As Lexi points to Leah she said a few words to her friend, he shook his head and they make their way toward Leah. Lexi and her friend stop a few feet away.

"Leah is that you?" Lexi said.

Leah looks up, seeing Lexi.

"Hey gurl," Leah said with a smile.

"Hi," Lexi said. As she and her friend came over." I thought that was you."

Leah gets up as Lexi approaches, she greeted Lexi with open arms and a big hug. Lexi is a bit surprised by the warm welcome. Her friend stood off to the side watching their interaction. As Leah released Lexi from the hug they smiled at one another.

"It's a small world," Leah said. "So, how you been?'

"I'm all right," Lexi said. She motions to her friend. "This is my friend Cody." She points to Leah. "You know my roommate, this is her Aunt Leah."

"Hello," Cody said.

"Hello, Cody, nice to meet you," Leah said. "Y'all have a seat." She moves her purse. "Join me."

Lexi looks at her watch, then at Cody and nods.

"Okay..." Lexi said. "We can't stay long, Dana and I are going to Vegas for the week of Valentines. So, I need to pick up a few things and get back to the city."

"No problem," Leah said. "I'm just sitting here reading anyway. I took off a few days; I needed me some relax, relate and release time."

Lexi sits next to Leah and Cody sits across from them.

"I understand that," Lexi said. "Let me say this, I've been feeling so bad. Since I've known you, you've never treated me funny. So, I sincerely apologize for how I acted that day."

"Sweetheart, I thank you for the apology," Leah said. "We're good though. So how's everything? I heard my sister's been calling and leaving messages for Gigi. Has she called her back yet?"

"Not that I know of," Lexi said. "Gigi's real guarded when it comes to her mom. And I don't blame her either."

"Everybody deserves a second chance." Leah said. "And I must say, Shayna has changed a great deal."

"Well, she's done some awful things too," Lexi said. "Just because Gigi is gay."

"Lexi, you know Gigi wasn't always gay. She was saved and the family saw her grow in God. Then all of a sudden it seemed like she changed over night."

"Well you know, way before Gigi came out, the last three guys she went with hurt her. After that, she tried talking to her mom about what she was feeling for women. Her mom didn't want to hear anything and just shut Gigi down. The next thing I know-"

"Gigi came out," Leah said. "And Shayna told her to leave the house."

"No," Lexi said. "What she did was kick her out. You know, love is beautiful. God created it. So, why can't two people of the same sex experience that together, without all the criticism? And I'm so over all the abomination stuff. You've gotta come with something better than that."

"Okay... Okay, I feel you. God dislikes all sin. So, if I steal a piece of candy and you sleep with women. We both would still go to hell."

"Yeah, I've heard that one before too."

As Lexi and Leah talk, Cody pays close attention to their conversation.

"Okay, hear me out." Leah said. "Homosexuality is an abomination to God, because it doesn't reflect God. The word of God says, men and women were made in the image of God. So, look at this for a second."

Leah opens her Bible to a particular passage and moves the bible over to Lexi so she can see it.

"Here read Genesis 1:26," Leah said.

Lexi looks at Leah and shakes her head a bit. She looks down at the Bible and starts to read out loud.

"Let us make man in our image, after our likeness:" She moves the bible back over to Leah. "Alright so?"

"Well, we're going somewhere." She moves the bible back over to Lexi. "Please, read down to verse twenty-eight."

Lexi looks at Leah for a few seconds. Cody shakes his head and as he looks off to the side sucking his teeth. Leah looks at him briefly and back at Lexi. Lexi huffs and looks at the Bible.

"So God created man in his own image, in the image of God created he him: male and female created he them." She sighs. "And God blessed them, and God said unto them, Be fruitful and multiply, and replenish the earth, and subdue it." She moves the bible back over to Leah. "So your point?"

Cody turns his attention back to them.

"God's point is simple." Leah said. "God made men and women to create, create others in His image, meaning children. No matter how science tries, God meant it to be a thing that only a man and woman can do together. That's why be it two women or two men, nothing can be created from it because it was never meant to be. It represents the opposite of God, anti-god, anti-Christ, meaning the Devil, who's the father of lies."

Lexi takes a deep breath, as she exhales she leans back in the chair and looks at Leah.

"I get where you're coming from. I've got my own views and I'm not changing who I am, but I've never heard it broken down like that before either."

"Baby, the devil is the author of confusion. God don't make no mistakes. Look at nature, you don't see a horse wanting an operation to become a cow do you. Human beings are the only ones, that want to change what God originally created them to be."

"He'll Work It Out" Chapter 7. Taryn C. Atkins

Lexi clears her throat and shakes her head. She makes a face as she looks at Leah. Cody looks at Leah, huffs and looks away again. Lexi looks at Cody and then Leah. Leah looks at Cody.

"Excuse me, Cody, have I offended you?" Leah said.

Cody looks at Leah and leans on the table in front of him.

"Yes," Cody said. "I find your last statement very offensive. Cause I'm a trans man, my name used to be Courtney."

"Alright well," Leah said. "Lord knows I didn't mean to offend you. I love you though and Jesus loves you, just like He loves everybody else. He sacrificed himself for you too. So that you might not perish but have everlasting life. There's salvation and deliverance for you too in Jesus."

"Oh really," Cody said. "Well, I lived in the closet for years, cause I'm a PK, a preacher's kid. I came out at twenty, and had the surgery when I turned twenty-five. Once I did this. My family wanted no parts of me. My pop's straight up told me I was gonna bust hell wide open. I bounced right after that. I'm thirty-two now, living my life and happy with the decisions I've made. I believe in God; I know he loves me, and because he loves me, that means he should accept me for who I am. It says in the Bible somewhere that there is no respect of persons with God. So, it shouldn't make a difference if I'm a man or a woman."

"Sweetheart, I am not here to judge you," Leah said. "I don't have a heaven or hell to put nobody in. Let me ask you something though? After its all said and done, where would you like to go in the end?"

Cody huffs and laughs a bit as he looks over at Lexi.

"Well, I would like to go to heaven," Cody said. He and Lexi give each other a pound. "I mean, that would be kind of nice, but they want you to do too much, and I ain't down with jumping through all those hoops."

"I know that's right," Lexi said.

"I'm saying," Cody said leaning back in the chair.

"Alright, I get not wanting to jump through hoops," Leah said. "You being a PK should know, receiving Jesus into your heart isn't a complicated thing."

"Listen, all that church stuff ain't never been good to me anyway," Cody said. "I'm finally who I want to be, being true to myself and living life the way I want it. That's what's important to me."

Lexi looks at her watch as she stands up. Once Cody sees Lexi leave her seat, he follows suit.

"Look, we've gotta go," Lexi said.

"Okay, just let me say this to y'all," Leah said. "When our number is finally called, this *physical body*, goes right back to the ground. What's most important to Jesus is your soul, remember that."

"I can't promise I'll be in church on Sunday," Lexi said.

"Or the Sunday after that either!" Cody laughed.

Lexi agrees with a chuckle.

"I know," Leah said with a smile nodding her head. "Just think about what I said, and what you read. It's never too late to get right with God; I know that for myself."

"Alright, I'll see ya." Lexi said.

"Take it easy." Cody said.

"Take care." Leah said.

Leah watches as Lexi and Cody walk off. When they get on the escalator, Lexi looks back and waves. Leah smiles with a return wave watching them as they disappear from her view. Leah folds her hands on her chest and closes her eyes. While her eyes are closed, Wes and one of his ghetto fabulous females, are coming down on the opposite escalator.

Wes wears black leather from head to toe. While his ghetto hoochie has on her winter, freak me wear. When Wes and the female arrive on the food court level, he notices Leah from a distance and pulls the female off to the side out of Leah's line of sight. Leah sits with her eyes closed for a moment.

Under her breath, Leah said, "Lord, if that was the only reason I was here, it was worth it. Now Lord, I just planted a seed, send another to water and you send the increase. In Jesus name. Amen."

When Leah opens her eyes, her cell rings and she taps the Bluetooth in her ear to answers it.

"Hello." Leah said. "Okay, hold on for a moment please."

She mutes the call. Under her breath, she said. "Lord, you know and let your will be done, in Jesus name."

She unmutes the call. "Alright, go ahead." As she listens, she takes in a deep breath, exhales and swallows.

"Okay... .Thank you." She ends the call. "Yes-negative."

Her hand goes up. "Thank You Jesus."

Wes pushes the female up against the wall, kissing her for a moment and then pulls away. She fans herself.

"Oh, Mr. Manager!" She said, chewing on her gum. "I love it when you get spontaneous like dat."

"I know you do," Wes said. "What's your name again."

Wes looks around the wall and watches Leah, who has gone back to reading her bible.

"It's Alize, you know when we met." Alize said. 'It was what they call... Fate."

"Yeah," Wes said watching Leah. "Fate, that's what it is."

"I just knew Mr. Manager." Alize said. "I knew, I would meet somebody important at that karaoke spot sooner or later. My natural talents are waisted there."

"Don't worry," Wes said. "Those natural talents will be put to good use."

Wes goes into his pants pocket and pulls out his wallet.

"It feels good to be appreciated for a change."

"Yeah its all good, now look here." Wes takes some money out and gives it to her. "Go to Macy's, get yourself something nice, then jump in a cab and meet me over at BBQ's. I've got some business to handle. Call me once you're at to the restaurant."

"Whatever you say, Mr. Manager."

Alize takes the escalator up heading to Macy's. Wes makes sure the coast is all clear as he proceeds over to Leah. He quickly takes a seat in the chair across from Leah.

"Well look a here." Wes said.

Leah raises her eyes and they focus on Wes, sitting there with a big Cheshire cat smile.

"Hey, sexy." Wes said. "I'm telling you this is fate."

Leah slowly shakes her head as she looks at Wes.

"I just got back in town." Wes said. "Got off the plane and came by here to pick up something. Something for you actually, and look who I see." He leans back in the chair and opens his arms wide. "Come show me love gurl."

"Hi, Wes." Leah said. She takes a tract from the back of her Bible and puts it down on the table in front of him. "Here you go. Jesus loves you. So get right, He's coming back soon."

Wes picks up the tract, gives it a once-over, and sucks his teeth as he looks at Leah.

"Come on Lee." Wes said. "Show me some love. You handed me this tract like I'm just anybody, when we got a kid together."

"First off." Leah said. "I gave you a that tract because Jesus does love you and desires none to perish. Jesus is the worlds hope of escape. Second, yeah we have Reggie but whatever was between us is over."

Wes rolls his eyes, he notices Leah has her Bible out on the table. He scans the area around them, looks at Leah and nods.

"Right, you doing the church thing again and we all out in the open." He gets up, sits next to Leah, leaning in a bit closer to her and whispers. "Slip me the house keys. I'll meet up with you later."

Leah laughs and moves over.

"Wes, that person is gone and I've come too far to turn back now."

"Come on, you know we have something special."

"If it was so special, I wouldn't have learned you're HIV Positive by finding your medication. A real man would've told me."

"Who told you I have HIV?"

"He'll Work It Out" Chapter 7. Taryn C. Atkins

Leah looks over at Wes, rolls her eyes shaking her head in disgust gathering her belongings together.

"Look I don't know what you're talking about. I'm safe."

"Wes, you've never been honest with me;" She stands. "I don't expect you to start now. Look, I've got to go."

Leah walks away and heads toward the escalators. Wes watches her get on the up escalator. Just when she's about to disappear from his view, Wes abruptly gets up and goes after her. He rushes up the steps of the escalator, gets off on the first level and looks around for Leah. He notices her waiting by the elevators. Wes rushes over to Leah and grabs her arm. Leah quickly turns around snatching her arm out of his grip.

"Easy," Wes said. "Now hold on a moment."

"What Wes?" Leah said.

Wes looks around as mall patrons pass by, he motions over to the wall, he and Leah step to the side out of everybody's way. Leah looks around realizing she's somewhat in a corner, Wes stands in front of her laying his hand against the wall.

"Now Leah, we never had any problems, but umm..." Wes glances left and right then eyes Leah. "If... If, I was positive, and you tried to use that against me. Well, I could sue you for slander."

Leah's jaw drops as she leers at Wes, seeing the elevator doors opens Leah pushes pass him.

"I don't believe you!" Leah said

Leah rushes into the elevator and Wes makes it in too. There are a few mall patrons in the elevator as Leah presses the button for third level. As the elevator goes up, Wes smiles at the female patron next to him. Leah patiently waits for her floor to come. When the doors opens on the third level Leah rushes off and Wes quickly pursues her.

Leah walks through the hall to the parking lot with Wes right behind her. When Leah goes to touch the parking lot door it opens, a woman covered from head to toe in her hijab and niqab walks through rolling a baby carriage. A man wearing a gold rope chain with an Italian horn charm on it sports a New York Rangers jersey steps in right behind the woman. He towers over Leah as he holds the door open for her. Leah hurries through it with Wes still on her heels she heads to her car.

"Look, Lee, I'm just saying," Wes said. "I'm a businessman; I've got to protect myself."

Leah stops in her tracks and abruptly turns to Wes.

"How dare you!" Leah said. "Sue me for slander!? When every time we laid down together, you were willing to give me a death sentence." She goes to walk away but turns back to him. "Oh, I found that little bottle with your date-rape drug. Now that, brought a lot into perspective."

Leah turns away and heads to her car. Wes is close behind.

"You know-So what!" Wes said. "Don't try to stand here and play Ms. High and Mighty with me!"

Wes follows Leah to her Jeep Grand Cherokee. When she goes to open the driver's side door Wes stops her, he slams the door shut and points in her face.

"You knew I slept around and you chose to ignore it. So don't be surprised you got the baggage that comes with it. I'm just sharing the love baby! Like someone shared it with me! So have a good life, for however long that is."

Wes turns around to head back to the mall.

"I'm so glad Jesus has the final say." She follows Wes for a few steps. "Because, he's already given me a clean bill of health." She stops. "And as long as I keep Jesus first in my life, not you or anyone else can hurt me."

Leah turns and walks away from Wes. He turns around and watches Leah as she goes over to her jeep. Leah gets in, starts it up and rolls down the window. Wes rushes over, slams his hand on the roof and looks at Leah through the drivers window.

"Yeah okay, you've got so much to say right now. Let's see how you feel, when lesions show up on that smooth skin and pretty face of yours."

Leah looks at Wes and slowly shakes her head.

"Even if that happens. I'm still going on with Jesus. You take care."

Leah pulls her jeep out the parking space and drives away.

"Go on, you'll be back. Hear that! You'll come running back Lee! Nobody else wants ya! You'll be back, watch!"

She look in her rear view mirror and sees Wes standing off in the distance still yelling. Leah lifts her head up, looks straight ahead taking a deep breath and exhales with a beaming smile.

~REBUILDING RELATIONS~

It's the last Friday in the month of January. After a hectic work week, Lexi and Gigi spend their down time at home. Lexi takes a big bowl out the kitchen cabinet and places it on the island. While the microwave prepares the selection of popcorn for the evening Lexi talks on the phone.

"Not tonight Bobbie," Lexi said. "All we're doing is chillin' in our favorite pj's, maybe next week... Gigi's been knocked out for the last three hours..." She leans against the kitchen counter. "Well, after we got in from work, she talked to Cassandra then Gina for a while, after that she jumped in the shower and went right to bed... Yeah, she'll be up soon... She's supposed to watch a movie with Dana and me... Nah, Cassandra's not coming over tonight either... I think their waiting till we leave for Vegas... Well, they'll have the place to themselves for a week. So I'm sure they're making plans..." She yawns.

"Like I said, next week we'll hang out before Dana and I leave for Vegas... Alright, Lata Bobbie."

The microwave beeps as Lexi puts the house phone on the island. Lexi goes to it and grabs the bag of popcorn.

"Hot hot," Lexi said.

Lexi throws the popcorn bag on the island by the big bowl and blows on her fingers. She opens the popcorn, pours it into the bowl, brings it to the living room and sits it on the coffee table. Lexi plops down on the sectional, picks up a stack of DVD's off the coffee table and rifles through them. Her back is to the hallway, she hears the front door slide open and shut.

"See," Lexi said. "That's why I left the door cracked. You

go to the store so fast. Have you decided what you want to watch?"

Lexi continues to parous the DVD's, she hears footsteps coming up the hallway and hears when they step out the hall.

"Dana, did you remember to get my fruit snacks?" After getting no reply, Lexi lets out a harsh breath. "Dana?!"

Lexi turns around, seeing Shayna standing there she drops the DVD's on the sectional and quickly rises to her feet.

"Hello," Shayna said.

"What are you doing in this house?!" Lexi said.

"I... I just wanted to-" Shayna said.

"I don't care!" Lexi said, she points toward the front door. "That rainbow flag over the entrance," She moves by the end table. "It means no straight people allowed!"

"I deserve that," Shayna said.

"What you deserve- Lexi said moving toward Shayna. "Oh Honey, believe me... That isn't nothing compared to what you really deserve!"

"Look, I didn't come here to fight," Shayna said.

"The fact you've got the nerve to even walk up in here, makes me want to fight!"

Lexi huffs and she tensed her shoulders walking pass Shayna going to the kitchen. Shayna turns to Lexi as she moves to side of the island.

"All I want to do is speak with my daughter."

Lexi's eyes go to Shayna, she stares at her for a bit as she walks to the kitchen side of the island.

"Your daughter?! Wow! You must be talking about Regina, from my understanding, that's the only *daughter* you got!"

"Look, I know I've done terrible things and I want to make amends. That's why I'm here, I want to speak to Gisele. Please Alexis."

Lexi quickly gets face to face with Shayna.

"It's Lexi to you! And you formed all that so well, but you see people of my kind, don't mix with people of your kind." Lexi walks about as she continues. "See, I'm a femme-aggressive or soft butch. My best friend," She rushes over to Shayna. "Your daughter is a femme or lipstick lesbian. We associate with those under the title of dyke, butch or lesbian. You... Don't fit any of those categories, in other words." Lexi points down the hall. "You can get the he--"

"Lexi," Shayna said. "I understand, you have a right to protect her." She steps away and goes to the living room. "When Gigi needed me most, I pushed her away; I turned my back on her."

Lexi rushes over to Shayna once again.

"You kicked her out!" Lexi said.

"I know." Shayna said.

Shayna turns away and walks to the candle fireplace.

"I was there, when she'd cry through the night!" Lexi said. "I was there, when she got depressed and wouldn't eat! I was in the ambulance with her, after she slit her wrists!"

Shayna promptly turns around and approaches Lexi.

"Wha... What?!"

"Oh, you didn't know that did you?! Where were you and your so called God then?!"

Gigi rushes out her room and up the hallway.

"Lexi what's with all the screaming?!" Gigi said.

When Gigi comes out the hall she freezes seeing her mother standing in her living room. Lexi approaches Gigi.

"She, wants to talk to you." Lexi said. "I know, you're not interested in anything she has to say, right?!"

"I... No. I'm not," Gigi said.

"Exactly," Lexi said.

Gigi proceeds to the kitchen and leans up against the counter. Lexi goes to the hallway and points to their front door.

"So do us favor, get out!"

Shayna takes a deep breath, she walks to the hallway as she exhales but then rushes over to the island.

"Please Gigi," Shayna said. "Give me a few minutes."

"No!" Lexi said, going to Shayna. "There's no way, I'm letting you-"

Lexi's cell rings, she quickly picks it up off the end table, looks at it and answers.

"Hello! What?! Why didn't you take your license!?" Okay... okay, I'm coming."

Lexi dashes over to the sectional, sits and speedily puts on her sneakers. She swiftly grabs her jacket off the coatrack.

"Gigi, I'll be back." Lexi runs down the hall. "Dana, don't let them tow my car!"

A second later the front door slides open and slams shut. The tension is thick in the room as silence takes over for a moment.

"I know, I'm the last person you want to see," Shayna said. "And I'll understand if you want me to leave, but please Gigi, can you just hear me out?"

"I have all the right to kick you out." Gigi said. "Grandma taught me better than that though. So, come with it!"

Gigi rushes pass Shayna as she goes to the living room

"Gisele," Shayna said, turning in Gigi's direction. "I know we've always had tension in our relationship."

"We never had a relationship."

Gigi walks about the living room, keeping her distance.

"Yes, and it's been my fault. I know, I've been an awful mother to you."

"You've been awful period. I would've never treated a bum on the street the way you've treated me."

"I'm sorry for hurting you. The past few months, I've realized so much."

"This revelation is supposed to wipe away the years of hurt you caused me? Just make them magically disappear." Gigi snaps her fingers. "Just like that! Not gonna happen!"

Gigi rushes pass Shayna again going to the kitchen.

"I know the hurt can't go away just like that, if we talk though and get our feelings out, at least the healing can begin."

"Well, you're already inside right? So talk."

"Gisele," Shayna said, "There's so much I need to explain to you. You see, for a long time, I didn't want to confront my own issues and demons. I didn't want to face or even accept my own mistakes, and because of that. It caused me to treat you and your father so unfairly. I've realized a lot over the last few months and one of them is that, I don't want to lose my daughter."

"Really..." Gigi said. "You must have practiced that in the mirror. Cause you actually sound sincere."

"I am sincere Gisele; I'm here because I want to fix things between us. That's why I want us to sit down and talk."

"Hmph."

Gigi walks to the fridge and gets a bottle of wine. Shayna takes a deep breath and exhales as she takes off her coat. Gigi gets a wine glass out of the cabinet and pours herself a drink. She leans up against the kitchen counter watching Shayna lay her coat across the back of the sectional. Gigi walks to the island studying her mother as she nurses on her wine.

"Let me get this straight." She puts her wine glass down.

"Oh, I do know the word *straight* mom, even though I'm not actually. So... I'm supposed to drop everything, just because after all these years, you decide, you want to talk and fix things." She gave a mirthless laugh. "You got some nerve."

Gigi huffs, taking a healthy swallow of wine.

"I understand why you feel like that."

"No! You don't! After that day, I made up my mind." Gigi moves toward the living room. "I didn't want anything to do with you. I didn't want you or anything you stood for in my life." She stops by the end table. "So excuse me for not making time for you, just because you've suddenly seen the error of your ways."

"Gigi please, just hear me out."

"The fact I let you even stay in this house should say something."

"Mind if I sit down?"

"Whatever."

Lord, give me strength. I can't do this without you. Shayna thought, walking into the living room.

Gigi goes back to the island, gets her glass of wine and proceeds into the living room. She takes a seat on the far side of the sectional by the candle fireplace, she runs her hand through her hair as she leans back trying to get comfortable. Gigi tensed up as Shayna took a seat beside her. When Shayna scoots closer Gigi sits up.

"Don't!" Gigi said. She motions to the other end of the sectional. "Just... Sit over there, please."

Shayna rises to her feet and walks over to the island. She stands collecting herself then turns to Gigi, who's nursing on her glass of wine.

"Gisele," Shayna said. "When I got married, I was young. I was only twenty and I got pregnant so quick."

"So you blame me for that?" Gigi said. "All your resentment was toward me though and Gina's not far behind me. Yet, you never shoved her to the side."

"Yes, I did blame you; I'm able to admit that now. When Regina was born, thankfully, I was more settled with being a mother."

Gigi puts her wine glass down on the coffee table.

"Well how fortunate for her."

"Gisele, Please understand, for me life was on hold."

Shayna walks back to the sectional and takes a seat. Gigi moves over, preferring to keep distance between them.

"I wanted to go back to school for my Masters in Accounting, but I couldn't-I had you. Gina came three years later. Then, your dad's business took off and he was traveling all the time. When I finally went back, you were eight, Mama helped out by letting you stay with her and Gina was with me.

"Fine! I get it. I was the kink in your plans... Now, let's fast forward eleven years. Why kick me out? Why disown me?" Gigi's eyes begin to water. "At a time when I needed you the most, you threw me out like I was trash!"

"I know,"

Gigi fights to hold back her tears as Shayna reaches out to console her, but when she gets close, Gigi pulls away.

"Do you remember what was going on at that time?" Gigi said. "I just got saved, remember? I'm trying to live right before God, but at the same time, I'm struggling with all these feelings and emotions that the Bible and my spirit are telling me is wrong. All this turmoil is going on inside me."

"I know but I couldn't face-"

Shayna reaches for Gigi again causing her to abruptly get up and move away. Gigi paces around the living room as she expresses her feelings.

"When I try to go to the one person I thought I could be honest with, my Mother, who's in God herself. You didn't want to hear it!" She lets her tears go. "Instead of compassion, I get told to get out! Get out?! Mom-you threw me out! That's why Lexi is like a sister to me, she's been there through it all."

Shayna gets up from the sectional.

"Gigi, please let me explain!"

Gigi abruptly turns to Shayna.

"Everybody was there for me! Grandma, Leah, Regina, you didn't even want Daddy to have anything to do with me. Regardless, he's been there for me too; I even had to sneak into the hospital to see Grandma, just so we didn't bump into each other. You see-I didn't want us to argue, especially at a time like that. I thought of you, in spite of how you treated me. Lexi's parents were there for me when you kicked me out, and all I wanted was you. I needed my mother more than anyone else." Gigi shakes her head no, mimicking her mothers actions at that time as she wipes her tears. "Not you though, you made it perfectly clear that you couldn't stand the sight of me." She gets her wine glass off the coffee table. "I may not have gotten it before, but after the repass, I get it now!"

She strolls off to the kitchen. "So, I'm done, you don't have to worry about being bothered with me period!"

Gigi pours herself another glass of wine finishing off the bottle. Her back is to Shayna as she drinks her half full glass straight down. Shayna cautiously approaches Gigi.

"Gigi please, I don't want that! I've never wanted that! You have to understand. I was ashamed! I was so ashamed of myself. Ashamed, and afraid that... that it was because of me you were gay."

Gigi shakes her head a bit turning to Shayna.

"You thought it was because of you? How could me liking women be your fault?"

Shayna steps away from Gigi as she walks back to the living room. Gigi gets a fresh bottle of wine out the fridge, grabs the cork screw out the drawer and brings it over to the island.

"Well," Shayna walks around the living room. "When I went back for my Masters, everything appeared fine to every body else. In reality, I was feeling useless, empty, like I was dying inside. I kept up appearances, making it seem like everything was okay."

Gigi takes the wine, corkscrew and empty glass, and sits on one of the barstools at the island near the sectional.

"One of my classes was so difficult, that I needed a tutor, and that's all it was at first. Your dad was my best friend, but he was always gone and he wasn't there for me anymore. Every time I needed him to be there for me, he wasn't, but they were." She turns away from Gigi and walks over to the candle fireplace." Anyway, we started talking and really sharing with each other. I was able to take off the mask, be real, finally open up and be myself. The devil was setting up a trap." She turns around and walks toward Gigi. "Our friendship grew and we got closer."

Shayna walks pass Gigi and over to the living room windows. Gigi turns the barstool in her mother's direction and studies her staring out at the cities skyline.

"Your dad and I were constantly arguing, and it was

always about him traveling for his business; It was always about him leaving us, and him always being away from me. Well, one day, after a huge argument, Cliff left went out of town. That's when things got intimate. I felt unique and beautiful again. I felt like someone with something to offer this world... It started when you were eight and ended not too long after you turned twelve."

"So! You had an affair with some man, why blame yourself for me being-"

Shayna abruptly shifts toward Gigi.

"It was a woman!"

Gigi looks at her mother stunned as her mind begins to process what she just said. Shayna returns to observing the city lights as she takes a deep breath and exhales. Shayna's head slowly drop as she folds her arms and walks over to Gigi. Shayna leans against the back of the sectional and looks at Gigi.

"I had an affair with a woman Gigi."

Shayna and Gigi stare at each other for a moment. Gigi looks away, she opens the new bottle of her wine, pours herself a fresh glass and turns to Shayna as she takes a healthy sip.

"Can I get some water please?" Shayna said.

"Help yourself" Gigi said. "There are bottles in the fridge."

"Thanks."

Shayna stands, she goes to walk away but stops.

"Listen, before you say anything. Let me finish okay."

Gigi nods her head in agreement.

"You're grown so I won't leave anything out."

Shayna goes to the fridge and gets a bottle of water.

"Mom there's clean glasses in the dishwasher. I know you don't like drinking out the bottle."

"Oh, you remember."

Gigi acknowledged. Shayna gets a glass, pours herself some water and drinks a healthy portion of it. Shayna returns to the living room sitting on the sectional by the end table. She puts the glass and the bottle of water down. Shayna's still feeling the perspiration bead up on her face while her heart pounds within her chest. She closes her eyes and rubs her hands over her face trying to calm herself.

Lord, help me to continue. Shayna thought turning to Gigi "Okay so where was I?"

"Oh, I remember," Gigi said getting up from the barstool. "You had an affair... With a woman... For five years. For real?"

"Yeah..."

"You were my age when you met her, huh?"

"Yes, but it wasn't a physical thing between us; We had become good friends. Best friends, actually. We had a lot in common, we could talk about anything and be ourselves around each other. I still miss her friendship a lot."

Gigi nurses on her glass of wine walking over to the sectional. She takes a seat at the far side of the sectional, sitting back and comfortably crosses her legs.

"So, let me clarify." Shayna said. "At the time, you were living at Mama's so you never met her. Gina was young, so she knew her... Well, knows her, but Gina never saw us together, not like that. Mama never knew either, nobody in the family did. The only person that found out was your father. He caught us together in our pool's grotto."

As Gigi takes in her mother's story her eyebrow raises.

"She left for California the next day; I met her at the airport before she left and... That's when she told me she was in love with me. She wanted me to leave with her, but I couldn't go. It wasn't like that for me. Looking back now, I'm able to say a part of me did love her. I knew I wasn't in love with her though, our relationship was just filling a void I had at the time. I've always been in love with your father. When I left the airport that day, it was over between us."

Shayna pauses taking a drink of water. She holds the glass in her hands as she crosses her legs.

"So," Gigi said. "Did you ever contact each other again?"

"It was over and years went by," Shayna said. "Then, your dad started drinking, a lot. We constantly argued and one day, he hit me. After that, I couldn't take anymore. So... I-"

Gigi sits up.

"You left-I remember that. I was seventeen, Dad kept saying you were on a business trip. You were gone for close to two weeks until Gina got hit by that car. I remember at grandma's birthday party years ago, I overheard you and Aunt Leah arguing about that. You said, you were in Texas for that business trip." Gigi folds her arms. "So, what exactly is the truth? Were you on a business trip? Or, with her?"

Shayna drinks more water, she clears her throat and puts the glass down.

"There was no business trip. I was in Texas with her. Gigi, we hadn't spoken in like six years, but... After Cliff hit me, I was a wreck. So, I called her, we talked and when she invited me out there I went. I was so upset with your father, I wouldn't answer any of his calls or texts, not even his emails. When she rented a villa for us in St. Martin, I left my phone in Texas. We had a great time too, I wish I could say different but... I can't." Shayna takes the bottle of water, empties it in her glass and takes a few swallows. "While we were in St. Martin, she pulled out this beautiful ring and proposed to me. I asked her for a few days to think about it. When we got back to Texas, I saw the messages about Gina. That night, I left the ring and a note beside her. Got on a plane and never looked back."

"Wow, does Dad know what happen in Texas?"

"He does now, we're doing our share of counseling. God's restoring our marriage. I'm praying God can restore our relationship Gigi. I pray you want that too."

"I don't know, I haven't made any decisions. You wanted me to hear you out, right? Let's finish this first."

"Alright, the main thing I wanted to tell you. Is how I

realize now, I allowed the issues in my life back then to open me up to do anything."

Shayna stands, stretches her arms out a bit then walks back to the living room window and gazes out. Gigi turns to her mother.

"See Gisele, at the time I needed something... Someone to make me feel better about myself. Your father and I went for counseling at the church after the pool incident and God restored our marriage. Your father forgave me, God forgave me but I couldn't forgive myself. I allowed condemnation to change me into a terrible person, and because of it, I just couldn't handle what was going on with you. Seeing you just made me feel more guilty about what I did. Then, to top it all off, about two years ago the woman I had been involved with was back... and with all the churches, on every corner in New York, she ends up joining Full Gospel. She's even one of the leaders there. When I first saw her at Full Gospel, I couldn't believe she got saved. Instead of praising God about that, all I did was worry about someone finding out about our past. I knew her before she had a title, she's Minister Cassandra Pauls now."

While Shayna admires the view, Gigi nonchalantly turns away putting her hands over her face and shaking her head.

This can't be happening. Gigi thought smirking.

"Cassandra's held the affair over my head at Full Gospel, threatening to expose it." Shayna said. "That's only because I haven't been exactly cordial to her. She has tried to make peace with me, several times. I just shut her out every time. She has a right to be angry with me. She was always there for me and rather than be honest with her, I ran away more than once. Rather than just talk to her, I hurt her so much, just like I hurt your father and you. None of you deserved that, and it's all my fault. Now that I'm able to accept everything I've done; I can talk about it, be honest about it and finally forgive myself for everything. I can't say sorry enough to everyone."

Shayna walks away from the window and sits beside Gigi on the sectional.

"That's why I'm here," Shayna said. "I'm sorry Gisele-I am so sorry for all the hurt and pain I've caused you, and I pray you can forgive me."

"So when I came out," Gigi said. "It reminded you of what you did. That's why you feel you're to blame. You feel like you opened the door to a generational curse."

"Yes, and even though I repented, was forgiven by God and delivered, I was still filled with so much guilt and shame. It kept me bound in my heart and mind. I forgot once you repent and confess your sins, they're covered by the blood of Jesus." Shayna gets up and walks about. "Instead of facing it when you came out to me. I ran the other way. All I could do was get rid of it, get it out my sight!"

Gigi abruptly stands and approaches her.

"Not *it* Mom! Not it! Me, your daughter! You got rid of your own flesh and blood! Every time you saw me, you'd rather hurt me, over and over than ever deal with it! And that's what's messed up!"

"And for that... I'm truly sorry."

Shayna tries to hug Gigi but she moves away once again.

"Don't... Okay, just don't! Please! I'm just... I'm not ready for that. Not right now, everything you've told me... It's... It's a lot to process. And, I... I need some time. Right now, I can't promise anything will change for me."

Shayna goes over to the sectional and puts her coat on.

"Well, I'm glad you know everything now. I've finally forgiven myself for the mistakes I've made. All I can do is pray you can forgive me too."

Shayna walks to the hallway but turns to Gigi before leaving.

"In February, all of Full Gospel Temple is going to Dr. Wilson's RAW gathering. I remember you going with your grandmother every year. You loved going so much. That's where you first got saved too."

"Mom, don't."

"All I'm saying is I would love for you to come. Gigi for me it's a brand new day. I pray you allow our relationship to start on new ground too. I love you so much, honey."

"Mom, I've tried hard not to, but I love you too. Thanks for finally being upfront and honest with me. It's too bad it didn't happen years ago."

"I know, but at least you know everything now."

"Look mom, I can't tell you what's gonna happen with our relationship. So I can't promise anything either."

"I understand that. I hope we talk again soon."

"Hopefully."

"Okay. Well, good night sweetheart."

"Good night, take care."

Shayna walks down the hallway and leaves. Gigi walks about her living room.

"God, what does she expect from me, after the years of pain that she's caused." Her eyes start to tear. "And now my hearts been broken again, why would she do this to me." Her tears fall from her cheeks. "Lord I need you right now, cause my mind and emotions are raging like the sea... today I've learned and discovered so much. Besides the hurt, I feel my anger growing within me. All of it's tossing me back and forth. I can't see through my tears, Jesus, please help me find the right path."

Shayna walks out of Gigi's building and the sounds of the city go forth. Shayna takes a few steps away from the building and looks up to the heavens.

"Father, I know I've caused this storm that rages between us, and for that, I'm so sorry. Only you can fix it now. The wind's and waves obey your will Lord. So, please Jesus, speak peace to this storm."

~CHAPTER 8~

~*His Ways Are Not Our Ways*~

~MOVING FORWARD~

It's now January 31st, the last Friday of the month, it's late at night and the large rehab meeting room has been remarkably transformed into an elegant wedding reception hall. All for the nuptials of Kisha Carrington and Reginald Jacobs. The room has been decorated in the colors of black, dark purple and silver for this truly special occasion. Pamela, Leah, and Shayna have simple casual clothes on as they sit at a table in the back and watch the staff of caterers, florist and decorators move about finishing up last minute details.

"This is absolutely incredible," Leah said. "Pam, you have out did yourself."

"Yes, you have," Shayna said. "Everything looks fantastic."

"Thank you ladies, but we did this together," Pamela said. "I just took all our ideas and made it one."

Shayna's cell goes off making a sound like Morse code. She picks her cell up from off the table and checks it. The other two stop talking and watch her for a moment. Shayna starts to type on her iPhone, as she sends a quick reply back, she takes a deep breath, exhales and puts her cell back down on the table.

"Everything okay?" Leah said.

"Yeah, that was a text from Elder Mays," Shayna said. "She's headed out of town, there's a family emergency, so she can't bring the gift from the women's department. She asked Minister Pauls to bring it tomorrow."

"Oh... alright," Leah said.

"Well, I was just about to say," Pamela said. "I saw the menu and the cake. You two surely made that caterer work for his money."

"Now, that's all Leah," Shayna said. "My sister knows

how to put together an excellent meal."

"Thank you honey," Leah said. "I can't believe y'all found the carpet we talked about. I looked everywhere, and nobody had a dark purple silver paisley carpet."

"Shayna did that all by herself," Pamela said. "I don't know how she found it either."

"Well, being an auditor has its perks sometimes," Shayna said. "A project I had a few months ago was a custom design carpet firm. I saved the owner thousands after he said, if I ever needed anything, just ask. So... I did."

"Ladies," Pamela said glancing at her watch. "It's now eleven fifteen. Let's get going. We've got to get home, get some sleep, and be back here tomorrow before 10 AM, looking all types of attractive."

"Gurl, you are so right," Leah said.

"I've already spoken with the staff, still here," Shayna said. "So they know what they need to do."

"So let's go," Pamela said.

The ladies get up, put their coats on and leave.

The sun has risen and the birds go about singing their lovely songs on Saturday, February 1st, a brand new day has arrived and the Lord has blessed us with a beautiful one. The time is now 9:40 AM and in the transformed meeting room instrumental gospel music is playing. The crowd is an intimate thirty people: consisting of family, close friends, a few Full Gospel Temple Church Members, and select Rehab staff and clients. Everyone's dressed to impress but those in the wedding party looked stunning. The wedding party consisted of Leah, James, Ron Pemberton, Moses and Pamela Carrington, Cliff and Shayna, Minister Andre Randall and Regina, Dray and Nola Lavell, and Paris and Nikita Beaumont.

The ladies of the wedding party looked lovely, all chic and stylish, no matter what they wore, be it a gown, dress or skirt suit with fancy hat included. They all adorned themselves in dark purple silver with of course matching high heels. All the gentlemen looked equally handsome, all dashing and sophisticated, they wore in unity, a black pinstripe tuxedo with a gray paisley print waistcoat, matching cravat tie, pocket square, and black patent-leather shoes.

Most of the wedding party and guest wait inside the large meeting room for the ceremony to begin. Ron stood by one of the rehab offices, speaking with Suzette, who was clad in a black leather faux dress, which stopped mid-thigh and it was just a splendid accessory to the curves on her naturally fit body. Presley was with her, his Stacy Adams, gold label vested suit, was black with white stripes, he stood to the side as they spoke.

"I peeked in the room when I first got here," Suzette said.

"They really transformed it for the wedding."

"I know it surprised me too," Ron said. "I'm glad you made it. Reggie appreciates you letting him have the wedding here."

"Not a problem."

"I've gotta check on the food. I'll see you inside."

"Okay."

As Ron walks away, Suzette and Presley step into her sizable office; Presley closes her office door behind them. Presley follows Suzette toward her large mahogany desk. He stops midway and as if it's a natural reflex he stands at attention. Suzette places her Prada bag on her desk and turns to Presley.

"You may rest my pet," Suzette said.

On her word, Presley changes his stance to the military at rest position. Suzette moves closer and starts to fix his tie. Presley is taller than her, but as she adjusts his tie, he keeps his head up and eyes straight ahead.

"You look so handsome my pet," Suzette said.

"Thank you, Mistress Zett," Presley said. "You're always so breath taking, its a pleasure to serve you."

"When I dropped by that auction a few months ago," Suzette said. "I stopped in just to see a friend. I must say, it was a pleasure to have acquired you that day. You're such a well-endowed and prize stallion. While I've been waiting for everything to transfer over, I've thoroughly enjoyed our time together. Your last owner must have been extremely frustrated to let a stud like you go. I'm not surprised either, he's a novice. I'm sure he's only been doing this for a year or two. Turn around my pet."

Presley quickly turns around and she starts to brush off the back of his suit jacket.

"I've booked you for two exclusive shoots, one is in New York but those won't take place for another three months. Now, after the title of ownership is transferred over, and it's in my hands, I require that all new horses in my stable be it stallion or mare, are trained and conditioned to my liking for at least three months. Face me my pet."

Presley quickly turns back around, as she takes a few steps back her eyes carefully scan her newly acquired property. She takes a deep breath, exhales and approaches him.

"Of course everyone's training is different, depending on what I desire them to be. I've spoken with your last three owners and from what I've heard, the consensus is that you can't seem to control yourself-isn't that right?"

"Yes, Mistress."

"Well, that tattoo you received means you're mine. I've broken wild horses before, so know this-you're going to learn that, your *manhood*, what you think is your pleasure, belongs to me. So, it's my pleasure now and I'll control what it does."

Presley nods twice as he stares straight ahead, she sees him swallow and notices his body tremble.

"Mmm... A tremble, now that's lovely my pet because hearing my voice, should make you tremble. Look at me!

Presley tilts his head carefully looking into his Mistress's eyes. She softly places her hand on the side of his face.

"You will learn how to control yourself and obey me without question, one way or the other. Understand, my pet?"

"Yes, Mistress."

"He'll Work It Out" Chapter 8. Taryn C. Atkins

Suzette heads over to her desk, she walks around it and sits down in the huge leather chair behind it. She opens the desk drawer to the right, takes out a medium black box and places it firmly on the desk. She gets up, walks around to the front of the desk and sits down on top of it. Suzette looks away for a moment to get the black box as she moves it beside her, Presley steals a peek at her legs as she crosses them. His eyes revert back to their original focus just as Suzette returns her attention to him.

"Come closer my pet and look at me."

Presley comes over, he stands at rest in front of her. Presley's eyes meet hers, she reaches out, grabs each of his suit jacket lapels and slowly pulls his face down to hers. Suzette softly and ever so sensually kisses Presley's lips. After kissing him twice, she stops and looks into his eyes.

"You may kiss me back."

The next kiss they share is a long steamy one. As they kiss, the passion shared between them starts to take both of them over and Presley wraps his arms around her. Suzette stops, she moves back from Presley and they stare into each others eyes. Presley breathes heavy; as he looks into her eyes, wanting to continue, he moves forward trying to kiss Suzette again. She roughly pushes him away.

"Stand at attention!"

Presley's eyes look straight ahead as he assumes the position trying to catch his breath. She stares at him, slowly shaking her head.

"See-no control."

"I'm sorry Mistress."

"Oh, you will be my pet."

Suzette gives Presley the once-over, it's quiet for a moment as she contemplates him.

"Your real name is Presley Beaumont, and that's what you use for the special porn films and magazines you're in-correct?"

"Yes, Mistress."

"You're a proud one... You got the swagger, and the looks, and are ever so proud of everything about yourself. Which is why, you proudly use your real name.

"He'll Work It Out" Chapter 8. Taryn C. Atkins

I haven't named you and you won't be given a name either, I'll call you my pet because that's all you are. You're my pet, to do with whatever I like. You see... My pet, I know exactly what a submissive like you needs, what your very being craves. You must have been a handful growing up. I'm sure you probably got into all types of mischief, didn't you?"
"Yes, Mistress."
"Yet, there's this submissive side. That apparently only the right dominate can control. So, who was it? Who was it that took control of that spirited little boy in secret? Who was it that purposely reached inside him and not only planted that submissive seed but cultivated it as well? Whoever they are, they have either grown tired of you or they're just not around anymore. See... I do my research, you've run through five owners in such a short time. That's because you're still searching for the right one. Aren't you?"
"Yes, Mistress."
"So my pet, who was it? And make sure you tell me everything."
"Yes Mistress, when I was eleven, my parents put my twin brother and me into an after-school program at this Catholic church. The nuns were in charge of the program there. While my brother was the good one. I've always been the rambunctious and unruly."
"Continue."
"After having gotten in trouble so many times during the school year, the following year, the head nun placed me under the strict care of Sister Davenport. So once I got there after school, I went to her quarters and stayed there until it was time for my brother and me to get picked up. We were in that program for two years."
"Okay, get to the point."
"Sister Davenport left me alone for a while one day. When she returned, she caught me in her bathroom with one of my dad's porn magazine's. She told me I was

improper and that I needed to be disciplined. She had me bring more porn magazines with me. When I'd arrive, she'd make me strip, then tie me up to a chair or in the bathroom. She'd show me the magazines. When I got aroused, she'd use various devices to tease and torture me. Davenport said if I ever told anybody, she'd castrate me and my brother. I never told; I still got aroused by the magazines though, but then-I started to get excited when she messed with me too. So her discipline got more sadistic. I started to want it though, it was all I could think about. I would rush over to the program when I got out of school. One day she was transferred and I never saw her again."

"Well, she certainly ignited that kinky flame. You were so young, only twelve when it was lit, and then she disappeared. Leaving you my poor pet, with this fire burning deep within and you had the slightest idea how to quench it. You're thirty-eight now correct?"

"Yes, Mistress."

"I'm sure you lost your virginity early too, growing up you probably looked at all types of porn, whatever you could get your hands on... and probably still do. The more you fanned that flame, the more intense it got. That's why you star in specific types of porn, no matter the venue. You're chasing that euphoric high Sister Davenport gave you years ago... that's what drives you in your search, isn't it my pet?"

"Yes... yes it is Mistress Zett. You know me so well."

"Of course I do, and my pet, you're most definitely with the right owner. I've decided, your reconditioning will begin now, and that a stallion such as yourself-one with so little control, needs chastity. So, I've got a special gift in this box, custom made just for you my pet. Which I'll be locking on to my pleasure, and then we'll attended the wedding."

"Yes Mistress."

"He'll Work It Out" Chapter 8. Taryn C. Atkins

"There are two keys but I'll be keeping both."

"Of course Mistress."

Suzette picks up the black box, places it on her lap and sensually caresses the top of it. She moves her hands to the sides of it and lifts up the top. While Presley sneaks a view of Suzette opening the black box, beads of perspiration arise on his brow when feasting his eyes on the shiny metal device she takes out. He quickly returns to staring forward just as Suzette brings her focus back to him. She observes his chest rise and fall from rapid breaths, when Suzette spots the sweat running down the sides of his face a wolfish grin emerges from her lips.

A few moments have passed and the wedding ceremony has not started, in the wedding reception hall standing by the window are Minister Casey Thomas, Dray, Nola, Paris, Brother Marcus Hamlin and his wife Patricia.

"It's a small world," Nola said.

"I guess it is," Paris said.

"Man, how long have you known?" Dray said.

"I didn't realize until Cliff and you two walked into the rehearsal last night." Paris said. "I never thought that the wedding you and Nola mentioned was the same one that Nikita and I were going to be in."

"Well, for Nikita and Kisha to be cousins all this time, is wild," Dray said. "With you here my brother, it will just be a better celebration."

"So true," Paris said. "What time is it now?"

Dray takes a deep breath as he looks at his watch and as he exhales he looks over at Paris.

"It's going on 10:30," Dray said. "Shayna said the minister is close, but he was stuck in traffic. That was about fifteen minutes ago. He should be here any minute."

"I hope so," Paris said.

"We caught traffic too." Brother Hamlin said. "We're surprised we got here before things started."

"We made it, thank God," Patricia said. "Everything and everybody looks so lovely."

"Feels good to get away from the job." Brother Hamlin said. "Working for Corrections is no joke. The money is good and all but it comes with a load of stress. I was happy to put in for this day."

"How's your family Tricia?" Nola said. "Are things going alright with Kia now?"

"Not at all," Patricia said. "She met someone. So, right now she's in her own world. Just keep her in your prayers, please."

"I certainly will," Nola said.

"Casey," Dray said. "Your plus one is waving at you."

They all look over at the seats, Minister Thomas raises his hand, smiles and waves back to none other than Sister Carlton. She smiles back as she crosses her legs and faces forward.

"So, of all the people to bring," Nola said. "You bring the church gossip."

"It wasn't planned believe me." Minister Thomas said.

"Minister McDaniels was supposed to come with me but she got the flu. I don't know how Sister Carlton found out, but when I got ready to walk out my house, there she was. Sister Carlton told me Minister McDaniels said she could take her place. She showed up at my house. Apparently, Sister Carlton lives right around the corner from me, so I couldn't actually say no to her."

"I would of," Nola said.

"Me too," Dray said. "You should have told her you were picking up a family member or something."

"I wasn't gonna lie to the woman." Minister Thomas said.

"You could have repented in your car," Dray said.

Minister Thomas looks at Dray and shakes his head.

"So, Casey," Paris said. "Speaking of family, I never hear you talk about yours."

"There's not much to talk about." Minister Thomas said.

"Well, you're standing here with us," Dray said. "So we're pretty sure you got parents. You an only child, got siblings or what? Give us a little something."

"Give y'all a little something." Minister Thomas said.

They all look at him nodding their heads.

"Yeah... please," Paris said. "Indulge us."

"I'll try to keep it short and sweet." Minister Thomas said. "I'm from Mississippi; I have two older brothers, a older sister and then it's me. I was nine when my parents adopted my little sister. When the older ones left for college, they never bothered with the family again. We haven't spoken in years either. I was twenty-one and she just turned ten when our parents died in a plane crash. Right after that, I was given custody of my little sister. So, that's basically it."

When he finishes, an awkward silence fills the atmosphere around the small group for a moment.

"Whoa... Man, I'm sorry," Paris said. "I didn't mean to pry."

"Casey, we're so sorry for real," Nola said. "You have my deepest condolences."

"Yeah, I'm so sorry." Patricia said.

"Me too man." Brother Hamlin said.

"Yeah Casey," Dray said. "It must have been rough. I get why you don't talk about them."

"It was rough, especially for me." Minister Thomas said. "All our grandparents were dead. My aunts and uncles just turned their backs on us. Our parents left a little something but not much. We would've lost my families cabin, land, everything. So, I had to make some hard and quick decisions. Anyway, the founder of this local foundation, he took care of everything, and just looked out for us.

"It's great someone stepped in and helped you out," Dray said. "That was a blessing."

"Everything happened so fast," Minister Thomas said. "I mean I was just twenty-one, it's legal, but I was a kid, concerned about girls and video games. I realized our parents were gone and we had no other family. So, I'm trying to deal with that... I blink my eyes, and I'm given custody of a kid. Not even a little boy, but a little girl. My mom used to do everything for her. Just like that, I'm the sole parent for my ten-year-old little sister; Man, she was a lot to deal with too, besides worrying about bills and school. I had to figure out a way to handle things, and I did. That founder, he stepped in and really handled everything for us, watched out for us for a while. So I did what I had to do. I had no choice."

"You were looking out for your family," Paris said. "That's what's most important. Anybody could understand that."

"You're right," Minister Thomas said. "I did what I had to do for my family. My sister and I meet up at our family's cabin, the founder comes over and we show our respect by spending time together. So it's all good."

"There's nothing more important than family," Nola said. "Look guys. I'm gonna help Pam and Nikita with Kisha, the lovely bride."

"Alright," Dray said. He smiles. "Nola loves weddings."

"Marcus, we should get our seats." Patricia said.

"Let's go," Brother Hamlin said. "We'll see you guys after the ceremony."

Brother Hamlin and Patricia go to take their seats. Nola walks away too and heads over to the meeting room doors. The doors open and in walks Presley and Suzette. Paris looks over and sees his brother. Presley sees his brother across the room too, he raises his hand and waves.

"What's he doing here?" Paris said.

"Hey!" Nola said. She hugs Presley. "What in the world are you doing here?"

"Hi, Nola," Presley said. He hugs her and as they release each other. "I came with my new agent-she's the head director here as well."

"Hi," Suzette said with a smile.

"Wow, I love your accent," Nola said. "You sound so, War of the Roses, Kathleen Turnerish if you don't mind me saying."

"Not at all, thank you." Suzette said. "I hear that a lot."

"I'm sure you do," Nola said. She looks at Presley. "Well, like I told your brother it's a small world. Look, I'm on my way to check on the bride."

"Okay now." Presley said.

Nola strolls out the room.

"While we're here," Suzette said. "You may relax and be yourself, within reason my pet." She moves to his side and takes his arm. "You may use my full name to introduce me. Now smile my pet and let's enjoy the festivities."

They smile and go over to Paris, Dray and Minister Thomas.

"Well now, what are you doing here? Presley said.

"This is Nikita's cousin's wedding," Paris said. "What are you doing here?"

"My new agent works here," Presley said, motioning to the woman on his arm. "This is Suzette Scarsboro. Suzette, as you can see that's my twin and these, are his friends."

"Hello all." Suzette said.

Dray nods in her direction.

"Hello Suzette," Paris said wearing a smile.

"Nice to meet you," Suzette said with a smile as her eyes take in Paris. "Presley did say he had a twin, but seeing you together-mercy! It makes a girl like me dream." She takes note of Dray. "You're handsome yourself."

"Me?" Dray said pointing to himself. "You're too kind."

"Now this is the first, I'm actually meeting one of my brothers agents," Paris said. "Pres has complained about others... I hope you know how to treat him."

"Oh, believe me," Suzette said. "I do."

"Suzette?!" Minister Thomas said.

"Yes," Suzette said.

"You don't remember me?" Minister Thomas said.

"Sorry, I guess I don't," Suzette said.

"It's me Casey Thomas, Ivy's brother." Minister Thomas said. "We met in April, at a dinner party my sister and her husband had at their home in Connecticut. We fellowshipped at their church first and then went back to their place. My sister's a Chef and her husband Bryce is a Cardiologist."

"Right! I remember." Suzette said. "I don't normally do church, it hasn't been my thing for quite sometime. I only came to drive up to the club with them the next day."

"Well, I didn't know their exact plans." Minister Thomas said. "I just knew they were going out of town."

"You're the minister," Suzette said. "Yes, I do remember now. It was interesting that you two were siblings. You and Ivy are so... different from one another." She looks at Presley. "Darling, you remember Ivy and Bryce, that May and December couple? We've gotten together with them before-we were just with them at the clubs New Years party."

"Yeah... I remember Ivy now." Presley said. He looks at Suzette. "You and Bryce even recommended my friends and I put Ivy to good use at a few of our parties." He looks at Minister Thomas. "Whatever cooking school she went to, they taught her well. She can handle a crowd."

"She always loved to cook." Minister Thomas said. "The master chef' at the school she attended, found Ivy enjoyed catering for special occasions and can manage cooking for five or fifty. It's taken time and serious training, but it paid off cause Ivy's good at what she does."

"That's cool your sister being a chef," Dray said. "Me, I can burn ice water."

All those around Dray laugh at his statement.

"That not a joke!" Dray chuckles. "I'm serious, I can literally burn ice water."

"So what do you do Casey?" Paris said.

"Nothing as flamboyant like being a chef." Minister Thomas said. "Since I was raised in the country, I always had a passion for nature. I'd help my mom out with her garden, she couldn't stand that I liked collecting insects, and dad could always find me helping out at one of the neighbor's farms. I would be milking the cows, riding the horses or I'd be volunteering at the local kennel. It just came naturally to me and I loved it. So, I figured, why not be a specialist; I'm a triple threat, a certified qualified Botanist, Entomologist and animal Vet, all rolled up in one. If it has leaves, creeps, crawls, barks or moo's, I know about it."

"So in laymen's terms, you a geek." Paris said.

"Basically." Minister Thomas said laughing a bit. "But a good looking geek."

"Well, you ain't gonna get no girlfriend or wife collecting bugs," Dray said. "I could tell you that right now."

"You got that right brother," Paris said.

Paris and Dray give each other a pound. Presley smiles and nods his head. Minister Thomas looks at Suzette, she gives him a slight smirk and folds her arms.

"You know, the last time I was told to use Ivy," Presley said. "There was only about ten of us. Suzette's having a special dinner party. Since you've let us know what Ivy's capable of handling, we'll have to add more peeps to the guest list. Suzette stopped at fifteen, let's make it thirty and see if Ivy's available." He looks at Suzette. "Is that alright with you?"

Presley smiles as he looks at Suzette. She smiles back at him and slowly approves nodding.

"That's fine," Suzette said. "Getting Ivy to cook shouldn't be a problem. I know Bryce is attending; I'm sure she'll be with him..."

"If you want her to cook." Minister Thomas said. "Give her a call, because she'll need time to prepare."

"Well if Ivy's available to be used for the dinner party," Presley said. "I'll be letting her know every moment, that her big brother said she could handle it."

"I'm curious," Suzette said. "What exactly does Bryce and Ivy do at their church?"

"Well, Bryce is usually working." Minister Thomas said.

"I'm sure he attends services when he can. Ivy travels a lot too. When she's home, I believe she sings in the choir."

"She sings too? I gotta remember that." Presley said. "So Casey, have you ever gotten the chance to see your little sister in action, at any of the parties she's catered?"

"Actually, no I haven't." Minister Thomas said. "We have such different schedules. We only see each other once a year, at our families cabin in Mississippi."

"That's special." Suzette said. "Does Bryce go?"

"He goes." Minister Thomas said. "It's an anniversary thing for all of us. Anyway, since Ivy gets a lot of work out of town catering in New York, it's usually a private party. Sometimes I'm just not able to attend. I'm either out preaching or on assignment for my church."

"My dinner party is in a few weeks." Suzette said. "My loft is in the city. Please drop by, come see what skills your little sister uses to serve a crowd."

Minister Thomas's phone goes off, he unclips it from his belt and answers it.

"Excuse me." Minister Thomas said preparing to walk away. "I've got to take this call it's Pastor Gorham. Nice to see you again Suzette."

"Glad to see you." Suzette said. "Casey, you should really make an effort to attend my party. Come and see for yourself what your little sister is up to. I'm sure Ivy seeing you there, would be a great surprise for her. Please think about it."

"I'll let you know." Minister Thomas said.

Minister Thomas walks away focusing on his cell. Suzette watches him and huffs as he leaves the room.

"Gentlemen, excuse us too," Suzette said. "I'm gonna take a seat. While Presley goes to my office and gets the wedding gift, we left in there. See you all after the ceremony. Let's go my pet."

"Alright," Presley said. "Later guys."

"He'll Work It Out" Chapter 8. Taryn C. Atkins

Paris and Dray watch Suzette and Presley go to their seats. Suzette sits handing Presley a set of keys and he walks out.

"What's up with your brother?" Dray said. "And I don't know what it is, but that woman's kinda scary."

"I'm not sure what's up with him," Paris said. "I hope she's good for him."

"Why does he need an agent?" Dray said.

"Well, I'm not proud of it, but it's his life." Paris said. "My brother's an adult film actor and model. He's been an escort before too. He don't tell me everything but I know he's into some kinky stuff."

"Okaay... So, you telling me that Pres is a porn star?"

"Yep... True dat"

"All families have their issues, you know that, but you being his identical twin... Man, that's got to affect your life."

"It does at times, but you manage the hand you're dealt. He's my brother, what am I suppose to do?. They say everybody has a twin right. Mine's a porn star. I rather he's that, then some deranged serial killer out there."

"I understand that, but I'm sure your wife isn't too thrilled with his choices."

"You know that."

"I know one thing. I read between the lines, and they ain't foolin me. I know how their dealing with Casey's sister."

"Yeah." Paris shakes his head. "I know my brother too, and after that conversation; I'm sure the way Pres knows Ivy, isn't for her catering."

"For real," Dray said. "I'm surprised Casey didn't pick that up. They were rather bold with it."

"He might have caught it," Paris said. "That's his little sister though, and Casey just may be one of those that chooses to ignore what's right in front of him. Whatever Ivy's story- Apparently Pres plays a part."

"Well, just leave it." Dray said. "We'll learn more later."

"I heard somewhere," Paris said. "That there're six

degrees of separation between us all. Nevertheless, like Nola said earlier. It's a small world."

"Apparently smaller than we thought." Dray said.

In the rehab center hallway, the elevator doors open up and a Titanic style hat is seen, it's a"Lady Olivia" it's designed over a gorgeous navy wool hat. The hat band and the bow are gray and white silk taffeta and there're two gray organza roses accented with gray satin leaves adorning the side of the crown. The hat in itself was stunning and caught one's attention when the wearer looked up, it was Minister Pauls. She walked out of the elevator carrying a generous size wedding gift- The Armani, blue, rounded collar, fitted formal crepe dress, stopped right at her knee and it underscored her figure.

Minister Pauls sees the signs directing people to where the wedding was taking place. As she walks over to the meeting room, Presley is on his way back carrying Suzette's wedding gift under his arm. Presley and Minister Pauls reach the meeting room door simultaneously. Presley opens the door for her, he looks at her and does a double take. Presley checks her shape as he walks in behind her, he starts to head toward Suzette but changes direction.

"Excuse me," Presley said. "I don't mean to bother you but I've gotta ask you something."

'Yes." Minister Pauls said.

"I'm an actor," Presley said. "You look so much like an actress I've worked with, her name is Chastity Chase. You two could be sisters. Really... Both of you got the long jet black hair, those curves that are not hard to miss and... are absolutely gorgeous. You're a little older, but minus the glasses. You two look so much alike."

"Chastity Chase?" Minister Pauls said. "That sounds like a porn stars name."

"Yeah... Actually it is, she is. So... is she your sister?"

Minister Pauls looks at Presley and smirks.

"Okay let me get this straight." Minister Pauls laughs. "You've chosen to boldly come up to someone you don't even know, and have the nerve to ask, if Chastity Chase, the porn star, is my sister?"

Presley nods his head, "Basically."

Minister Pauls looks at Presley, takes a step back, huffs, moves forward and through gritted teeth.

"No, she isn't."

"Okay, sorry to offend." Presley walks away but looks back at Minister Pauls. "The resemblance is amazing. Look her up online and see for yourself."

Minister Pauls huffs again as she shakes her head, she rolls her eyes as Presley walks away. She turns toward the table filled with wedding gifts, takes a deep breath and exhales.

Chastity Chase will never be my sister. Minister Pauls thought.

Presley places Suzette's wedding gift with the rest of them, then returns to his seat. Cliff and Shayna see Minister Pauls and approach her.

"Here, let me take that." Cliff said.

Cliff puts his hands on each side of the sizable gift and takes it out of Minister Pauls hands.

"Thank you Deacon Greye." Minister Pauls said.

"No problem." Cliff said. "No titles today, we're all here to celebrate this joyous occasion. So it's Cliff, if that's alright with you Cassandra?"

"Okaay?" Minister Pauls said.

"Great," Cliff said. "I'll put this with the rest."

"Thanks again." Minister Pauls said. "Appreciate it."

"You look stunning," Shayna said. "Love the hat."

Shayna and Minister Pauls watch as Cliff walks away and heads to the table filled with wedding gifts. Minister Pauls turns to Shayna.

"Thanks, you too." Minister Pauls said. "What's going on Shayna?"

"Relax," Shayna said. "We come in peace."

"Well, why is he so friendly?" Minister Pauls said. "Wait- hold that thought. Why are you so friendly?"

"Cliff's always been cordial," Shayna said. "I'm the one that's been unkind."

"Both are true." Minister Pauls said.

"I know," Shayna said. "I want to apologize for it all too. I know I've hurt you in so many ways Cassandra. I wasn't even in the place to admit that, or face all that I've done... It's because of God's grace and mercy, that I'm in a new place now, and I just want to tell you that I'm sorry."

Minister Pauls looks around casually seeing if anybody is paying attention to them.

"And you decide to tell me this here, today." Minister Pauls said. "Really, why now?" Her voice slightly raises.

"You've never cared about me or my feelings before."

Minister Pauls clears her throat dropping her eyes away from Shayna as she takes a few steps, moving away from those around them. Shayna follows her.

"Like I said, I'm in a new place." Shayna said. "And I've always cared about you Cassandra. Remember, we were best friends before anything else. I'm telling you now because tomorrow's not promised. I want to clear the air between us; We can't go back to the way things used to be. We are sisters in Christ and I don't want there to be strife between us anymore. I hope you want that too."

"When I realized you were attending Full Gospel," Minister Pauls said. "I *did* try to clear the air, several times, but you wanted no part of it. Why should I let bygones be bygones now?"

"I can't force you or anyone else to do anything. All I can do is come to you and tell you that I'm deeply sorry for how I treated you, and all the ways I hurt you. You didn't deserve none of it, and I am truly sorry. I hope you're able to forgive me one day."

Cliff comes over to Shayna and Minister Pauls.

"Excuse me, ladies," Cliff said. "Shayna, Pam wants the wedding party to line up outside the room."

"Okay, I'll be right there," Shayna said.

Cliff walks away and joins the rest of the wedding party leaving the room.

"Cassandra, I do miss our friendship and I pray you can forgive me. It's a blessing to know you're a child of God now, I couldn't accept that before, now I can, and I'm happy for you. Whether we start our friendship anew or remain sisters in Christ. I'm praising God for what he's doing in your life either way. Look, I've got to go out."
"Alright."
"Listen, don't rush off after the wedding." Shayna starts to walk away. "Stay and celebrate with us."
Minister Pauls looks at Shayna and nods her head.
"Sure."

Leah and Reggie are in one of the smaller meeting rooms. Leah looks at her watch as she walks over to Reggie. She smiles as she looks at him. Reggie's wearing a gray pinstripe tuxedo with a dark purple paisley print waistcoat, matching cravat tie, pocket square, and gray patent leather shoes.

"Pastor Gorham should be here any minute," Leah said. He was caught in traffic. Minister Thomas is outside waiting for him."
"Alright," Reggie said.
"You look so handsome Reggie," Mother Livingston said.
"I'm sure right now, Mae's looking down at you with smile from ear to ear. I know she's so proud of you, and so am I son. So am I."
"Thank you ma'am," Reggie said.
"I'm gonna head on into the room." Mother Livingston said. "See y'all inside now."
"Alright mother," Leah said.
"Okay," Reggie said. "Take your time, mother."
"I will." Mother Livingston said.

Mother Livingston makes her way out of the room. Reggie nervously repositions his tie but Leah fixes it.

"Look at you." Leah said. "Looking all handsome. I'm so proud of you. I wish Mama could see you."
"She does see me Ma." Reggie said. "Grandma is up there bragging up a storm to the angels right now."
"I know that's right." Leah said. She laughs as she

brushes Reggie's jacket. "My baby, you got yourself together and about to... about to..."

Leah gets welled up with emotion.

"Come on Ma." Reggie said. "Don't start."

"I know... I know," Leah responded. "I promised." She tries to hold her tears back. "I know I said I wouldn't... I wouldn't." Her tears start to flow. "Cry, but..."

"Ma." Reggie said.

"Leave her alone Reggie." James said.

They look over and see James. He walks over to them.

"Moment like this, your mother's allowed to cry." James said. "Besides, we've all seen Leah's mascara run before."

Leah nudges James as Reggie smiles looking at him.

"Oh, shut up you!" Leah said.

Leah hugs James and as they part she smiles at him.

"Let me fix my face." Leah said. "I'll see y'all inside."

"Alright." James said.

Leah walks out the room. Reggie and James shake hands and hug each other. As they break Reggie smiles.

"Hey man, I'm so glad you're here." Reggie said. "After getting silence when we last spoke on the phone, I wasn't sure you would come."

"Yeah, it's been a moment." James said. "I'm sorry for what I did to you and for what went down here that day. I especially apologize for what I said to you. I'm sorry about what happen to Mario."

"No problem." Reggie said. "The past is the past. Besides, you honor Mario's memory by standing in for him as my best man. So, we're starting off fresh right here." He extends his hand to James. "Alright man."

They shake hands and hug again.

"Alright." James said. "You look good, like a new man."

"That's because I am." Reggie said. "When I got here, I was all torn up but once I got my head clear, the first thing I did was accept Jesus into my heart and gave him my life. I've been reading my bible, praying and God is helping me through this. It hasn't been easy but... God has been in this with me. Mr. Pemberton, my counselor, got me into this outpatient program, so this is my last day here. I'm about to move on in my life and it was only Jesus who got me to this place. So I'm blessed."

"You nervous?" James said.

"Surprisingly not. I'm just excited. This is truly a day that the Lord has made. Jesus is restoring me. He's given me back my family. And now I'm about to get married-"

"So, you're ready to do this handsome?" Kisha said.

Reggie and James look around and see Kisha standing in the doorway of the small meeting room. They are amazed by how Kisha looks. Reggie's speechless when his eyes take hold of her. Kisha's looking astonishing in a white beautifully crafted custom wedding gown. Reggie is stunned by her beauty and continues to admire Kisha as he slowly approaches her.

"My Lord, you're breathtaking," Reggie said.

"Thank you," Kisha said. "So are you."

As Reggie goes to Kisha, she comes over to him.

"I'm gonna go," James said. "See y'all out there."

James goes to walk out the small meeting room. He looks back at Reggie and Kisha and smiles as he closes the door behind him.

"So like I said, you ready to do this?" Kisha said.

Reggie takes Kisha's hands within his.

"You're my good thing." Reggie said. "So I'm more than ready. How about you? Are you sure?"

"Of course, I am," Kisha said.

As Kisha caresses his face, Ron Pemberton opens the door and steps half way inside the small meeting room.

"Okay, Pastor Gorham's here and in place," Ron said.

"We're all lined up and waiting for you two."

Ron steps back out the room and closes the door. Reggie looks at Kisha and smiles as he takes her hand.

"Listen, I just want to cut to the main event personally," Reggie said. "I can understand if you want to do all the pomp and circumstance."

"Oh please," Kisha said wearing a smile. "Let's just do it."

"He'll Work It Out" Chapter 8. Taryn C. Atkins

Reggie smiles as he nods, they hold each others hands and rush out the small meeting room.

"Here they come," Leah said.

They quickly stroll to the wedding party.

"Come on everybody," Reggie said.

"Follow us," Kisha said. "Change in plans."

Reggie opens the door to the large meeting room which has been remarkably transformed into the wedding reception hall.. He, Kisha and the rest of the wedding party go inside. All there watch as Reggie and Kisha head over to Pastor Gorham and stop right in front of him.

"Pastor Gorham if you don't mind," Reggie said. "Kisha and I want to move right to the main part."

"Not a problem." Pastor Gorham said.

"Thank you," Kisha said.

Reggie and Kisha turn around and face their family, friends, and guest in the room.

"Hey everybody," Reggie said. "We're gonna do things a little differently."

"So, we want everybody to stand up," Kisha said. "Push your chairs all the way back and make a circle around us. Pastor Gorham, you stand in the center with Reggie and me of course."

"Alright." Pastor Gorham said.

"Okay, let's go everybody! You and your plus one can stand together of course," Reggie said. "We're just skipping over things and going right to the main reason we're all here."

Pastor Gorham, Reggie, and Kisha stand in the center as everyone else forms a nice size circle around them. As everyone moves into position, Ron Pemberton is next to Leah and nonchalantly checks her out for a quick moment. As he looks off to the side, Leah looks over at Ron and checks him out also. Just as Ron looks back in her direction, Leah looks away.

"My my, you're looking stunning Leah," Ron said.

"Why thank you," Leah said. "You clean up real nice yourself. Things are getting started. Where's your plus one?"

"Well, I came alone actually," Ron said. "I needed to look decent in case you shoot me down, because I wanted to ask... Would you allow me to be your plus one? If you shoot me down, at least I'll still look good on the outside."

"Well, maybe I won't shoot you down then," Leah said with a smile.

As everyone settles in their spots, Reggie happens to look over at his mother. He smiles watching things spark between his mother and his counselor. Kisha looks around and sees that everyone seems to be in place. All of the wedding party and guest are standing in the circle around them. Kisha looks around the room again and leans over to Reggie.

"Where's your aunt and uncle?" Kisha said.

Reggie looks around and looks at his mother.

"Ma..." Reggie said. "Where's Aunt Shayna and Uncle Cliff?"

"They're not in here?" Leah said.

"They were lined up with us," Dray said.

"I saw them in the hall with us too," Regina said.

The room door opens, as Cliff holds the door open, Shayna rushes in and Cliff follows.

"Sorry, we're here," Shayna said. "We're right here."

"Sorry about that," Cliff said.

They rush over and stand by Dray and Nola. Dray nods his head and smiles looking at them. Kisha looks at Pastor Gorham.

"Pastor Gorham, we're ready," Kisha said.

Alright, let's get started. Pastor Gorham said.

Everyone's eyes in the circle are on Kisha and Reggie as the wedding ceremony begins. Nola leans over to Shayna.

"Ahh... Excuse me," Nola whispered. "Fix your slip."

Shayna looks down, sees her slip is a bit bunched up under her dress and speedily fixes it.

"Thanks," Shayna said smoothing out her dress. "Anyone noticed?"

"Your slip?" Nola said shaking her head a bit. "No... That

huge hickey on your neck... That's another story."

"What?!" Shayna's hand speedily moves to the left side of her neck as she controls her inside voice. "Oh my God, it's that noticeable?"

"Not at all," Nola said with a dismissive wave. "It's that one on your right side ya can't miss."

"Huh!" Shayna's hand quickly goes to the other side of her neck, she looks at Nola, blushing as she bit her bottom lip. "Lord, it's like we just got married."

Nola looks back with a huge smile. "Well, praise da' Lawd!" Nola chuckled. "Gurl, I'm not mad at ya... you two better go head."

Dray nudges Cliff's arm with his elbow. Cliff looks over at him. Dray takes his finger and motions to the left side of his mouth.

"Umm... You got some lipstick right there." Dray whispered.

Cliff wipes his mouth off, looks at Dray and shrugs.

"Hey, things happen," Cliff said with a smile.

"Niiice." Dray said. "And when they happen, it's a beautiful thing."

"Yes it is." Cliff said.

Cliff and Dray wiggle their fingers together and do their special handshake. They put their arms around the waist of their wives standing in front of them. Both couples wear smiles on their face as they watch and listen as the wedding ceremony begins. Shayna happens to look across the room and makes eye contact with Regina, standing with her arms folded, looking at her parents. Shayna looks at Regina with a bewildered expression. Regina points to the right side of her neck. Shayna touches the right side of her neck again and realizes what Regina is talking about. She looks at Regina, smiles and shrugs her shoulders. Regina looks back at her mother with a serious face and shakes her head.

Regina mouths the word, "Really??"

Regina looks away from her parents and looks over her shoulder at Minister Randall. Minister Randall wears a big smile as he looks across at Cliff and Shayna. Regina folds her arms as she looks at him.

"And what are you smiling at," Regina said.

"What?" Minister Randall said. "After so many years of marriage." He huffs and laughs a bit. "That's alright."

"Yeah, okay," Regina said, as she shakes her head. "Whatever."

Minister Randall puts his arm around Regina's waist and they return their focus to the wedding ceremony at hand. Pastor Gorham goes to speak, but Reggie raises his hand, motioning for him to stop.

"Wait, Pastor Gorham," Reggie said. "I want to say something." He turns toward those in the circle. "I just want to say, I know you're all probably wondering why I wanted to do this here. Well, since this was my last day here at the rehab center, this is a symbolic moment for me. It's a shift and a new season in my life. I came in here one way, and now I'm leaving another. I'm starting a new life, a new beginning; And I'm not going back or ever looking back again." He looks up toward heaven. "Grandma, I know now, that if God is for me, there's nobody who can stand against me. I love you Grandma and thank you for praying me through." He looks back at those in the circle. "So, I'm moving forward from this point on, in Jesus name and praising my God all the way. AMEN!!!"

All those in attendance proclaim AMEN!!! Reggie turns back toward Pastor Gorham and gives him the nod.

"Alright, let's do this." Reggie said.

"We've all gathered in this place." Pastor Gorham said. "Because we all have a great affection for Reggie and Kisha, we've all come here to witness and bless their union in holy matrimony. Marriage is a special union created by God and should not be entered into unadvised. The bride and groom should enter it carefully and reverently. Now, into this holy union, these two come to join together and become one flesh. No other human tie is more tender or sacred. May I have the rings?"

"He'll Work It Out" Chapter 8. Taryn C. Atkins

James steps out from the circle, as he approaches Pastor Gorham, he takes the rings out from his inside tuxedo pocket, James gets ready to hand Pastor Gorham the rings but stops-He looks at Reggie and Kisha.

"You two sure?" James said. "It's your last chance."

"James, stop it," Kisha said.

"Stop playing," Reggie said. "Give him the rings."

"Okay, I'm just saying," James said.

James opens up his hand and Pastor Gorham takes the rings. James returns to the circle as Pastor Gorham cups the rings in his hands, he closes his eyes and blesses the rings. After two or three seconds he opens his eyes. Pastor Gorham gives one ring to Reggie and the other to Kisha.

"Reggie and Kisha, you may now say your vows." Pastor Gorham said.

Reggie and Kisha turn and face each other. Reggie takes Kisha's hand in his:

> "Kisha, what I feel for you is so real, and I cannot picture myself without you. You have been and are my best friend. You've been there for me through thick and thin. You were there for me when I didn't want to be there for myself, and you loved me when I didn't want to love myself. I know that I was predestined by God to be with you, and from the first time that I saw you, I was speechless at your breathtaking beauty and I knew that I loved you. So, I Reginald Wesley Jacobs make this vow to you today, and as I take your hand within mine, I say to you that you are my good thing, orchestrated by God from the beginning of time. I promise to be the best man for you that I can be. I promise to take care of you and to cherish you. You are my heart and all that I have is for you. I will share all that I have with you. I need you and I cannot live without you. Kisha, I will love you for the rest of my life, and I am blessed that God has allowed me to find you, my wife. A love that was given to me that is true, and as I, Reggie, stand here today and look into your eyes-I say I Do!"

Reggie puts Kisha's wedding ring on her finger. Kisha takes Reggie's hand:

"Reggie, from the first time that I met you, I knew that there was something special about you. From that day forward you have shown me that I could trust you. You captured my heart with the love that you have shown me, and I thank God today for allowing you to find me. My heart belongs to you, and as my hands are in your hands, I'm asking you not to let go of it and hold on tight. I thank God today for making you my husband and making me your wife. I promise to love you with everything that is inside of me, for I was created for you and you were made for me. I promise to love you till death do us part, and as we embark on this new start of our lives, I promise to be there for you and to stand by your side, through sickness and pain, wellness and joy, no matter what comes our way. I Kisha Carrington stand here today, in the company of these witnesses to say, Reggie I love you and no one can take your place. Destined to be together, you and me, our love eternally, because Reggie, you complete me."

Kisha places Reggie's wedding ring on his finger. The wedding ceremony, though simple, is one that has touched every heart there and it has created memories that are sure to last a lifetime. Reggie and Kisha hold each other's hands and they look at Pastor Gorham.

"Reggie and Kisha-" Pastor Gorham said. "I now pronounce you man and wife. You may kiss your bride."

They lovingly share a passionate kiss and close hug, family, friends and all gathered, start to whistle, cheer, clap, whoop and holla in celebration congratulating them. As family and friends talk to each other, Reggie takes Kisha in his arms and looks at her. Kisha leans her head on his for a few seconds. She raises her head and softly caresses Reggie's face.

"I love you," Kisha said.

"And I do love you." Reggie said. "Forever."

They lean into each other and once again share a passionate kiss. Dray jumps into the middle of the circle, all eyes go to him.

"Since we're doing things a little different," Dray said. "I'm taking my cue from Reggie over there. So... Rather than wait, Nola and I have an announcement." He looks over at Nola and motions to her. "Come here, come over here and you tell everybody."

Nola smiles, she comes into the circle and stands next to him. Dray wears an enormous smile as he puts his arm around her.

"Dray and I are..." Nola said. "Having a baby!"

Dray bends and does several fist pumps.

"Yeah baby! Yeah!" Dray said.

The room explodes with excitement as everyone cheers and celebrates with them on hearing their news. Dray turns Nola toward him and they kiss each other. Andre rushes into the middle of the circle. Dray and Nola rejoin the circle wearing huge smiles. Cliff and a few other guys high five Dray. While Shayna and Nola hug each other for a bit, they turn their attention to Andre. As he goes to speak, Andre puts his hand on his chest.

"Okay... okay. Oh my God, I'm nervous!" Andre said. "I was outside, trying to figure out when the best time would be." He looks at Reggie. "Then you two changed things. Which is great cause spontaneity is awesome, but then I'm standing trying to figure out what to do."

"You're rambling son," Moses said. "Get to the point."

"Right right," Andre said. He turns to Regina. "Gina, I'm so glad my mom had met you before the Lord called her home a few years ago. And besides my own mother, you are the most incredible woman I have ever known."

Regina looks on and listens to Andre, her eyes start to fill with tears.

"Besides God having His hand on my back, pushing me to learn more about Him and me just wanting to be a real Son of God, I want to be the best man I can be for you. I love you with all my heart Regina." He goes into his pants pocket. "This has been burning a hole in my pocket all day."

Andre takes out a small red velvet box, he goes over to Regina, takes a deep breath, as he goes down on one knee he blows it out and opens up the small box. Regina's eyes widen seeing his mother's vintage diamond engagement wedding ring set.

"Okay, here it goes," Andre said. "Gina there's no way I can promise that every day will be perfect because we're imperfect people. I can promise that I'll love you each and every second that we're together... be it until the Lord calls us home or up until Jesus returns. No matter which one comes first, and everything between now and then, I want you by my side through it all. So, will you marry me?"

Regina looks at Andre with tears roll down her cheeks and she slowly nods her head twice.

"Gina! He can't hear a nod!" Leah said. "You better speak up gurl!"

Regina swallows and smiles as she looks into Andre's eyes.

"Yes," Regina said. "Yes, I'll marry you."

The room erupts with yells from all celebrating Andre and Regina's engagement. Andre puts the engagement ring on her finger and they share a quick kiss with each other. As everybody cheers in celebration, Minister Thomas's cell vibrates, he checks his cell and picks up the call. He walks out the room basically unnoticed. James rushes into the middle of the circle as well. He's holding the hand of his plus one Sister Juanita Cantres.

"I just want to say." James said. "For all of those that thought I would never be in a relationship, I just wanted to let everybody know-DRAY." He holds up Juanita's hand. "Me and Sister Juanita Cantres are... Wait for it...
A Couple! Yes yes, that's right, we're dating!! Boo-ya!!"

Everybody cheers for James and Juanita, James holds Juanita's hand, they turn around and James struts back to their place in the circle. Reggie raises his hands in the air and motions to everyone, trying to get their attention.

"Alright everybody," Reggie said. "Now if there's no more announcements or proposals. The buffet is ready. So, lets enjoy the menu my mom put together and get to cutting that cake."

"Amen to that!" James said. "LET'S EAT!"

"He'll Work It Out" Chapter 8. Taryn C. Atkins

Minister Thomas is on his cell, speaking in a low tone and standing over in the corner by the elevators, near the window.

"Hey there little sister... I'm alright... Yeah, it's good to hear your voice too.. You're stuttering-What's the matter? Ivy, I know you, what's going on? Well, tell me... Will you just say it... See-now you're getting me upset... Haven't you learned yet? Ivy will you just tell me already! Okay... When?! Three months ago! He was supposed to call me first. Well, then you should have... Listen-I don't care, I still have a say, understand?! Whatever Ivy... You'll pay for it in June. Trust me. Now put him on the phone!"

Minister Thomas paces for a few minutes.

"Bryce, you took her anyway... What happened to discussing it? We had her on a specific routine all year, and we got the desired results.... Bryce.... I created the therapy you asked for, it worked better than expected, and you still took her for the procedure... She didn't need any further enhancements! When I allowed you to marry her, we had an agreement... Listen-had I known all this, I would of never let you pay for anything. I was looking out for us, but you-it's disgusting what you got her doing out there. No! Look, I just do what you ask me to do every June, and I do it because it's the agreement. We can end that agreement now! You heard me! No! I won't hold--"

Minister Thomas paces around once again.

"Look-" He turns back toward the window. "I'm not that twenty-one year-old kid anymore, I don't need anything from you! Ivy's grown. So this agreement is over, and if you mess with my life... I'm sure, your prestigious colleagues, would be surprised to learn about your deviant lifestyle... wouldn't they Dr. Wilkins? Especially... how you purchased and married a thirteen year-old girl, then groomed her, just for your perversion! I'm sure that would be an interesting read for them, so I'm done with you and Ivy."

"He'll Work It Out" Chapter 8. Taryn C. Atkins

Minister Thomas ends the call. He turns around, leans up against the window, closes his eyes and puts his head back.

Under his breath, he said, "God forgive me, but Ivy-it's for the best." *I'm not gonna let you ruin my life again.* He thought.

Minister Thomas stands there a few minutes, he hears a woman clear her throat. He raises his head opening his eyes, and sees Suzette leaning against the wall.

"I was heading back inside." Minister Thomas said.

As he made his way to the hall doors Suzette approached him.

"Before you go," Suzette said. "I'd like a word with you."

"It's the reception Suzette," Minister Thomas said. "We don't want to miss anything."

"Well," Suzette said. "The wedding party just started giving their regards to the couple. So we have time."

"Okay... What do you want?" Minister Thomas said.

"Well, Bryce and I go way back." Suzette said. "We've known each other for at least twenty years. When I first met him, he was simply Dr. Bryce Wilkins, but later we discovered, we had some of the same interest, even socialized in the same circles. He's the founder of the local Wilkins Foundation in Mississippi. You're from there right?"

"I'm from Mississippi, and I'm aware of it." Minister Thomas said,

"Well, a close friend of his," Suzette said. "He and his wife died in a plane crash. They left two children behind, their son, a young man of twenty-one and their adopted daughter, a little girl of ten. He used the foundation so no questions would arise about him helping them. A few years later, Bryce married a young bride of thirteen."

"Well, in Mississippi, it's legal to marry someone thirteen." Minister Thomas said. "That's with parental consent, of course, So, it's..." He makes quotation marks with his fingers. "Perfectly legal."

"Oh..." Suzette said. "No question about that-it's all the

"He'll Work It Out" Chapter 8. Taryn C. Atkins

stories behind it that are quite interesting."

"Stories?" Minister Thomas said. "Hmph, more like gossip and rumors."

"Allow me though, Bryce told me that for thirteen, his young bride showed such desire. Seeing that, he said she could easily be bred and prepared to be a specialized type of concubine."

"Okay, and where are you going with all this?"

"Please, this is merely the beginning of the story. See after their parents died, all this little girl had left was her older brother. This young man of just twenty-one, got full custody of his ten year-old little sister and became a parent overnight. The girls in town his age didn't want to be bothered with someone who had a kid, and neither did his buddies. His friends actually teased him about it. So, he finds himself all alone. The situation he saw himself in, made him angry. He began to resent his little sister. To him, she stole his youth and that fueled his resentment with a passion."

"Sounds like it was rough for him."

"It was, the stories say he adapted and since his little sister caused this great change in his life, he made sure, she adapted too. After all, she wasn't his blood sister. The girl was adopted, so... he made his ten year-old little sister his girlfriend and introduced her to everything that went along with it."

"Nobody knows that for sure," Minister Thomas said. "People have nothing better to do then come up with their own stories."

"I'm sure you're right," Suzette said. "Indulge me anyway. Bryce and this young man's father who died, they were in the military together; Bryce said when the boy was in his teens, unlike most teenage boys, who wanted to hear their war stories, and about all the weapons they used. This teenage boy was more intrigued with how the military got their enemies to talk. Bryce happen to look at the boys bookshelf one time while he was doing homework. Some of the titles were: Chinese Tortures, Military Interrogation, Tortures from the Middle Ages. This boy even had books on using plants, insects and animals for specialized tortures, isn't that interesting?"

"It's not unusual, every teenage boy is different. While some are into detective or adventure comics. Others read Sci-fi, Anime or Graphic comics. Boys will be boys after all, so... doesn't sound strange to me."

"Well, that teenage boy grew up to be that young man of twenty-one, who now extremely resented his little sister and was using her as his girlfriend. She was still a child, who frequently gave him a hard time. The stories said, when she did that, he would punish her for not obeying him. He would discipline her with what he knew best, and with what was naturally around them, be it plant, insect, or animal. The stories say, he even used the family foxhound. Now, don't you specialize in all those areas?"

"Some do, especially those from the country. Look, like I said before-" He laughs and huffs again. "Sounds like nothing more than rumors and gossip that come with every small southern bible belt backwater town, across the US. It doesn't mean it actually happened, because there's no actual proof of it." He shrugs his shoulder. "Who knows if its fact or fiction."

"Not finished," Suzette said waving her finger. "Since this young man didn't have friends anymore, he went online and found some local ones with a particular interest in little girls. When the little girl was unruly and got on his last nerves, this young man would have these parties and invite all the miscreants over. He would have his little sister tied up in one of the bedrooms upstairs, then let each one go inside and have their way with her. Stories be told, he resented his little sister so much, he sometimes even sat in the room and watched. Apparently he enjoyed watching her life be destroyed. See-as far as he was concerned she destroyed his."

Minister Thomas looks at his watch and huffs. He looks at Suzette and points toward the meeting room.

"Yeah okay." Minister Thomas said. "Can we go inside now?"

"Not just yet. This young man slipped up one time, and when he emailed the invite to these offenders, he sent one to Bryce. The email caught his attention because the subject was a statement he heard the young man say frequently. He mainly used it when he planned to use the little girl as his girlfriend. The statement and the subject of those invites said: "It's Time to Poison Ivy" Ivy's your sister's name, correct? Wait... I know! I'm sure there are many women named Ivy, plus with all the hackers nowadays, anybody could have sent that email."

Minister Thomas looks at Suzette and laughs.

"Ever play telephone? The first person tells a story, by the time it gets to the sixth person, everything's all distorted. So again, nothing more than he said, she said." Minister Thomas's jaw clenched as he glared at Suzette. "Look, I'm getting tired of this."

"Tolerate me a bit longer," Suzette said placing a hand on her hip. "I'm just getting to the best part. I saw Bryce at an auction a few months ago, after, we had drinks back at his home in Connecticut. Ivy was out of town at the time. While I was there, Bryce showed me tapes of her dating back to when she was ten."

"Tapes?" Minister Thomas said. He shakes his head a bit, then glances at his watch. "Yeah... I really don't think so."

"Oh, yes he does." Suzette said. "Plenty in fact. He keeps them different places, even has them stored in a safe deposit box somewhere."

"I'm supposed to be afraid of some tapes? That's what Bryce thinks-well, I don't intimidate easily. Why should I believe you anyway? I grew up in that house; I would have noticed something."

"Not according to Bryce. See, he had a friend's son named Paton, you two went to school together, right? You know Paton has a learning disability, that apparently you teased him about. Turns out, he's creative at installing those tiny surveillance cameras. When Bryce asked him to install them, Paton happily set them up when Bryce took you and your sister to Disneyland. Surprise! It's a small world after all."

"That's supposed to be funny?"

"Oh come on, that's funny. Anyway-those tiny cameras are all over that cabin. I mean really, all over; I've seen a few tapes, some are actually right in front of you, but you'd never know it. The footage runs into equipment in the attic. Camera's have been there for years. Bryce said Paton installs new camera's every so often, he calls it remodeling. Every vile thing that young man did to his sister are on those tapes, including all those parties and everyone that attended. That young man's an adult now, and by the way, you've filled out nicely."

Minister Thomas jams his hands into his front pockets as he began to pace back and forth, staring at Suzette for the moment. As she takes note of him, she shakes her head a bit and smirks. Her phone sounds off with a ticker tape ringtone. She scans her text message then returns her attention to Minister Thomas. He lets out a harsh breath stopping short of being eye to eye with Suzette as he adjusts the sleeves on his jacket. He points at her as he steps a tad closer.

"You know what, go ahead..." Minister Thomas said. "Upload the videos, bombard the internet for all I care. People put out fake videos all the time, it's called editing. So whatever, I'm going inside."

The minister attempts to rush pass but she steps in his path.

"Bryce shared some other news with me," Suzette said. "He's held on to it a while because it might come in handy."

"Is that suppose to make me nervous? Cause I don't feel

myself shaking."

"My goodness, you're a cocky one aren't you? I think you just turned me on."

"Sorry darling, you're not my type."

"Right, you prefer adolescents."

"Funny."

"Oh honey, that wasn't meant to be. Now, that news I mentioned, Bryce apparently is the cardiologist for two people who attend the Full Gospel Temple. Their names are Elder Rayner and Sister Carlton, do you know them? Wait, isn't that the church you go to? And... the minister who just did the wedding, isn't he the pastor? Hmph."

Minister Thomas's whole countenance drops, he walks away for a moment heading over toward the window. Suzette slowly follows him over. He turns around, leans up against the window and threaded his hand through his hair as he glanced over at her. Suzette watches Minister Thomas as she smooths out her dress and folds her arms.

"So you know," Suzette said. "Bryce never planned to put those videos on the internet. Not at all. Instead, he selected the most illicit ones; Where Ivy was a child, experiencing all types of sadistic and perverse acts, being done by you, and several known pedophiles. He has them copied, packaged and ready to go out. He plans to send them to several police officials, patients of his who live in Mississippi, New York and Connecticut. From what I hear, pedophiles don't last long behind bars."

Minister Thomas body tensed, as he massaged the nape of his neck he slowly shakes his head.

"Bryce told me to tell you, he's looking forward to seeing you at the cabin in June. As stated in the agreement, and remember to bring Rudi with you like usual."

Minister Thomas stares at Suzette watching her move in front of him.

"Bryce actually recommended you to me, he said you're quite skilled with all that knowledge of yours. Well... I

"He'll Work It Out" Chapter 8. Taryn C. Atkins

recently acquired a rather wild stallion for my stable. He needs three months of intense training and reconditioning. I want all new and unique ways to do this, methods he'll never forget. Can you assist me?"

Minister Thomas wipes over his face with his hands shaking his head. When he removes his hands, he chuckles. This time, his laugh has taken on a corrupt and depraved undertone. He clears his throat and fixates on Suzette.

"Fine-you want to break him," Minister Thomas said. "I'll need to know as much about him as possible... His fears, what turns him on and off, all of it, and I'm going to need his medical records. This way the program I create to train and recondition him will be most effective. When it's over, he'll literally become whatever you want him to be. You just get me that information I need and I'll put it together. If you want, bring him to the cabin in June to start his training. I don't deal with all this stuff during the rest of the year. Only in June-got that!?"

"Alright, Mr. Minister," Suzette said nodding her head. "So tell me, is that what you did to Ivy?"

As he eyes Suzette his countenance turns cold.

"You best believe I did," Minister Thomas said. "Ivy deserved every twisted thing done to her too. I mean, she stole my life, so I savored taking hers. Bryce is her Master, he's done his part, but she was already thirteen when he got her. I'll always be her Owner; I got her at ten, sweet and impressionable. Yeah... I made her what she is, and once I broke her, it didn't matter that she was just ten." He snickers a bit. "Not to me anyway, because eventually she grew to love it. After all, she had no choice in the matter. Just like I had no choice. I'll never forget or forgive her. Every June I reinforce the words *I branded* on her at ten, making sure she don't forget the only thing she's good for is *"To Be Used."*

Suzette stares sharply into his eyes.

"And there they are," Suzette said.

"Who?" Minister Thomas said.

"I thought I saw them when we first met. You were looking across the dinner table at your sister when they peeked out for a moment."

"What? I don't know what you're talking about."

"You don't? All that rage, resentment and hostility you have for your sister. They're beastly now, all of them are, the revenge and hate. Plus several others are consuming you and that's what he wants. There's a part of you that still loves your sister, I don't know where right now, but it said in the bible somewhere-That love covers a multitude of sin. Try to remember that and forgive your sister. You don't have to let him win."

Suzette looks away.

I can't believe that still happens to me. She thought.

Suzette takes a few steps away from Minister Thomas, takes a deep breath and exhales as she goes back over to him.

"Can I share something?" Suzette said.

Minister Thomas nods his head okay. Suzette turns around and stands next to him as she leans back against the window.

"My mother was an avid church goer, for my mom it was Jesus all the way; Mom passed years ago when I was in my teens. Fast forward, I've been a dominatrix for about twenty-five years. During the Summer last year, I was driving in my car out in Lynbrook somewhere and listening to my music. I stop at the red light-I look over, there's a white Lexus SUV pulling up next to me. The woman driving had a chestnut complexion, a cheerful smile and a short curly doo going on. We both gave each other courtesy smiles and then looked forward."

"A few seconds later, I heard a horn beep but I paid no attention. The red light was taking forever. I heard a horn beep again, I looked over and it was her. She said something, but I couldn't hear her. I turned down my music, leaned over and mouthed excuse me I didn't hear you. She said to me, It's not over till it's over. Jesus loves you and you're called to be used for His glory. She then said, God wants you to know your mother's prayers for you weren't in vain. She said, Put your trust in Jesus, his hand is reaching out to you and it doesn't make a difference how far you've gone. The woman then said, She didn't know where I was at in my life, but that God said, He promised my mother while I was yet in her womb, that he had me in the palm of his hand and that nobody can pluck me out. The last thing she said to me was a scripture, it was: *"For I am the Lord: I will speak, and the word that I speak shall come to pass..."* The light turned green, the woman in the Lexus said God bless you and drove off."

Minister Thomas stands there listening to Suzette attentively as she continues telling him of her encounter.

"I froze and all I could do was sit there for a moment. I couldn't even drive off to catch her. I knew her license had *"Sonshp"* on it, minus the i. I remember all of it, as you see. It's the scripture the woman said that touched a part of me, a part I hadn't felt for years. You see, my mom, always quoted that scripture to me. She would tell me about God's promises, then show me in her Bible where God would speak a thing and then do it. I told you all that to say, no matter how it may look right now. Even with all that we've done, I don't know how or when, but those words that woman said they tell me. There's somebody greater watching over me, and there's a part of me that takes comfort in knowing that. So, regardless of how far out there we are, because I'm sure some people label us already damned, she said Jesus' hand is yet reaching out. That means it's attached to an arm that can reach who others deem unreachable, and I... I take comfort in that."

Suzette leans over, places her shoulder against his and lightly bumps him. Minister Thomas glances at her.

"So... There's still hope for *both* of us. Believe me, it's strange for me to be saying all this, but apparently it needs to be said. I'm sure God can help you get rid of all that hate and resentment, so you can forgive your sister."

Minister Thomas moves around and stand in front of Suzette toe to toe.

"Wait..." Minister Thomas said. "Did you just try telling me something about God? For real? Why would I listen to somebody like you?"

Minister Thomas looks at Suzette, laughs again turning away.

"Look, let me explain something." Minister Thomas said approaching Suzette. "When I leave the cabin and I'm back in New York, all those feelings go back in a box. I don't get caught up in all the guilt or condemnation anymore. I do what I'm supposed to do. On July 1st, I confess and repent, ask for forgiveness in Jesus name, and move on. Understand?" He stands beside her. "See, when June comes again, I go and give those feelings an outlet. It's one month out of twelve. We all mess up from time to time. I just choose my time, that's all. None of us are perfect. My once a year indulgence, doesn't make me like you, Bryce or Ivy." He walks away. "I'm going inside now but thanks for sharing."

Suzette folds her arms watching him casually stroll toward the wedding reception hall.

Under her breath Suzette said to herself rolling her eyes, "So that's given over to a reprobate mind."

Minister Thomas reaches for the door knob, the door opens and out walks Sister Carlton.

"Oh, I was looking all over for you." Sister Carlton said. "I've gotta go. Sister Richardson was baby-sitting my daughter but her mother was rushed to the ER. Could you please give me a ride home?"

"No problem."

"I don't know what to do now. My daughters only eleven, and I really don't want to leave her alone. I just started this new job, so I've already taken off twice because she was sick. I can't afford to take off again."

"Well if you want I'll watch her. I'm not doing anything

after this anyway."

"Really?"

"Yeah, Charlotte's been to the church. I'm sure she knows me."

"She knows you."

"Then it's up to you, do you think she'll be comfortable staying with me?"

"I'm sure she will, you're actually one of her favorite people at the church. Ever since you got her and the rest of the kids that ice cream during the summer, you're at the top of her list. She even calls you Uncle Thomas. So, I'm sure she'll enjoy spending time with you."

"I'm sure I'll enjoy being with her. You know, I've been wanting to tell you... you look beautiful Sister Carlton."

"Why thank you." Sister Carlton said blushing. "Call me Mavis."

"Well Mavis, call me Casey. I'm glad we came together. We never get the chance to talk much at the church."

"So true, I'm glad too."

"If you don't mind, I'd love for us to talk again sometime. I'd enjoy getting to know you better, you and Charlotte. I'd like *us* to get to know each other. Would that be alright with you?"

"That would be wonderful. I'm sure I would enjoy your company."

"Yes, I'm sure you and Charlotte, could easily adapt to me being around. So, let's get going."

"Okay, can we take the stairs."

"Sure."

They get ready to walk around the corner but Sister Carlton stops short. She turns to Minister Thomas.

"You know I love my daughter Casey," Sister Carlton said. "And... Please don't take this the wrong way... but I wanted to enjoy being out for a change. It's been a long time since I had any real time to myself... I don't regret having her. You would think by now I'd be used to things... It's just my whole life has changed. Charlotte's just a little girl, all she wants is her mother there all the time. She doesn't understand I need time for myself too. I'm... I'm sorry."

"Hey, I get it." Minister Thomas said putting his arm around her shoulders. "Look you do live right around the corner from me. If all goes well tonight with us, when you need a day or two for yourself, give me a call. I'll take care of Charlotte for you."

"Would you!" Sister Carlton said. "That's such a blessing, you just don't know. Now are you sure about doing this?"

"Sure, I can do that for you." Minster Thomas said. "Maybe in the future, once Charlotte is used to spending time with me, you'll be able to go on vacation for a week or so by yourself. You deserve a life too. Besides, God wants us to be well rounded people. We should have a life inside and outside the church, right?"

"You are so right Minister Thomas."

"After all, I'm sure Charlotte could understand you taking some time for yourself. Besides, now she'll have Uncle Thomas to keep her distracted. We'll have to be patient of course, but if we develop a routine, like me watching her two to three times a week, she'll get used to me. Charlotte's eleven, she'll adapt."

"Listen, if I can just get a day or two for myself out of this. She'll have to adjust."

They move toward the staircase door as they continue talking.

"Exactly," Minister Thomas said as his hand when to the middle of her back. "So you ready to go? You know, I hope this isn't too forward, hopefully in the future maybe we three can even go on a vacation together. I've got a cabin up in Mississippi, it's breath taking during the summer months, especially in June. I'm sure you two would love it there. I'm sorry-excuse me for being impetus, I enjoy your company that's all. Lets just see how things go tonight."

"No need to apologize, I like a man who knows what they

want. I'm sure things will go well, Charlotte's a good girl, not disrespectful and she listens to her elders," She chuckles. "I'm sure you won't have any trouble with her. You've taken a huge weight off my shoulders Minister Thomas. Just to be able to get a moment to myself is great. Thank you so much Casey."

"The pleasure's mine Mavis. Now let's get you home."

Suzette shakes her head watching Sister Carlton and Minister Thomas exit through the staircase door. Suzette then goes inside the hall to finish enjoying the reception. Footsteps are heard on the floor, and from around the corner steps out Brother Marcus Hamlin. He walks over to the staircase doors with a blank expression, shaking his head as he places his hand on the staircase door as it closes.

"Man Casey, why?" Brother Hamlin said. "Jesus..."

~FOUND OUT~

A week has passed, it's the second week of February. Although it's rather chilly out the inside of Lexi and Gigi's loft is feeling toasty. On this Saturday afternoon, Gigi sits on the far side of the sectional in a pretty silky robe and nighty. As Gigi talks on her cell, she leans back on the sectional crossing her legs.

"I'll see you soon," Gigi said in reserved tone. "Right now it's..." She looks at the time on her cell. "It's just 12:05... Hey, I know you don't want to do this, but I really need you to... I do, which is why it's not easy for me either... I've tried... Well, since I've found out, I've given her chances and nothing... Look... I've got to do this... Okay- thanks for coming Gina. It's snowing so drive carefully. So we're gonna say, around 2 p.m.? Alright... Bye."

Gigi ends the phone call. She looks at her cell, takes a deep breath, and exhales putting her cell on the coffee table. Gigi gets up from the sectional and stretches as she walks to the kitchen. She gets a glass out of the kitchen cabinet, goes to the fridge and grabs the container of orange-pineapple juice. As Gigi stands at the island pouring herself a glass she hears a door open in the hallway and footsteps draw near making their way down the hall. As Gigi nurses on her juice, she smiles when out of the corner of her eye she observes Cassandra stepping out of the hall. Cassandra's hair is tousled about and she's wrapped in a burgundy bed sheet. Their eyes lock on each other as Cassandra leans against the frame of the hallway entrance.

"Mmm, hello," Cassandra said with a satisfied smile.

"Good afternoon baby," Gigi said. "Sleep well?"

Cassandra looks at Gigi with a extended smile and stretches.

"Mmm, you know I did," Cassandra said.

"Very hot..." Gigi said. "You wear that bedsheet well."

"It was worth it," Cassandra said moving to the island. "Why didn't you wake me up?" She sits down on one of the barstools. "I would have cooked us breakfast."

"Well, I love watching you sleep." Gigi said. "Besides, I figured you needed your rest." She drinks some of her juice. "After keeping you up all morning."

"You don't hear me complaining." Cassandra said.

"No, I don't... Want some juice?"

"Yes, apple please." Cassandra stretches again. "So its true, Lexi and Dana left for Vegas yesterday, and we have the loft all to ourselves for two weeks."

"Yep," Gigi goes to the kitchen cabinets. "It's only me and you for two weeks. Lexi extended their vacation."

"Yeah I know, Dana wanted to stay after Valentines."

Gigi gets another glass out the cabinet and goes to the fridge. Cassandra gestures for her to wait just before it closes.

"Pass me the container with the pineapples please." Cassandra said.

"Okay." Gigi said.

Gigi places the glass of juice and Tupperware down in front of Cassandra. Gigi then gets two forks out of the kitchen drawer and takes a seat on one of the barstools. She hands Cassandra a fork and they both snack on the pineapples in the container between them.

"We've got two weeks," Gigi said. "Did you take time off."

"Of course," Cassandra said. "I'm all yours."

"Same here," Gigi said. "I'm sure CCNY will be okay without me. So, what do you want to do?"

"Well," Cassandra said. "It's already snowing and New York is expecting a storm. We went shopping, got more than enough food, snacks and drinks. Plus, all the seasons of The Walking Dead. So you can catch me up on all things regarding the Zombie Apocalypse. I think we're set."

"What if cabin fever hits?" Gigi said.

"I don't get cabin fever sweetheart," Cassandra gets up from the barstool and walks to the entrance of the hallway. "If you happen to get all irritable and restless." She turns to Gigi walking backward up the hall, unwrapping the bedsheet. "I can figure out something to keep you busy," The sheet falls to the ground. "I'm going in the shower, feel free to join me. I'd love your help, with those... hard to reach places."

"I already took a shower."

Cassandra stops in front of Gigi's bedroom door.

"So,"

Gigi slowly shakes her head as she watches her. Cassandra smiles seductively at Gigi, as she enters her bedroom. After a minute or two Gigi hears the sultry vocals of a cherished female jazz singer come on and a second or two later the shower starts running.

Gigi gets up from the barstool and walks up the hallway to her bedroom. She enters taking off her robe and throws it on her bed. While Gigi stands by her queen size bed gazing into the bathroom, she takes in Cassandra's silhouette behind the shower door and studies her for a few moments. Gigi notices the clock on her nightstand changed to 12:30 p.m.

Under her breath, Gigi said to herself, "Gina won't be here till 2. I got time." She admires Cassandra's silhouette once again. *Mm-hmm, one last time.* She thought.

When Gigi goes to take off her nighty, she glances toward her big dresser and her eyes go to the picture of her with her grandmother. She looks at it for a few seconds, shakes her head and sits down on the bed. Gigi closes her eyes, takes a deep breath, and as she slowly exhales she opens her eyes. Gigi looks over at the picture on the dresser once again.

Under her breath, Gigi said, "Yeah I know it's not right, but she deserves it too grandma..." She looks away. "Romans 12:19, Vengeance is mine; I will repay, saith the Lord." She looks toward the bathroom. "It's not fair, not after what she's done to me, to my mother." She releases a harsh breath. "Psalms 105:15, Touch not mine anointed and do my prophets no harm." She shakes her head. "After all she's done... All the lies she's told... Her? Your child... I haven't done half the things she has..."

"Baby," Cassandra said. "Where are you? I could use your warm sexy body right about now. It's getting cold in here."

"Well, I wouldn't want that," Gigi looks heavenward.

Sorry, I need her. She thought.

Gigi takes off her nighty, drops it on the carpet and goes to the shower. She steps in, closes the shower door behind her and two silhouettes merge.

About an hour has passed... Gigi's wearing an adorable Old Navy pajama set standing in the living room talking in a inconspicuous tone on her cell.

"Where are you?" Gigi said. "Okay you're in the elevator... The door is unlocked, when you come in go sit down in the living room... I'll keep her in the bedroom for a little while... She's drying her hair right now... she won't hear anything when you open the door... I'm gonna hang up."

Gigi walks over to the hallway and goes to her bedroom door. She still hears the hair dryer blowing in her bathroom. Gigi stands back from her bedroom door so Cassandra doesn't see her standing there. Gigi sees the front door slowly slide open, Regina comes in and pushes the door shut. Regina walks softly down the hallway, passing by Gigi, and continues down the hall into the living room. On the far side of the sectional, she takes off her coat, folds it and takes a seat. Regina fidgets in her seat repositioning herself a few times.

> *This is gonna be something.* Regina thought. She closes her eyes. Under her breath, she said. "Okay Lord, I'm here. Father, give me the right words to say for this situation. I sure can't do this without you. In Jesus name, Amen."

Regina takes a deep breath and exhales. She sits back on the sectional and waits for Gigi and Cassandra to walk out. Gigi goes to her bathroom and steps inside, Cassandra's in the bathroom wearing a charming classic Burberry check pajama set. Gigi smiles watching Cassandra standing at the bathroom sink, looking in the oval wall mirror while blow drying her hair.

> "Pleased with how the day is going?" Gigi said with gleam in her eye and a raised eyebrow.

Cassandra stops what she's doing, eyes Gigi as her mouth curves into a smile. She gives Gigi a full once-over as she draws in her lower lip between her teeth, and finally their eyes meet.

> "Mm-hmm," Cassandra said. "Thoroughly," She winks, kissing at Gigi. "And you?"

> "Definitely," Gigi blushes wearing a grin.

Cassandra readjusts herself in the bathroom mirror and continues blow drying her hair.

> "So, the agenda for the rest of the day is..." Gigi said.

> "You cook lunch... While we eat, we'll watch at least half of the first season of The Walking Dead, have some dessert, we'll play some Monopoly or Scrabble for a while on Lexi's PS4... I'll beat you real bad on Lexi's PS4, we'll talk some, flirt some, have another earth moving, multi-orgasmic lovemaking session, to which..." She points to Cassandra. "I'll knock you out again. Then... I'll come in the bathroom, point to myself in the mirror and proceed to say-that's how you do it."

> "Well," Cassandra said. "I see you've got the rest of day

all worked out."

"I do."

Cassandra finishes her hair, unplugs the dryer and puts it in the cabinet under the sink.

"Umm, you've forgotten a few things on your agenda."

"Like what?"

Gigi leans against the bathroom door, Cassandra draws near, grasping the tassels on Gigi pajama pants and pulls her close as she leans against the door frame.

"Some of us have our own agenda..." Cassandra said.

"Oh really..." Gigi said. "And what would that be?"

"My agenda would say... After I cook lunch, I kiss you on the neck... While watching The Walking Dead, I cuddle up close to you and whisper in your ear-I love you... After that earth moving session, we spoon and fall asleep in each other's arms, but... Since all that's not included on yours." Cassandra strolls to the bedroom door and looks back at Gigi. "Guess that won't be happening."

Cassandra walks out the bedroom with Gigi following close behind.

"Now, Hold on... Wait a second."

"No no..." Cassandra walks down the hallway. "I'm gonna go start lunch. That's on your agenda, right?"

They walk out the hallway, Cassandra heads to the kitchen and Gigi goes to the side of the island near the sectional. She pulls out one of the barstools and sits down. The way Gigi's positioned Cassandra can't see Regina sitting on the sectional in the living room. Gigi looks at Regina and motions for her to come stand by her. Cassandra goes to the fridge, opens it, takes note of what's inside then closes it. Regina places herself next to Gigi but leans against the back of the sectional. Cassandra's back is still to them. Cassandra walks to the kitchen counter, grabs the cordless phone and begins to dial.

"You know what, I don't feel like cooking." Cassandra said. She looks at the phone and starts to dial. "I do feel like Dallas BBQ's, and they deliver. I'm calling the one on 73rd and 3rd." She turns to Gigi and notices Regina.

"Hey Gina, so what do you want baby?"

Regina wiggles her fingers at Cassandra as the cordless phone slips from her hand, speechless and frozen Cassandra's eyes meet Regina's.

"Wow, you two know each other already." Gigi said.

"Well, let me ask a few questions then. Oh wait-How rude am I. Let me formally introduce you two."

Cassandra picks up the cordless phone and leans against the kitchen counter, folding her arms as she purposely looks off to the side toward the kitchen windows.

"Cassandra darling." Gigi said looking at her. "Please look at me."

Cassandra takes in a deep breath and exhales as she looks into Gigi's eyes.

"This is my younger sister Regina." Gigi said. She looks at Regina. "Regina, this is Cassandra Pauls, my girlfriend... She's the first person I've ever fallen in love with. She was at Game Night last month, the same day you and Aunt Leah showed up. You missed each other by minutes, she said, she had to rush off to take care of some business." She looks at Cassandra. "I'm pretty sure she saw the text from Aunt Leah on my phone."

Gigi reaches into her side pajama pocket, takes out a business card and looks at it.

"Regina, you gave me this business card that night, which is from a Minister Cassandra Pauls. Right?"

"Yes... I did." Regina said.

Gigi looks at Regina and points to Cassandra.

"Gina, is that Minister Cassandra Pauls, from Full Gospel Temple, where you, our parents and where grandma attended?"

Regina glances at Cassandra, nods looking at Gigi.

"Yes... She is." Regina said.

"Gina, is she also mom's friend and tutor from college?"

Cassandra slowly approaches Gigi.

"Yes." Regina responded. "Gigi, come on!"

"I'm not finished... Is she the one at the airport with mom that day, when you were little? Is she the one that left for California?"
"Yes, she is."
"Well Gina, I've got some new information about my girlfriend here, that mom told me herself. Did you know-"

Cassandra stands nervously by the side of the island near Gigi, drumming her fingers on top of the island as she shifts her weight from one foot to the other while listening to Gigi and Regina.

"Mom told me," Regina said. "Way before she came and talked to you."
"So you know already" Gigi said. "That my girlfriend, before she became "Minister Cassandra Pauls." Her and mom were lovers. Apparently, they had an affair right behind dad's back. He found out when he caught them together in that little cave part of the pool."
"Yeah, I know all about it." Regina said.
Cassandra touches Gigi's hand "Let me explain."
"Don't!" Gigi said snatching her hand away.
"When we first started I didn't know." Cassandra said. "Back in college, I never knew Regina had a sister."
"She's telling the truth," Regina said. "You lived with grandma and grandad at the time. She never even saw you."
"Wait a minute," Gigi said. She looks at Regina. "You're on her side about this!"
"I'm on God's side," Regina said. "Gigi, I'm here cause you asked me to come, but both of you are wrong. Both of you have backslidden, both of you need to go to the altar, repent and get right with God. Or, both of you are going to hell. Okay." Regina stands up and looks at Cassandra.
"Minister Pauls-"
"Don't you dare call her that." Gigi said.
"Oh please, Gigi!" Regina said continuing. "When I first learned all this I was mad too. I got over it. I had to. God

is a forgiving God. How can I expect him to quickly forgive me, if I can't forgive others."

Gigi sucks her teeth and abruptly gets up from the barstool. "Whatever!" Gigi said.

Gigi marches away from them toward the living room windows.

"Look," Regina said looking at Cassandra. "We've all made mistakes. I know you're not this terrible person, but you know what? Even if you are, God saved you for a reason. I don't know everything that happened to you along the way, or what caused you to give up on God. I know this-Jesus is still there for both of you." She looks over at Gigi. "And for you, love covers a multitude of sins, regardless of your past, present or future mistakes; God still loves you. It doesn't make a difference if you think you're too far gone. Jesus is still right there for you. And he's waiting for you to give him a chance."

Cassandra feels her eyes flood with tears, and to fight back her emotions she pretends to cough a little.

"Excuse me, Gina." Cassandra said clearing her throat.

Cassandra walks to the fridge and grabs a bottle of water. While Cassandra takes a few sips, Regina walks away and to the far side of the sectional.

"I know y'all don't want to hear what I have to say," Regina said. "But it needs to be said. I think where people miss it, they get saved thinking they can change and fix themselves." She puts on her coat. "We can't fix or change ourselves, that's why we need Jesus. If we're honest with God, if we confess and own up to our sins, there's deliverance through Jesus. Okay... I've said all that God wanted me to say." She looks out the living room windows. "I've got to go, the snow is really coming down now. Andre's waiting in the car and I don't want us to get stuck."

Regina heads over to the hallway but she stops at the end table by the sectional. Gigi looks over at her sister and Cassandra. Regina looks at Minister Pauls and smiles.

"Love you Minister Pauls," Regina said. "And I'm praying for you."

Gigi rolls her eyes, as she loudly sucks her teeth and goes back to looking out the living room windows.

"Love you Gigi-Oh, I forgot... Two things, first-the doorman said the building's parking lot door is broken, no car can get in or out until sometime Monday. Also, Mom knows nothing about you two. So, I'm asking both of you to please keep it that way." She looks at Cassandra. "I saw you two talking at the wedding. Mom said everything's been resolved between you two, correct?"

"It has," Cassandra said.

"Great-mom's in a good place and I don't want to interrupt what God is doing with her. So please, don't say anything to her about this alright?"

"Sure," Cassandra said.

"Gigi... alright?" Regina said.

"Fine," Gigi said.

"Okay, I'm gonna go," Regina said. "Remember sis, when you two discuss all this. When you point at her, you got four fingers pointing right back at you. Both of you did your share of wrong."

"Isn't Andre waiting for you Gina?" Gigi said.

"Yeah alright. Love you." Regina said.

"Love you," Gigi said. Be safe, and don't forget to text me when you get home."

"Alright, See ya Minister Pauls."

"See ya Gina."

Regina heads down the hallway to the front door. Gigi looks over at Cassandra and huffs.

"Minister Pauls... .Hmph Please,"

They hear the front door slide open and shut. Gigi promptly walks down the hallway. Cassandra hears a door open, after about a minute she hears a door close. Gigi returns carrying bedding and angrily throws them on the sectional.

"You can use the bathroom in the hall or in Lexi's room,

but you're sleeping out here. Whatever time that garage door is fixed on Monday, you can get out and I don't want to ever see you again."

"Gigi, we've got to talk."

"Not now... Probably not ever."

Gigi rushes down the hallway to her bedroom, Cassandra winces hearing the door loudly slam. Gigi dashes over to her bed collapsing on it, burying her head in a pillow, trying to release the throbbing pain within her heart by screaming and pounding her fist into her pillow repeatedly.

In the hallway beside Gigi's bedroom door, Cassandra sits on the floor leaning against the wall. She overhears Gigi's muffled howls, she places a hand over her own mouth as tears cascade down her face like torrential rain. Her other hand lays over her chest, dealing with her own heart's agony as it suffers from Gigi's distress.

Moments later Cassandra enters Gigi's bedroom. Gigi lays on her side under the covers, holding the pillow over her face, trying to hide from view her tears that continue to flow. Cassandra moves to the side of the bed and notices Gigi's pajamas bunched up on the floor. Cassandra disrobes, lifts the covers and slips in behind Gigi. They spoon; Cassandra wraps her arms around Gigi and lays her head softly on Gigi's back. As Cassandra holds Gigi close, her tears flow again and Gigi feels them on her skin as she weeps.

"I'm sorry... I'm so... so... sorry." Cassandra said.

A minute or two passes and Gigi turns to face her. Cassandra's head rest on Gigi's chest, their arms wrap around each other and they lay together feeling the warmth of each others skin. In the quietness, they hear each breath the other takes. When Cassandra's ear hears the beat of Gigi's heart, she pulls her closer.

"I didn't mean for this to happen," Cassandra said. "I love-"

"Don't say it-" Gigi said. "Please."

"Gigi, I just want you to know how much I love-"

"No! Just... Make love to me."

"Gigi--."

"Please Cassandra..." Gigi moves on top of her and kisses her throat. "Please..." Gigi kisses her ear and whispers.

"Make love to me..."

"If it's the last time, Gigi... then say it."

"Cassandra..." Gigi kisses and sensually bites the side of Cassandra's neck.

Cassandra changes places with Gigi and looks into her eyes.

"Say it!"

As they look into each others eyes. Gigi takes a deep breath, and exhales, running her fingers through Cassandra's hair.

Gigi silently mouths, "I love you."

"And I love you." Cassandra said.

Gigi and Cassandra focus on one another, trying their best to escape and forget about everything between them for just a few hours, losing themselves in each other once again.

It's now around 10 PM at night. Gigi has on a NY Giants, candid, plaid flannel pants and tank sleep set. Cassandra wears a black plaid DKNY boyfriend sleep shirt with black biker shorts underneath. The bedding Gigi threw on the sectional earlier lays next to the end table.

They sit at opposite ends of the sectional, with sofa pillows behind their back, legs straight out and feet crossed. Gigi's sitting up while Cassandra's laying down. They sit in silence, but every so often one will look at the other, stare for a moment, get ready to say something, stop and look away. This process repeats itself for thirty minutes before they finally lock eyes.

"So..." Cassandra said.

"So..." Gigi said.

Gigi gets up from the sectional, Cassandra sits up as she watches Gigi head over to the kitchen. Cassandra fixes the pillow behind her and sits up. She watches Gigi go to the fridge, open it, sees her grab the bottle of wine and closes it.

Yes please, drink some wine. Cassandra thought.

Gigi gets ready to walk away from the refrigerator, but glances over at Cassandra. Gigi looks at her for a few seconds, turns around, and puts the bottle of wine back inside. She grabs a bottle of water, instead.

I don't need any wine right now. Gigi thought.

"He'll Work It Out" Chapter 8. Taryn C. Atkins

Gigi closes the fridge and as she goes to the island. Cassandra notices Gigi opening a bottle of water.
Dag... Cassandra thought. "I thought you were getting some wine, cause I wanted some."
"I changed my mind," Gigi said and drank some water.
"Well, I want a glass." Cassandra said.

Cassandra gets up off the sectional. As Gigi goes around to the other side of the island, she takes one of the barstools, moves it closer to the sectional and sits down. Cassandra walks to the fridge and proceeds to prepare her own glass of wine.
"So, what do we do about this?" Cassandra said.

Cassandra looks at Gigi as she takes a healthy sip of her wine. Gigi crosses her legs, as she drinks some of her water. Gigi puts the bottle on the island, looks off to the side, and takes a deep breath. As Gigi exhales, her eyes return to Cassandra's and they exchange looks.
"Gigi... What do you want us to do?" Cassandra said.
"Well, I'll tell you what we're not doing," Gigi said. She looks away. "I don't want to say this, but I know I've got to," She looks at Cassandra. "We can't be together." Gigi motions to her bedroom. "Not like that anymore, and I'm serious. That was the last time." She points at Cassandra. "Its gotta be that way for both of us."
"Only Gina knows," Cassandra said picking up her glass she heads toward the island. "And I think we're good together." Cassandra comes near Gigi and leans against the back of the sectional. "And I do mean in every sense of the word." She reaches out and softly caresses Gigi's arm. "Baby come on, you've got to admit that."

Cassandra nurses on her wine as they talk.
"Yes," Gigi said. "I do love being with you, spending time with you, all of it, but regardless... It still has to end."
"See, that just doesn't make sense to me." Cassandra said walking away, she puts her glass on the island. "This is something we both want." She turns to Gigi and points toward the bedroom. "We both said we love each

other in there." She comes over to Gigi. "Gigi I don't get that."

Cassandra moves into the space between Gigi and the island. Gigi watches Cassandra as she gets closer. They stare deeply into each other eyes.

"Cassandra, we can't do this."

Cassandra reaches out and softly caress the side of Gigi's face.

"Gigi, this works, we work..."

"Look... We can't..."

Gigi looks away, Cassandra tenderly guides Gigi's face back to focus on her. She then sensually takes Gigi's face in her hands.

"Gigi this doesn't have to end. You know we both want this."

Cassandra moves in to steal a kiss. Gigi raises her head and moves in also. Their eyes close but before their lips touch, Gigi eyes open and she moves her face away. When Cassandra feels Gigi move she releases a soft gasp.

"No, I... I can't..." Gigi gets up and moves away from Cassandra. "We can't do that anymore."

Cassandra abruptly turns toward Gigi.

"Why?!"

Gigi swiftly turns to Cassandra.

"You know why, Minister Pauls!" Gigi said grabbing her bottle of water. "Oh and I still don't believe that!"

Gigi walks away, Cassandra rushes over to her, reaching out grabbing Gigi's hand.

"Gigi wait a second!" Cassandra said.

Gigi snatches her hand away as she turns in Cassandra's direction.

"No you wait! Your a minister and attend my family's church! Seriously! And then, you say nothing, but hide it! Are you kidding me! Didn't you think I'd want to know that!? Now! I'm suppose to just believe you didn't plan any of this, right?!"

Gigi walks away from Cassandra again rushing into the living room and Cassandra follows after her.

"There was no way I could tell you," Cassandra said.
"And you not think this was some elaborate seduction."
Before Gigi sits, she turns to Cassandra.
"Wasn't it though, Cassandra?" Gigi said.
"No, it wasn't." Cassandra said.
"You sure about that."
"There's no scheme. You're just determined to find one."
"That's because, I'm sure there's one."

Gigi sits at the far end of the sectional. Cassandra gets ready to sit by her, but Gigi points directing to the other side.
"Sit over there," Gigi said.
"Fine," Cassandra said.

Cassandra walks to the island, gets her glass of wine and returns to sit on other side of the sectional. Cassandra softly sucks her teeth putting her glass on the coffee table. She tucks one leg under her as she faces toward Gigi.

"Happy now?" Cassandra said motioning to the space between them. "Is that enough space for you?"
"Yes, it is," Gigi said. "And let's keep it that way, because apparently you don't know the meaning of the word *no*."
"Come on Gigi!" Cassandra said. "Now there's a motive behind me wanting to kiss you too?"
"All I'm saying is," Gigi said. "There's no longer personal space, when we get close. We let our desire for each other just take over, and right now we need to seriously talk."
"Personally, I think you're over thinking things."
"Oh my goodness! Really Cassandra, that's how you want to play this?"

Gigi laughs leaving her seat shaking her head in disbelief.
"I'm just saying," Cassandra said. "You're letting your mind run away with this conspiracy of yours. I do have a right to voice my opinion right? Free country and all."
"Cassandra we've been together since my grandmother passed." Gigi said. "That's about seven months now. I know how to work what I got, and baby, you know you do too." Gigi laughs again. "So please, don't sit there, and

act like we don't know how to get to each other. Cause if that was the case, *we* wouldn't be sitting here in our third set of clothes, now would we?"

Cassandra reaches out grabbing the sofa pillow closest to her and sucks her teeth. She glances over at Gigi putting the pillow behind her back. Cassandra lays back on it crossing her legs and folding her arms as she stares at the ceiling for a moment.

"Actually," Cassandra said. "I'm in my second set of clothes."

They look at each other, Cassandra smiles trying to lighten the mood with some humor but Gigi just rolls her eyes.

"Nevertheless," Gigi said taking a seat. "My points has been made."

They sit in silence for a few moment or two.

"Okay... You want to talk," Cassandra said. "Where should we start?"

"When did you meet my mother? Gigi said picking up the bottle of water. "Better yet, how old was she when you two met? From what I understand, you were her tutor when she was finishing up her Masters."

Gigi takes a few gulps of water.

"I was 25, Shay was--"

Gigi stops drinking her water mid gulp and looks at Cassandra.

"Wait-Shay?! Oh no... No Shay, let's just keep it Shayna, thank you. I don't want to hear none of your little nicknames or anything, alright? I'm still processing the fact that my mom and I shared the same lover. I'm still freaked out over that one, okay?"

"Well, you two didn't actually share me..."

Gigi drinks from her bottle of water again, but stops to glare at Cassandra as she sits up and takes few sips of wine.

"Don't go there." Gigi said.

"I'm not," Cassandra said. "I just don't think *share* is the right word."

Gigi continues to stare at Cassandra.

"Cassandra."

"Anyway, I was 25 and Shayna was 28 when we met at

Hofstra. I had finished my Masters in Psych and Accounting. I was in my residency at New York Presbyterian at the time. For extra money I would tutor at Hofstra and do personal accounting."

"You were 25 and already finished 2 Masters. When did you get your Bachelors? Well, for that matter-when did you graduate from high school?"

"Learning, it came easy to me; Teachers told my parents I processed information quick. So, I've always been in advanced classes and driven. I graduated high school at 16, got both Bachelors at 21, decided to continue and got both Masters at 25."

"So... You're not just intelligent, you're brilliant."

"Well, I'm no genius; I still had to apply myself and study."

Cassandra sits up, pushes the sofa pillow back against the arm of the sectional, scoots herself back to rest against it.

"Wait, I saw Minister, Dr. Cassandra Pauls on your card. So, you've got a Ph.D.?"

Cassandra confirms with a nod.

"Okay, you must have got saved at some point and time, you are a minister, did you study theology too?"

"Well, I got saved in 2000; I was out in California at the time. A patient of mine invited me to her church and I attended. The preaching and worship was wonderful, so I started to attend more often and considered it my first church home. One day, the pastor did the altar call as they do, and I found myself walking up the aisle to the altar." She laughs a bit and smiles, "I got baptized and filled with the Holy Spirit that day-I'll never forget it either. Anyway... After that, I wanted to make sure I knew all about the God I gave my life to; You know, study to show thyself approved. I attended theology school and went seminary. I earned my Bachelors and Masters in Theology, focusing on Biblical Counseling."

"Wow, your eyes just lit up talking about yourself... Sounds like you loved it, going to church, God, all of it.

What happen, why this double life?"

"Gigi, I... I'd rather not talk about all that right now."

"Cassandra you owe me a explanation! I deserve one."

"I'm not saying I won't talk about it. I'm just saying later, that's all... Maybe tomorrow, okay? I mean we do have two whole weeks together right."

"Alright... Fine... How old was my mom when you two met?"

"Shayna was 28."

"I'm 28 Cassandra, isn't that a coincidence?"

"I knew you were in your late 20's. I didn't know your exact age."

"Mm-hmm, okay."

"I didn't Gigi, honestly-I never knew your exact age, or that you were Shayna's daughter. Regina even told you that, I never even saw you back then, so how would I know."

"And how am I suppose to be so sure you didn't already know either? There's a lot I didn't know about you, isn't there. It's just when I look back at everything, I can't help but question things now... I mean every time I was vulnerable, you were there. You knew what to say and what to do. Knowing now, that you're a psychologist. Come on, what am I suppose to think."

Cassandra abruptly gets up, face tensing with eyes intensely fixed on Gigi.

"Think about the fact I'm in love with you! Why is it easier for you to believe I'm deceiving you!? Well, excuse me for thinking you felt the same way?!"

Cassandra snatches her glass off the coffee table and heads straight to the fridge, drinking down what's left, takes the wine out the fridge she refills her glass.

"Cassandra," Gigi said turning in her direction. "You can't be upset at me for having questions and doubts. I mean, there's so much you didn't tell me. I've given you chances, but you always sneak around the topic."

"You talk about me telling the truth," Cassandra said.

"You could have been honest with me, Gigi, You could have just came right out and asked me anything. Instead you set me up and get Gina involved. What was that!?"
Gigi jumps up from her seat.
"I had to make sure all the cards were on the table. You should've been honest with me from the jump, especially after we slept together." Gigi points toward the hallway. "I was honest with Lexi about us and our friendship is even better because I did."

Gigi grabs her bottle of water and takes a few sips. Cassandra returns the bottle to the fridge, takes her glass, cutting her eyes at Gigi she storms over to the living room window closest to the island, pulls a barstool out and sits down.

Cassandra nurses her wine gazing through the window; It's dark out but the city illuminates from its lights and the fresh blanket of snow transforming NYC into a lovely Winter Wonderland. After a few moments, Cassandra sits her glass on the island, she embraces herself and calmly rocks back and forth. Her head lowers for a few seconds then rises as she slightly turns to look over at Gigi.

"Gigi, every time I came here and we talked, I saw your turmoil from coming out. When your grandmother passed, and then with what happened between you and your mother, you were hurting so much. I just wanted to be there for you. That's all. When we made love that night, it felt so good to be with you, and for the first time, in a long time, it felt right. It wasn't a calculated move, Lexi and I had plans that night, remember?. You weren't even supposed to be home, but everything changed."

Cassandra's tears break free, she turns away fighting to hold them back. Trying to keep her sniffles quiet with her back to Gigi.

"I really didn't plan for this to happen between us, but it did." Cassandra's tears freely flow. "The last few months have been incredible, I thought you felt the same way... Am I suppose to regret falling in love with you? Well, I don't... I'm sorry but I don't regret any of this."

Cassandra buries her face in her hands allowing the dam of tears to break. Gigi gets up, rushes to the kitchen, pulls a few tissues from the box and goes to Cassandra. She hands them to her, taking them Cassandra catches her streaming tears.

"Calm down... Relax," Gigi said. She pulls over a barstool and sits. "I don't want you to regret anything. I don't regret being with you that first time, I needed you. I don't regret falling in love with you either."

Cassandra tries to calm herself. Gigi laughs a little using her fingers to comb Cassandra's hair.

"All this hair... I can't see you." Gigi combs Cassandra's hair to the side. "There you go beautiful,"

Cassandra smiles turning to Gigi, taking Gigi's hand in hers and looks into her eyes.

"Gigi, its been a long time since anyone could see me, I mean the real me; The me behind the physical part. You and only one other person has, and was able to love me and wanted me, for who I am."

Gigi takes a tissue and softly pats Cassandra's cheeks and chin, drying her tears.

"I'm not talking about Shayna either," Cassandra turns away once again. "We were platonic friends for a while before getting intimate. I was just a distraction for her anyway, Shayna never really loved me."

Gigi softly caresses her back. Cassandra lets out a harsh breath brushing away left over tears.

"Looking back, it was only during their rough times that Shayna wanted to be with me."

Gigi tugs on the left side of Cassandra's shirt exposing her shoulder. Gigi leans in closing her eyes and breathes in the scent of Cassandra's perfume. Gigi's lips come together and delicately roam Cassandra's shoulder. The amorous, silky sensation of lips to shoulder causes Cassandra's lower lip to tremble. Her eyes flicker paying attention as Gigi's lips part applying a sensual kiss.

"Gigi..." Cassandra looks away with bated breath, licks her lips and exhales as her eyes return to Gigi. "Ahem..."

Gigi's eyes open looking up at her.

"Remember what you said." Cassandra said.

"Yes..." Gigi softly huffs. "Sorry." She covers Cassandra's shoulder and puts space between them. "Continue."

Cassandra turns herself in Gigi's direction and takes Gigi's hands in hers again.

"Gigi," Cassandra said. "There was a time after I got saved, that I really allowed Jesus to come in and have his way in my life. I even let this life go. I was living for God and growing too. I did at one time have a real relationship with God. You remember that story I told during game night? The one about my friend and the first lady?"

"Yeah, I remember." Gigi said.

"Lexi was right, that was me." Cassandra said. "You want to know what happen? Well, that story was about everything that happen to me, in church. What Lexi said, while looking at me, was exactly what those leaders said too. There's no way God would use someone who looked like me. That... I'd just be a distraction for some and a temptation for others."

"That was just the devil, trying to stop you." Gigi said.

"Well, when those physical situations kept happening with leaders in the church, and I kept hearing that over and over. I started to believe it, and I didn't try anymore. I thought God wouldn't be using me anyway. So, I just lived my life as Minister Pauls and Cassandra."

"That's serious church hurt."

"I'm telling you all this to say, that beside you, the only other person that could see me and loved the real me was my fiance at the time; He really loved me. I was going to him marry too. After everything with those leaders. I just broke it off with him and stopped even trying to go anywhere in God. After all, It was easier than trying and having God reject me. I've lived like this a long time. I'm sure he wouldn't want me back, after all I've done."

"Cassandra..."

Cassandra gets up and walks to the hallway.

"I'll be right back, my face is a mess. I'm just gonna go use the bathroom for a moment."

As Cassandra steps through the hallway entrance, Gigi stretches a bit.

"Okay, I'm gonna make us a snack." Gigi said stopping by the island. "Nothing heavy, it's late. Umm... How about some champagne, strawberries and whip cream?"

Cassandra's stops at the bedroom door and she looks at Gigi.

"Champagne, strawberries and whip cream?" Cassandra gives Gigi a look. "Really?"

"What? It's for consumption only, I swear."

"Yeah... okay. Make some popcorn too, this way it won't feel so much like a set up."

"You think you funny."

"I'm right though."

Gigi drops her head, then raises it wearing a smile looking at Cassandra.

"Okay... I'm busted."

"Mm-hmm, look who's scheming. Make the popcorn with movie theater butter please."

"Alright."

Cassandra strolls inside the bedroom. Gigi goes to the kitchen to prepare their snacks. Cassandra stands at bathroom sink letting water run, she grabs her wash cloth and drops it into the water; She stares in the mirror, takes in a deep breath and blows it out. Cassandra leans over the sink, dips her hands in the water, cups them and wets her face. She straightens up and gazes at her wet reflection for a few seconds. Cassandra wrings out the washcloth and wipes her face, then places it back on the rack. Her eyes go to image and contemplates her persona once again.

"Okay, you've got to do this-you can't put it off any longer, if you do it'll be worse. I gotta tell her."

Cassandra affirms to herself with a nod.

"Yes... she'll be upset and angry with me, but at least I'll be telling her the truth. And that's what she wants. I love her, and she deserves to know the truth. That's what's most important; She loves me. I love her. So hopefully, we'll get through whatever happens, alright."

Cassandra leaves the bedroom walks through the hall, she notices the lights have been dimmed and hears soft jazz playing. The candle fireplace is burning when she steps into the living room. A spread awaits Cassandra sitting on top of the coffee table. Gigi is seated on the living room carpet, holding a glass of champagne in each hand as Cassandra approaches her.

"I know what you're thinking," Gigi said with a smile.

"And no... this isn't a setup. I just wanted some ambiance, that's all."

Cassandra smiles a bit, kneeling down on the carpet with Gigi. She makes herself comfortable, leaning back against the sectional as Gigi hands her a glass of champagne. Cassandra takes the glass and they look at each other at the same time.

"Ambiance?" Cassandra said. "Feels more like setting the mood to me."

"Some would call it that," Gigi said. "This, is all strictly platonic."

"Lies and lesbian tales." Cassandra said.

"Well, that's my story and I'm sticking to it. So, cheers."

They clink their glasses together, and each take a healthy sip.

"Ooo, nice," Cassandra said.

"Taste good, right?" Gigi said. "I know I said a lot about personal space and all, but... can we just enjoy what we have right now... For this moment at least."

Gigi moves in a closer, Cassandra looking deeply into her eyes, studies them contemplating her next step.

"Look," Cassandra said taking Gigi's glass and places them on the coffee table. Her attention returns to Gigi. "I really need to talk to you,"

"Okay," Gigi reaches over, takes a strawberry and eats it. "Mmm, try one of these."

"I will, but lets talk first."

"Okay." Gigi brushes off her hands. "Alright, I'm listening."

"I left New York in 97. When I came back a few years ago

and joined Full Gospel Temple, I didn't know your family attended there. There are a lot of members, plus several services taking place on different days. I never ran into Shayna or Cliff until I was there for about 6 months. I saw Regina a few times, but I didn't even realize it was her until we talked. The last time I saw Regina she was nine."

"Okay." Gigi said.

"Once your mother knew I was attending there," Cassandra said. "She wasn't happy. I tried to make peace with her several times as a matter of fact, I wasn't there to cause her grief or anything like that, but she wouldn't be civil and it ticked me off; Especially with of our history, she was just unreasonable and it got me angrier."

"Right," Gigi nods. "I get being angry with her. I know how she treats me; I could just imagine how she acted toward you."

"Exactly, I did try though, but nothing worked. She tried to intimidate me one time, and I told her, if she told my secret, I would tell hers. I never intended to do that, but Shayna made me so angry."

Gigi leans back, folding her arms and listens.

"When I met Lexi at the bar, I didn't have any idea you were Shayna's daughter. How would I? Like Gina said, I never even knew Shayna had another daughter.."

"Right, you had no idea I existed."

"I didn't Gigi-I really didn't..."

"So what are you telling me?"

"We had those moments that showed there was chemistry between us and we found ourselves drawn to each other. We kept it in its place for a while, but we both knew we were attracted to each other and we wanted to be together, in every sense of the word. We clicked so fast, it was intriguing and exciting, but it caught me off guard Gigi."

With her brow raised Gigi agrees with another nod.

"I went to visit your grandmother; It was after she got out

the hospital. I'm one of the leaders at Full Gospel, we all had to visit and I wanted to. I loved Mother Babcock. Anyway, while there, I saw a picture of you and Shayna at your high school graduation. It was sitting on-"

"The fireplace mantle-I'm the one that put it there."

"When I took a closer look, that's when I realized *you* were Shayna's daughter."

"Oh really."

Cassandra sees Gigi's whole countenance change as Gigi's face goes blank.

"Wait! Okay, just wait!" Cassandra said. "Hear me out, just let me finish."

Gigi shifts her position, picks up the remote, cuts off the music and tosses the remote on the sectional.

"Go ahead, I'm listening." Gigi said.

"The way your mother was treating me made me so angry. I was at your grandmother's the same day you and Shayna had some big argument. Your grandmother said you left upset. When I came over that day and you were still upset. Being angry with Shayna at the time, and now knowing who you were, made it a perfect situation for me. I just wanted to get back at her! That's when I planned to sleep with you."

"I knew it!" Gigi rushes to her feet. "I'm so stupid!"

Cassandra gets up. Gigi folds her arms pacing about the living room.

"Baby... it started out as a way to hurt Shayna, but it changed Gigi. We got closer, my feelings for you grew and I just wanted to be with you. Before I knew it, I fell in love with you and before I got the chance to say it-You did. And I love you Gigi, I do."

"Well, that's just too convenient."

Angrily, Gigi continues pacing shaking her head in disbelief.

"I know you're upset, but can the fact we love each other count for something?"

"Why should it, huh?! Why?! Apparently it didn't to you

because you continued to lie to me."

"I wanted to tell you-I did... but after you said you loved me, I was so scared to tell you all this. I had a feeling you would react like this and I didn't want to lose you... Can you please understand that?"

Cassandra reaches out for Gigi's hand.

"Get away from me!"

Cassandra's tears fill her eyes backing away to give her space.

"Gigi, I know you're angry, and you have every right to be. I told you the truth though, regardless of what happens after this, you know everything now. I've poured my heart into this, my intentions were wrong, all it took was that first time and my feelings changed. Baby, all I want is you. Can you please forgive me?"

Gigi pays Cassandra not attention as she takes herself to the hallway entrance. Gigi gestures to the bedding by the side of the sectional.

"You can sleep out here, or in Lexi's room, that's where you started anyway."

"Baby, please-"

"Either way, I could care less what you do. I know one thing, my door will be locked so don't bother checking!"

"Gigi please," Cassandra said rushing to her.

Cassandra grabs Gigi's arm, she swiftly snatches it away.

"Don't you dare touch me!"

"Please, Gigi don't do this."

Gigi steps to Cassandra pointing in her face as angry tears roll down her cheeks..

"I didn't do this! You did!"

"Talk to me then, don't walk away"

"I'm done talking!"

Gigi goes to the intercom and buzzes down.

"Hi, is that garage door fixed yet? Right... Monday.... What time will it be ready? After 6 AM? That works... Oh, 6 PM..." She looks at Cassandra, huffs shaking her head. "Well, that's fine too... I was just checking... Thanks."

"Gigi please."

"He'll Work It Out" Chapter 8. Taryn C. Atkins

Gigi hangs up, cutting her eyes at Cassandra as she returns to the hallway entrance. Cassandra tries reaching out to her once more.

"Don't!" Gigi points, "At 6 PM on Monday, not 6:01 or 2, but at 6 PM on Monday, I want you gone! Don't call me... Don't email.. Don't text... Don't even think about sending flowers... None of it! As far as I'm concerned, this is over!"
"Gigi, please try and understand."
"No, you understand this! Whatever we had is over!" Gigi points to the door. "When you walk out that door on Monday. I never want ever see you again!"

Gigi quickly walks to her bedroom with tears streaming down her face, slamming the door and locking it behind her. Cassandra grabs the sofa pillow, buries her face crying profusely. Emotionally exhausted both eventually fall asleep.

Sunday comes. From dusk to early evening Gigi mainly stays in her bedroom, only coming out when necessary. Cassandra on the other hand with unsuccessful attempts through out the day realizes Gigi simply refuses to have anything to do with her.

It's a little after 11 AM on Monday. Earlier when Cassandra was headed into Lexi's room, Gigi was in the kitchen drinking a cup of coffee. Hair and makeup done, she's lounging in a Bugs Bunny, off the shoulder big t-shirt, black biker pants and white ankle socks. While Cassandra, was in Lexi's bedroom getting dressed for the day sporting a sexy oversize top, black leather skinny pants and black stilettos. Occupying Lexi's bathroom, as Cassandra brushes her hair out, she faintly hears Gigi's voice, along with a few others.

Cassandra places her brush down, spritzes her perfume in a few places, then tucks them away in her LV tote. Checking herself in the mirror, her cell vibrates catching her attention. Cassandra considers the caller and answers.

"Hi there... I've texted you several times you know..." Cassandra leans against the sink. "I haven't heard from you in weeks... I was concerned... Of course you were... You need to stop doing those movies... Cassi, you don't even need the money-When Mom passed in 97 she left us five million each, remember? Or have you finally run through it? I was just wondering little sister... Cassi, I'm not saying don't enjoy it! I know I do... It won't last forever... Well, I'm an accountant, I know how to make it work for me... Yeah yeah... I know... You'd rather handle it yourself... I'm just saying though... By the way, are you still a blond? When did you go back to your natural jet black? Oh... Okay... Now, I understand..."

Cassandra studies her reflection again, running her fingers through her hair, styling it a bit.

"Cause somebody you apparently worked with asked me if I was your sister... And, I'm not Chastity Chases sister! I'm Cassidy Cavanaugh's, you do understand that right?! Okay, I just wanted to make that clear... It annoys me that you kept our father's name anyway, regardless of how he treated mom. That's why I took mom's maiden name and you should've too... Fine... Anyway Cassi, what's up? You're gonna be filming in New York? " She huffs shaking her head. "Wonderful... I want to see you too... I don't know right now... Just call me a week before... Cassi, you won't be here for another three months... My plans may change so just call me first... Look, I gotta go... You and those movies... Well, like I always tell you, please use protection at least... Love you too... Be safe, see ya."

Cassandra finishes her call and gives her reflection the once-over.

"Looking good, sexy," Cassandra said to herself. "You're right, Gigi. I know exactly how to work what I got, and you will not ignore me today. Watch." She looks at the clock on the bathroom wall. "Not even 11:30 yet. Great, I got until 6 PM, that's more than enough time."

Cassandra listens, hearing Gigi's voice and background noise. "Alright, who's out there?"

Cassandra places her phone back in her bag and comes out of Lexi's bathroom, she places her LV tote bag on top of Lexi's bed, goes over to Lexi's bedroom door and opens it. Cassandra carries her bags to front door and closes Lexi's bedroom door behind her.

Cassandra tiptoes down the hallway, listening to Gigi talk and respond to someone familiar. She realizes the voice belongs to Regina. Picking up her pace as she walks down the hall. When Cassandra exits the hallway, turning toward the living room she sees Gigi and Regina sitting on the sectional. She comes to a complete stop, speechless when taking in Pastor and Lady Gorham seated there too. Regina notices Cassandra standing by the hallway entrance.

"Hi, Minister Pauls," Regina said. "Look at you!"

All eyes are on Cassandra, Gigi sits silent but slightly smiles.

"Hey there," Gigi said.

Gigi sits silent, trying to keep her attraction and feelings for Cassandra under wraps.

"Hello, Pastor Gorham, Lady Gorham," Cassandra nervously said.

"Hello, Minister Pauls," Pastor Gorham said.

"Hi, Minister Pauls," Lady Gorham said. "I've never seen you without your glasses, or your hair out for that matter. You look lovely."

Pastor Gorham nods his head in agreement with his wife, all Cassandra can do is lean up against the wall. She's speechless, and focused on Pastor and Lady Gorham. Regina gets up and approaches Cassandra.

"Listen to me," Regina said. "I know what's running through your mind. You can relax, because it isn't what you think."

"Daughter," Pastor Gorham said. "We're just here to have a word with you. So, no need to get yourself all flustered."

"Honey, just relax." Lady Gorham said. "Have a seat, it's gonna be alright."

Regina takes Cassandra's hand and feels her trembling.

"Minister Pauls," Regina said. "It's okay, I asked them to come. So, trust me, you've known me since I was little."

Cassandra lets out a breath nodding as she looks at Regina and they proceed to the sectional. Cassandra's eyes meet Gigi's for a moment but Gigi looks away moving over on the sectional. Gigi sits back crossing her legs. Cassandra sits down at the far end and Regina sits between them. Cassandra glances at Gigi as she crosses her legs fidgeting in her seat. Their eyes meet again but both look away putting their focus on Pastor and Lady Gorham.

"This won't take long," Pastor Gorham said. "You see, its come to our attention that-"

"Pastor-sorry to interrupt," Cassandra said. "You don't have to explain anything, I understand what's happening here, after everything you've heard, I know why you've come..."

"You do?" Lady Gorham said.

Pastor Gorham and Lady Gorham look at each other and then back at Cassandra. Gigi fights to keep her eyes off Cassandra.

"Yes, I do," Cassandra said. "I won't be difficult either because you have every right to do this. The garage door to the buildings parking lot is broken, it won't be fixed till 6 PM so I can't leave right now. I know there's a leadership meeting tonight and service tomorrow night. If it's alright with you Pastor, first thing tomorrow morning, I'll clean out my office and leave my keys in your mailbox. I'll be gone before anyone arrives, don't worry, I know not to come back."

Pastor and Lady Gorham look at each other again and then back at Cassandra once more.

"Look Cassandra," Pastor Gorham said. "When you came to Full Gospel and became a member, God revealed certain things about you good and bad. God showed me as he does with all those he intrust to me, how to handle them and their situations; Now, there are times he wants me to just leave them in His hands, I said all that to simply say this, I may not say much or address situations right away, that doesn't mean I don't know about them. Now daughter, I and First Lady, by no means came here to, blast you out, cut you open, let you bleed and just leave you to die."

"No, we didn't..." Lady Gorham said. "Now a few months ago, being brutally honest, after hearing certain things I did have some choice words for you, Yes, I did child."

"I did too daughter." Pastor Gorham said. "The God We serve is a forgiving God and he extends his grace and mercy to everyone. So, if I'm following in Jesus footsteps, striving to be more like him, then I can surely forgive you and extend grace and mercy to you also."

Lady Gorham affirms her husband's statement with a nod.

"Cassandra," Pastor Gorham said. "Whom the Lord loves he chastises and God is pulling on both you and Gisele's coattails."

As Cassandra keeps focused on Pastor and Lady Gorham, in her peripheral, she's aware Gigi is staring.

"Now Deacon and Deaconess Greye," Lady Gorham said. "Shared information with us concerning you in their counseling sessions. So, we're aware of that situation. Which is over now, correct? Shayna and you have spoken?"

"Yes, we spoke at her nephew's wedding," Cassandra said. "Any problems myself and Shayna had are over and there's no animosity or anything like that between us."

"So, we're clear," Pastor Gorham said. "All other relations between you and Shayna are resolved."

"Yes, Pastor," Cassandra said. "We haven't had any dealings like that in years. Our relationship is platonic."

"Okay," Lady Gorham said. "Now, Regina told us you two are together."

Cassandra and Gigi exchange stunned expressions and then cut their eyes to Regina, who simply looks back.

"Yes... I told them," Regina said. "I'm not gonna have them come here and lie about that part, duh."

"So, you two are together?" Lady Gorham said.

Gigi and Cassandra look at each other for a moment.

"Well?" Cassandra said."

"Umm?" Gigi said.

"It's a yes or no answer." Pastor Gorham said.

Cassandra sits back, shakes her head, takes a deep breath, and as she exhales, she gives Lady Gorham a long hard stare.

"I don't know." Cassandra said.

Gigi looks at Cassandra again, then turns away looking off toward the kitchen gesturing with her hand.

"Honestly-" Gigi said. "Right now, I don't know either."

"Well," Lady Gorham said. "We'll deal with that later."

"Cassandra," Pastor Gorham said. "We're simply here to give you a chance. Regina, you go ahead, say what you need to and I'll continue when you're done."

"Alright, Pastor," Regina turns to Cassandra. "So, yesterday Gigi and I were talking on the phone. She told me about those physical encounters with the church leaders you sat under. Well, I spoke with Pastor and Lady Gorham about what happen to you. Please, forgive me for sharing that information but I thought it was important for them to know." She looks at Pastor Gorham. "I'll let Pastor take it from here."

"Considering what you went through," Pastor Gorham said. "The fact you never bad mouthed them or even spoke about the situations you encountered there with them either, is commendable. We've talk to those pastors, and although they released you without question. They were quick to state their feelings about you to us."

"Now, we as pastors," Lady Gorham said. "Sometimes we hear things about our co-laborers in the vineyard. We haven't come here to speak about those leaders or situations. We're gonna leave them in God's hands and let him deal with it. God will handle it whether we see it or not."

"So daughter," Pastor Gorham said. "As I stated before, we're here to give you a chance. Although we've heard the negative things you've done. We've also heard the positive too."

"From those you've counseled at Full Gospel," Lady

Gorham said. "You've assisted in their deliverance while at the same time thinking you didn't deserve deliverance."

"Cassandra," Pastor Gorham said. "Speaking as a pastor, I'm godly angry with those pastors who stomped out your zeal for God. Cause that's not what any leader or any child of God should do to another."

"Yes," Lady Gorham said. "And God is no respecter of persons. If he can use a donkey, he can use whoever he wants."

"Daughters, I say daughters because this is for you and Gisele." Pastor Gorham said. "When you got saved you didn't walk down to the altar that day just to have something to do, Jesus knocked on the door of your heart and you answered. You invited Him in so He could be your Savior and the Lord over your life. You had the Holy Spirit and was growing in God. Okay, so you went off the road for a moment. We all have at some point and time, but now Jesus is knocking at the door of your heart again. I know you both feel him cause I see it. Now, you're here at this fork in the road and it's your choice which way you want to take. Jesus has called you out of darkness into his marvelous light."

"Ladies you have to remember," Lady Gorham said. "This journey isn't a sprint, it's a marathon. You've got to know if He's called and chosen you, He'll make you holy and sanctify you too. Just yield yourself to God, confess and own your sin; Whatever it is, be honest with God about those things that hinder you and there's deliverance for you. We can't fix or change ourselves, that's what God is for-it's His job. If we yield to God and say yes, God is faithful and he'll do the rest."

Pastor Gorham looks over at his wife and smiles.

"I liked that," Pastor Gorham said. "That rhymed and everything."

"Thank you darling," Lady Gorham said. "God is good."

"He'll Work It Out" Chapter 8. Taryn C. Atkins

All ladies smile watching the interaction between Pastor and Lady Gorham.

"Now Cassandra, if you truly want God," Pastor Gorham said. "We'll do all we can to help you. As your pastor, I'm supposed to do that. Lady Gorham and I will be at the church for that leadership meeting tonight. We'll be there till about 11. So, if you're ready to come out of this here lifestyle, rededicate your life to Jesus and begin a fresh relationship with God. Then show up tonight and we'll speak with you further. Okay, daughter?"

"Thank you, Pastor," Cassandra said.

"Wait a minute," Lady Gorham said. "In case you don't know what you want to do yet, we don't want you to stay away or disappear either, cause you're still one of our daughters. So, show up and after, like Pastor said, we'll sit down and talk. Now, we can't stop you or make you do anything, but our doors are open to you."

"Thank you so much," Cassandra said. "I appreciate it."

"No problem." Lady Gorham said. "Gigi, that goes for you too. Our doors are always open, you hear me?"

"Yes I do," Gigi said.

"So, if you want to come by tonight as well," Pastor Gorham said. "You're more than welcome too."

"I'll remember that," Gigi said. "Thanks."

"I think all has been said," Pastor Gorham said. "We're gonna get on outta here. Get ourselves back to Queens before traffic gets crazy."

Everybody rises to say their goodbyes, Gigi and Cassandra keep making eye contact here and there, while everyone else puts their coats on preparing to leave. They all show their love and say their farewells to Gigi and Cassandra and move toward the front door.

"We're headed to the RAW gather in a few days." Lady Gorham said. "A few buses are scheduled to leave from the church at 5 PM this coming Wednesday, Thursday, and Friday. It's gonna be a great time."

"I'm sure it will be," Gigi said.

"He'll Work It Out" Chapter 8. Taryn C. Atkins

Pastor and Lady Gorham step out the front door and head to the elevator with Cassandra following. Regina approaches Gigi before leaving.

"Listen Gigi," Regina said. "I know you love Cassandra, but if she's ready to go back to God, don't stop her."

"What makes you think I can stop her?" Gigi said.

"Cause I've seen it happen with couples." Regina said. "It doesn't matter either if it's a straight or gay couple. One wants to get right with God and get their life together, while the other one isn't feeling it, or just doesn't want to let go. So, I'm saying to you, the same thing I would say to her, don't try to hinder or stop what God is doing for both of you-You just have to allow yourself to see it."

"I know Gina," Gigi said.

"Fine, I'm going." Regina said, embracing her sister.

"Love you sis."

"Love you too," Gigi said.

Regina steps out the loft as Cassandra returns.

"Gina the elevator's there," Cassandra said.

"Alright, see ya," Regina said, hugging Cassandra. "Love ya."

"Love you too Gina," Cassandra said.

Regina rushes to the elevator as the doors quickly close behind her. After returning to the loft Gigi and Cassandra have settled in the living room, each contemplates the conversation they just took part in.

Gigi lays flat on the carpet with a sofa pillow behind her head, playing catch with a blue handball. Cassandra kicks off her stilettos and lays down on the sectional opposite Gigi, her eyes stay fixed on the ceiling for a moment. She then turns on her side, resting her head on her hand and stares at Gigi.

"So," Cassandra said.

"So," Gigi said. "You look beautiful."

"Thank you," Cassandra said.

"It's extremely distracting too," Gigi said.

"Apparently," Cassandra said. "From your looks here and there."

"You noticed that, huh?" Gigi said.

"He'll Work It Out" Chapter 8. Taryn C. Atkins

Gigi sits up and leans back against the sectional.

"It made me smile, at least you weren't ignoring me like yesterday. Still upset with me?"

Gigi looks over at Cassandra.

"You did tell me the truth, and that's what I wanted."

"And now you know everything."

"I do."

Gigi lifts herself up off the floor and stretches. She gives Cassandra a looks.

"You are stunning." Gigi said.

Cassandra smiles as she reaches for Gigi's hand and without malice or anger Gigi takes her hand.

"Bugs Bunny's looking every so sexy."

"It's what we do..." Gigi said with a sexy smile included.

Cassandra holds Gigi's hand, as she softly kisses it their eyes stay locked on each other.

"Come here, I miss you."

"I miss you too."

"Then come here, it's been over twenty four hours since we've kissed. I'm experiencing withdrawal."

Gigi and Cassandra smile as they observe each other.

"Withdrawal? Come on, it wasn't that bad."

"Mm-hmm, maybe not for you... Now please, kiss me."

Gigi smiles watching Cassandra, enjoying her seductive expression. Gigi continues to smile and shakes her head.

"Mmm... you are inviting. We still have things to talk about though. And umm... If I come down there, we won't be talking at all. So, why don't you get up."

Gigi pulls Cassandra up into a sitting position, she releases her hand and steps back.

"We have more to talk about?" Cassandra said.

"Of course," Gigi said. "Especially after that visit. So, lets sit at the island." She moves toward the kitchen. "I'll fix us something to drink and snack on and we'll talk."

"Okay, make us some Mimosa?"

Gigi stops mid stride, turns around and looks at Cassandra.

"No... I'll be getting us some juice, meaning a

nonalcoholic beverage. Cause we need to have a serious discussion, without one distraction."

"You did just say I was distracting."

"Yes, that's why we're sitting over there, across from each other with the island between us. You see-boundaries."

"I see."

The ladies sit on opposite side of the island as agreed while snacking.

"You couldn't answer when Lady Gorham asked if we were together," Gigi said. "Even though I said it was over."

"Well, I couldn't answer because I don't want it to be over," Cassandra said. "You didn't answer either."

"Part of me doesn't want us to be over." Gigi said.

"And the other part?" Cassandra said nursing her juice.

"Well, that part isn't about what I want, it's about what God wants."

"What does that mean?"

"Of all people, you should know what that means. You lit up when you talked about getting saved. How much you loved learning about God. You have a chance to get your relationship back with God, and be who God wants you to be. I won't stand in the way of that because I want to be selfish."

"Gigi, I can do both."

"No, you can't. Not if you really want to be used by God."

"I've seen others do it. I've seen pastors and other leaders live two entirely different lives. They live one way before the church and another behind closed doors. God still uses them, and in mighty ways too. So, why can't I do both, if I choose?"

"Cassandra the ones who do that, they're not getting away with anything. In the end, they still have to stand before God. Do you want to be like that? Or do you really want God to use you? Those leaders who said, God couldn't use someone who looked like you. Don't you want to prove them wrong?"

"A part of me does, but I don't want to lose you. I love you and want to be with you. Gigi you love me too, don't you want us to be together?"

"Cassandra I do love you." Gigi smiles and laughs. "You're actually the first person I've ever fallen in love with, and yes-I love us being together, in every sense of the word. The problem is, I know the *word* too, just like you do. We know that this... Us... This isn't supposed to happen."

"How can you say that, you don't know that."

"I do know, because of what happened with those leaders. You broke it off with that guy you were going to marry. The fact that you were going to marry him; Tells me you loved him. You would probably be married to him now. You don't know where he's at, but if you're meant to be. God has a way of making it happen, and you deserve to be happy."

"So, what are you saying to me?"

"God is giving you a chance, and I think you should take it. I'm not going to get in the way either. God wants you to come home, and you should want to. If you want to ignore God, it won't be because of me. I'd rather us not be together then have you walk away from God again... So... What I'm saying is..." Gigi gazes deeply into Cassandra's eyes, takes a deep breath and exhales. "We can't be together."

The intercom rings, catching them off guard and in unison they stare at it. It rings again. Gigi gets up and picks up the receiver.

"Hello... Good afternoon Cesar... Oh wow! So soon... They said 6 PM... Alright... So, there's valet parking again? Okay, thanks for letting me know." Gigi hangs up, glances at Cassandra, heads back to the island and sits down. "The garage door is working."

"Well, it had to happen."

"Yeah."

"Baby, if it has to be like this. Let's be together one last time."

"Cassandra..."

"Gigi, let's make love one last time. Then I'll go... I promise."

"Cassandra, I... I can't do that... right now, I'm not strong enough to be with you like that. For me to make love to you, then let you leave and us not be together. I can't..."

Gigi smiles, crossing her arms. "How about, we do a Waiting to Exhale?"

Cassandra smirks as she looks away, she then returns her eyes to Gigi and shakes her head.

"No... I can't do that... There's no way I can be that close to you, and not want to make love to you. I'm not strong enough to do that."

"Okay... Where do we go from here?"

"Well, I guess that's my cue. I'm gonna go, my stuff is packed and at the front door. Lexi and Dana won't be back for a while, I'm concerned about you. Will you be alright?"

"I'll be fine, I'll figure it out."

"I'm sure you will."

Cassandra gets up preparing to depart. She puts on her stilettos, goes to the coat rack where Gigi meets her. Gigi takes Cassandra's full length, burgundy leather shearling coat, holds it open for her and Cassandra slips into it. Cassandra buttons her coat and turns to Gigi. They embrace holding on to each other for a few moments, Gigi takes the initiative softly releasing Cassandra first.

Cassandra moves in as she reaches out and caresses the side of Gigi's face, she leans in and tenderly kisses her cheek. As Cassandra moves away, they rest their foreheads against each other. Gigi notices Cassandra lick her lips and carefully steps back. Cassandra taking a breath turns around and heads down the hallway, she takes a few steps and as Gigi is about to follow Cassandra stops her.

"Stay here, please. I'd rather remember you... Well, remember us like this... Than saying goodbye at the door."

Gigi nods in agreement.

"Gigi... To be perfectly honest with you, I may not fully agree with what's happening with us, but.. I understand why it is. After this, I'm really not sure what I'm gonna do yet-A part of me will always love you though."
"Same here."
"I'll see ya' Gigi,"
"See ya', Minister Cassandra Pauls,"
"Hmmph, you think?"
"I think you can do it, if you want to."
"True, the same goes for you. That invitation to return to Jesus is open to you as well, and you should be thinking about it too."
"You're right... And I will. And you?"

Cassandra smiles at Gigi and shrugs her shoulders.
"Maybe."

Gigi smiles as Cassandra turns and walks down the hall, midway, Cassandra turns back to Gigi.
"Question-What happens if fate steps in, and we meet at a fellowship or a service one day?"
"Well, I'm sure I won't act like my mother." Gigi chuckling.
"I hope not."

They both laugh.
"If that happens, when it happens, I think it would be cool. And... I'll look forward to meeting your husband."

Cassandra grins and slightly laughs.
"Or my wife... Ya' never know."

Gigi tilts her head and shakes it a bit.
"Yeah... But I highly doubt it."
"I guess... Only time will tell."

As Cassandra heads down the hall one last time, Gigi walks to the center of the living room. Gigi brushes away a tear rolling down her cheek while hearing the clack echo of Cassandra's heels on the hallway floor. There is a brief pause, then the front door slides open and slides shut. There's a calm silence as Gigi stands in the middle of her living room. Closing her eyes she takes in a deep breath, holds it in for a few seconds and then exhales.

"What now?"

When Gigi opens her eyes, they focus on a African-American painting hanging over the candle fireplace. She stares at it for a few moments then with barely any movement she nods. The painting her eyes took in, is titled: "The Road" its of a woman standing on a path and off in the distance is the shadow of a cross upon it.

~HIS MYSTERIOUS WORKS~

After the storm hit leaving the state of New York covered in snow, it took just a few days but all five boroughs finally dug their way out. The temperature outside is currently forty degrees on this early Friday evening, which happens to be Valentines Day. Pastor Gorham's in his office, sitting behind his desk talking on the phone.

"Well, Thank God nothing happen," Pastor Gorham said. "Brother Hamlin said he'll be taken back to Mississippi soon... From what I understand, the guy who took care of the cabin gave them the tapes... And with his sister's statement, he's going to do some time... Her husband hasn't been charged yet, simply because wives can't testify against their husbands... Right now? Besides God, Thomas need someone there... So I told him we'll keep in contact... I know honey... but God is able..."

Pastor Gorham stands, goes to his office window and looks out into the church parking lot. There sits one bus with exhaust going and he watches it pull off.

"The last bus just left... Honey, I'll be there in time for evening service... I'm waiting to see if any stragglers come by... Okay, go check in and pick up our things from the RAW registration table... Yes... Yes, I already told Minister McDaniels and Minister Randall to make sure everybody from the church was checked in and registered... I'll be locking the church up soon... Good, I'm sure Minister Nelson will fill you in on everything."

Pastor Gorham sits on the corner of his desk.

"Yes... Hello to her too." He laughs. "Yeah I hear them... Tell Mother Brenda and Sister Ada, I look forward to seeing them as well... Oh, remember to tell Dr. Carlett to tell Bishop we want to take her, the pastors and elders out for breakfast. Okay... Yes darling, love ya... See ya soon."

Pastor Gorham hangs up, turns toward his desk, picks up an envelope and places it in his inside jacket pocket. He prepares to leave and does a little shout.

"Yes Lord, it's RAW time."

Pastor Gorham is getting his things together when Gigi rushes into his office carrying a few bags. As she stops in her tracks she's slightly out of breath.

"Pastor Gorham!" Gigi said. "Please don't tell me the last bus left?"

"Yeah daughter," Pastor Gorham said, shaking his head.

"It left a few minutes ago."

Gigi, with disappointment on her face, plops down in one of the leather chairs in front of his desk. Releasing her bags they drop to the floor.

"Gisele the one thing I've learned while being a pastor is, God's time is not our time."

Pastor Gorham's office door opens and in walks Gilbert closing the door behind him.

"The jeep is warmed up and ready Pastor Gorham," Gilbert said. "Excuse me Pastor, but umm... Do you mind if someone else comes with us? It's only one other person."

"Well, who is it son?" Pastor Gorham said.

"It's my sister," Gilbert said. "I've been asking her to go for the longest. This morning, she said yes. God is up to something pastor. Anyway, she's right outside your office."

"Well, bring her in." Pastor Gorham said.

Gilbert opens the office door.

"Come on in," Gilbert said.

"He'll Work It Out" Chapter 8. Taryn C. Atkins

Gigi stands up when she sees Suzanne walk through the Pastor's office door.

"Suzanne!?" Gigi said.

"Gigi!?" Suzanne said.

"Oh my goodness, I can't believe this!"

"It's so good to see you!"

They greet one another with big smiles and share a tight hug.

"I guess you two know each other." Pastor Gorham said.

Pastor Gorham looks at Gilbert, who in turn looks at him and shrugs his shoulders.

"What in the world are you doing here?" Gigi said.

"Gilbert's my brother," Suzanne said. "You know, the one I spoke about at game night. He's been telling me about this RAW thing. Normally, I say no. When he asked this time, I decided why not."

"You two can finish talking in the jeep." Pastor Gorham said. "Gilbert, please grab Gisele's bags and take your sister to the jeep with hers. We'll be right there."

"Yes Pastor." Gilbert said.

Gilbert takes Gigi's bags. Suzanne waves and smiles at Gigi as she and Gilbert walk out. Gigi smiles and shakes her head.

"Wow, it's a small world," Gigi said.

Pastor Gorham reaches into his inside jacket pocket, takes the envelope out and gives it to Gigi.

"Gisele," Pastor Gorham said. "I do believe somebody was praying you show up." He puts on his coat and throw his duffel bag over his shoulder. "I'll be in the jeep. Just turn out the lights and close the door behind you when you leave."

"Alright Pastor," Gigi said.

Pastor Gorham leaves. Gigi opens the envelope, pulls out the letter and begins to read i:

Hi Gigi, Lord knows baby; I wish I could just wipe away all the hurt life has dealt you, but that which I can't do the Lord can.

Gigi's eyes tear up, seeing the letter is from her grandmother. She slowly sits, continuing to read hearing Mama Mae's voice ever so clearly:

It was at RAW where you first allowed Jesus to come into your heart, baby. I'm praying that you'll allow Jesus to come in again and heal all those hurts. So, I paid for your hotel room, plus registration with meals included of course; Grandma's gonna make sure you eat now.

Gigi laughs as her tears still flow.

Listen Gigi, you go and enjoy yourself. While you're there open up, let Jesus in and allow Him to have his way in your heart and your life. Jesus loves you baby, and so do I. You're always in my prayers and I'll always love you, Grandma.

Gigi looks heavenward.

"I miss you so much. I'll always love you too grandma."

Gigi wipes her tears and places the letter in her pocket. She walks to Pastor Gorham's door, turning off the lights as she steps out closing the door behind her.

After Gigi checked into the hotel and received all she needs from the RAW registration table, she steps out the elevator and into the hotel lobby, buzzing with movement from all the RAW staff and attendees moving about. Many were checking in, getting their packets at the registration table or simply greeting fellow attendees. As Gigi walks through she survey's the crowd sharing a smile with others from time to time. She enters the RAW conference room lobby and a woman greets her with a loving smile as she approaches her.

"Hello, I'm Minister Workmen. Welcome to RAW, we're so glad you made it."

"Thank you," Gigi said. "I am too."

Two years have passed and it's now the Summer of 2016, Gigi leans on the podium as she stands in the front of a sizeable conference room. There's an enormous banner draped on the wall behind her, across it is printed the name of this gathering and it reads, "AWE PETALS". Under the title, in script, the meaning of the acronym *AWE* is written stating, "All Women Empowered" and the gathering is being presented by, "Karyn Rayner Enterprises." Right below the organizations name their mission statement simply said, "Empowering Women... One woman at a time."

Gigi looked out into a room that easily holds between one hundred to a hundred and fifty people, a score of women are in attendance. They weren't sitting in your usual conference stacking chairs either, but in sofas lined up across the room and back.

"... Well, I've been going to RAW ever since," Gigi said. "I'm even a member at KAGM. I joined right after RAW. There's no place like it either. It's truly a place where you can encounter God and experience change. I've always loved Dr. Wilson, and I'm blessed to call her my pastor. Jesus is having his way in my life and I say Yes to the process. Believe me, it's by no means an easy journey, but... it's a road I'm willing to travel. I know we did Q and A in the last segment, but I'll take two more before we end. So, any more questions or comments?"

Gigi sees various people quickly stand from all over the room. A young woman, in the middle of the crowd raises her hand and waves it, another woman, a conference worker rushes over and hands her a microphone.

"Hi," The young lady said as her voice quivered. "I just wanted to say that I was so blessed by your transparency."

Various people from all around the room applaud, agreeing with her, thunderous claps roars out and then quiet.

"Praise God," Gigi said. "To God be the glory, please keep me in your prayers." Her eyes inspect the room. "Someone else?"

A middle age woman on the other side gets the mic.

"I was wondering..." The middle age woman said. "Do you know what happen to Cassandra? Did she stay in church or leave? I'm just curious, that's all."

"It's okay," Gigi said with a smile. "Well, she didn't show up that night or the next. It was about two months later that my sister Regina told me, she saw Cassandra talking with Pastor and Lady Gorham outside his office.

"He'll Work It Out" Chapter 8. Taryn C. Atkins

She finally rededicated herself to the Lord, even agreed to be counseled and mentored by them-She thrived too. About a year ago, Pastor Gorham released her and she moved back to Chicago. She's a part of an excellent church there too. Jesus is using her, she's preaching and teaching. I heard she's doing awesome things in God and helping so many people. So, let's Praise God!

The attendees clap and cheer, Gigi moves to the side of the podium with mic in hand. As the jubilation comes to a rest, Gigi glances up to heaven for a second, smiles and looks out into the sea of women of different races, backgrounds, for some religious affiliation, and some even came just to see what's it all about.

"My grandmother's first name was Maven, it means one who is experienced or knowledgable... An expert... And when it came to Jesus, spiritual things and just... Having a relationship with God, Grandma was an expert. So, ladies... I guess to wrap it all up, I'll say what my grandmother always told us, *"When you find you've done all you can do, and you finally give everything over to God. You've got to have faith and know, he'll work it out."*

~The End~

~Please Share Your Thoughts Or Write A Review~
Send Your Email To: ireadhwio@tcaproductionsinc.com

TCA Productions Inc, Taryn C. Atkins

& He'll Work It Out

Like, Connect & Follow Us On

Facebook, Instagram, LinkedIn & Twitter

www.ingramcontent.com/pod-product-compliance
Lightning Source LLC
Chambersburg PA
CBHW071958150426
43194CB00008B/919